Reflective Naturalism:

An Introduction
to Moral Philosophy

An Introduction
to
Moral Philosophy

Vincent C. Punzo

St. Louis University

Reflective
Naturalism

Macmillan Publishing Co., Inc., New York
Collier-Macmillan Publishers, London

PRINTING   78910   YEAR   789

Library of Congress catalog card
number: 69-15095

MACMILLAN PUBLISHING CO., INC.
866 THIRD AVENUE, NEW YORK, NEW YORK 10022
COLLIER-MACMILLAN CANADA, LTD.

Printed in the United States of
America

To
Professor Vernon J. Bourke

Preface

If a college ethics course is to fulfill its responsibility to the student, it should provide him with an opportunity to reflect on the major problems of ethical theory and to examine the more concrete ethical problems of his day in the light of such reflection. This book was written to make a contribution to the realization of such an opportunity. I have tried to write a book that would serve as an introduction to some of the major issues currently under discussion in the technical philosophical community and that would also examine problems of a more general interest, such as the morality of premarital coition, of capital punishment, and of war. The discussion of such technical issues as the naturalistic fallacy and the difference between utilitarianism and deontologism will provide a reasoned framework within which some of the concrete ethical issues of our day can be discussed and explored. The consideration of these latter issues will give an opportunity to show the relevance of moral theory to the concrete issues of life.

The method used in dealing with the problems discussed in this book may be described as an "expository-critical" method. This method involves an attempt to give a straightforward exposition of some of the more significant positions taken with respect to a given problem and to use a critical examination of these positions to argue for what one considers to be a more satisfactory resolution of the problem. The use of this approach has the advantage of making the student aware of the pluralism that exists with respect to certain issues and of seeing how a philosopher tries to use this pluralism to fashion and to defend what he considers to be a more satisfactory handling of the problem.

If one's aim is to provide a student with the opportunity to establish a reasoned ethical outlook of his own and to gain a certain independence of thought concerning ethical issues, it seems to me that this approach is preferable to a recital of the plurality of positions that exist in the philosophical community. This approach not only introduces him to a variety of positions, but also gives him the opportunity to reflect on an attempt to ground a coherent and consistent ethics within the context of pluralism. He is thus not only challenged to make the same attempt himself, but he is also able to learn from what he may find to be the strengths and weaknesses of the attempt made by another.

I have dedicated this book to my colleague and former teacher Vernon J. Bourke as an expression of gratitude. Because he not only suggested that I begin the project, but also took the initiative to make arrangements with Macmillan for its publication, it is no exaggeration to say that the book would never have come into being without his aid. My debt to Professor Bourke also reaches beyond the immediate circumstances surrounding the publication of this book to the time of my graduate studies. My interest in ethics and the germ of some positions taken here were developed in several seminars that he conducted. Those seminars were marked by an openness and experimental spirit that made a student feel that there was yet work to be done in the field of ethics and that he might be able to make a contribution.

I also wish to thank Dr. Robert Cunningham of the University of San Francisco and Dr. Maurice Holloway of Edinboro State College, Pennsylvania, who read the chapters dealing with matters of ethical theory. Because they played the role of critic so well, I am satisfied that the book in its present form is philosophically stronger than the drafts that they criticized. Because I know that neither agrees with all that I have written, I must take full responsibility for the final version.

I am also indebted to Dr. Patrick Coffey, Dr. and Mrs. James Reagan, Drs. Paul and Marie Mathews, and Rev. V. R. Gorospe, S.J. Their friendship, encouragement, and interest helped ease the burden of what appeared to be an unending task. In the last analysis, none of the help which I received would have resulted in the publication of this book had it not been for the patience, faith, and good cheer of my wife. She helped me through the darkness of a shared tragedy and eased the frustrations connected with trying to write a book while at the same time carrying a heavy and often unyielding academic load.

Finally, I wish to thank Rev. George Klubertanz, S.J., Chairman of the Department of Philosophy, Saint Louis University, who financed the typing of the final draft.

V. C. P.
Saint Louis University

Contents

CHAPTER I

Types of Ethics and the Possibility of a Normative Ethics

The purpose of this chapter is to give a brief statement of the major ethical positions espoused in contemporary philosophical discussions in the English-speaking world in order to provide a schematic view of the problematic context within which issues will be discussed in this book.[1] It is also hoped that this statement will direct the reader's attention to a variety of ethical positions that are presently open for consideration and discussion. With the exception of the emotive theory, which will be described and evaluated in some detail in the concluding sections of this chapter, I shall put off a more detailed consideration of these positions for those places in our discussions where they will be especially relevant.

In a rather popularized and nontechnical assessment of the contemporary status of philosophy, Mortimer J. Adler points to the lack of significant communication among philosophers as a major factor hindering the advance of philosophy as a humanly significant cognitive enterprise. "The most crucial failure of philosophy so far is the failure of philosophers to face each other in clear and genuine disagreements, to join issue and engage in the debate of disputed questions."[2] It should be noted that the failure of philosophers rests not in the failure to achieve complete agreement, but in the character of their disagreements. For disagreement is a part of every human intellectual undertaking, whether it be physics, biology, sociology, or psychology. However, the men working in these other areas seem to be more successful than the philosophers in clarifying their disagreements so that there is some reason to hope that issues will be effectively joined and that the scientific community in question will thereby profit from the disagreement.

The problem with the disagreements among philosophers is that too often these disagreements have led many philosophers to withdraw into the isolated safety of a particular school of thought, thus contributing to the breakdown

[1] The following books provide a good survey of ethical positions. Richard Brandt, *Ethical Theory* (Englewood Cliffs, New Jersey: Prentice-Hall, 1959). Thomas E. Hill, *Contemporary Ethical Theories* (New York: Macmillan, 1957).

[2] Mortimer J. Adler, *The Conditions of Philosophy: Its Checkered Past, its Present Disorder, and its Future Promise* (New York: Atheneum, 1965), p. 180.

1

rather than to the enrichment of the philosophical community. If this problem is to be met, it is necessary, first of all, to try to understand the different philosophical positions taken on various issues. It is then necessary to try to join issue with these different positions by weighing the possible reasons for agreeing with certain positions and disagreeing with others, and by trying to see whether a unified and coherent view of the issue can be established—a view that can incorporate what is of value in other positions with certain factors of human existence that may have been overlooked or misinterpreted in these other positions. In general, this is the type of procedure used in this book. It is hoped that this procedure will help the reader gain a grasp of different philosophical positions and a sense of the dialogue that is possible within the philosophical community. In the last analysis, the issues discussed in this book and the positions taken can only help the reader in his own thinking; they cannot substitute for his personal reflection.

In trying to probe into the moral basis of man's life, this book will focus on three questions that are central to contemporary ethical discussions: (1) What is the task of moral philosophy? (2) What are the grounds upon which one can base the distinction between moral good and evil, and what role does knowledge play in this distinction? (3) What is the role, if any, that a supernatural God plays in man's moral life? It is hoped that the discussion of these issues will contribute depth and substance to the consideration of problems such as the morality of induced abortions and of limited war.

1. WHAT IS THE TASK OF MORAL PHILOSOPHY?

The question of defining the task of moral philosophy will eventually be broadened to include problems concerning the relationship between man's knowledge of general moral principles and the particular moral questions that face him in his day-to-day life. These latter problems will be explicitly treated in Chapters IV and V. This section will simply mention two conceptions of the task of moral philosophy.

The following statement by R. M. Hare represents one conception of this task: "The function of moral philosophy—or at any rate the hope with which I study it—is that of helping us to think better about moral questions by exposing the logical structure of the language in which this thought is expressed."[3] Being thus restricted to determining the logical rules of moral reasoning through a clarification of the meaning and function of moral words, ethics does not directly deal with such questions as, "How can a standard be established for the distinction between moral good and evil?" "Is the private property system immoral; is socialism immoral?" Such an ethics is not concerned with establish-

[3] R. M. Hare, *Freedom and Reason* (New York: Oxford University Press, 1965), p. v.

ing what is moral or immoral. Charles L. Stevenson points out that this type of ethics has been described as "analytic ethics," "Metaethics," and "critical ethics."[4]

Normative ethics is concerned with establishing a norm upon which a distinction between moral good and evil can be rationally based. It is not content with simply describing those acts which certain societies happen, or happened, to consider moral or immoral. Hence, it is distinct from such studies as sociology and anthropology in that it does not set out to simply describe or explain the factors accounting for certain types of human behavior. It is concerned with discovering a way to evaluate the morality of human acts.

There is agreement between the normative ethician and the linguistic conception of ethics exemplified by R. M. Hare in that both stress the fact that moral philosophy is concerned with clarifying man's moral situation. They differ in their respective conceptions of the nature and scope of such clarification. Whereas the analytic approach limits this clarification to an analysis of the logic and function of moral discourse, the normative ethician holds that in addition to this type of clarification the philosopher can offer a further clarification by reflecting on man's existential situation in the world in order to gain a more thorough, systematic, and profound intellectual penetration into the moral dimensions of human existence. The difference between these two conceptions of moral philosophy may be described as a difference between a view that sees moral philosophy as being only logically normative and a view that sees it as both logically and morally normative.

Hare's approach restricts moral philosophy to the task of establishing the logical framework of moral discourse. The establishment of such a framework enables one to accept or reject positions in terms of their consistency or inconsistency with the logical rules governing moral discourse, but it does not enable him to distinguish between acts as being either morally good or morally evil.[5] For example, one could use this type of moral philosophy to show that race prejudice is not in keeping with the logical rules of moral discourse, but he could not use it to show that such prejudice is immoral. As Hare shows in his *Freedom and Reason*, such a moral philosophy can make a significant contribution to man's moral life.[6]

Unlike Hare, I think that moral philosophy can also be morally normative, meaning by this that it can provide a standard upon which one can ground distinctions between acts as morally good or morally evil. The establishment of the possibility of such an undertaking will require an investigation into the issues raised by emotivism and by G. E. Moore's naturalistic fallacy. The first set of issues will be discussed in this chapter, and the second set, in Chapter III. It will also be necessary to present a reasoned defense for the moral

[4] Charles L. Stevenson, *Facts and Values: Studies in Ethical Analysis* (New Haven: Yale University Press, 1964), p. vi.

[5] See footnote 3, pp. 89, 97.

[6] *Ibid.*, pp. 203–224.

standard advanced and to show that this standard is significant and useful in helping man solve his concrete moral problems. This latter point must be established because a standard that is too vague to be of any use in solving such problems must be rejected in that it fails to do precisely what is required of a standard. However, one must avoid making excessive claims for what moral philosophy can accomplish in this regard. The moral standard advanced in this book can function as an aid to an individual's reflections on the moral problems of his particular situation, but it cannot substitute for such further reflections. These issues will be considered in Chapters IV and V.

2. ETHICAL DISTINCTIONS AND KNOWLEDGE

The answers given to the question concerning the basis for man's distinction between moral good and evil can be divided into two classes, noncognitivism and cognitivism. The emotivists, who represent the noncognitivist response, maintain that in the last analysis, moral distinctions are grounded in human emotions, and not in knowledge. The cognitivist position can be subdivided into deontologism and utilitarianism. The deontologists maintain that moral distinctions are grounded in the very nature of certain acts or rules.

According to W. D. Ross who is a deontologist, "An act is not right because it, being one thing, produces a good result different from itself; it is right because it is itself the production of a certain state of affairs. Such production is right in itself, apart from any consequences."[7] For example, a reflection on the nature of promises reveals that intrinsic to this nature is the obligation to keep a promise, although one might not be particularly pleased with all the consequences that may flow from meeting this obligation.

Ross criticizes utilitarian ethics for oversimplifying man's moral life in that such ethics "recognize only one type of claim, the claim that we shall act so as to produce most good, while in fact there are claims arising from other grounds, arising from what we have already done (e.g. from our having made a promise, or inflicted an injury) and not merely from the kind of result our action will have, or may be expected to have."[8] As seen from this statement, deontologism maintains that the morality of an act cannot be decided simply in terms of the consequences produced by such an act. Immanuel Kant is usually regarded as giving the classic statement of the deontological position. He held that moral obligation is absolute in that it demands that man act morally, not for any extramoral effect or consequence, not out of any natural feeling that one may have, but for morality's sake, and out of a sense of moral

---

[7] W. D. Ross, *The Right and the Good* (Oxford: Oxford University Press, 1930), pp. 46–47.

[8] W. D. Ross, *Foundations of Ethics* (Oxford: Oxford University Press, 1939), p. 189.

duty, even though one's natural inclinations may not find such a demand satisfying.[9]

The utilitarians disagree with the deontological view, pointing out that the distinction between moral good and evil is to be grounded in a consideration of the consequences that flow from performing a certain act or from following a certain rule. Although he does not believe that he can offer a final disproof of the deontological position, J. J. C. Smart does find a certain persuasive objection which he thinks will be convincing to those who are concerned with the welfare of humanity. Smart maintains that there must be some cases in which human misery could be avoided only by a refusal to act in accordance with the demands of deontological ethics. The deontologist who asks us to act in accordance with a rule even when such an act will lead to a great deal of human misery seems to be more interested in preserving rules than in the prevention of human misery.

Smart acknowledges that the deontologist may meet this objection by taking the position that although such an opposition between duty and human welfare is logically possible, it never occurs in fact. To the extent that the deontologist could prove this point, Smart would have no quarrel with the position. For if the point were proved, there would be no practical difference between deontologists and utilitarians. However, Smart has never seen a deontologist position which did not, as a matter of fact, differ from utilitarianism in both theory and practice. Hence, he concludes that although deontologists may view his argument against their position as the result of a soft-hearted sentimentality, the fact is that once deontologism is seen to be infected with the disease of "rule worship," it loses much of its philosophical vitality.[10]

3. GOD AND ETHICS

In Plato's *Euthyphro*, Socrates poses the following question: "The point which I should first wish to understand is whether the pious or holy is beloved by the gods because it is holy, or holy because it is beloved of the gods."[11] This problem raises the issue of the relationship between man's knowledge of God and his knowledge of the distinction between moral good and evil. Is a prior knowledge of God necessary to the distinction between moral good and evil, or can man ground this distinction apart from such knowledge.

John Dewey emphasizes another aspect of the problem of the relationship between God and man's moral life. He is concerned with the dualism which

[9] For example, see Immanuel Kant, *Foundations of the Metaphysics of Morals*, trans. by Lewis White Beck (New York: The Liberal Arts Press, 1959), pp. 14–15.

[10] J. J. C. Smart, *An Outline of a System of Utilitarian Ethics* (Australia: Melbourne University Press, 1961), pp. 2–3.

[11] Plato, *Euthyphro*, in *The Dialogues of Plato Vol. I*, trans. by B. Jowett (New York: Random House, 1937), p. 391.

the acceptance of a supernatural God introduces into man's natural existence. The acceptance of a supernatural God leads man to see himself as existing in two realms, a supernatural and a natural realm, with all the value and significance of man's life being found in the supernatural realm. Such a state of affairs detracts from man's natural concerns. If all value rests in some supernatural order, it would appear that man need not concern himself with trying to advance the cause of human justice and freedom here on earth. One might be able to use the power of God as a way of frightening people into doing the moral thing, but this use of a supernatural God hardly appeals to what is best in man. It is Dewey's contention that the acceptance of the existence of a supernatural God not only is not necessary to man's moral life, but is detrimental to this life. The issues raised by Dewey's position and the problem of whether or not a prior knowlege of the existence of God is necessary to ground the distinction between moral good and evil will be discussed in Chapter IX.

4. THE EMOTIVE THEORY OF ETHICS

Whether one ultimately agrees or disagrees with the emotivist, his philosophical grasp of the respective roles of reason and of the emotions in man's moral life will be broadened and deepened by the emotivist's attempts to show that ethical statements, precisely in so far as they are valuative, are grounded ultimately in human emotions rather than in human knowledge. This exposition of the emotive theory will begin with A. J. Ayer's brief and unqualified statement of the emotive position and will proceed to C. L. Stevenson's more complete and qualified statement.

According to Ayer, it would be just as meaningless to ask whether the statement, "Stealing is wrong," is true or false as it would be to ask whether the cry, "Ouch!" which a man makes after hitting his thumb with a hammer, is true or false.[12] The point of this comparison is that ethical statements are similar to cries of pain or joy in that they are expressive of an emotion. Statements possessing valuative terms such as "good," "bad," "virtue," and "vice" do not describe facts that might be examined by rational investigation, but simply express the emotions of the speaker. Hence, the statement, "Stealing is wrong," is no different from the cry of disgust, or horror, "Stealing!"

The emotive character of ethical statements has not been generally recognized because in so far as these statements use the copula *is*, they do not seem to differ from descriptive statements. The statement, "Stealing is wrong," appears to be no different from the statement, "Chicago is three hundred miles from St. Louis." However, the use of the word *wrong*, in the first statement shows that it expresses the speaker's feelings about stealing and that it, therefore, cannot be either proved or disproved as can the second one.

[12] See A. J. Ayer, *Language, Truth and Logic* (New York: Dover, 1946), p. 107.

In addition to their function of expressing the emotions of a speaker, ethical statements may also be used to arouse similar emotions in a listener. Viewed from this perspective, the statements are simply imperatives. For example, the statement "You ought to tell the truth," may express not only the speaker's approval of truth-telling, but may also be a less emphatic way of expressing the command or imperative, "Tell the truth."[13] Again, in so far as ethical statements possess this imperative character, they can be neither true nor false. Thus, a student taking a "true-false" examination could not classify an imperative such as "Close the door," as either true or false. The emotive character of ethical statements leads Ayer to conclude that the task of philosophy is not to make ethical pronouncements or to try to establish the truth or falsity of ethical norms.

Ayer has presented us with the bare outlines of an emotivist view of ethics. Before trying to evaluate this view, it will be well to consider a more detailed and fully worked out statement of the position. Such a statement is found in Charles L. Stevenson's *Ethics and Language* and his collection of essays entitled *Facts and Values*. Although he will qualify Ayer's statement of the emotive position, Stevenson maintains that the works of such men as Ayer, Bertrand Russell, and Carnap do not "discredit" ethics. He bases this interpretation on the following three points. First, the comparison of ethical judgments to imperatives does not necessarily involve the denial of the importance of such imperatives in human life. Secondly, to say that ethical statements are expressive of feelings is not to say that men are to inhibit all their feelings. Finally, to say that ethical judgments are neither true nor false does not commit one to the view that these judgments "are to be made capriciously, in ignorance of one's self, or the nature and consequences of the object judged."[14]

The first two points in Stevenson's defense do not touch what is the essential difficulty involved in an emotive interpretation of man's moral experience. Granted this interpretation, it may be true that ethical judgments will remain useful to man as a means to convince others to do his bidding. It may also be true that there will be no need to inhibit our feelings. As we see it, the major problem, which the position raises, lies in what appears to be its denial that reason has any significant and decisive role to play in man's moral judgments. If it is true, as Stevenson indicates, that an emotive position need not involve the view that ethical judgments are to be made "capriciously, in ignorance of one's self, or the nature and consequences of the object judged," does this mean that the emotivist maintains that ethical judgments *can* and *ought* to be based on a knowledge of one's self and of the objects with which one is dealing? If the answer to this question is affirmative, it would appear that the emotivist does not deny the possibility of establishing ethical norms on a cognitive basis. In short, Ayer's type of emotivism has raised the following questions. Can reason play any role in man's moral life? If it can, what is the precise character

<hr>

[13] *Ibid.*, pp. 107–108.

[14] Charles L. Stevenson, *Ethics and Language* (New Haven: Yale University Press, 1960), p. 266.

and significance of this role? Or putting this matter in another way, "What is the scope and limitation of reason's role in man's moral life?" Stevenson does address himself to these questions in working out his own statement of the emotivist position.

He tries to work out a *via media* between what he considers to be overstatements of the emotive position and what he terms the "naturalist" position. Whereas exaggerated emotivism gives one the impression that reason plays no role at all in ethical judgments, the naturalist seems to make these judgments a matter of reason alone, thus denying a role to emotions in moral discourse. He maintains that ethical disagreements and problems involve both descriptive elements, or man's beliefs concerning himself and the world in which he lives, and man's attitudes toward himself and his world. He describes an "attitude" as "any psychological disposition of being *for* or *against* something."[15]

5. THE EMOTIVE CHARACTER OF ETHICAL JUDGMENTS

We shall begin our brief exposition of Stevenson's position by considering his views concerning the emotive character of ethical judgments. Although he does not deny that ethical problems and disagreements involve cognitive dimensions, he maintains that it is the fact that such problems and disagreements are ultimately grounded in conflicting attitudes that marks them as *ethical* problems as distinct from *scientific* problems. What makes a problem an *ethical* problem is that it is centered in a conflict of attitudes or emotions.[16] A consideration of the reasons that Stevenson advances to sustain this position will clarify this point.

It is important to realize that these reasons are based on Stevenson's reflections on ethical language and on the ethical discussions that man carries on in his daily life. In presenting his reasons, he is taking no explicit stand concerning the nature of man or of the world in which he lives. His evidence is gathered from an analysis of moral language and moral discourse.[17] Thus, he maintains that the character and aim of moral discourse show the primary and decisive role that attitudes play in ethics. Attitudes are seen to be decisive in moral disagreements, in that they determine which factors will be considered relevant and significant evidence for or against an ethical position. That ethical reflection or disagreement aim at resolving conflicting attitudes is seen by the fact that such reflections or disagreements are usually terminated when the conflict of attitudes has been resolved, although problems and disagreements may persist with respect to beliefs. If, for example, in a disagreement between union and management, management agreed to meet the union's demands, although it was

---

[15] See footnote 4, pp. 1–2.
[16] See footnote 14, p. 13. See also footnote 4, p. 3.
[17] See footnote 14, p. 13.

in complete disagreement with the union's position concerning the present state of the economy, the disagreement would have been terminated. However, if they both agreed in their views of the economic situation, but they could not agree on whether a wage increase would be "good," the disagreement would continue.[18]

This view of the aim of ethical discourse conforms with Stevenson's contention that the function of moral judgments is to recommend things or actions for one's approval or disapproval. This recommending function of moral judgments indicates that they speak not only to a man's intellect, but also to his emotions.[19] They are used not only to inform a man about a certain state of affairs, but also to move him to react favorably or unfavorably to this state of affairs. They serve to encourage, alter, redirect, or strengthen attitudes.[20] A value judgment such as, "A minimum wage law is good," involves the following elements, "I approve of a minimum wage law, [and] you ought to also." If two men are in disagreement concerning this judgment, their disagreement concerns the second part of this judgment, since it is taken for granted that the one who favors the law has a favorable attitude toward it and the one opposing the law has an unfavorable attitude toward it. Each is aiming at getting the other to share his attitude toward the law. There is a kind of imperative character to the second element of the judgment, and it is this imperative or recommending factor that is at issue in all ethical judgments and reflections.[21] This recommending element is present not only in judgments of the type, "X is good," but also in attempts to define such terms as courage, justice, and injustice. "To choose a definition is to plead a cause, so long as the word defined is strongly emotive."[22] For example, Plato's attempts to define the true essence of justice was determined by his own attitudes so that he was satisfied with a definition only if it accorded with these attitudes.[23]

It is important to note that in equating definitions with pleading a cause, Stevenson indicated that this equation is justified "so long as the word defined is strongly emotive." This is an important qualification because it seems to have played a role in leading Stevenson to conclude that ethical judgments and definitions are directed primarily to altering or strengthening human attitudes. His point seems to be that the emotive character of the words used in moral discourse controls such discourse, thus accounting for the central and decisive role of attitudes in this discourse. This point is clearly expressed in the following statement: "The emotive meaning of a word is the power that the word acquires, on account of its history in emotional situations, to evoke or directly express attitudes, as distinct from describing or designating them. In virtue of this kind of meaning, ethical judgments alter attitudes, not by an appeal to

[18] See footnote 4, pp. 4–5.
[19] See footnote 14, p. 13.
[20] *Ibid.*, p. 21.
[21] *Ibid.*, pp. 26, 28–29, 153
[22] *Ibid.*, p. 210.
[23] *Ibid.*, p. 225.

self-conscious efforts (as in the case with imperatives), but by the more flexible mechanism of suggestion."[24] Moral discourse evokes or expresses attitudes because it employs and deals with words that have the tendency to express and to evoke feelings, emotions, and attitudes.

Finally, Stevenson presents what we might term a "logical" defense of the view that "X is good" means "I approve of X," although he does not press this defense too hard. He points out that one can conceive of certain situations in which a person might say, "I approve of X, but it is bad." An intractable child might make such a statement, meaning by it that he approves the act, but that his parents disapprove of it and scold him for it. A man with a troubled conscience might also make the statement. In this case, the statement might mean that his selfish attitudes approve the act, whereas his altruistic ones disapprove of it. However, if one were to say, "I wholly and unqualifiedly approve of X, but X is wholly and in every respect bad," it is difficult to see how this statement could be anything but a contradiction. Stevenson concludes these reflections with the following observation: "It can be of no service to ethics to insist that 'I approve of X and X is bad' is always a contradiction—as the alternative interpretations [of the intractable child and of the man with the troubled conscience] above will show; but it lends itself to that interpretation unless explanatory remarks are made."[25] Therefore, Stevenson places the burden of proof on anyone who would disagree with his view that "X is good" means "I approve of X."

In summary, we have seen that Stevenson's account of the emotive character of moral discourse revolves around the following points: First, attitudes determine which facts are relevant to the solution of ethical conflicts or problems in that the aim of moral discourse is the resolution of disagreements in attitudes. In so far as ethical statements include a quasi-imperative meaning (i.e. "X is good" means "I approve of X, *you ought to also*"), they are directed to altering or strengthening attitudes. Secondly, in so far as ethical judgments and definitions involve value words, they plead a cause or try to redirect attitudes, since value or emotive words are directed to such an end. Finally, Stevenson seems to place the burden of proof on anyone who would disagree with him, asking such a person to prove that it would not be contradictory to say, "I approve of X wholly and unqualifiedly, but X is wholly and unqualifiedly bad."

6. STEVENSON ON THE ROLE
OF REASON IN ETHICS

Stevenson rejects the view that knowledge has "only an inconsequential, secondary role in ethics," on the grounds that such a position is "foreign to the

[24] *Ibid.*, p. 33. See also footnote 4, p. 21, footnote 8.
[25] See footnote 14, pp. 96–97.

most obvious facts of daily experience."[26] Thus, he points out that the ethical judgments made in a book defending a particular form of government are often supported by a systematic body of beliefs, which is logically ordered and which involves truths from the fields of economics and psychology, as well as conclusions gathered from a study of such fields as history and sociology.[27]

In trying to specify the exact role which reasons play in justifying or substantiating ethical judgments, Stevenson maintains that these reasons are related to the judgments *psychologically* rather than *logically*. This distinction means that the reasons advanced to substantiate a moral judgment do not logically imply this judgment as an axiom implies a theorem. The reasons and the judgment are not related as logical ground to consequent. Moreover, the facts gathered by reason do not provide the same sort of inductive foundations for ethical judgments as they might for general scientific laws.[28] An example may serve to bring out the psychological relationship that exists between the work of reason and man's ethical judgments. I may advance a logically impeccable argument in defense of a piece of welfare legislation, but may be unsuccessful in getting a committed anticommunist to agree with me because my argument fails to influence his unfavorable attitude toward everything that resembles communism. Another person may present a fallacious argument in defense of this same legislation and may succeed where I have failed. For although it was logically fallacious, the argument may have presented the legislation in a way that appealed to the person's patriotic sentiments and that offset his unfavorable attitude toward everything resembling communism. In short, logic and induction are involved in moral discourse, but it is not the logic or illogic of an argument, or the strength or weakness of one's inductive procedures, that will be the decisive factors in the making of moral judgments. It is rather the way in which the argument affects one's emotional responses to the matters at issue.[29]

Because the relationship between ethical judgments and the arguments supporting them is ultimately of a psychological character, Stevenson maintains that it would be misleading to speak of these arguments as being either valid or invalid. For they are valid only in the sense that one is psychologically disposed to redirect or strengthen his attitudes because of them. However, we usually use "valid" or "invalid" in judging the logical or inductive grounds of a position, and not in considering the way in which these grounds may psychologically effect one's attitudes.[30] Stevenson does not want to go so far as to say, unqualifiedly, that ethical judgments are neither true or false. "It is more accurate and illuminating to say that an ethical judgment *can* be true or false,

[26] *Ibid.*, p. 24, also p. 23.
[27] *Ibid.*, p. 129.
[28] *Ibid.*, pp. 113, 115, also pp. 118, 236.
[29] *Ibid.*, pp. 27–31, 153. See also footnote 4, p. 28.
[30] See footnote 14, pp. 170, 171.

but to point out that its descriptive truth may be insufficient to support its emotive repercussions."[31] For example, in so far as the statement "X is good," means, "I approve of X," the statement is either true or false in that one either does or does not approve of X. Turning to that aspect of this statement which makes it a specifically *ethical* judgment—i.e. that quasi-imperative aspect which says, "you ought to share my attitude,"—Stevenson says that there is a certain broad sense in which this aspect can be said to be true or false. For example, I may say that a mother's judgment that her son is a good boy is true, meaning by "true" that I share her favorable attitude toward the boy.[32]

In concluding this section, we have seen that Stevenson does not deny that beliefs and reasons play a significant role in moral discourse in that they may, and certainly do, serve to strengthen or redirect attitudes. However, the connection between reasons and the attitudes which they change is a psychological one, so that in so far as moral discourse and conflicts are directed to redirecting or strengthening certain emotive aspects of man's life, ethics is not purely a cognitive or rational enterprise, grounded in the laws of logic or inductive reasoning.

7. EMOTIVISM AND THE POSSIBILITY OF A NORMATIVE ETHICS

In assessing the work of the linguistic analysts in ethics, Brand Blanshard observes, "The school has not touched bottom," meaning by this that there are many possibilities inherent in the school that remain to be explored before one can arrive at a complete and definitive evaluation.[33] This observation can be applied to Stevenson's work. As a result of considering his position, we are left with the following question, "Is a normative ethics possible?"

By a normative ethics, I mean, in general, a unified, systematic, and cognitive attempt to discover a standard or norm upon which man can rationally base distinctions between moral good and evil. Such a study would also consider the way in which this standard can be used in solving particular moral problems. Although Stevenson maintains that reason plays a significant role in man's moral life, the major thrust of his work seems to militate against the possibility of such an ethics. However, in his preface to *Facts and Values*, he intimates that his "analytical ethics" is propaedeutic to normative ethics in that it "makes no effort to answer the questions of normative ethics—withholding answers to them because, in the interest of a temporary division of labor, it must restrict attention to its selected tasks."[34] Without claiming to know how Stevenson

---

[31] *Ibid.*, p. 267.

[32] *Ibid.*, p. 169, See also p. 267.

[33] Brand Blanshard, *Reason and Goodness* (New York: The Macmillan Co., 1961), p. 263.

[34] See footnote 4, p. vi. See also footnote 14, p. 161.

himself would move from his emotivism to a normative ethics, I shall advance my reasons for holding that his emotivism does not destroy the possibility of a normative ethics.

The emotivists have performed a service in showing that human attitudes or appetites are an essential ingredient in man's moral life. The moral dimensions of human existence are not grounded exclusively in the fact that man possesses reason. Unless man were also an appetitive being living in a world full of frustrations and fulfillments, he would not be a "moral" being, one trying to discover which of these fulfillments are "true" fulfillments which ought to be pursued, and which are disguised frustrations which ought to be avoided. Moreover, in emphasizing the fact that man's moral decisions are not always the work of reason alone, but that human emotions very often play a conclusive role in the formation of these decisions, the emotivists have brought up a legitimate point, which the philosopher working in the quiet of his study is prone to overlook. It is undoubtedly true that the value judgments made by many politicians, social reformers, advertisers, and editorial writers—to mention only a few—are often expressive of emotions and intended to arouse similar emotions in others.

However, the emotivist position is open to question in so far as it seems to imply that the very nature of ethical discourse is such that all such discourse must be ultimately grounded in emotions and must be directed toward changing or strengthening emotions. We have arrived at the crux of the problem, and must undertake an evaluation of those aspects of Stevenson's work that lead to this conclusion. If it is true that all moral discourse must aim directly and immediately at changing or strengthening attitudes, it would follow that a normative ethics that proceeds from reason and appeals to reason would be impossible. The task of the normative ethician would be that of discovering the psychological techniques which he might employ to convince others to share his attitudes.

8. EMOTIVE WORDS AND THE TASK OF NORMATIVE ETHICS

Stevenson holds that ethical statements and definitions must be directed toward influencing attitudes, because the words found in these statements and definitions, are emotive in that they both express an emotion and recommend an emotion. This position is valid only if we accept the view that the words which men use control them. Certainly man may be victimized or imprisoned by words, and perhaps, more so by evaluative words than by "descriptive" or "factual" ones. However, it is necessary to move beyond Stevenson's linguistic analysis of judgments and definitions to discover whether or not the power of words over the human mind is such that every time man uses a term such as "good," he can use it only in an emotive way, i.e., as expressing his own attitudes and trying to change the attitudes of others. We must ask, "What is the character of human beings and the world in which they live that renders them incapable of using value words in such a way that they are expressive primarily of the human intellect's grasp of the human condition and are directed toward communicating this grasp to the minds of other human beings?" This question will not be completely handled until we have dealt with the problem of the relationship between empirical facts and values in the third chapter.

We have raised the question here to indicate that the mere analysis of the content of a proposition cannot of itself tell us whether the proposition is ultimately expressive of human attitudes toward that content or of a man's reflective comprehension of that content. For example, the Pythagorean theorem may or may not be expressive of an attitude, depending on whether it comes from a child who states it as being true because a teacher toward whom he had a favorable attitude told him so, or from a mathematician who has considered the question of the possible justification for the theorem.

Moreover, the work of Stevenson himself indicates that man is not completely at the mercy of the value words which he uses. For the human mind is imprisoned by the words that it uses when it does not recognize the influence that these words exercise over it. For example, in our own day, many men will accept something as true simply beause they have been told that it is "a scientific fact," although they have no idea what a scientific fact is, how it has been demonstrated, or why it must be true. The fact that man can reflect on human language, as Stevenson has done, and see that words have a history, which allows them to exercise an influence over both speaker and listener, shows that man possesses the intellectual resources to master and control his language, to put it at the disposal of the human intellect.

Human minds engaged in a moral universe of discourse need not be wholly passive and subject to the words that they use in this universe. Man's mind can take control of this universe and subject these words to his purposes, making them the *tools* and not the *masters* of communication. For example, depending on the circles in which one moves, "capitalism" and "socialism" may have either a pejorative or approbative meaning. The moral philosopher must reflect on the conditions and situations that these words describe, in order to discover what is involved in either a capitalistic or socialistic economy that makes it moral or immoral. The task of the moral philosopher is to move beyond the emotive meaning of words and to explore the moral dimensions of human existence in order to discover values to which he can give a reflective meaning and content.

9. PERSONAL APPROVAL AND MORAL VALUE

Another feature of Stevenson's treatment of moral discourse that seems to militate against the possibility of normative ethics is the view that moral statements involve an expression of emotive approval or disapproval on the part of the speaker. We are here dealing with what we have termed Stevenson's logical defense of emotivism, namely, the fact that it appears to be very odd, if not contradictory, to say, "I wholeheartedly approve of X, but X is completely bad." Such an oddity seems to indicate that ethical statements must be grounded primarily and ultimately in a man's attitudes and not in his intellect. Again, we cannot deny that when many men use pejorative or approbative words they may be simply expressing their own unfavorable or favorable emotive response to a situation. However, this fact need not mean that this is the only way in which man can deal with questions of good and evil.

It is undoubtedly true that when I say "X is good," my emotive response to X must involve some favorable attitude, however slight, toward X. This truth is not identical with the view that whenever one says, "X is good," he is saying so *because* of this favorable attitude. It is certainly possible that one's favorable attitude toward X is a result of one's cognitive grasp of X. I may come to have a favorable attitude toward X because my intellectual penetration into X has led me to see that it is good. Hence, it is an intellectual grasp of X that ultimately grounds the judgment that X is good, as well as the favorable attitude toward X.

This matter will be considered further in the examination of the relationship between human reason and value in Chapter III. At this point, I think that I have established the necessity of moving beyond an analysis of moral language to a reflection on man and his environment in order to discover how it is possible for human reason to be at the basis of man's value judgments. The prima-facie evidence certainly points to the possibility that when a man judges something to be good, he may have a favorable attitude toward the thing, but that both the attitude and the judgment are the result of his intellectual grasp of the thing as being good.

10. AIM OF MORAL DISCOURSE AND NORMATIVE ETHICS

Stevenson maintains that ethical discourse is emotive not only because it is expressive of attitudes, but also because it involves a quasi-imperative meaning and thus is directed to changing or strengthening attitudes. He relies heavily on this quasi-imperative character to sustain the view that ethical statements cannot be said to be valid or invalid and that they can be said to be "true" only in a very broad sense. He has clearly seen that the reasonableness or logic of a position does not automatically or logically guarantee that the position will change a person's attitudes or appetitive response to a situation. Hence, to the extent that induction and logic are directed to changing attitudes these processes are neither valid nor invalid, in any cognitive sense, but are simply successful or unsuccessful in so far as they do or do not change an attitude.

My disagreement with Stevenson lies in his conception that all moral discourse is directed to changing attitudes. He has failed to distinguish two levels of moral discourse, namely, moral philosophy and moral counseling. The primary aim of the moral philosopher is not to change attitudes, but to try to get at the truth of man's moral existence, to try to discover from an examination of man's existential status in the world whether there is any standard for distinguishing between moral good and evil, and if such a standard is found, to discover its scope and limitations in resolving the particular moral problems that confront man in his day-to-day life. The moral philosopher is primarily and directly concerned with contributing to the increase and development of man's knowledge of the moral dimensions of his existence, including the character of his moral problems, and the tools available in human experience to help him move toward a solution of these problems. The moral counselor is primarily concerned with discovering and changing the attitudes of his listeners.

For example, we might note the difference implied in attempts to *prove* that premarital sex relations are immoral and to *convince* someone on this matter. When I try to prove this point, I have achieved my aim if I have brought him to see the intellectual soundness of my argument, although he may not feel constrained to put this conclusion into practice in his own life. Although in the quiet of our study or in the classroom, such a state of mind may appear unreal or contrived, reflection on the human condition reveals that man is not disembodied reason, but that he is a complex being motivated by factors other than reasoned arguments. As Immanuel Kant points out, although man is capable of knowing the moral law, he "is affected by so many inclinations that he is not so easily able to make it concretely effective in the conduct of his life."[35] Hence, if we are to convince a man to put into practice a position that may have been philosophically substantiated, we must try to influence these inclinations, i.e., we must move to the level of moral counseling.

Whereas in moral philosophy, the primary concern is with the evidence that sustains the truth of a position, in moral counseling the center of interest shifts to the character of the listener, trying to discover what language, what examples, what images will strike the proper emotive response in that character. Interest has shifted from that of exploring the morality or immorality of premarital sex relations to that of trying to motivate a person to act in accord with what one has discovered to be a sound philosophical conclusion.

Although Stevenson does not avert to this point, there is implied in his view of a gap between proving a belief and changing an attitude, a rejection of the Socratic notion that virtue is identical with knowledge. As our discussion of the virtues will show, we are in substantial agreement with this implication. A growth in one's knowledge of his moral condition is not identical with the development of a proper appetitive response to one's environment. As Thomas Aquinas points out, knowledge is a *condition* for moral virtue, in that moral virtue consists in acting according to the demands of reason. However, moral virtue is essentially a perfection of the appetitive dimensions of human exist-

---

[35] See footnote 9, pp. 5–6, also p. 21.

ence.[36] Thus, the work of moral philosophy is directed toward man's cognitive grasp of his general moral situation, which can provide a basis for the moral development of his attitudes, but it itself is not directed to this development.

Stevenson sees no significance in a purely cognitive type of moral philosophy. "But perhaps the reader does not care whether his ethical subject matter is an object of approval. In that case he will have this to consider: having convinced certain men by reasoning that X is good, in his sense, he may find that in consequence they have a much greater desire to destroy X. How could such an ethics be of interest to anybody? Why, indeed, would one study ethics at all, in preference to some pleasantly innocuous subject like the stamp issues of Andorra? It will not help him to rest content in assurance that all men *ought*, in his unsanctioned sense, to approve of what he finds good. They may admit that too, and thereupon take a special pride in doing what, in his sense, they oughtn't to do."[37] Stevenson has clearly put his finger on the limitation of the type of study that we are undertaking. However, this limitation does not mean that the study has no value at all.

Immanuel Kant has pointed out that a cognitive type of moral philosophy possesses both speculative and practical value.

A metaphysics of morals is indispensable, not merely because of motives to speculate on the source of the . . . practical principles which lie in our reason, but also because morals themselves remain subject to all kinds of corruption so long as the guide and supreme norm for their correct estimation is lacking.[38]

An appreciation of Kant's point here need not commit one to an acceptance of the whole Kantian ethical system. A reflective inquiry into morals fulfills a speculative need in so far as man is interested in discovering a rational basis upon which he can ground his moral judgments. Should I lead my life according to Marxist principles, and should I try to convince others to do so? Or should I defend capitalism as the only moral economic system? Moral philosophy would appear to be a matter of interest to anyone concerned with discovering some sort of rational standard which would help him decide which attitudes, which ways of life, ought to be developed as being moral and which ought to be avoided as being immoral. The practical value of normative ethics lies in the twofold fact that there are many factors in man's world that can lead him to lose sight of the moral demands of his existence and that such an ethics, in providing man with a moral standard, helps him to recognize these factors and to subordinate them to the demands of morality.

[36] Thomas Aquinas, *Summa Theologiae* I–II, Q. 56, a.2, ad.2; trans. in *Basic Writings of Saint Thomas Aquinas*, Vol. II, ed. by Anton C. Pegis (New York: Random House, 1945), p. 421. Hereafter this work will be cited in its standard abbreviated form. S.T., with the Roman numerals following to indicate the major subdivision of the work; I–II refers to Part I of the Second Part.

[37] See footnote 4, p. 70.

[38] See footnote 9, p. 6.

In stressing the practical value of normative ethics, Kant does not deny that man may in many cases discover what his moral duty is without the help of moral philosophy, and may do so with less confusion than the philosopher who is in danger of being led astray by a mass of confused irrelevancies. However, he thinks that this danger is worth the risk.

> Innocence is indeed a glorious thing, but, on the other hand, it is very sad that it cannot well maintain itself, being easily led astray. For this reason, even wisdom—which consists more in acting than in knowing—needs science, not to learn from it but to secure admission and permanence to its precepts.[39]

Kant's point here is that the values which we hold without the help of moral philosophy are in danger of becoming empty and meaningless clichés unless there are men in the community who are capable of probing into the foundations of these values so as to give them some meaning and substance for human consciousness. Without such probing, conformity to these values is in danger of becoming "merely contingent and spurious."[40]

Emotivism's emphasis on the emotive character of values gives substance to Kant's observations concerning the practical need for a reflective inquiry into the basis of our moral values. In so far as a value has only an emotive meaning in a society, man does not control that meaning; it controls him, thus creating a rather dangerous situation. For example, to the extent that the value of "capitalism" is based on the favorable emotional responses of a society to that word, it will be possible that men may continue to cling to "capitalism," no matter what the evils and hardships which such a system might cause for a vast majority in that society. Because the value is grounded in an emotive response, man loses the control, which knowledge allows him to exercise over the system, by making him aware of the difficulties it may come to embody and by providing him with an intellectual penetration into the possibilities inherent in his situation that will be useful in overcoming these difficulties.

This defense of the value of normative ethics does not mean that the establishment of a moral standard on a rational basis will necessarily lead men to adjust their attitudes to this standard. Because man is motivated by many factors other than reason, he can always decide to act against the conclusions of a reflective inquiry. To admit this limitation is not to deny the value of normative ethics, but to recognize that those engaged in other areas of human endeavor such as the artist, the novelist, dramatist, and the poet who have a more direct access to human emotions also have a role to play in the formation of the human character.

Finally, having discussed the cognitive character and aim of normative ethics, as well as its values and limits, we shall try to specify its object or area of interest. With what aspect of reality is normative ethics concerned? It is con-

---

[39] *Ibid.* p. 21.
[40] *Ibid.*, p. 6.

cerned with that aspect of reality which comes under the voluntary control of man in so far as this aspect fulfills or frustrates the being of man. A moral philosopher reflects on this aspect of reality in order to try to discover a standard upon which man can judge the morality or immorality of these fulfillments and frustrations. A man certainly has the natural means to take his own life. The frustrations of life have become unbearable to him. Would it be moral for him to commit suicide? A man has committed a terrible murder. He has been tried and found guilty. The state certainly has the facilities for putting him to death. Would it be moral or immoral for the state to use these facilities? Can we establish some sort of basis for judging one way or the other concerning such questions? These problems are concrete examples of the areas of human existence with which the moral philosopher is concerned and of the perspective from which he tries to view them.

When one speaks of normative ethics as being concerned with those human acts that come under man's control, he is not speaking of an area of existence whose scope and limits are fixed once and for all. For example, in discovering the results produced by a certain combination of natural forces, physics has put these results under human control in that man can produce these results if he wills to do so, and granted that the necessary materials are available to him. Similarly, biology and chemistry, in discovering how certain features of man's environment can lead to sickness and disease, and how certain chemicals and organisms can be used to combat these, have extended man's control over himself and his world. As man thus comes to exercise more and more control over himself and his environment, the area of his moral responsibility is expanded. This increased control does not necessarily mean that man's moral life is made easier. There is a sense in which it is made more difficult. For man is confronted with more moral issues and problems. As man increases his control over his world, the areas of reality which he can ignore as being simply out of his hands become more limited.

This need not mean that scientific advances must be viewed as a moral setback. For in increasing the areas of human responsibility, they have increased the areas of moral opportunity. Hence, if we are to view these advances in their proper perspective, they should be seen not as solutions to moral problems, but as welcomed challenges; welcomed in that they provide man with the opportunity to make nature and human society work for the moral betterment and advancement of mankind. The moral philosopher tries to discover a standard for judging what constitutes moral betterment.

CHAPTER II

Freedom
and
Moral Responsibility

The primary purpose of this chapter is to explore the problem of the nature, limits, and scope of human freedom in so far as this problem is relevant to an understanding of man's moral situation. This problem brings one to the very center of man's moral universe because it deals with those human resources that render man capable of living and acting within a moral sphere. Because we will be at the very heart of man's moral existence it will be proper to conclude the discussion with a comparison and contrast between the legal and moral spheres of existence. Such a comparison and contrast is especially called for in view of the fact that much contemporary discussion fails to distinguish the question of the function and significance of freedom in the moral order from that concerned with the significance of responsibility in the legal order.

1. INDETERMINISM AND INDIVIDUALISTIC DETERMINISM

In an excellent brief survey of the contemporary discussion of freedom in the moral order, William Frankena discusses two approaches to the question, namely, determinism and indeterminism. Determinism holds that all events, including human choices and decisions, are caused, and hence determined, by past occurrences. The indeterministic view holds that human choices, along with some other events, occur without any determining cause.[1] There is a third alternative, which Frankena merely mentions, but does not explore, both because he thinks that it has not been adequately worked out and because any discussion of it would take him out of the field of ethics and into metaphysics. This is the view that freedom consists in some sort of self-determination.[2] It is this

---

[1] William Frankena, *Ethics* (Englewood Cliffs, New Jersey: Prentice-Hall, Inc., 1963), p. 57.
[2] *Ibid.*, pp. 60–61.

last notion of freedom that I shall try to establish as being at the basis of man's moral universe.

Perhaps most people would be inclined, at first glance, to accept indeterminism as being most compatible with man's moral experience. For in so far as man's choices are not determined at all, man alone would be responsible for his acts. It would appear that a position that sees man as performing acts in complete independence from his historical, social, and physical environment accounts for the existence of man as a moral agent. However, a closer examination reveals that there are certain elements involved in this position that are destructive of the moral enterprise.

David Hume points to a major difficulty in the indeterminist position in the following statement:

> Actions are, by their very nature, temporary and perishing; and where they proceed not from some *cause* in the character and disposition of the person who performed them, they can neither redound to his honour, if good; nor infamy, if evil. The actions themselves may be blameable. But the person is not answerable for them; and as they proceeded from nothing in him that is durable and constant, and leave nothing of that nature behind them, it is impossible he can, upon their account, become the object of punishment or vengeance. According to the principle, therefore, which denies necessity, and consequently causes, a man is as pure and untainted, after having committed the most horrid crime, as at the first moment of his birth, nor is his character anywise concerned in his actions, since they are not derived from it, and the wickedness of the one can never be used as a proof of the depravity of the other.[3]

Although this statement does seem to involve an excessively legalistic approach to morality which will be questioned later, it does make two points that show the inadequacy of indeterminism alone to ground moral experience. First of all, a wholehearted indeterminism would be forced to deny any causal connection between the self performing an act and the act he performs. If there were no causal connection between the self and his act such that the self would be said to have determined the act, this would mean that the self could not be said to have exercised any control over the act. In which case, the act could not be said to be the act of the self in question. It would not have been *his* act, properly speaking. The point here is that a complete and unqualified indeterminism would be destructive of man's moral experience in that it would involve a denial of the fact that man can be said to cause his own acts. In short, such an indeterminism cannot account for the control, however limited it may be, which man must exercise over himself and his world, if he is to be a moral agent.

Secondly, Hume's observation that an unqualified indeterminism sees man as being as pure and untainted after having committed the most horrid crime

---

[3] David Hume, *Enquiry concerning Human Understanding* (Oxford: Oxford U. Press, Selby-Bigge ed.), p. 98. For a contemporary statement of this position, see footnote 14, Chap. I, p. 313.

as at the first moment of his birth involves a fruitful insight. For any position which denies that there is any sort of continuity existing between a man's past and his present situation denies the significance of a central feature of man's moral life. Man does not possess a moral character at birth. A major task, if not the major task, of man's life is the formation and development of a moral character. This task is accomplished in so far as there is a continuity in his life so that the acts which he has performed in the past, do not die at the moment they have been performed, but live on in the self, contributing to the growth and development of a certain type of moral character.

Man deludes himself, if he thinks that what he does today will die when "today" becomes "yesterday." A man does not escape his acts. They remain a part of him. Any position which denies that man is conditioned, and to some extent at least, determined by his past experience, is not only destructive of the human moral enterprise, but also does not conform with the facts of human existence. A man who has been an alcoholic may give up his alcoholism. However, he can never be in exactly the same position with respect to alcoholic beverages as one who has never been addicted. The degradation that goes with excessive drinking, the agony of trying to overcome the habit will always be a part of his character.

Spinoza provides us with a notion of freedom which he applies only to God, but which is worthy of consideration here because, although it does involve the notion of determination, it is as destructive of the moral dimensions of existence as is an unqualified indeterminism. "That thing is called free which exists from the necessity of its own nature alone, and is determined to action by itself alone."[4] According to this definition, a free being must be completely self-enclosed, i.e., must exist in complete independence from everything else and must be determined to act in complete isolation from any context. Spinoza is right in maintaining that finite beings, such as man, cannot be said to be free in this way. For man is a conditioned being, living and acting in a historical, social, and physical environment—to mention only a few dimensions of this environment.

Moreover, not only is such freedom impossible for man, but such freedom would render many aspects of his moral existence meaningless. This conception of freedom involves an excessively individualistic view of human existence, in which individuals are seen to live and act in splendid isolation from their fellow man. As Josiah Royce points out, there can be no moral order in a world in which agents exist in "sin-tight compartments and in evil-tight compartments."[5] In such a world my acts could not contribute to the growth or destruction of another's moral character. A view of man as completely self-enclosed and cut off from any significant relationships to, and dependence on, his fellow

[4] Benedict Spinoza, *Ethic Part I*, Definition VII, in *Spinoza Selections*, ed. by John Wild (New York: Charles Scribner's Sons, 1930), p. 95.

[5] Josiah Royce, "The Problem of Job," *Studies of Good and Evil: A Series of Essays upon Problems of Life and Philosophy* (New York: D. Appleton and Co., 1898), p. 13.

man cannot account for the fact that in many cases men are either morally obligated to, or responsible for, other men.[6] Such obligations and responsibilities exist among men only because men exist in relationship so that what one man does or fails to do may make a great deal of difference to the lives of other men. If what I do makes absolutely no difference to the being of other men, and if what they do makes no difference to my being, it is difficult to see how I can be said to be obligated to or responsible for others. If man were completely self-enclosed and independent of his social environment, there would be no reason to be concerned with whether one's economic or political institutions were of a democratic or totalitarian character. The whole enterprise of trying to build a more humane society would be meaningless, since such a society would make absolutely no difference to men who could exercise their freedom and thus lead their lives in complete independence from such a society.

Moreover, such an individualistic conception of freedom would involve a denial of the significance of man's concern with the legacy which he is leaving to future generations. For since those who follow us would, according to this view, be so free that they could act in complete isolation from the history which we are making, it makes no difference to them what type of world we have left to them.

Both a negative and positive conclusion result from this investigation. On the negative side, it appears that a complete indeterminism and an exclusively individualistic or intrinsic type of determinism are destructive of the moral dimensions of existence. The positive conclusion is that man's moral experience demands that human freedom be of a limited and conditioned type, i.e., limited and conditioned by such factors as the historical and social dimensions of human existence. This conclusion is certainly not without its problems. John Hospers states this problem very clearly and succinctly.

> How can anyone be responsible for his actions, since they grow out of his character, which is shaped and molded and made what it is by influences—some hereditary, but most of them stemming from early parental environment—that were not of his own making or choosing?[7]

We seem to be caught in a dilemma. On the one hand, both the limited character of human existence and the demands of man's moral experience point to the fact that human freedom must be limited and conditioned by such features as the physical, historical, and social dimensions of human existence. On the other hand, as Hospers' question indicates, the conditioned character of

[6] Josiah Royce, The World and the Individual, Vol. II (New York: Dover, 1959), p. 283.
[7] John Hospers, "What Means This Freedom?" Determinism and Freedom in the Age of Modern Science, ed. by Sidney Hook (New York: Collier Books, 1961), p. 131. Hospers advances his own defense of human freedom in his book Human Conduct: An Introduction to the Problems of Ethics (New York: Harcourt, Brace, and World, 1961), pp. 469–521.

human existence seems to militate against the possibility of man's being free. The demands of moral experience seem to be self-contradictory in that they require that man be "free" and that he be determined by the historical and social facets of his existence.

Paul Edwards maintains that the conditioned character of man's existence is incompatible with freedom and responsibility. "The reflective person, I should prefer to express it, requires not only that the agent was not coerced; he also requires that the agent *originally chose his own character*—the character that now displays itself in his choices and desires and efforts . . . From the fact that human beings do not ultimately shape their own character, it *follows* that they are never morally responsible . . . I mean 'follow' or 'imply' in the same sense as, or in a sense closely akin to, that in which the conclusion of a valid syllogism follows from the premises."[8] Is there a sense in which man can be said to be free and morally responsible, granted that he does not originally choose his own character? This is the question which Edwards' position raises.

2. FREEDOM AS SELF-DETERMINISM

This section will be concerned with ~~discovering whether man has the power or potentiality to act freely and in what this power consists.~~ This means that the major issue will focus on establishing the conditions for the possibility of human freedom, and not on proving that this or that man is actually free.

The human intellect is an absolutely indispensable and essential ingredient of human freedom. It renders man capable of dealing with universal conceptions both in the speculative and practical orders. In the speculative order, for example, man is concerned with the laws applicable to *all* falling bodies. He cannot only add the sum of two apples plus three apples, but also wrestles with the question of the nature of numbers and of the general principles grounding various number systems. As a metaphysician, he moves from an acceptance of the reality of a multiplicity of different particular beings to question whether there is any community among these beings and what accounts for this community. Examples such as these point to the fact that although man's knowledge is dependent on the particular, sensible things of his experience, it is not restricted to these things in their particularity, but can deal with them as universals, as belonging to certain communities of being.

What is more pertinent to the particular issue at hand is that man can form certain conceptions of perfect happiness or of something that is wholly and completely good without any admixture of unhappiness, evil, or frustration— a good that is permanent and abiding, that cannot be lost. Whether such a good actually exists independently of man's conception is not important to the present

[8] Paul Edwards, "Hard and Soft Determinism," *Determinism and Freedom in the Age of Modern Science,* pp. 123, 125.

question. The point is that man does possess such knowledge, and also possesses an appetite, which is naturally attracted to such a good, an appetite that is denominated "will." It must be emphasized that I am not saying that man is actually free simply because he possesses the capacities to form a concept of an absolute good and to will this good. Unless he exercises these capacities, he is not existentially free. Man can be said to be born free only in the sense that his nature provides him with the capacities for freedom. He actually is free only when he exercises these capacities. Hence, man must make himself free by using his natural resources.

We come now to the heart of this section. How can man be said to become free by the exercise of his intellect and will? None of the particular objects of man's concrete situation is an unqualified, absolute good. They are all partial goods, at least in the sense that they all share in the precariousness of man's present existence, and hence, unlike that which is absolutely good, are in danger of being lost. For the man who knows that he lives in such an environment, there is nothing in that environment that can determine him to exercise his will. For there is no absolute good in the environment that would necessarily determine the will to act. Hence, such a man is free in that it is he who determines whether or not he will exercise his will. Although it is perhaps most difficult to explain this area of human freedom, and although the full burden of my case for human freedom will not rest on this type of freedom, it does appear to be a very significant area of human freedom. For it involves man's commitment to use his will, a commitment, which is essential if he is to assert himself as a being who will try to exercise some control over himself and his world. If man determines not to exercise his will, he has, in effect, decided that in that particular situation other forces will determine his character and his world. Of course, it is also possible that once man does commit himself to exercising his will, he may voluntarily enslave himself to some human emotion or to some object in his environment. This commitment to act or not to act voluntarily, shall be referred to as the liberty of exercise. More will be said about this type of freedom in the following section.

Having determined himself to consider the value of the objects found in his experience, man may come to see certain things or situations as being so good that whatever shortcomings they may have make no difference to him. To the extent that man comes to know things in this way so that, for all intents and purposes, they become absolute goods for him, he is naturally and necessarily attracted to them. In so far as man comes to apprehend anything as being unqualifiedly good, it becomes an end for him and he is necessarily determined by it, since the will is necessarily determined by that which man sees as an unqualified good. Hence, in so far as man is dealing with objects as ends, he is not free. It will be necessary to qualify this point after discussing man's choice of means.

Once having been committed to an object as an end, man must choose the means by which he is to achieve this end. It is in choosing means that man is said to be free. For in so far as objects are seen as means to an end, they themselves are seen as partial goods, i.e., not as goods in themselves, but as ways to achieve what is apprehended as an end or an unqualified good. For example, a man may decide that there is nothing wrong with possessing a great deal of money. Money may appear to him as an unqualified good. Seen in this light, it becomes an end for him, and he necessarily wishes to possess it. He must now consider the means to achieve this end. He may discover three possible alternatives. One may be to court a wealthy woman, with the idea of marrying her for her money. Another alternative may be to embark on a long and arduous educational program leading to the attainment of a degree in a lucrative profession. A third alternative may be to take some sort of position immediately, although the position might not be lucrative, with the idea that he would spend money only for bare essentials and by hoarding the rest, would eventually achieve the end of possessing a great deal of money.

Within this framework, each of these alternatives is a partial good in that none is actually the end itself, namely, money. As simple means, each is only a partial good so that no one of them necessarily determines man to choose one rather than the other. Man is free in this case in that it is he himself who determines which alternative he will pursue as a way to achieve his end. Freedom does involve determination, but it is the determination of the human agent to realize or actualize one of several possible alternatives known to him as a means to an end.

This discussion provides the material for qualifying what was said concerning the necessary determination of man when he is dealing with an object that he apprehends as an end. From what was said, it would appear that once a commitment has been made to an end, man is not free to change that commitment. However, it can now be said that as a result of a man's reflection on the possible means to the end, he may discover values that he now thinks outweigh the original end, thus supplanting this end, or he may come to see that the difficulties connected with the achievement of this end are so intimately tied in with the end that the end ceases to be seen as an unqualified good, and hence no longer necessitates the human agent. In the example used above, a man may come to see that a happy marriage is more important than money, thus surrendering the latter as an end. Money is no longer acknowledged as an unqualified good, in comparison with a happy marriage. Or he may have come to the realization that the difficulties connected with the alternatives open to him for obtaining the money detract from its goodness.

This discussion of the way in which a man's consideration of means may alter his commitments to certain ends points to a rather paradoxical feature of man's relationship to his ends. In so far as an object becomes an end for man, he necessarily wills it. Viewed from this perspective one's commitment to an end constitutes a limitation of one's freedom. However, it should be noted that unless a man has a goal to work toward, there is no possibility of his reflecting on means to an end, and hence there is no freedom of choice. The man who finds nothing that can function as an end for him is no moral agent. He is simply a plaything of his environment. He is a physical conductor of the aims of others.

The young man who is wholly indifferent to the prospects of going to college, of getting a job, or of entering military service may, as a matter of fact, go to college because his parents had this goal for him and pushed him into it. So long as this man remains wholly indifferent, he is not free. Whatever activities may proceed from him are not truly his own in that they do not stem from his own wishes. Thomas Aquinas states the case as follows:

> It is evident that the will can be moved to the end without being moved to the means; whereas it cannot be moved to the means, as such, unless it is moved to the end.[9]

In tying together this discussion of freedom of choice, we have seen that this freedom is the work of the human agent as a thinking-willing being. For a man has no freedom of choice if he sees no means to achieve his end. The less a man knows about his own capacities and about the possibilities for action inherent in his world, the less free he is. "The fact that man is master of his actions is due to his being able to deliberate about them; for since the deliberating reason is indifferently disposed to opposites, the will can proceed to either."[10] Put in other words, human ignorance, and all that contributes to ignorance, constitute basic limitations to man's freedom of choice.

The conception of freedom discussed in this section could best be classified as a self-determination theory. A man is said to be free in so far as he, acting on the basis of his deliberations and reflections on a situation, chooses one alternative way of acting over the other possible alternatives of which he was aware. This is self-determination in the area of man's choice of means. Since all the means were only partial goods, no one of them necessarily determined the man to his choice. The choice was made, i.e., determined by the man himself. The same point may be made with respect to man's liberty of exercise. Since he recognizes both willing and not willing as partial goods, the determination to will or not to will must come from man himself.

A consideration of the difficulties which P. H. Nowell-Smith finds in a self-determination theory will help clarify the position advanced in this section. As he sees such a theory, it maintains not only that the choice made by the self was not determined by external forces, but also that this choice was not determined by a desire or by the character of the self making the choice. The self-deter-

---

[9] S.T. I–II, Q. 8, a.3; see footnote 36, Chap. I, p. 249. See also Thomas Aquinas, *Summa contra Gentiles* III, 2; trans. in A. C. Pegis *et al.*, *On the Truth of the Catholic Faith* (Garden City, N.Y.: Doubleday, 1955–57), Bk. III, Part I, p. 37. Hereafter this work will be cited in its standard abbreviated form as *ScG*, with the Roman numerals following indicating the Book and the arabic number following indicating the Chapter in that Book.

[10] S.T. I–II, Q. 6, a.2, ad.2; see footnote 36, Chap. I, p. 229. See also Thomas Aquinas, *De Malo*, q. 16, a.5.

minist does not accept the view that the choice is determined by the self's character because this view denies that the choice is a result of the creative activity of the self, and thus denies the freedom of choice. Nowell-Smith challenges this theory to specify the relationship that seems to exist between the creative self that is said to make the choice and the character that would appear to be different from this "self."

Moreover, he thinks that the theory may simply lapse into a camouflaged indeterminism. If a choice is not determined by one's character, then it would appear that in so far as this character is concerned, the choice is not determined.[11] He thinks that some sense can be made of the notion of freedom as self-determination, if it is understood to mean that one is determined by his own motives and character, as opposed to being compelled to do something either by circumstances or by other people. However, he does not believe that self-determinists are willing to accept this interpretation.[12]

Without undertaking a consideration of Nowell-Smith's own views of the character of human freedom, I shall attempt to use the opportunity, which his criticism affords, to try to clarify the view of self-determination taken in this section. This view does not deny that the acts of a free man proceed from his character. Hence, it does not imply a distinction between one's character and one's "creative self." Rather, I have tried to specify the difference between those acts that proceed freely from one's character and those which proceed necessarily from that same character. In short, the distinction between human acts that are free and those that are not is grounded in the different ways in which these acts proceed from the human self, rather than in the fact that they did or did not proceed from this self or character. This means that the fact that an act did proceed from, or was determined by, one's character does not, of itself, imply that the act was either free or not free. If the act was determined by the self's reflection on alternatives and his choice of one of these alternatives, the act was free. If it was determined in such a way that the character's rational capacities of intellect and will did not function in a way that enabled the self to make a commitment to an end and to choose among alternate means to that end, then the act has proceeded from the self or from motives in a way that was not free.

The way in which an act can be determined by one's character, but not freely determined, will be specified in the following section dealing with the limits and conditions of human freedom. It is sufficient to note here that a free act is not a wholly unmotivated act. Both free acts and those that are not free are motivated, i.e., tend to some end, some good. A motivated act is free in so far as the motivation comes out of the workings of man's rational capacities of intellect and will. For example, a man who wants money and who has discovered the alternatives of working for it, robbing a bank, or marrying a rich widow, is

[11] P. H. Nowell-Smith, *Ethics* (Baltimore, Md.: Penguin Books, 1954), pp. 282, 283.
[12] *Ibid.*, p. 283.

motivated. However, in so far as his choice of marrying a rich widow was grounded in his deliberation concerning means—no one of which was wholly good—he was free, because it was he himself who determined to marry the widow.

In trying to show that the theory of freedom explained in this section does not imply a distinction between one's character and a rather amorphous "creative self," I am in substantial agreement with Nowell-Smith's observation that the rigid separation between a completed and formed character, on the one hand, and a creative self who freely chooses, on the other, must give way to "a conception of continual modification of character in both its moral and non-moral aspects. A man can grow more or less conscientious as time goes on, just as he can become better at tennis or more fond of Mozart."[13] There is no separation between a human character and his free acts. A human self is a being in process. He can use his rational capacities to act freely, and, thereby, become free; or he can act in such a way as to by-pass these capacities, with the result that the character that is in the process of formation in this case is a character that is becoming less and less free, in so far as such a character will find it more difficult to use its rational capacities as the principles of its activities.

3. HUMAN FREEDOM AS CONDITIONED AND LIMITED

The quotations from Hospers and Edwards in section one of this chapter indicate that a man is not free, since he is born into a world and a society which he did not make, and since his character is formed by this world. The obvious fact that man is a historical being, born into a world which influenced him before he had an opportunity to shape his own character certainly destroys the validity of any position which would attempt to apply the Spinozistic conception of divine freedom to man. For according to such a conception, freedom is predicated only of that which exists and acts in complete independence from all external factors, from all historical or social conditions.

However, the conception of human freedom advanced in the previous section was not based on the misconception that man is a being without a past or a being acting wholly outside of any context of relations, but rather on the view of man as a being whose intellect and will provide him with the opportunity to act freely in his contextual situation. In so far as man is a finite being, he can exercise his intellectual capacities, and hence his freedom, only within a context. Indeed, in so far as knowledge is an essential ingredient in human freedom, and in so far as man is not born with knowledge, but must acquire it through

[13] *Ibid.*, pp. 289–290.

a temporal process, the historical dimensions of human existence are essential to the growth and development of freedom. The same point can be made with respect to the social character of man's existence. In so far as man requires other men to grow both intellectually and emotionally, the social dimensions of his existence are essential to his freedom.

All this is not to deny that human freedom, just as human existence, is limited and conditioned, but just as an admission of the limited character of human existence need not entail a denial of such existence, so also an admission of the limited character of human freedom need not entail a denial of such freedom. Moreover, in maintaining that man can be free only within an historical, social context, I am not denying that such a context can stifle and destroy freedom. For example, a man's childhood may have been such that his rational capacities of intellect and will were not provided with the proper conditions for their development so that as an adult he is unable to use these capacities in the manner required for acting freely. His environment may have so shaped him that certain emotive factors or passions such as fear, anger, or despair have stifled his rational capacities so that he is unable to exercise these capacities in a way enabling him to take control of himself and of his world. Such a man acts not out of a rational consideration of alternatives, but out of the emotion that dominates him. Physical or neurological disorders may also stunt the development of man's rational capacities and hence deprive him of his freedom. In short, whatever factors in man's world contribute to the frustration of man's intellectual capacity—whether these factors be physical, social, or emotional—constitute the limiting factors of human freedom. For the extent and depth of a man's freedom depends on the extent and depth of his cognitive grasp of the alternatives available to him in his pursuit of a certain end and of the consequences accruing to him in such a pursuit.

John Hospers calls attention to a point that cannot be ignored by any theory that places such a heavy emphasis on the role played by human reason in making man free. He argues that a man's reasoning power does not provide him with a means of escaping from unconsciously motivated behavior. This power is simply pressed into the service of his neurosis. Thus, reason plays a "rationalizing" role in human life in that it presents reasons to justify activities that were not, as a matter of fact, grounded in reason, but in some neurosis.[14]

As should be clear from what was said above, I do not deny that a man's response to a situation may be controlled by whatever appetite or emotion controls him. Thus, in so far as goodness involves a certain relationship of suitability among things, a thing may appear to be suitable to a man either because of the character of the thing itself or because of the character of the man who is considering it. For example, an angry man may view as good something which does not appear to him to be good when he is calm.[15] There is no deny-

[14] See footnote 7, p. 129.
[15] S.T. I–II, Q. 9, a.2; see footnote 36, Chap. I, Vol. II, p. 252. See also *De Malo*, q. 3, a.6.

ing that the relationship between the cognitive and appetitive dimensions of human existence is a very complex one in which reason may well be controlled and imprisoned by an emotion. Moreover, precisely in so far as reason is controlled by an emotional disorder, man is not free. For in such a case, man acts not out of his rational resources, but necessarily follows the impulse of the emotion which may be controlling him.[16]

Any so-called "reasoning" which is carried on by such a man is nothing but "rationalizing," which consists in using reason to justify behavior that proceeds independently of reason in such a way as to give the appearance that the behavior is actually grounded in reason. For example, an alcoholic who is so addicted that there is nothing more important to him than whiskey may try to hide his addiction from both himself and his friends by quoting an article from a medical journal which stated that alcoholic beverages may serve a good function in helping a man to relax. My account of human freedom was not predicated on the view that all men are always free or that reason is always and in all cases playing its liberating role in human affairs.

However, there is a vast difference between the view that reason may be sometimes abused in rationalizing a certain type of behavior and the view that the character of human existence is such that the sole function of reason is to "rationalize" behavior. The very statement of this latter position involves the denial of the position. For if it were true that human reason is necessarily imprisoned by and at the mercy of human emotions, it would be impossible for man to be aware of this imprisonment. A man is truly imprisoned by his emotions only when he is not aware of the fact that his reasoning is only rationalizing. However, as this present discussion indicates, human reason can gain a perspective on itself and its relations to the appetitive dimensions of human existence and distinguish between reasoning and rationalizing. Moreover, it would appear that the major aim of the psychiatric treatment of one who cannot distinguish reasoning from rationalizing is to try to help free this person's reason from its enslavement to a man's desire for alcohol, drugs, power, or any other form of addiction. Hence, the existence of rationalization in the lives of men in no way means that the very nature of human reason is to "rationalize" human behavior. In summary, precisely in so far as human reason is controlled by emotions man is not free. However, evidence has been presented which indicates that it need not be so controlled. In so far as it is not controlled, man is free.[17]

The question raised by Edwards' position can now be considered. Can man be free and morally responsible, granted that he does not originally choose his own character? In so far as the question is based on the view that an act that is determined by one's character is necessarily not free, it is based on a false premise. The fact that an act flows from one's character does not necessarily

---

[16] *S.T.* I–II, Q. 10, a.3; see footnote 36, Chap. I, Vol. II, p. 263.
[17] *Ibid.*

mean that it is not free. An agent is free in so far as, by deliberating on his situation, he uncovers certain possible alternatives to an end, and acting out of this cognition, he himself chooses to realize one alternative rather than any other. An act proceeding from one who has thus deliberated and chosen is free. An act proceeding from one who has not deliberated and chosen is not free. What renders an act free or not free is the *way* in which it proceeds from a certain character, not the *fact* that it either has or has not proceeded from a given character.

Moreover, Edwards' observation that a man is not free because he did not mold his own character from birth, is open to the charge of committing the fallacy, *Post hoc, ergo propter hoc* (After this, therefore on account of, or because of this). The fact that I have a past need not necessarily mean that this past is actually causing me to do what I am now doing. This is not to deny that my past does play a role in my present situation. However, this role need not be that of a necessitating cause. As was seen, the past may function both as a limiting factor in a person's present situation in so far as it limits the alternatives available to him and as an enriching factor in that it provides him with certain opportunities. Edwards seems to have ignored these roles of the past, and seems to have concluded that since the past precedes the present, it must necessarily be related to the present as a wholly necessitating cause is related to its effect.

Hospers' view of the relationship between the past and present demands that this relationship be examined in some detail. He presents those who would argue for the possibility of human freedom with the following difficulty. If a man is able to overcome the influences of his early environment, this ability is itself an effect of this environment. If he is unable to overcome these influences, this inability is also a result of his early environment. Thus, a man is not responsible either for his ability or inability to overcome early environmental influences, since both are determined by these very influences.[18]

It is true that in so far as a man's ability to act freely is a result of his early environment over which he had no effective control, he is not responsible for this ability. If a man's childhood or physical condition were such as to deprive him of the possibility of using his reason, he could not be held to be morally responsible for his situation. In so far as man's capacity for freedom is viewed simply in its relationship to those factors of his existence over which he had no control, it is true that man is responsible neither for lacking nor for possessing this capacity. However, granted that he does possess the capacity, he is responsible for what he does with this capacity. Granted that he does possess such a capacity, he is responsible for freely willing either to exercise this capacity so that it will grow and develop or to reject this exercise in favor of the easier life of going along with the crowd, or of letting others do the thinking, while he goes out and enjoys himself. At this point, we are dealing with freedom considered as the liberty of exercise. Because growth and development in freedom

[18] See footnote 7, p. 138.

may require an arduous job of deliberating, and may require that one challenge
certain fashions, man is not necessarily determined to commit himself to a life
of freedom and to the exercise of his rational capacities. In short, man may
freely reject freedom as his end.

Perhaps to a philosopher working in an ivory tower or to students relaxing in
the reflective atmosphere of the classroom, the notion that man can freely reject
a free life seems utterly inconceivable. However, the reality of this fact was not
lost to Dostoyevsky's Grand Inquisitor in *The Brothers Karamazov*. The Grand
Inquisitor scolds the Christ-figure for not recognizing that man is not interested
in being free.

> I tell Thee that man is tormented by no greater anxiety than to find some one
> . . . to whom he can hand over that gift of freedom with which the ill-fated
> creature is born . . . In bread there was offered Thee an invincible banner; give
> bread, and man will worship Thee, for nothing is more certain than bread. But
> if some one else gains possession of his conscience—oh! then he will cast away
> Thy bread and follow after him who has ensnared his conscience . . . For the
> secret of man's being is not only to live, but to have something to live for. With-
> out a stable conception of the object of life, man would not consent to go on liv-
> ing, and would rather destroy himself than remain on earth, though he had bread
> in abundance . . . Nothing is more seductive for man than his freedom of con-
> science, but nothing is a greater cause of suffering . . . Instead of taking posses-
> sion of men's freedom, Thou didst increase it, and burdened the spiritual kingdom
> of mankind with its suffering forever . . . But didst Thou not know he would
> at last reject even Thy image and Thy truth, if he is weighed down with the
> fearful burden of free choice?[19]

The Grand Inquisitor has emphasized the fact that there are goods other than
the free life to which a man is attracted. In weighing goods such as material
comforts and the security of having others make decisions for us against the
value of freedom, most men, according to the Grand Inquisitor, will choose the
material comforts and the security of having no responsibilities. There are those
who reject the "fearful burden" of freedom, the burden of living in a world in
which everything is not settled. The world of the free man is a world in the
making, and within limits, it is the free man who is to decide the character of
his world. Although the Grand Inquisitor's view that most men do not want to
be free is open to question, he has put his finger on some dimensions of human
existence which may lead a man to reject a life of freedom.

It is necessary to recognize the rather tragic fact that man can exercise his
freedom in such a way as to develop a character that will deprive him of his
freedom. He can freely perform actions that will contribute to the development
of a character that is so dominated by certain emotional factors that he will be

---

[19] Fyodor Dostoyevsky, *The Brothers Karamazov*, trans. by Constance Garnett, with introduction by Marc Slovina (New York: The Modern Library, 1950), p. 302.

unable to use his rational capacities effectively. This is the truth behind the view that real freedom consists in doing what is in keeping with one's nature. A man who freely pursues a line of conduct that places him under the control of his emotions is actively engaged in enslaving himself to some object or emotion.

Spinoza describes such enslavement in pointing out that a man controlled by his emotions "is not his own master, but is mastered by fortune, in whose power he is, so that he is often forced to follow the worse, although he sees the better before him."[20] The lives of dope addicts and of alcoholics, who may have been able to control themselves at one time, provide the most obvious examples of such men. These men find themselves in a situation in which it is they who are ruled and controlled by dope and alcohol, rather than vice versa. Unfortunately, alcohol and dope by no means exhaust the innumerable objects or needs to which man may become slavishly attached. Whatever the objects or needs to which one becomes enslaved, the situation is the same in all cases in that these men may be able to be free once again, but only with great difficulty and with the help of others who can try to establish certain types of environments in which the rational capacities of such men may once again assert themselves.

Dictators have abused this notion of freedom as the right to do what one ought to do or what is in keeping with one's nature by interpreting it to mean that man has the right to do only what the dictator wants him to do. They have undertaken the contradictory task of "forcing man to be free" by attempting to control and mold him through a reign of terror, fear, and suppression. They have tried to make man free by establishing an environment which is diametrically opposed to the growth of freedom, i.e., an environment in which human knowledge cannot develop and mature. They have either lost sight of the fact that no man can actually force another to be free, or they have conveniently chosen to ignore this fact in pursuing their selfish interests. No man can force or *coerce* another to perform an act freely, because in order to act freely a man must be acting for some end, something that he himself sees as an unqualified good, whereas coercion involves using physical force in trying to get a man to do something which he does not see as a good.

However, a man living under the threat of violence may perform the acts demanded of him out of the sheer fear and terror which this threat introduces into his life. To the extent that such fear controls man's rational capacities so that he cannot use them as principles of his actions, he is not acting freely. It must also be admitted that the threat of physical violence may lead a man to freely perform an act which he would not have performed had the threat not existed. For example, it may be true that certain Nazis may not have helped in the extermination of Jews, if no threat were hanging over them for failure to cooperate. When faced with the concrete choice between exterminating Jews

[20] See footnote 4, *Ethic*, Part IV, Preface, p. 282.

and having themselves exterminated or imprisoned, they may have freely chosen the former course. Hence, the fact that a man is confronted with two rather unpalatable alternatives need not mean that he did not act freely or that he was not morally responsible. It is practically impossible, of course, for one human being to judge when another human being has been so terrorized that he was unable to exercise free judgment. This discussion does not contradict the view that coercion cannot make a man free. A man may freely act in the face of the threat of coercion, but he must possess the capacity to act freely. In so far as coercion itself is directed toward physically forcing a man to act, without the use of his rational capacities, it contributes to stunting the growth of these capacities, and, therefore, of human freedom.

In summary, I have tried to show that it is erroneous to view the historical and social dimensions of human existence as if they were only limitations of human freedom. These dimensions are also essential factors in the growth of human freedom. Whether they function as principles of limitation or principles of growth depends upon whether they frustrate or contribute to the development of man's rational capacities. Because the exercise of these capacities makes man morally free, whatever frustrates such exercise is destructive of this freedom. Finally, it was also acknowledged that psychological and physical factors may frustrate the exercise of man's intellect and will.

4. FREEDOM IN THE LEGAL AND MORAL ORDERS

The problem in this section will be that of exploring the relevance of freedom to morality. Why and in what sense is freedom essential to human morality? The exploration of this question will lead to a consideration of the relationship between the legal and moral orders of human endeavor. The reason for moving to the latter consideration is that many seem to think that the significance of freedom to morality lies in the fact that man must be free, if praise, blame, and punishment are to have a legitimate role in man's life. For example, Paul Edwards implies that people hold to a certain type of determinism, which allows for human freedom, because such a position allows them to continue punishing their enemies and their children.[21] One might suffer from a bad conscience if he could not convince himself that those whom he is punishing freely performed the acts for which they are being punished. I hope to show that the essential role of freedom in human morality does not lie in the fact that it permits us to praise and punish others or ourselves. The issues in this section will be discussed under the following three subheadings: a. The Case for Morality Without Freedom, b. Freedom As Essential to the Morality of Aspiration, and c. Against Moralism and Positivism in Law.

[21] See footnote 8, p. 119.

a. The Case for Morality
   Without Freedom

Charles Stevenson considers the question of freedom's role in morality in terms of whether or not one must say that a man is free in order to render moral judgments concerning his acts significant. He points out that the ethical judgments, which are passed on the behavior of others, are usually made to achieve a mixture of purposes, but that an essential ingredient in these purposes is usually that of trying to control the future acts of our listeners. Ethical judgments are directed toward changing "avoidable" acts, i.e., acts which would not have occurred had a person made a different choice from the one he actually made.[22] Stevenson maintains that avoidability so viewed is compatible with either a completely or a partially deterministic world. Even if a "bad" choice were completely determined by extrinsic forces, it would be meaningful to pass an ethical judgment on this choice, if this judgment could determine attitudes so that *in future* situations these attitudes would replace the extrinsic forces as the determining factors in bringing about a different choice.

Stevenson deals with the question of the role of freedom in morality from the point of view of the role which ethical judgments play in changing or controlling certain forms of human behavior. He is concerned with whether freedom is necessary to ground the significance of ethical judgments as means of changing or strengthening human attitudes and the behavior that flows from these attitudes. Seen from the point of view of this question, the significance of an ethical judgment passed on a certain activity is not destroyed either by the fact that this activity was wholly determined by some factor extrinsic to the agent or by the fact that it was not fully determined by extrinsic factors. For an ethical judgment can play its role of determining or guiding conduct in either case. A completely determined world would preserve the significance of ethical judgments in that these judgments could function as one of the determining factors in such a world. Thus, by telling a child that his behavior was bad, I would insure that his future behavior would be different. Morality is also compatible with a partial determinism because such determinism still allows for the control of future behavior by ethical judgments, although the control is not as exact as it would be in a completely determined world.[23]

The logical positivist Moritz Schlick takes a similar tack in trying to show that moralists have created a pseudo problem for themselves in their concern with the role of freedom in man's moral life. He points out that the significance of responsibility to ethics can be seen by investigating a man's aim in imputing responsibility to a person. The aim is clearly to reward or punish a person for certain actions. Because we do not usually have judges to reward people, Schlick

[22] See footnote 4, Chap. I, pp. 298–302.
[23] *Ibid.*, pp. 313–314.

examines the relationship between punishment and responsibility in order to see whether or not this relationship requires a notion of freedom.

He grounds his opposition to the view that freedom is a necesssary basis for human morality by pointing out that punishment is directed toward reforming the wrongdoer and intimidating others. Punishment is directed toward developing certain motives both in the wrongdoer to keep him from repeating his evil acts and in others to keep them from becoming wrongdoers.[24] Granted that the aim of punishment is to reform or to intimidate, and granted that punishment is meted out only to responsible people, it follows that a responsible person is one who can be reformed or intimidated by punishment.

This understanding of what constitutes a responsible person means that there is a difference between the question concerning who is responsible for an act and the question concerning who originated an act. For example, Peter's great-grandparents may be originators of his evil act, because this act was determined by the character he inherited from them. However, we consider Peter to be responsible for this act, if we know that by punishing him we can reform him. If, however, the character he inherited made him insane, and hence incapable of being reformed by punishment, we would not hold him responsible for his act.[25] Hence, it is clear to Schlick that such central moral concepts as responsibility and punishment do not require that man be free, if one means by free that man determines himself to one course of action rather than to another.

b. FREEDOM AS ESSENTIAL TO THE MORALITY OF ASPIRATION

There is one point in Stevenson's and Schlick's treatment with which I am in agreement. Both are searching for a conception of responsibility in which the moral agent is seen to be open to the influence of other beings. In their view man does not exist in a "sin-tight" compartment, completely oblivious to and untouched by the judgments and reactions of others to his behavior. The conception of freedom presented in this chapter tries to do justice to this facet of human existence.

There are two rather major difficulties in Stevenson's and Schlick's positions. First of all, they seem to have unconsciously introduced the problem of making a decision and a free choice into the life of the one who is judging the behavior of others. The judge must decide whether or not to punish or to pass a condemning judgment on a certain type of behavior. He must decide whether or not his judgment or punishment would in any way change the behavior of the wrongdoer himself or keep others from performing the same sort of act. Hence, it appears that the judge is confronted by alternatives among which he

---

[24] Moritz Schlick, *Problems of Ethics,* trans., and with a new introduction by David Rynin (New York: Dover Publications, 1962), pp. 151–152.

[25] *Ibid.,* pp. 153–154.

must choose. This notion of a choice to be made on the part of the judge permeates both Stevenson's and Schlick's handling of the problem.

However, it is not inconceivable, especially in Schlick's case, that they could deny that the judge is confronted with a choice. They could maintain that the relationship between the wrongdoer's act and the judgment of the spectator is a stimulus-response relationship. The act of the wrongdoer automatically and necessarily triggers a judgment of condemnation by the spectator. If this is their position, then the position would seem to lose all relevance to man's moral situation. There is no longer any moral problem, any choice to be made between alternatives by the judge, and it would appear that the wrongdoer had no choice, having been determined by his character or his past. If this is what Stevenson and Schlick had in mind, they have described a mechanistic world in which granted act X by Agent A, Judge B will pass judgment Y. There are no decisions to be made, no alternatives to be faced, no problems for either the judged or the judge. A description of a world without problems certainly does not seem to apply to man's moral world.

Either Stevenson and Schlick have introduced a certain freedom of choice in the life of the judge (a point which apparently both would deny) or they have described a world and a universe of discourse in which there are no alternatives to be faced by the judge since he automatically responds to the behavior of the one whom he is judging, in which case their description fails to do justice to the problematic aspects of man's moral life. However, the burden of my criticism of the Stevenson-Schlick approach does not rest on this point. It was brought up simply to force the issue, to get one thinking concerning whether or not, and in what sense, if any, the judge can be said to be either free or determined. Schlick and Stevenson seemed to be so concerned with the status of the wrongdoer that they ignored the question of the judges' freedom or lack thereof.

The brunt of my criticism will be directed to the "spectator" view that they took with regard to the question of the relevance of freedom to morality and that led them to a legalistic view of man's moral life. They took a spectator view in that they considered the problem of the role of freedom in morality by asking whether a spectator's judgment or condemnation of an act required freedom on the part of the one performing the act. They took a legalistic view of moral life in that their analysis of the significance of freedom in this life was limited to the question of whether or not freedom need be posited in order to make judgments of praise and blame, acts of rewarding and punishing morally significant. Against this position, I hope to show that, although praise and blame do play a role in morality, they are not at the center of the moral situation.

Rather what is at the heart of man's moral life is what Lon Fuller terms "the morality of aspiration."[26] Man as a moral being is a being engaged in the task

---

[26] Lon Fuller, *The Morality of Law* (New Haven: Yale University Press, 1964), p. 5.

of trying to *real*-ize (to make real) the possibilities for what is best in himself and in his world. Hence, when asking whether or not freedom is essential to man's moral existence, it is on this attempt that one must center his attention and not on the role of praise and blame.

Although one need not agree with the "individualistic" interpretation that Henry David Thoreau would probably give to the following statement, he can appreciate the fact that it does capture the spirit of what is central to the moral enterprise:

> If a man does not keep pace with his companions, perhaps it is because he hears a different drummer. Let him step to the music which he hears, however measured or far away. It is not important that he should mature as soon as an apple tree or an oak. Shall he turn his spring into summer? . . . Shall we with pains erect a heaven of blue glass over ourselves, though when it is done we shall be sure to gaze still at the true ethereal heaven far above, as if the former were not?[27]

Thoreau's statement leads us to recognize that a man lives morally not by trying to pursue those ends which others have set for themselves, but by trying to work toward those ends which seem to enrich and fulfill him. He must try to mature and develop those resources that he finds within himself according to the time schedule, which he finds such growth to require, not according to the schedule and means that may be fitting to something external to him. If he tries to lead his life any other way, he will find that all his labors have been directed toward encasing himself in a pseudoworld, while still haunted by his "true ethereal heaven."

A man's moral task consists in trying to discover what he is to make of himself and of whatever part of the world with which he comes in contact. He must ask himself what sort of man can he be and how can he work toward being such a man. Once morality is seen in this light, freedom as self-determination is seen to be essential to man's life. There is no moral life for a man who is not in the process of considering what good he is to work for and the alternatives he is to pursue in working toward this good. The good for which a man works and the way in which he tries to achieve it are the ingredients that constitute his moral character. This process and the problems that it implies would be meaningless if man were not free.

This conception of the role of freedom in man's moral life is helpful to defining the proper role of punishment and condemnation in morality. Stevenson and Schlick are right in holding that it is meaningful to punish or condemn someone, although the one condemned or punished is not free. For we certainly show our displeasure to dogs and children when they perform an act which we do not like and which we realize can be avoided in the future. However, it would appear that there is a difference, or at least, there *should be* a difference, in the results which we hope to achieve in the respective cases. In the case of a

---

[27] Henry David Thoreau, *Walden* (New York: Harper and Row, 1965), pp. 241–242.

dog, we hope to establish a stimulus-response pattern so that the dog will in the future automatically perform the act which we desire. The establishment of the same sort of pattern in the education of a child would mean that he has been reduced to an automaton. Such a result would mean that the educative process had failed.

Praise and blame function properly in the education of a child, when they have contributed to the growth and development of his rational capacities, when they have provided these capacities with the opportunity to assert their mastery of the emotional aspects of the child's life. A child is disciplined not so that he will become an adult who gives unquestioning obedience to certain authorities or to certain commands. He is disciplined so that he may have the opportunity to become a reflective agent, an agent who tries to "step to the music which he hears however measured or faraway," a music which is not imposed upon him from an external source. A child is disciplined not so that he will passively repeat the values of his parents, but so that when he achieves maturity he will reflect on these values preserving what he finds worthwhile in them and adding to them those values which he himself has discovered.

Viewed from this perspective, it seems clear that praise and blame have a moral significance, only in so far as they are aimed at a being who has the capacities to be free and to exercise these capacities by assuming his own responsibilities. Freedom and responsibility are thus seen as essential constituents in morality and not as an excuse or justification for punishment and blame. They are essential to morality because a being who is not free and responsible cannot actually be a moral being in the proper sense, a being who has reached the level of the morality of aspiration. Freedom is important to morality, because unless a man is free, he does not see himself and his world as involving possible values and alternatives whose *real*-ization depend ultimately on the decisions and choices which he alone can make. It is in this way that freedom and responsibility become so intimately connected in the moral order. For the man, whose reflections make him aware of the various capacities for human fulfillment inherent in his life, realizes that he is responsible—perhaps in a limited way, but nonetheless responsible—for which among these capacities will be fulfilled and how they will be fulfilled. In short, without freedom and responsibility, the very heart of morality—what Fuller has termed the morality of aspiration—becomes impossible.

Moreover, within such a moral context, the value and success of punishment and reward are not judged by their ability to bring one to conform his external behavior to our demands. They are judged by their success in helping a person think for himself, to pursue a way of living which he has seen, through his own reflection, as most properly fulfilling those capacities for the good life that are found in himself and his world. If it could be shown that praise and blame could secure only unthinking conformity to demands which society imposes on the individual from without, then praise and blame would have no role at all to play in the moral order. This point is made in order to emphasize that praise and blame have moral significance only in so far as they detract from or contribute to the development of those capacities within man which, if exercised, will render him a free, i.e., a moral, agent.

c. AGAINST MORALISM AND POSITIVISM IN LAW

In so far as they have lost sight of this aim of praise and blame, Stevenson and Schlick seem to have mistaken the purely legalistic function of praise and blame for its moral function. For the legal order, as distinct from the moral order, is primarily concerned with establishing rules regulating the external relations existing between men. Thus, the law cannot require that one man love his neighbor, but it can require that he not injure the other physically, whatever may be his thoughts concerning him. Hence, in the legal order, punishment or the threat of punishment has succeeded in so far as it has prevented a man from doing harm to his neighbor, although it has not thereby convinced him to view his neighbor as a man deserving all the respect that any man deserves.

From what has been said up to now, it would appear that morality has absolutely nothing to do with the legal order. This appearance must be qualified, although I will try to show that the two orders ought not to be simply identified. It is necessary to avoid the extremes of an excessively "positivistic" view of law and an excessively "moralistic" view.[28] The positivistic view states that law and morals are and ought to be completely separate so that there are no moral issues involved in a legal system. The moralistic view identifies law and morality, with law being seen as a means to enforce moral demands.

First we shall deal with the way in which the legal and moral orders can and ought to be connected. In so far as legal systems influence human lives, they have moral dimensions. This position does not deny that such systems also involve the historical, cultural, and economic dimensions in the life of a people, but it does insist that laws are always open to moral scrutiny. In general, the task of the legal order is directed toward regulating the external relations between man and man so as to allow men to live peaceably in a community secure in their persons.

There are certain ways of fulfilling this task that do not involve moral issues For example, there was no moral issue involved in the decision concerning which color should signify "stop," and which, "go," on traffic lights. However, there is a moral issue involved in a law that maintains it is essential to the peace of the community that public speeches or writings, which disagree with the

---

[28] For a good survey of the views taken on this issue, see Roscoe Pound, *Law and Morals* (Chapel Hill, N.C.: The University of North Carolina Press, 1924). For a more recent discussion on this point see H.L.A. Hart, *The Concept of Law* (London: Oxford University Press, 1961), pp. 181–207.

official government position, be suppressed and subject to legal penalties. For in so far as such a law hinders the free, public exchange of ideas, it hinders the intellectual growth that is essential to the development of man as a moral being. Man cannot develop his intellectual capacities in a vacuum. He needs a society of men whose ideas he can come to know and to whom he can submit his own ideas to see whether or not, and to what extent, they can retain their validity in the face of criticism. Although the law cannot make a man moral, it can and must provide a social order that allows the members of that society to grow and develop as moral agents. A "peace" and "security" that frustrates such development is open to moral criticism.

The fact that law is concerned with regulating external relations among men constitutes a limitation on the role law should play in man's moral life. For law is restricted primarily to dealing with those actions of man that affect the peace and security of others in the community. This would mean that a moralistic approach to law is unacceptable in demanding that law attempt to regulate man's private morality. For example, the law ought not penalize an alcoholic for being intemperate, although it may penalize him if he makes himself a public nuisance by going out in a crowded area and embarrassing others by his behavior, or if he drives an automobile in a drunken condition, thus endangering the lives of others. If, however, he drinks himself into a stupor in the privacy of his own home, there is nothing that the law can or ought to do about it.

The same sort of reasoning should apply to homosexual behavior. If such activities are practiced by consenting adults in privacy, it is difficult to see how they constitute a threat to the peace and security of other members of the community. This does not mean that homosexual activities practiced in private are not immoral. It simply means that so long as they are performed in private by consenting adults they do not appear to impinge on the right of other members of the community to be spared from being subjected to practices they find revolting.

The point of this position is that the legal resources of society must, as much as possible, be restricted to those external acts that threaten the peace (which includes not being forced to witness behavior that is wholly contrary to community tastes) and security of an innocent party.

The reason for this position is that the character of man as a free moral agent is not simply a theoretical fact that must be admitted, but is also a reality that must be respected in the practical order. As a moral agent, man is not a purely "public" being who is simply an object to be viewed and examined whenever others are interested in him. As long as his actions are not directed to harming an innocent party, his privacy or subjectivity must be respected. However, in order to enforce private morality, it would be necessary for the law to deny such privacy to man. If such a law were to be meaningful and effective, it would be necessary to give law enforcement agents the right to observe a man at any time and in any place. There would be no area of a man's life that would not be open to public scrutiny. He would be the object of such scrutiny in every moment and in every area of his life, even in those areas not affecting the community directly.

Such a situation would amount to reducing man to the same level as an object in a museum, and would constitute a denial, in the practical order of daily living, of his character as a moral subject. For in such a situation, it would be literally true to say that man exists only for the law, i.e., his whole reality would be as an object for legal scrutiny. However, man's capacity for freedom—his ability to determine himself, to develop and remake his own character—makes him a being who does not exist only as an object for others, but also as a subject, a being whose life is in his own hands, as it were. It is true that this subjectivity is limited and precarious, but to say that it is limited and precarious is not to deny its reality.

In summary, it is necessary to reject both an excessively moralistic view of law, which simply equates the legal and moral orders and which sees law as an instrument to "make" men moral, and an excessively positivistic view, which gives the impression that there is no moral dimension whatsoever connected with legal systems. Basically, I have tried to show that law does have moral dimensions in so far as it influences human lives. It is open to moral criticism if its regulations are of such a nature as either to frustrate the development of man's moral character or to deny his character as a moral subject.

5. SUMMARY AND PROBLEM AREAS

In dealing with the problem of human freedom, we have not been considering an issue that is merely propaedeutic to man's moral life. Freedom is not a basis to this life in the sense that man must *first* be free and *later* enter into the moral sphere. The free man is the "moral" man—the man who has moral problems, the man who actually lives and moves within a moral universe. The free man lives in a world of possibilities, a world constructed by the interaction between his reason and imagination, and his environment. Living in this open world, man bears the responsibility of deciding which possibilities to actualize in himself and in his environment. It is up to him to decide what he is to make of himself and whatever part of the world to which his acts extend. He is thus faced with the problem of trying to discover some sort of standard upon which to base his decisions.

There are those who might maintain that a moral standard is necessarily destructive of the freedom that has been discussed in this chapter. For standards must necessarily be imposed on a man by some external source. Thus, to try to impose a standard applicable to all men is to reduce morality to the legal order in that man is then expected to conform to an external rule established by a source outside of himself. The same difficulty applies to the view of morality as being primarily a morality of aspiration. It might appear that to attempt to impose a general moral standard on man involves a denial of the morality of aspiration, as we have interpreted it. In a morality of aspiration, the free agent must find his good life for himself. It would appear that a moral standard spelling out what constitutes the good life and applicable to all men is incompatible with the morality of aspiration.

Moreover, the discussion of the morality of aspiration, the quote from Thoreau, the discussion of the contrast between the legal and moral orders—all seem to imply a highly "individualistic" approach to morality, an approach oblivious to the social demands of morality, which were so strongly emphasized in the rejection of any notion of freedom, completely cutting man off from any influence from his fellow man. These problems will be considered in Chapters IV and V.

CHAPTER III

Nature
and
The Moral Order

In evaluating the emotive conception of ethics, an attempt was made to show that Stevenson's analysis of moral discourse does not justify the view that all such discourse must necessarily be emotive. It was also pointed out that both the problem raised by Stevenson's position and the stand that was taken with respect to this position demanded that one move beyond the analysis of moral language to an investigation of the character of human existence in the world. More specifically, the issues raised in the evaluation of emotivism require an investigation of the question concerning the relationship between nature and values. This question also raises the issue of the relationship existing between human reason and the world in which man lives. Finally, an examination of this complex question is also necessary if the view that ethics need not necessarily be restricted to a study of the logic of moral discourse, but can be morally normative, is to be substantiated.

The purpose of this chapter is to state and explore the problems surrounding the relationship between nature, moral values, and human reason. The writings of John Stuart Mill and G. E. Moore will be used to state and clarify the issues involved in these problems. It is to the credit of these men to have exposed, each in his own way, the difficulties involved in man's attempt to ground a moral standard in human reason's reflections on nature. An indispensable feature of any philosophical undertaking is to probe a problem with the hope of gaining an appreciation and understanding of its depth and complexity. For one's philosophical position can only be as profound as is his conception of the problem which that position is intended to meet. Hence, it is important to grasp the nature of the problem which Mill and Moore present.

In the interest of historical accuracy, it is necessary to point out that this chapter will be restricted to dealing with the problematic aspects of Mill's and Moore's thought, and only in so far as these aspects relate to the question of the relationship between nature and morality. Moreover, in presenting Moore's thought, I shall rely primarily on his views as presented in his *Principia Ethica*. For although in later life Moore himself indicated that he was not in full agreement with the positions taken in this book, the fact is that the book itself has

achieved something of the status of a classic in the English-speaking philosophical world in the sense that later philosophers have used it either to show
that their own positions are able to resolve the problems raised by Moore or to
show that these problems prove or help to substantiate the view that morality
is purely emotive or that moral philosophy must be restricted to a study of the
logic of moral discourse.

After completing the expositions of Mill's and Moore's statements of the difficulties revolving around the relationship between nature and moral values, I
shall try to show that although there is much in their arguments which is destructive of an overly facile identification between nature and morality, an
ethics based on reason working within and reflecting on nature is possible and
that such an ethics is not open to the valid criticisms made by these men against
a simple identification of nature and morality.

1. JOHN STUART MILL'S OPPOSITION TO IDENTIFYING NATURE AND MORALITY

Because Mill thinks that the confusion concerning the meaning of such
terms as "natural" and "nature" has led to a great deal of difficulty, and has been
the source of erroneous views in ethics, he set out to clarify the meaning of
"nature," before undertaking an examination of its role in ethical theory. He
distinguishes two meanings of the term. First, nature is the sum of all the
phenomena that actually exist, including the causes for these phenomena and
the capacities within these causes to produce other phenomena.[1] This description equates nature with the whole of reality, or, as C. S. Lewis once put it,
nature is taken to mean "the whole show."[2] A second meaning of "nature" is
one based on the distinction that is often drawn between nature and art, with
"nature" being understood as the brute, given facts of existence, whereas "art"
is seen to refer to the transformation that occurs in nature under the influence
of human volition and action. Understood in this context, "nature" means that
which occurs apart from the voluntary agency of man.[3]

The fact that a certain action which is said to be "according to nature," or
"demanded by nature," is usually viewed as a morally good act, whereas an
action that is said to be "unnatural" or "contrary to nature," is usually viewed
as an immoral act would seem to imply that there must be some third meaning
for the term "nature." This third meaning seems to be required because the two
meanings already discussed involve the notion that nature is that which is or
can be, whereas ethics deals with "what ought to be." Hence, it would appear

[1] John Stuart Mill, "Nature," in Nature, the Utility of Religion and Theism (London:
Longmans, Green Reader, and Dyer, 1874), pp. 5–6.

[2] C. S. Lewis, Miracles: A Preliminary Study (New York: The Macmillan Co., 1947),
p. 10.

[3] See footnote 1, pp. 15–16.

that if nature is to function as a moral standard for "what ought to be," its meaning cannot be reduced to that which is or can be. However, Mill attempts to show that there is no need for a third meaning that would account for the view that nature is seen as a moral standard. He maintains that those who speak of nature as a criterion for what ought to be are guilty of confusing the given state of affairs, that which already exists, with that which ought to exist.[4]

Mill divides his investigation into the possible identification of nature and moral goodness into two parts, considering first whether goodness can be identified with nature considered as the aggregate of phenomena and of their causes, and secondly whether it can be identified with nature viewed as that which occurs apart from the intervention of human agency. To demand that one follow the laws of nature, when "nature" is taken to mean all that is, is nonsensical, since the only way in which man can act is by using the powers of nature. Because every action involves the exercise of some natural power and because the results of these actions are those that naturally flow from the exercise of these powers, man has no choice but to act according to nature. Mill holds that the command to "follow nature" can be meaningful only if it is interpreted as suggesting that man "observe nature" in his attempts to live a moral life.[5]

Whereas the command to follow nature seems to make nature a standard of moral behavior, the suggestion to observe nature means that man must use the means available to him in nature in order to work toward that which he considers morally good and to avoid that which he considers morally evil. This suggestion views nature not as a standard for morality, but as a means which man must use in trying to be moral. Since man acts within a natural context and must use natural capacities, he must examine this context and these properties in order to discover those features inherent in them, that will either further or hinder whatever goal he may wish to achieve. Thus, a study of nature can uncover ways to achieve a morally good end or to avoid an immoral result, but such a study does not provide a criterion for distinguishing between moral good and evil.

Mill next examines the possibility that nature considered as the spontaneous activity of things acting independently of human agency may provide a standard for moral behavior. He maintains that to accept the spontaneous course of nature as a moral standard is both irrational and immoral.[6] Such a position is irrational in that it implies that the spontaneous order of nature is perfectly good and satisfactory. This implication is justified only if it can be proved that nature, when left to itself, is always beneficial to man. However, floods, droughts, plagues—to mention only a few of the evils perpetrated on man by nature—point to the fact that the spontaneous course of nature is not to be pas-

---

[4] *Ibid.*, pp. 9–13.
[5] *Ibid.*, pp. 15–16.
[6] *Ibid.*, pp. 64, 65.

sively accepted by man, but that it challenges man's ability to alter and to improve it.

> Everybody professes to approve and admire many great triumphs of Art over Nature: the junction by bridges of shores which Nature has made separate, the draining of Nature's marshes, the excavation of her wells, the dragging to light of what she has buried at immense depths in the earth; the turning away of her thunderbolts by lightning rods, of her inundations by embankments. . . . But to commend these and similar feats, is to acknowledge that the ways of Nature are to be conquered, not obeyed.[7]

The spontaneous course of nature provides man with problems, not with a standard to be imitated. Man must study nature in order to discover those facets which he can use to resolve the problems and difficulties with which nature confronts him.

Moreover, it would be immoral to accept the spontaneous course of nature as a moral ideal to be imitated because this order is one in which every being tries to take advantage of and destroy other beings. We find that a constant state of war exists among many species of animals. Certainly, it would be immoral for man to set out to imitate this order. We also find that nature fails to distinguish between the just and unjust in its treatment of men. Some of the most just among men are often victims of the greatest natural disasters whether in the form of terribly debilitating, painful and long illnesses, floods, or fires, whereas many of the unjust seem to be spared from such disasters. Finally, both the just and the unjust must suffer the ignominy and pain of death. It is difficult to see how an order so devoid of moral factors, and indeed so replete with injustices can be accepted as a model for man to imitate in his voluntary activities.

In the face of these difficulties, those who would want to insist that nature is to be taken as a model for moral behavior may shift their emphasis from the spontaneous course of natural forces external to man to the spontaneous movement of natural impulses found within himself. Against such a position, Mill makes the following observation: "That a feeling is bestowed on us by Nature, does not necessarily legitimate all its promptings."[8] However, in defense of the position, it might be argued that a distinction must be drawn between man as he comes from the hand of his Creator and man as he has made himself. Since what man does as a result of his own reflections and deliberations can most clearly and easily be accepted as that which man has made of himself, this position seems to say that the more an impulse can be seen as being cut off from and uninfluenced by human deliberation, the more acceptable it is as a moral standard.

Mill does not think that such a naturalism can be consistently held.

---

[7] *Ibid.*, p. 20.
[8] John Stuart Mill, *Utilitarianism* (London: Parker, Son and Bourn, 1863), p. 61.

I do not mean, of course, that this mode of judgment is even pretended to be consistently carried out: life could not go on if it were not admitted that impulses must be controlled, and that reason ought to govern our actions. The pretension is not to drive Reason from the helm but rather to bind her by articles to steer only a particular way. Instinct is not to govern, but reason is to practice some vague and unassignable amount of deference to Instinct.[9]

Mill has clearly touched a weakness connected with this type of position in stressing the fact that reason is expected to practice "some vague and unassignable amount of deference to Instinct." To leave the whole of man's moral life to instincts and to deny reason any role whatsoever in the formation of man's moral ideals would mean that whatever a man felt inclined to do, he ought to do. If this were the case, man would be free of moral problems or dilemmas. If he felt inclined to thank one who gave him an unexpected gift, he ought to thank him. If he felt inclined to shoot a stranger who accidentally stepped on a particularly sore and sensitive bunion, he ought to shoot him.

Those defending the primacy of natural instincts might protest against this characterization of their position on the grounds that they do not advocate that man follow *indiscriminately* any and all of his instincts, but only those that are "natural." It is at this point that reason is asked to pay its "vague and unassignable deference to Instinct." How is reason to decide which instincts are "natural" and which are not? If the answer is that those instincts which are "good" are "natural," then it is the "goodness" of instincts that leads us to conclude that they are "natural." This outcome is a complete reversal of the original statement of the position which implied that we come to know which instincts are good by first knowing which are natural. Moreover, if we are not to follow any and all instincts indiscriminately, and if reason is to discriminate between good and bad instincts, does this not mean that the ultimate basis for the distinction between moral good and evil is to be found in the work of human reason? Thus, it would appear that reason, not instincts, is the ultimate court of appeal in moral matters.

In concluding this section, it will be well to consider Mill's observation that the emphasis on natural instincts fosters a prejudice against accepting the findings of reason when these findings do not conform with established custom.[10] Thus, although one might be unable to find any rational argument to offer against a well-reasoned defense of a certain type of behavior, he may reject the behavior by saying that it is "against nature." What he really means by the phrase "against nature," is that it is not the type of behavior to which he has become accustomed. That Mill should offer such arguments against equating moral good with nature is paradoxical in view of the fact that his defense of his own utilitarianism is open to the charge of having equated what men

[9] See footnote 1, p. 45.
[10] *Ibid.*, pp. 44–45.

ought to desire with what they *actually* desire. This matter will be explored in Chapter IV.

2. G. E. MOORE'S CRITICISM OF NATURALISTIC ETHICS

G. E. Moore's conception of a naturalistic ethics is described in the following statement:

> Whether good be defined as yellow or green or blue, as loud or soft, as round or square, as productive of life or productive of pleasure, as willed or desired or felt: whichever of these or any other object in the world, good may be held to *mean,* the theory which holds it to *mean* them, will be a naturalistic theory.[11]

There are elements in Moore's criticism of naturalistic ethics that are similar to Mill's criticism of the identification of nature and moral values. For example, Moore also holds that although it is true that man must follow the necessities of nature in working toward a certain end, this truth does not necessarily imply that these necessities must be equated with the highest good.[12] However, Moore's case against naturalism is much more extensive than Mill's criticism. The purpose of this section is to provide a brief exposition of the major features of Moore's criticism of naturalism.

He points out that many ethicians have missed the importance of the issues involved in defining "good" because they have not been sufficiently clear in distinguishing between two ethical questions. The first question asks, "What sort of things ought to exist for their own sakes?" The second asks, "What kind of actions ought we to perform?"[13] The first question is concerned with defining "good" or "intrinsic value," whereas the second asks whether an action ought to be performed because it leads to such a "good," or leads to a state of affairs that would be better than the one which would occur if the action were not performed. The question concerned with the definition of "good" is the most important question for ethics. This question is important because the resolution of moral problems must be based not only on factual premises, but also on strictly ethical premises, premises that are statements of value.

For example, if taking a capsule of heroin involves a moral problem, this problem cannot be resolved by a factual statement which describes the feelings that will be caused by taking the capsule. An ethical proposition which tells us whether the feelings are morally good or bad is also required. Basically, Moore's position is that it is impossible to draw a moral conclusion—a conclu-

---

[11] G. E. Moore, *Principia Ethica* (Cambridge: Cambridge University Press, 1959), p. 40.

[12] *Ibid.,* p. 44.

[13] *Ibid.,* pp. 22–23.

sion concerning what I ought to do or not do—from purely factual premises that describe what is or what will be the case.[14] Hence, it is important to probe the meaning of good which grounds the propositions of value that must play a part in all ethical reasoning. Unless the problem of the definition of good is faced, there is no possibility of coming to a valid ethical conclusion concerning what state of affairs I ought to bring into existence.

Turning to the conception of good, Moore holds that it is a simple concept that cannot be broken down into parts and that is thus indefinable.[15] For example, the concept "man" can be defined because it is a complex concept including the notion of animality, which places it in a generic class and the notion of rationality, which serves to distinguish it from other things included in the class of animality. Failing to recognize the indefinability of good, naturalistic ethicians have committed the *naturalistic fallacy* which consists in identifying or confusing good or intrinsic value with things that may be good, but that certainly are not that which is "good in itself."[16] In exposing the naturalistic fallacy, Moore does not deny that there are many realities such as pleasure, which are truly goods, but he does deny that any of these constitute the very definition of good.

One argument that runs throughout Moore's criticism of the attempts to identify intrinsic good with some other reality is what has come to be called the "open question argument." Moore's procedure in this argument is to point out that the supposed identification between any natural or metaphysical (supersensible) reality and good is seen to be fallacious by the fact that if this reality is posited, it is always legitimate to ask whether it is good.

> Whatever we may have proved to exist, and whatever two existents we may have proved to be necessarily connected with one another, it still remains a distinct and different question whether what thus exists is good; whether either or both of the two existents is so; and whether it is good that they should exist together. To assert the one is plainly and obviously *not* the same thing as to assert the other. We understand what we mean by asking: 'Is this, which exists, or necessarily exists, after all, good?' and we perceive that we are asking a question which has *not* been answered. In face of this direct perception that the two questions are distinct, no proof that they *must* be identical can have the slightest value.[17]

[14] *Ibid.* David Hume has made the same point in expressing his surprise at the fact that demonstrations directed toward a moral conclusion—one that tells us what ought or ought not to be done—are supposedly grounded in purely factual premises, i.e., premises telling us what is or is not the case. He states that such demonstrations cannot be accepted unless one is able to show how from purely factual propositions one can derive propositions concerning what ought or ought not to be. David Hume, *A Treatise of Human Nature,* Vol. III (Oxford: Oxford University Press, L. A. Selby-Bigge, ed.), p. 469.

[15] See footnote 11, pp. 7–10.
[16] *Ibid.,* p. 9.
[17] *Ibid.,* p. 126.

The fact that we can know that a thing or a group of things exist and still ask whether they are good, substantiates the contention that good is not identical with either the thing or the group. Moore points out that when one is dealing with the question concerning whether a thing is good, he recognizes that both the question and his own state of mind with respect to the question differ from what they would be if he were asked whether a thing is desired, approved, or pleasant.[18] This more specific statement of the open question argument shows, Moore thinks, that good is not identical with being desired, approved, or pleasant.

In making his open question argument, Moore points out that there is a difference between "good," or any other predicate of value such as "beautiful" and other types of predicates such as "yellow" and "round."[19] He tries to specify this difference between predicates of value, which he denominates "non-natural intrinsic properties," and other predicates, "natural properties," in the following statement:

> Properties which are intrinsic properties, but *not* natural ones, are distinguished from natural intrinsic properties, by the fact that, in ascribing a property of the former kind to a thing, you are not describing it *at all,* whereas, in ascribing a property of the latter kind to a thing, you are always describing it *to some extent.*[20]

The difference between a predicate of value and other predicates is that the former is wholly nondescriptive, whereas the latter does describe in some way that of which it is predicated. For example, if I tell someone that a certain thing is good, I am not describing the thing at all, whereas if I tell him that it is yellow and soft, he knows something about it. If a person overhears me talking about X, and if he asks me what it is, he would undoubtedly be disappointed if I were to answer X is good. To say that it is good in no way helps him understand what it is, because the predicate good is nondescriptive.

Moore's open question argument and his distinction between descriptive and valuative predicates lead him to oppose any facile identification of "good" with that which actually exists. For example, he opposes any one who would say that intrinsic good is to be found in the realization of the "true self." Such a position suggests that the self is good because it is real or true.[21] In opposition to this position, Moore holds that it would appear that if the realization of a particular kind of self is intrinsically good, it is good whether the self is real or imaginary.

It is necessary to distinguish between the basic ethical significance of the question, "What is good?" and other secondary issues involved in this question.

[18] *Ibid.,* pp. 16–17.

[19] See G. E. Moore, "The Conception of Intrinsic Value," *Philosophical Studies* (Paterson, New Jersey: Littlefield, Adams, and Co., 1959), pp. 273–274.

[20] G. E. Moore, "A Reply to My Critics," *The Philosophy of G. E. Moore,* ed. by Paul Arthur Schilpp (Chicago: Northwestern University Press, 1942), p. 591.

[21] See footnote 11, p. 114.

Such secondary issues would be concerned with discovering what existent things may be said to be good, whereas the basic ethical issue centers on the discovery of the nature or character of intrinsic good, whether this nature exists or not.[22] A similar distinction is required to avoid the possible ambiguity in the assertion, "This is good." The assertion may mean that certain actually existing things are good, in which case it would be necessary to show that the things which we claim to be actually existing do, as a matter of fact, exist. However, the assertion may also be taken to mean that a thing is good in the sense that although it does not exist, it ought to exist.[23] The second meaning shows that a thing is intrinsically good is not the same as to assert that the thing actually exists. This means that there is no need to establish the reality of a thing in order to hold that it is intrinsically good.

Moore points to two difficulties that confront one who fails to draw any distinction between good and reality. First, if good is equated with reality or with that which exists, ethics, as it is usually understood, disappears. For taking the point of view that some actually existing things are good and others bad, the ethician sets out to discover some sort of rules to aid in acquiring the good and avoiding the evil.[24] Moreover, if the good which ethics seeks is identified with some natural object, then there is no need for ethics as a discipline distinct from that which studies that object. For example, if good is identified with what man favors as a matter of actual fact, it would follow that there is no need for a study of ethics as distinct from psychology or sociology. For one task of both these sciences is to discover what men actually do favor, and what factors lead them to favor certain things over others.[25]

Moore also finds three difficulties connected with the attempt to establish a criterion for judging values by disengaging a certain property from a complex state of affairs that is said to be good, and using this property as such a criterion. He points out that a certain common property can be established as the criterion for intrinsic good only if a consideration of this property itself as isolated from all else shows it to be good. For example, if one were to argue that the property which makes everything else good is "the realization of the true self," it would be necessary for him to show that what is meant by such a realization would be of value even if it were to exist alone, even if it were the only thing existing in the world. Moreover, if the objects which are said to realize the true self can be seen to have some value of their own part from such a realization, it follows that the realization of the true self cannot be the sole criterion for value. A final point that must be taken into consideration in trying to discover some common property that is the criterion of all value, is the fact that it may be possible that the complex state of affairs of which this criterion is a part may be more valuable when viewed in its totality than the property that is purported

[22] *Ibid.,* p. 118.
[23] *Ibid.,* pp. 120–121.
[24] *Ibid.,* p. 42.
[25] *Ibid.,* p. 20.

to be the criterion of all values. Such a possibility serves to show that there are certain specific features in a given complex state of affairs in addition to the common property, which contribute to its value, but which do not come under the criterion that has supposedly been found in this common property.[26]

3. THE PROBLEM OF REASON AND MORAL VALUE

Mill's and Moore's probings into the relationship between nature and moral values raise problems with respect to the grounding of man's knowledge of moral values. If the identification between nature and moral values must be surrendered, it would seem that man's knowledge of moral goodness cannot be accounted for by a view which sees him as simply looking out on the given existential state of affairs and pronouncing that which he finds there morally good. Such a view presents man's knowledge of moral values as being a copy or reproduction of what actually exists. Whatever one's ultimate judgment on Mill's and Moore's criticism of such an identification may be, it must be acknowledged that the identification of moral goodness with what actually exists involves such morally repugnant conclusions as that the extermination of six million Jews was morally good because it actually did exist. The purpose of this section is to state the problem concerning the basis of man's knowledge of moral values that arises if one does not accept the simple identification of nature and moral goodness.

It would appear that Mill's and Moore's positions provide reason with no leverage within nature for the construction of a moral standard. Thus, it would seem to follow that if reason is to play any role in the formation of this standard, it must do so in complete independence from the given order of nature. This means that morality would be grounded in reason functioning on its own, apart from any examination of nature, i.e., in reason *a priori*. In his *Elements of Law*, Gottfried Leibniz presented a case in defense of this position. He pointed out that the theory of law belongs to those sciences (among which ethics is included), which are founded "not on experiments but on definitions, not on the senses but on demonstrations according to reason; it deals with questions, as we say of law and not of fact."[27] For example, the meaning of justice remains independent of whether anybody actually does justice to others or is himself justly treated, just as numerical relations remain true regardless of whether anyone does any counting or whether anything is counted.[28] This fact indicated that man's idea of justice does not come from observing just acts in his sense experience. Sciences such as ethics and mathematics are thus seen to involve

[26] *Ibid.*, p. 188. See also the discussion of the criterion of beauty, p. 202.
[27] Gottfried, Leibniz, "Elements of Law and Justice," *Leibniz Selections*, ed. by Philip R. Weiner (New York: Charles Scribner's Sons, 1951), p. 1.
[28] *Ibid.*

propositions that are eternally true, since these propositions are grounded not in the contingent facts of existence, but in definitions that are the work of reason itself. Leibniz concludes that the point of departure for these propositions is not the senses, but a clear and distinct intuition, or, as Plato called it, "idea."[29]

It is interesting to note that John Locke who, being an empiricist, is usually taken as representing a position that is diametrically opposed to the rationalism of Leibniz, takes a position with regard to reason's role in man's moral life that is strikingly similar to Leibniz's position. Although he denies that there are any innate moral ideas, Locke does hold that moral ideas are to be included among those ideas that are not grounded in an examination of the real existence of things or verified by patterns found to be actually existing in nature. Man himself puts together such ideas as incest and adultery so that the truth or rightness of these ideas are not dependent on any pattern existing in the natural order.[30] That man can reason about moral ideas, although these ideas may have no corresponding reality in nature, can be seen in the fact that lawmakers have often made laws concerning certain types of activity that were only creatures of their own minds.[31] Although we do not want to push this similarity between Locke and Leibniz so far as to deny that there are substantial areas of disagreement between them, the fact remains that they shared similar views in holding that the moral ideas which man possesses are not simply the result of human reason's imaging of patterns given to it in sense experience.[32]

It was Immanuel Kant who most forcibly and explicitly made the point that morality is grounded not in experience but in reason a priori. The concern of the moralist is with actions that may have never been performed in the world, and the feasibility of which might be seriously doubted by those who would ground everything in experience. For example, the moralist may discover that every man is morally obliged to be sincere in his friendships, although a truly sincere friend may never have existed.[33] Since morality is concerned with what ought to be, reason cannot derive the moral law from observing the ways of the world, what people actually do, and how they actually behave.[34] Kant maintains that the attempt to ground morality in experience paves the way for a denial of true morality, since it is extremely doubtful whether virtue is ever actually found in the world. Hence, granted that morality is grounded in experience alone, it would not be too difficult for one to show that what is called moral obligation is a matter of selfish interest, pure and simple, and that man is interested in getting away with as much as he can for himself, with the "moral

---

[29] *Ibid.*

[30] John Locke, *An Essay Concerning Human Understanding*, Vol. II (New York: Dover 1959), p. 44.

[31] *Ibid.*, p. 45, also pp. 157–158.

[32] *Ibid.*, pp. 208–211. See also Vol. I, p. 65, footnote 1.

[33] See footnote 9, Chap. I, p. 24.

[34] Immanuel Kant, *The Doctrine of Virtue*, trans., with an introduction and notes, by Mary J. Gregor (New York: Harper and Row, 1964), p. 13.

man" being he who is most successful in advancing his own interest, while giving others the impression that he is working for some higher good such as the moral law.[35]

This is not the place to go into a full epistemological investigation of the possibility of knowledge based on the work of reason apart from human experience. I shall restrict myself to considering the implications for moral philosophy involved in the view that moral ideas, or moral values, are the work of reason a priori. The difficulty with the view that ethics is similar to mathematics is that it seems to involve an excessively abstract and formalistic conception of ethics. As will be seen in Chapter V, I do not think that moral philosophy deals directly with the concrete moral issues facing given human individuals. The ethician deals only with a general framework which can be helpful to the reflective individual in meeting his own moral problems. Hence, the rejection of reason a priori as a basis for ethics on the grounds that it is excessively abstract should not be interpreted to mean that I am committed to the view that moral philosophy can replace the human individual's reflections on his concrete moral problems.

Rather, my point is that if moral philosophy is to provide an adequate general framework for such reflections by providing a moral standard that can be useful to these reflections, it would appear that this standard can arise only out of a probing into the character of man's existence and of the world in which he lives. It is difficult to see how reason can provide this framework out of its own resources and apart from a consideration of man in his world. Because mathematics deals with purely formal systems, a much stronger case can be made for the view that it is the work of reason a priori than can be made for the view that ethics is grounded in reason a priori. The description of mathematics as dealing with purely formal intelligibilities means that it is concerned with the logical consistency of a given system of numbers. It does not attempt to ground this system of numbers in man's existential world. A certain system is postulated and the logical possibilities and difficulties inherent in this postulated system are explored.

Because moral philosophy purports to have more relevance to man's existential situation than simply sharpening his logic, it would appear that moral philosophy cannot be satisfied with a *postulated* system. It must be able to show that the standard for moral behavior which it advances is grounded in man's real situation. For example, a standard based on the postulate that man is a wholly immaterial being, who exists in complete independence and isolation from the material dimensions of existence may be the basis for a perfectly logical system of behavior, but it will suffer from the fact that the postulate on which it is based does not accord with the real character of human existence.

Perhaps Hegel's criticism of what he considered to be the excessive formalism of Kant's ethics may help shed further light on the difficulty of trying to base ethics on reason a priori. Hegel argues that if the basis for moral obligation

[35] See footnote 9, Chap. I, pp. 23–24.

is the absence of contradiction, there is no possibility for moving to a specification of particular duties nor is there any criterion upon which one can decide whether any given state of affairs is or is not his duty. Hegel's point is that purely formal or logical consistency alone is not sufficient to ground man's moral life.

To exemplify the point, he presents the following considerations:

> The absence of property contains in itself just as little contradiction as the non-existence of this or that nation, family, etc., or the death of the whole human race. But if it is already established on other grounds and presupposed that property and human life are to exist and to be respected, then indeed it is a contradiction to commit theft or murder; a contradiction must be a contradiction of something, i.e., of some content presupposed from the start as a fixed principle.[36]

The last phrase of this statement, pointing out that a contradiction must be the contradiction of some context nicely summarizes the ethical reason behind our rejection of reason a priori as a basis of moral philosophy. The content which must be involved in an ethical standard must be more than a postulate of reason. For this standard must be meaningful to man as he exists in this world, not as he may exist in a world that reason may be able to construct whole-cloth out of itself and without any reference to this real world. As Hegel has pointed out, to murder or to steal are not in *themselves* and considered apart from any content contradictory. If we want to say that murder is contradictory, we must indicate precisely what it contradicts and *why* such a contradiction is immoral. The position which we have taken is that reason a priori cannot provide an answer to these questions.

Since reason a priori cannot form the foundation of man's moral life, it would appear that this foundation must be provided by some factor which is natural in the sense that it is something which is *given* to reason. David Hume provides an excellent statement of the factors which seem to justify this conclusion. He examines the following argument which purports to show that man's moral life is grounded in reason alone. The argument states that man's acts can be characterized as moral or immoral, whereas those of animals cannot because man possesses reason which enables him to recognize the morality or immorality of his acts, whereas animals do not possess this power. For example, sexual relations between an animal offspring and one of its parents are not immoral because animals do not possess the knowledge to recognize the turpitude of their acts; whereas incest is immoral among men because, possessing reason, they are able to know the immorality of such acts.

Hume rejects the argument on the following basis: "Before reason can perceive this turpitude, the turpitude must exist; and consequently is independent of the decisions of our reason, and is their object more properly than their effect."[37] Hume's point is that the argument purporting to show the primacy of

---

[36] Hegel, *Philosophy of Right*, trans., with notes, by T. M. Knox (Oxford: Oxford University Press, 1942), p. 90.

reason in ethics actually must presuppose a prior immorality in the acts of sexual relations between parents and offspring. Reason is not primary in ethics in the sense that it is a constitutive factor in the distinction between moral good and evil. The distinction must exist as a fact that is given to reason, if reason is to discover it. As Hume puts it, the turpitude which reason perceives must exist before reason can perceive it so that such turpitude is the object which reason perceives rather than the product or effect of reason's work. A universe in which there is a distinction between moral good and moral evil must exist independently of human reason, if reason is to perceive this universe.

We have now seen the essential ingredients of the problem that challenges the basis of the position taken in Chapter I, which pointed to the possibility of a normative ethics. On the one hand, reason a priori, reason working independently of man's experience of his world, does not provide a valid basis for the distinction between moral good and evil. On the other hand, it would appear that reason reflecting on man's world can only repeat what is given there. If one accepts this position, he is saying that the distinction between moral good and evil is given in nature, and is thus confronted with the difficulties raised by Mill and Moore. Hence, if a normative ethics is to be shown as being possible, it will be necessary to see whether these difficulties can be surmounted.

4. VALUES IN THE NATURAL ORDER

Mill was right in recognizing that if the issue concerning the relationship between nature and morality is to be resolved, some consideration must be given to what is meant by "nature." The purpose of this section is to evaluate Mill's treatment of the relationship between nature and moral values, and to try to establish what I consider to be a more adequate conception of nature. A reflection on these issues will lead to an investigation of what is meant by "good," and an evaluation of Moore's distinction between descriptive and valuative predicates, as well as of his open question argument. It must be emphasized that this section will deal primarily with a consideration of the relationship between nonmoral goods or values, and nature, leaving the issue of the relationship between moral good and nature for the following section. The task of this section will be pursued under the following subheadings: a. The Meaning of "Nature," b. The Meaning of "Good" and the Place of Values in Nature, and c. Intrinsic Value and the Criterion for Good.

a. THE MEANING OF "NATURE"

Mill has a valid point in emphasizing that the attempt to establish the spontaneous order of nature as a criterion of moral behavior implies that this

³⁷ David Hume, *A Treatise of Human Nature*, Vol. III, pp. 467–468. See also Hume, *Enquiry Concerning Principles of Morals*, pp. 288–289.

order of nature
is perfectly moral

order is perfectly moral. The truth of the matter is that nature conceived as the spontaneous activity of things occurring apart from any intervention of man's voluntary activity is nonmoral. It is interesting to note that Thomas Aquinas, whose natural-law theory of ethics appears to be particularly vulnerable to the criticisms offered by Mill and Moore against attempts to equate nature and morality, distinguishes between acts considered according to their natural character and those same acts morally considered. For example, he points out that sexual intercourse between a man and a woman may lead to the birth of a child, whether the act is performed in wedlock or in an adulterous union.[38] Aquinas' point is that nature takes its course, whether the sexual union be moral or immoral. In so far as acts are considered apart from their relationship to human reason and will, they do not possess a moral character. Hence, Aquinas goes so far as to say that moral ends are "accidental" to natural occurrences, and conversely that the character of natural ends or results are "accidental" to the moral order.[39]

The problem in Aquinas' position is with the word "accidental." Perhaps, an example will help clarify his position. Viewed naturally, i.e., apart from the intervention of man's intellect and will, the act of killing a man has one obvious result, namely, the death of a man. However, this same act which involves one result naturally considered can be either moral or immoral in so far as it is viewed in its relationships to human reason and will. Seen in this relationship, it may be either moral in so far as it was done out of self-defense, or immoral in so far as it was done out of hatred or a desire to be rid of a man in order to inherit his money. Thus, from a knowledge of the natural fact that a man has been killed, one cannot move to a knowledge of its moral character without considering its relationship to the human intellect and will. This indicates that there can be no simple identification of the natural and moral orders. This point is in keeping with Mill's observation that nature fails to distinguish between the just and unjust in its treatment of men, often inflicting on the just such natural disasters as disease, fires, floods, whereas the unjust may be spared much of these.

As was indicated in the exposition of Mill's criticism, I think that his argument against the view that there are natural impulses in man which provide a model for human behavior is also sound. The fact is that these impulses considered apart from reason and human agency are neither moral nor immoral. The spontaneous course of nature, whether it be nature external to man or nature as found in man's impulses, does not provide man with a moral order. Rather the spontaneous order of nature constitutes a challenge to man's ability to build a moral order. It is up to man to work toward the realization of a moral universe within this natural order.

[38] S.T. I–II, Q. 18, a.5, ad.3; see footnote 36, Chap. I, Vol. II, p. 324. See also De Malo q. 2, a.4 and ScG III, 10; see footnote 9, Chap. II, Bk. III, Part I, p. 58.

[39] "Finis autem morales accidunt rei naturali et e converse ratio naturalis finis accidit morali." S.T. I–II, Q.1, a.3, ad.3.

This position is in agreement with G. E. Moore's view that the necessities of nature must be taken into account in order to discover the means within nature which are to be utilized in working toward that which we consider to be morally good. For if man is to bring a moral order to fruition within the natural context in which he finds himself, he must come to know those features of this context which will contribute to his moral task and those which will frustrate it. The question as to the contribution which nature can make to a criterion for distinguishing between moral good and evil remains open. It is clear that when "nature" is equated with the whole of reality, the advice to follow the laws of nature cannot be taken as providing such a criterion, because man can act only from these laws of nature, there being no other principles of operation open to him. In order to pursue the issue of the relationship between "nature" and moral values, it will be necessary to move beyond the equation of "nature" with "reality." There can be no question here of a full and complete exploration of the meaning of nature. The discussion will be restricted to exploring one meaning of the notion of nature which can be grounded in human experience and which is important to any consideration of the relationship between nature and value.

In his *Metaphysics*, Aristotle includes the following points in his conception of the central meanings of nature: "(1) the genesis of growing things . . . (2) that immanent part of a growing thing, from which its first growth proceeds. (3) the source from which the primary movement in each natural object is present."[40] The fact that nature is thus seen to be intimately connected with activity has a good deal of significance for the problem at hand. Nature is seen to be the intrinsic principle of activity within a thing. Nature is thus not some inert material. Hence, when we speak of the nature of a dog or of a tree, we are referring to the intrinsic principle of the activities performed by these beings. In so far as a thing performs any sort of activity at all, e.g., in so far as it grows, matures, reproduces its own kind, nourishes itself, senses, actively unites with other things, it is said to have a nature which is the intrinsic principle at the basis of these activities. This means that whatever does not perform activities that proceed from some principle intrinsic to it cannot be properly said to be a "nature." For example, such artifacts as a screwdriver, a dish, a piece of paper, a pen, act only in so far as man uses them so that properly speaking they have no nature of their own. In so far as their activity is dependent on man, whatever "nature" they may be said to have is a "nature" that is imposed on them by man.

A further point worth noting is that to speak of nature as an intrinsic principle of activity does not necessarily mean that a natural thing must act in complete isolation from everything else. For example, it is a tree, and not the soil in which it is planted, that actually grows, that is the subject of growth. How-

[40] Aristotle, *Metaphysics* 1014b, 15–20, *The Basic Works of Aristotle*, ed. and with an introduction by Richard McKeon (New York: Random House), p. 755.

ever, it is true that the tree is dependent on the environment provided by the soil for its own growth. This means that there is a passive, as well as an active sense, connected with the notion of nature. The passive sense denotes that a thing's nature is open to and dependent on the influence of other things in its environment so that we can speak of a certain type of soil as being "natural" to a tree, meaning that it is congenial to the tree's intrinsic principle of growth and permits it to function so that the tree may mature.

In so far as man also acts from an intrinsic principle of activity and is dependent on certain environmental factors, he is part and parcel of the order of nature, an order of acting and interacting beings. Furthermore, there is no denying that man's intellect and will, seen as intrinsic principles of action, can be said to be natural capabilities. However, the character and scope of these specifically human natural capacities justifies the distinction which Mill recognizes as often being made between man and the rest of nature. "Nature" has been described as an intrinsic principle of action. To say that it is a *principle* of action, is to say that it is a tendency to a certain type of action. The interplay between man's will and intellect also is a principle of action or a tendency to action. What justifies the distinction between voluntary (human) actions and natural actions is that in so far as the former actions issue from man's rational capacities they are not determined to one result, to one end, whereas the latter actions are determined to a single result.

In so far as a tree or a horse acts out of its natural resources, its acts are restricted within rather definite limits. For example, in its interaction with its environment, the tree can transform the environment by spreading its roots to various levels in the soil, by spreading its branches to a greater or less extent. The horse can run, can jump, can transform its environment by eating certain grass. Alfred North Whitehead has captured this character of natural activity in the following statement:

> In its lowest form, mental experience is canalized into slavish conformity. It is merely the appetition towards, or from, whatever in fact already is. . . . This lowest form of slavish conformity pervades all nature. It is rather a capacity for mentality than mentality itself. But it *is* mentality. In this lowly form it evades no difficulties: it strikes out no new ways: it produces no disturbance of the repetitive character of physical fact.[41]

Although I would speak of natural tendency where Whitehead speaks of "mentality," the fact is that this quotation does capture the spirit of what I am trying to say when I say that the scope and character of the activities of natural agents other than man, and also of man himself when he is not acting out of his rational capacities, are restricted, or as Whitehead puts it, "canalized" into certain rather definite activities and results.

[41] Alfred North Whitehead, *The Function of Reason* (Boston: Beacon Press, 1958), pp. 33–34.

Because of the universal character of human knowledge, the activities of man as a voluntary agent so surpass the scope of those issuing from other natural beings that they justify the distinction often drawn between man and nature. Karl Marx has caught the spirit of this point in observing that whereas other species can act only according to the laws of their own species, man can act according to the laws of all species.[42]

For example, in the technological sphere, man's knowledge frees him from the limitations imposed upon him by his physical nature and allows him to fly as the birds do, indeed he now is able to fly faster and higher than any bird, and to travel the oceans as fish do. Moreover, he can imitate the shape of a whale in building his submarines because he has found that this shape enables whales to move through the water more easily. His knowledge of the soil and of the way in which plants grow and bear fruit has enabled him to advance the art of farming so that he can cultivate the soil to bear fruit and vegetables that are helpful and necessary to his subsistence. He has been able to make clothing, to fashion shelters, to heat and to cool these shelters so that he is not wholly at the mercy of the elements. Man's cognitive capacities have thus provided him with the opportunity of using not only his own physical powers, but the powers of other natural beings. They have literally opened the rest of nature to him so that he can make use of the powers and capacities of other natural beings to further his own aims.

This discussion of the factors distinguishing man from the rest of nature ties in with the discussion of human freedom in Chapter II. For the factors that serve to distinguish man from the rest of nature are ultimately the same factors that make man capable of freedom, of self-determination. It is man's capacity to reflect on truths as universal and his capacity to commit himself to that which is good in itself that is the intrinsic foundation of both his freedom and of the control over nature which we have been discussing as his distinctive characteristic. Without these capacities, man would be unable to exercise such control or to see things in general contexts and relationships and to be concerned with matters beyond the needs of the immediate moment.

This discussion may be summarized by referring to natural beings other than man as natural "agents," whereas man is a "subject." The description of natural beings as "agents" acknowledges the fact that they do act from an intrinsic principle of agency and that this principle is a tendency to a certain end. When man is spoken of as not simply an "agent," but also as a "subject," attention is drawn to the fact that man acts not simply from a blind tendency, but from a knowledge of the end toward which he directs himself. Put more succinctly the distinction acknowledges the fact that man alone among all natural beings is free, with "free" meaning self-determination and all that is involved in this meaning.

[42] Karl Marx, *The Economic and Philosophic Manuscripts of 1844*, edited with an introduction and notes by Dirk J. Struik, translated by Martin Milligan (New York: International Publishers, 1964), pp. 113–114.

b. THE MEANING OF "GOOD" AND THE PLACE OF VALUES IN NATURE

What are the repercussions of the conception of nature which has been presented up to this point for the problem of the relationship between values and nature? It serves to break down the separation between nature and value, or between fact and value, that seems to be implied in Moore's and Mill's criticism of the identification of good with nature. It will be necessary to explore the meaning of good as a first step in the justification of this contention. Moore's position in *Principia Ethica* that good is indefinable in that it simply is what it is and not something else can be sustained only if one sees a definition as equating one reality with another.

However, in exploring the meaning of good, we shall not attempt to equate good with any other quality. Rather our purpose is to make human consciousness more explicitly aware of what is involved in its predication of good to many things and activities in our experience. It is obvious that "good" cannot be simply identified with any one of these things. To be good certainly does not mean to be a fountain pen. For if to be good were identical with being a fountain pen, we would be involved in the ridiculous position of saying that when I speak of a good horse or a good man, I mean that these are fountain pens. The fact that there are a great multiplicity of things in man's experience which can be said to be good, with "good" not being reducible to any one of them, simply means that "good" cannot be identified with any one thing in experience.

The fact that "good" cannot be equated with any of these things need not mean that when a thing is said to be "good," it is simply "good," and no further questions can be asked. Granted that "good" cannot be equated with any of the things of which we may predicate it, it is legitimate to try to explore the meaning of this term with the hope of seeing what is involved in such predications. The emotivists maintain that when "good" is predicated of a thing, we express a favorable attitude toward the thing and commend it to others, implying that they also should have a favorable attitude toward it. So long as this position is not taken as exhausting the meaning of "good," I have no quarrel with it. When man says something is "good," he undoubtedly has a favorable attitude toward it, and is commending it. However, it is my contention that there is another factor involved in such a predication.

It seems fairly obvious that when we speak of such inanimate objects as automobiles, fountain pens, and dish washers as being good, we mean that these things are "suitable" to the performance of a certain task, a task which is imposed on them by man. Granted that we know that the task of a fountain pen is to be used by man in such a way that he can put clear marks on a paper, we would think that a person is peculiar, if he were to say that this is a good fountain pen, although it blots the paper every time I try to write with it. We would be led to ask him what he meant by saying it is good, because his description of it has indicated that it is obviously not suited to the task of writing. It would then be necessary for him to justify the predication of "good" with respect to this fountain pen by pointing out some sense in which it could be said to be suitable for something or other. The point of this example is to indicate that "good" involves the notion of "suitability." Admittedly, this identification of "good" with "suitability" does not define "good" in terms of a genus and a specific difference. However, I hope to show that it helps specify the character of the ethician's search for a norm that grounds judgments concerning moral good.

The problem that now confronts us is whether there is any basis in nature as it has been described in this section to justify the view that natural things can be said to be suitable or unsuitable to one another. If there is such a basis, it will follow that the separation between facts and values, between "good" and natural objects is not so great as Moore's distinction between valuative and descriptive predicates would seem to imply. The question at this point is not one concerning the relationship between *moral* values and nature. This question will be left for the next section. The immediate issue concerns the possible way in which "good" understood as "suitable" can be predicated of natural objects.

That "good" can be predicated of natural objects is seen in a point which was made earlier in this section. In making the point that "nature" as an intricate principle of activity does not mean that natural objects must act in complete isolation from everything else, I used the example of a tree which is dependent on a certain type of soil for its growth. It was pointed out that a certain type of soil can be said to be "natural" to that tree, meaning that the soil is "congenial," or, as we may now put it, "suitable," to the tree's intrinsic principle of growth, providing the conditions for the tree's development.

The notion of good as suitable involves either the conception that a certain thing contributes to the completion, development, and perfection of another's capacities or the conception that a thing itself is so disposed and constituted that, placed in the proper environment, it can exercise its capacities for growth and maturation. It is true that because man uses natural objects for his own benefit, he may mean that they are good in so far as they serve his own purposes. For example, when an avid gambler says that a horse is good, it is most likely that he means that the horse can run fast enough to enrich the gambler's financial status. In this case, "good" means suitable to the fulfillment and perfection of the gambler's economic life. However, in addition to these man-imposed tasks, natural objects as agents, perform tasks of their own. Some only eat, drink, grow, and reproduce their own kind. Others, in addition to performing these tasks, run, fly, and exercise certain sensory activities such as seeing, hearing, smelling, or touching. Thus, there are plant physiologists who explore issues relating to the health and diseases of plant life. There are veterinarians who deal with similar problems relating to animal life. It is undoubtedly true that these professions would not have existed had not man been interested in these forms of life and had these lives not proved beneficial to man.

Nonetheless, the fact remains that a veterinarian can describe a dog as being in "good health," meaning by this that the dog's physical condition is such that its capacities will be able to function so that it will be able to nourish itself, grow, hear, see, smell, run, and perform all the activities connected with being a dog. The veterinarian will not think that the dog is in poor health because it cannot fly or philosophize. For we have come to realize that there are certain capacities that belong to the character of being a dog so that when we say that a dog is in good health, we are referring to the condition of the dog which is suitable to the development of these certain capacities. Once it is seen that natural objects possess an intrinsic principle of agency and that the functioning and development of this principle can be fulfilled or frustrated either by external environmental conditions or by certain physical dispositions in the natural beings themselves, it is clear that value words such as "good" or "bad" can be predicated of them and of their respective environments.

Before moving on to a consideration of how these observations influence my interpretation of Moore's distinction between valuative and descriptive predicates and his open question argument, it will be well to emphasize that in equating good with suitability, I am not committed to the view that all things can be said to be "good" in exactly the same sense. This point is pertinent to Moore's view that "good" is not reducible to any single common property. This view is correct in so far as it can be interpreted to mean that "good" is not reducible to a single property that is always exactly or univocally the same whenever and wherever it is found. It is more proper to say that good is common to many things in an analogical way. This means that all things that are said to be good are at one and the same time similar and different in their very character as good.

An example may help to explain this point. Things are not said to be good in exactly the same sense, because the character of suitability is not exactly the same when applied to a mechanical dishwasher and a baseball player. Although it is true that when we speak of a good dishwasher and a good baseball player, the notion of suitability is involved in both cases, the fact remains that the task for which a dishwasher is suitable is different from the task to which a baseball player is suitable. In this case, to say that both are good is to say that both are suitable to some purpose or task, but since the character of the purpose or task is different in both cases, the character of the suitability or good is also different. To be "suitable" as a dishwasher is not the same as to be "suitable" as a baseball player. Hence, things that are said to be good are similar in that they are suitable to some task or to the perfecting of some character, but they also differ in their suitability in that to be suitable to one task or nature is different from being suitable to some other task or nature. This means that there is no single definition of good which is inclusive of all other goods and from which a knowledge of these goods can be deduced. If one wants to know what is meant when a horse is said to be good, he must know something about horses. However, a knowledge of horses is no help in discovering what is meant when a tomato plant is said to be good.

This last point has a bearing on Moore's open question argument. I have already expressed agreement with Moore's observation that good is not to be simply identified with any one given object, since it can be predicated of many objects. The analysis of good as suitability shows that the validity of Moore's open question argument lies not in the fact that there is an unbridgeable gap between good and natural objects, but that we must know something about the character or task of a thing before we can say that it is good. Granted that "good" means suitability to some task or nature, what the open question argument actually proves is that we must know something about the task or nature that is at issue before we can make a value judgment concerning a given object or state of affairs.

For example, Moore was right in pointing out that there is a difference between showing that two things exist together and that one or both of them are good. The reason for this difference is that unless one knows something about the character of the things in question, he could not know whether their coexistence was good or bad for one or both of them. If, for example, one of the things is food for insects and the other is an insect, then I know that the food which nourishes the insect, which suits his needs, is good, whereas if one thing is insecticide and the other an insect, I would say that the insecticide is not good for the insect. Any given case of coexistence might be said to be good from the perspective of one of the beings and bad from the perspective of the other. The existence of sheep is good for the wolf in so far as they are suitable to his need for food, whereas the existence of the wolf is bad for the sheep in so far as the wolf is destructive of the sheep's life.

Moore has pointed out that there is a difference in the question itself and in our own state of mind when we ask whether a thing is good and when we ask if a thing is desired, approved, or pleasant. The plausibility of this position rests on the fact that what is good or suitable in one context may not be good or suitable in another. For example, knowing that something is approved by, or pleasant to, another person, we may yet question whether that thing is good, because the task or character of that thing may not be simply to be pleasant. Thus, no matter how pleasant the odor of an insecticide may be to a man, it is not good precisely as an insecticide if it fails to kill insects. However, in this case, we would say that the insecticide is good in so far as it is suited to producing pleasure, but that it is bad precisely as an insecticide in that it is not suited to killing insects. Hence, the open question argument and the conception of good as suitable point not to the fact that there is some sort of gap between that which is approved, pleasant, or desired and good, but to the need to establish a certain context, a certain universe of discourse, in order to engage in a meaningful discussion of whether something is good.

There may be a difference in our state of mind and in the questions when we ask concerning whether a thing is approved or whether a thing is good. That this difference exists proves not that there is a dichotomy between that which is approved or desired and that which is good, but that it is possible for that which is good *in so far as it is approved or desired* to be bad considered in another context. For example, Adolf Hitler may be said to have been good in so far as he suited Eva Braun's desires, or in so far as he met with her approval. However, the fact that he was good in this sense does not necessarily mean that he was morally good. The fact that a thing may be good in so far as it is considered in one context, but bad considered in another indicates that the task of the ethician is to try to establish some sort of perspective that would function as a norm which would help man to distinguish between moral good and moral evil. This point will be discussed more thoroughly later in this section.

Before moving on to this matter, it will be necessary to consider the bearing of the evaluation of Moore's open question argument on the validity of his view that valuative predicates are nondescriptive. It is true that to predicate good of an unknown X is not to describe it. However, the reason for the truth of this position lies in the fact that the conception of good is so intimately linked with what a thing is, that good has no meaning unless I know something about the thing of which it is predicated. Hence, Moore's argument does not support the view that there is a dichotomy between nature and value. What gives the argument its cogency is that a person must know something about a thing before he can make any value predications about it. Granted that he does know something about a natural object, he would find it impossible to *describe* it without using some sort of value predicates. We cannot get very far in describing a natural agent without discussing what things are suitable or not suitable to it.

For example, one cannot proceed very far in describing the character of a certain species of plant or in understanding this species without considering what sort of soil, climate, and fertilizers are suitable or unsuitable to its growth and maturation, i.e. what conditions are good or bad for that particular species. The same point can be made with respect to any attempt to describe any animal or organism, including man considered as a physical organism. Any description of these things which does not include what is suitable or not suitable to them is a very incomplete description. Thus, once I know something about a thing, "good" does become a descriptive predicate in that I actually come to know more about a given thing when I know what things are suitable or unsuitable to certain facets of its reality and those features of reality for which it is either suited or unsuited.

The outcome of this section is that the natural order in which man lives is inherently charged with values, with good and bad. Values are not something that must be injected into man's natural context from some unknown external source. As a natural being, man himself is implicated in this world of "goods" and "bads." The given fact of human existence is that man's life is one of fulfillments and of frustrations. Man finds himself in contexts and situations, or confronted with objects, that actually are suited or unsuited to him or to some dimension of his being.

In concluding this subsection, it will be well to refer to certain observations made by C. S. Lewis and by John Dewey that might help explain the fact that philosophers have tended to take the view that values are somehow external to natural phenomena, thus creating the problem of accounting for the reality of values and of explaining the relationship between "facts" and values.

These philosophers may have been influenced by what C. S. Lewis refers to as the "Methodological Idiom," in their conception of nature. This idiom is at work when one equates nature with whatever is studied by a particular science, e.g., physics. Using this idiom, one need never ask what nature itself is. Nature is simply what you discuss and study when you are doing physics.[43] Granted the use of this idiom, it is easy to oppose the view that nature is alive with values and that values are intrinsic to the natural order on the grounds that this view is not sustained by nature as studied and presented by the physicist. Throughout this discussion, I am giving those who would make a dichotomy between nature and values the benefit of the doubt by admitting that nature as studied by the physicist is valueless.

There are two difficulties in a position which employs the methodological idiom to substantiate the view that there is a dualism between nature and values. First, it may be true that the quantitative, or mathematical, approach which physics takes in dealing with nature may lead it to depict a nature in which there are only mathematical relations of equality, identity, more or less, but no relations of suitability or unsuitability between things. The very approach which physics takes toward nature would lead it to prescind from the relationships of value found in nature. Because physics in thus limited by its very method of dealing with nature, its findings cannot be used to justify a denial of the value relationships in our experience of natural organisms such as plants, animals, and men—relationships which are confirmed by the life sciences such as biology and botany, as well as by the art of medicine.

Secondly, since physics restricts itself to the study of a limited field of nature, one that does not include living organisms precisely in their character as living, i.e., as growing, nourishing, reproductive, sensing, desiring, and knowing, it is not legitimate to take what this science offers as constituting the whole story of the character of nature. Indeed, a case might be made for the view that sciences such as physics and chemistry study those features of nature that constitute the conditions for the activity of natural organisms. Since they are thus dealing with the conditions for these activities rather than the activities themselves, it is not surprising that the relationships of suitability or unsuitability which are inextricably bound up with activity are not immediately evident in these sciences.

John Dewey points out that there is a tendency to assume that those facets of nature that do not play a part in scientific discourse either have no reality, or, at least not the same sort of unquestionable reality that can be attributed to "mathematical, mechanical or magneto-electric properties that constitute mat-

---

[43] C. S. Lewis, *Studies in Words* (Cambridge: Cambridge University Press, 1960), p. 69.

ter."[44] He also grounds the failure to accord values an intrinsic place in nature in what he terms "intellectualism."

By 'intellectualism' as an indictment is meant the theory that all experience is a mode of knowing, and that all subject-matter, all nature, is, in principle, to be reduced and transformed till it is defined in terms identical with the characteristics presented by refined objects of science as such. The assumption of 'intellectualism' goes contrary to the facts of what is primarily experienced. For things are objects to be treated, used, acted upon and with, enjoyed and endured, even more than things to be known. . . . The isolation of traits characteristic of objects known, and then defined as the sole ultimate realities, accounts for the denial to nature of the characters which make things lovable, contemptible, beautiful and ugly, adorable and awful. It accounts for the belief that nature is an indifferent, dead mechanism; it explains why characteristics that are valuable and valued traits of objects in actual experience are thought to create a fundamentally troublesome philosophical problem.[45]

Thus, although the philosopher and the scientist may be concerned with the facts of experience only as objects of knowledge, the fact is that man's transactions with the world are not simply and exclusively cognitive. As a being in the natural order, man is fulfilled and frustrated by other men and other beings in this order. The task of the ethician is to try to establish a standard upon which man can base his distinctions between those fulfillments that are moral and those that are immoral.

c. INTRINSIC VALUE AND THE CRITERION FOR MORAL GOOD

One might argue that the conception of good developed in this section does not come to grips with a major issue raised by Moore's *Principia Ethica*, viz., the search for a definition of intrinsic good. The conception of good as suitable does not appear to be the answer to this search. However, Moore's view that the definition of intrinsic good is a major task for the moral philosopher is open to question. Unless intrinsic good is equated with moral good, there appears to be no reason for the ethician to undertake a search for the definition of intrinsic good. Granted the validity of the position taken in this section that good means suitable, the task of the ethician is to discover a criterion for distinguishing between those suitabilities or goods that are moral and those that are immoral.

It may appear that the equation between intrinsic good and moral good is gratuitous. However, there is a reason for it. Granted that the leading of the moral life is of utmost significance for man, it is legitimate to speak of moral good as being the intrinsic good, meaning by this that a certain good is good

[44] John Dewey, *Experience and Nature* (New York: Dover, 1958), p. 25.
[45] *Ibid.*, p. 21.

within the context of man's moral endeavors. The adjective "intrinsic" refers to the good as being good within a moral context and carries with it the connotation that so long as a thing is good in this context, it need not prove its goodness in other contexts. For example, to say that friendship is good in itself is to say that it is good as fulfilling the moral demands of human existence and that in so far as it is seen to fulfill these demands it needs no other credentials to attest to its goodness. Thus friendship differs from such things as wealth and the development of atomic power in that, seen within a moral context, these latter things are only useful goods to moral fulfillment, depending on how man uses them.

Moore's discussion of the conditions that must be met by a criterion for intrinsic value indicates that he thinks that this criterion must be a criterion for all value. Thus, against the possible use of the "realization of the true self," as a criterion of value, he points out that if the thing, which realizes the true self, has a value of its own, it does not owe its value to the fact that it realizes the true self. Moore has saddled the ethician with the impossible task of establishing a criterion of value that will apply to all values. This would mean that the ethician must establish a criterion that would apply to all the different, possible contexts in which a thing might be said to be good. He would be required to establish some super class of discourse that would include within it all other classes, or perspectives according to which things could be said to be good. However, the ethician's task is of a much more limited and managable nature. He must establish a criterion for *moral* good. The fact that there are things that may be said to be good apart from this criterion does not invalidate the criterion, since it was not meant to be a criterion for *all* values.

5. HUMAN REASON AS A CREATIVE FACTOR IN NATURE: TOWARD A NATURALISTIC FOUNDATION OF MORAL LIFE

Granted that man is a valuing being living in a world of values (of goods and evils), the issue before the ethician is not how man moves from a completely valueless universe to a universe of moral values. Rather, the question is, "What factors of human existence serve to give these natural values their specifically moral character?" As we have seen, man lives in a world full of frustrations and fulfillments. He is not a spectator standing outside of this world. As intimately engaged in this world, he finds himself fulfilled and frustrated. The purpose of this section is to show the role which human reason plays, as a factor in nature, in the constitution of man as a "moral" being, i.e., a being concerned with discovering which fulfillments he ought to pursue and which fulfillments he ought to avoid. As a being capable of morality, man does not passively accept whatever fulfillments and frustrations happen to come his way. Not only does he try to distinguish among fulfillments that ought and ought not be pursued, but he also tries to distinguish among frustrations that ought to be avoided and those that are only superficial frustrations hiding certain fulfillments that ought to be pursued. The purpose of this section is to try to show that reason working within the context of man's universe plays a constitutive role in the establishment of these distinctions.

It is true that nature considered as exclusive of human reason, and as simply given to reason, is nonmoral so that if human reason were able only to repeat this given order of things there could be no hope of grounding moral distinctions in this interplay between nature and reason. The exposition of the thoughts of Leibniz, Locke, Hume, and Kant in this chapter indicated that there is a common element underlying the differences that separate these men. In dealing with the problem of the role of reason in man's moral life, they seem to agree that if there is any interaction between reason and nature or the facts of experience, the character of this interaction is such that reason can be said only to repeat what is already given in experience. The outcome of this agreement is that either there must be some fact given in experience that is given to reason as moral (this seems to be the alternative accepted by Hume) or the moral order is grounded in reason a priori (the view taken by Leibniz, Kant, and apparently Locke, at least in his *Essay concerning Human Understanding*). In this section, I shall present considerations that provide a foundation for a third alternative—one which allows for an interaction between human reason and nature without reducing reason to the status of simply repeating what is already given to it in the "facts" of experience.

As we saw earlier, David Hume maintained that if reason is to declare an act immoral, the immorality of this act must have existed as prior and given to reason so that reason could be said to be a spectator of the act, but could not be said to have been involved in the act itself which it judges to be immoral. The immorality of the act is a fact given to reason. Reason has no part to play in the constitution of this act as either moral or immoral. It is simply presented with the fact of the morality or immorality of the act. Although Alfred North Whitehead is not dealing with morality in the following statement, he does provide a good starting point for dealing with Hume's position: "This contrast of fact and thought can be conceived fallaciously. *For thought is a factor in the fact of experience. Thus the immediate fact is what it is, partly by reason of the thought involved in it.* [Italics mine]."[46] The italicized words are very pertinent to the issue raised by Hume. Reason does not stand outside of and apart from the "facts of experience." It is implicated and involved in these experienced facts.

Turning specifically to Hume's position, human reason need not be treated as a mere spectator of activities which are presented to it as facts. It may itself be involved in these activities and it is only because human reason discovers itself as a factor in these acts that it places them in a moral universe of discourse.

[46] See footnote 41, p. 80.

For example, the act which in animals is nonmoral becomes moral or immoral in the case of man because reason is seen to be a factor in this latter act. Hence, reason is said to function in the formation of the moral character of human existence not because it comes on the scene after an act has been performed, surveys it, and declares it to be moral or immoral, but because it is a factor in the act which is later reflected upon either by the reason of the one who performed the act or by some other man's reason.

Moore's case against the naturalistic fallacy is perhaps unassailable so long as the creative character of reason in nature is not recognized. So long as the interaction between human reason and the natural facts of experience is so interpreted as to treat reason as simply repeating or mirroring these facts, there can be no hope of grounding the moral dimensions of human existence in this interaction. John Dewey points to the implications involved in viewing human reason as merely mirroring the given facts of experience.

> The fact that thought is an intrinsic feature of experience is fatal to the traditional empiricism which makes it an artificial by-product. But for that same reason it is fatal to the historical rationalisms whose justification was the secondary and retrospective position assigned to thought by empirical philosophy. According to the particularism of the latter, thought was inevitably only a bunching together of hard-and-fast separate items; thinking was but the gathering together and tying of items already completely given, or else an equally artificial untying—a mechanical adding and subtracting of the given. It was but a cumulative registration, a consolidated merger; generality was a matter of bulk, not of quality. Thinking was therefore treated as lacking constructive power; even its organizing capacity was but simulated, being in truth but arbitrary pigeon-holing. Genuine projection of the novel, deliberate variation and invention, are idle fictions in such a version of experience. If there ever was creation, it all took place at a remote period. Since then the world has only recited lessons.[47]

There are two points in this statement that have a bearing on the problems being considered in this section.

First of all, Dewey's charge that both rationalism and empiricism fail to see thought as an intrinsic feature of experience conforms with the point of similarity between empiricism and rationalism that I emphasized above, namely, both interpret any interaction between thought and experience as meaning that thought merely repeats what is fully given in experience apart from thought. The rationalistic position is justified only if this interpretation is accepted. Granted that the moral dimensions of human existence cannot be grounded in an interaction between thought and the facts of human experience, it follows, according to the rationalists, that these dimensions must be found in reason alone apart from experience.

---

[47] John Dewey, "The Need for a Recovery of Philosophy," On Experience, Nature, and Freedom, ed., with an introduction by Richard J. Bernstein (New York: Bobbs-Merrill, 1960), pp. 34–35.

Dewey points out that the rationalistic position cannot explain how reason, viewed as a factor external to experience, could play any fruitful role in guiding and expanding the course of human experience. Because reason a priori is cut off from experience, it has no leverage within experience to provide man with any meaningful and constructive guide for meeting the changing demands of his existence in the world. A reason cut off from experience can only point out the logical inconsistencies and absurdities in existing beliefs. It cannot provide a constructive guide for the replacement of these beliefs.[48] Moral philosophy must move beyond the limits of a purely logical consistency if it is to be of any help to man in his attempt to establish a norm of moral behavior. The second, and major point, of Dewey's statement is that the empiricist notion of experience denies the possibility of any genuine novelty, of "deliberate variation and invention," arising from the interaction of thought and experience. Nothing new can arise out of this interaction. Everything must be given once and for all in experience so that man has only to recite the lessons given in experience.

A consideration of the role of human reason in the technological area of human endeavor will help call attention to the fact that the interaction between human reason and nature as given to man in experience is a source for novelty in the world. Nature, as separate from human reason, does not of itself pour out to man such technological advances as are embodied in atomic power plants, spaceships, refrigerators, and television sets. Unless human reason were an active factor in nature, these advances simply would not *be*. Nature is sometimes spoken of as providing the tools or raw materials for these advances. It is certainly true that things existing in nature are rich in inherent possibilities. This point should be kept in mind for future reference when we come to discuss the apparent dichotomy between what is and what ought to be. However, at this point, it is sufficient to note that these possibilities possess the character of "tools" or of "raw materials," only because human reason is a factor at work in nature. Nature without reason is no tool for technological advances.

In addition to the possibilities inherent in natural things other than man, there is in nature a being called man whose reason provides him with the ability to 'view these possibilities from a general or universal perspective, and who—thanks to this perspective—can transform these possibilities into the technological artifacts that are so much a part of our contemporary environment. Man's ability to introduce new mechanical utilities in reality is grounded not only in the human intellect's ability to come to know the possibilities inherent in things, but also in its capacity to move beyond a mere mirroring of the particular objects, as given, to viewing these objects in a somewhat universal perspective, which enables it to envision possible communities of objects without actually having these communities given to it as fully actualized in experience.

This discussion of human reason's role in technological inventions was meant only to set the stage for an investigation of the possible role of human reason

[48] *Ibid.*, pp. 35–36.

in the establishment of the moral character of human existence. The discussion cannot be simply transferred to the moral issue with which this section is concerned. Turning to this issue, it was pointed out above that in so far as man is an appetitive being, fulfillments and frustrations are intrinsic to his relationship to his world. The problem is not to show how reason can place a valueless world in a moral context, but to show how reason can perform this function in a world full of frustrations and fulfillments.

— The essential factor in the performance of this task lies in the fact that human reason enables man to reflect on himself and his world from the perspective of a being sharing in a certain community, i.e., the human community. The function of human reason which places it at the very heart of man's moral existence is that function which Ludwig Feuerbach sees as the distinguishing feature of human consciousness. Whereas the consciousness of brutes is restricted to a feeling of the "self as the common centre of successive sensation," human consciousness is the consciousness of "a being to whom his species, his essential nature, is an object of thought."[49] It is precisely the reality of this perspective of himself as a member of a certain species or community—a perspective that would have no reality apart from the work of human reason—that is an essential ingredient in the formation of the moral dimensions of human experience.

If human reason were restricted to dealing with particulars, only in their particularity, if it could not rise from these particulars to the level of universal thought, this conception of the human community could play no role in nature, and the interaction between man and his world would still involve fulfillments and frustrations, but it is very doubtful that there would be any moral problems connected with these fulfillments and frustrations.

Mill's criticism of a simple identification of nature and morality, and Moore's observations on the naturalistic fallacy are unassailable so long as one fails to recognize that reason does not simply repeat or mirror the particular, external facts with which it is directly confronted, but that reason adds its own dimension to this confrontation in so far as it is able to see these facts in the context of their relationship to the human community. In short, the fact that human reason is involved in man's transactions with his world makes these transactions different from what they would be if reason were not a factor in them. Reason does not simply repeat the transactions. As a factor in the transactions, it makes a difference to their very character. Dealing with the specific issue at hand, it is my contention that man's transactions with his world involve not only matters of what is or what is not the case, but also matters of what ought or ought not be the case because these transactions involve a knowledge of himself as a member of a certain community of being.

Before moving to a justification and explanation of this contention, it will

---

[49] Ludwig Feuerbach, *The Essence of Christianity*, translated by George Eliot (New York: Harper and Brothers, 1957), p. 1.

be necessary to discuss what is meant by the "human community" in this context and how this notion can be grounded in man's interactions with his world. There can be no hope of undertaking a complete discussion of these issues, since such an undertaking would require an investigation of metaphysical and epistemological matters that are beyond the scope of this book. These matters will be considered only in so far as they serve to clarify man's moral life. The "human community" which is known by human reason does not exist as a universal apart from the work of human reason. Only individual men exist. However, human reason discovers that these men possess certain capacities, which, as actually existent, are individual, but which also allow men to enter into the lives of other men in a more intimate and complete way than they can enter into the lives of any other beings. For example, the capacity to communicate ideas to one another not only concerning their own individual states, but also concerning their respective views of the nature of the universe, of man himself, and of man's place in this universe allows men to share their lives with other men in unique ways. It is a type of sharing that man can enjoy only with his fellow man among the beings found in the natural order. Not only can men exchange and debate abstract theories of numbers and of the universe, but they can also share human feelings through drama, poetry, and art. Moreover, through dialogue, a process using a set of symbols called words, one individual can bare his innermost and private emotions and thoughts to another who, using these same symbols, can influence him to change these emotions and feelings.

Man also seems to be unique among the beings of the natural order in the way in which he confronts the temporal dimensions of existence. He does not simply accept the changes involved in a temporal existence. He tries to make this experience an object of his thought. Thus, in myth and legend, as well as in the most painstaking type of historical study, he shows himself to be concerned with his past. His concern with an afterlife and with his posterity shows him to be equally concerned with the future. He is not simply an existent in time, but he is one who tries to gain some perspective on the temporal process in which he finds himself. Man is also seen to be a being who is concerned with what he ought to do and what he ought to avoid. He is thus a being capable of guilt, whether this guilt be grounded in taboos, religious beliefs, customs, or philosophical reflection. Finally, man's freedom, as described in Chapter II, serves to distinguish him from other natural beings.

In saying that human reason's conception of the human community is grounded in the points listed above, I am not maintaining that these facts alone ground this conception, nor am I saying that human reason possesses a full and exhaustive grasp of what it means to be man. However, the fact remains that human reason has gained a sufficient grasp of those functions and capacities that serve to distinguish man from other natural beings and can use this distinguishing grasp in evaluating the courses of action open to man. It should also be noted that the conception of the human community was grounded in a recognition of man's capacity for freedom, among other things. This fact would appear to meet the possible criticism that this conception does not allow for the rich varieties of activities man may undertake. For this conception is based on a knowledge of the capacities that serve to characterize man, without claiming to know precisely how man will actually use these capacities in the future.

The fact that man is a free being existing in a world of values and the fact that he is able to know himself, through reason reflecting on his experience, as a member of the human community serve to break down what appeared to be a complete dualism between what is (the so-called factual order) and what ought to be (the moral order), without simply identifying what ought to be with what is. Man is directly involved in his moral tasks when he is free, when he is confronted with a world that is "open," i.e., a world offering him alternatives. In this case, man is not confronted with a world that simply is what it is, but with a factual order that offers possibilities for frustrations and fulfillments. The free man finds in what is, not a brute, given existential fact, one that is simply what it is, and can be nothing else. Rather, he sees in the fact or situation that is, possible fulfillments that might be pursued and possible frustrations that might be avoided.

Reflecting on these fulfillments in the light of his conception of the human community, he may come to see that certain fulfillments *ought to be* pursued and others *ought to be* avoided, being either suitable or unsuitable to the character of the human community. Thus, "what ought to be" can be seen to arise out of man's reflections on what is, but is not simply identified with what is. For human reason in its reflections on what is, reveals to man the possibilities inherent in the facts for the fulfillment or frustration of the human community—a community which is also the result of human reason's reflections on man and his world, and a community which could have played no part in man's decision had it not been for human reason's ability to form a universal conception of it on the basis of its reflection on individual human beings and human cultures.

Man as fully and humanistically integrated with himself and his world is not a given existential fact. Human reason must uncover the possibilities inherent in man's morally fragmented and disconnected world for such an integration and must make these possibilities the object of human consciousness so as to provide man with a basis for distinguishing between those possibilities destructive of a fully integrated human life and those which contribute to it. That man, in his moral life, is not limited to repeating the brute facts of his experience is seen in the lives of moral reformers. Whereas other men accept existing injustices as being given "natural" facts, without recognizing that these facts are unjust, the moral reformer not only recognizes the injustice, but also discovers possibilities inherent in the situation for a life or society that contributes to the fulfillment of the character of the human community. Thus, human reason's ability to discover possibilities in the given state of affairs and to relate these possibilities to its conception of the human community can account for that tension which characterizes man's moral existence, i.e., the tension between the given world which *is* and man's understanding of what this world *could be* in terms of his grasp of this world as related to him as a member of the human community and what *ought to be* if the situation is to accord with the character of this community as seen by human consciousness.

This account of man in the world serves to show that emotivism is wrong in holding that moral obligation can be grounded only in the appetitive dimension of human existence. It is undoubtedly true that when many men say that one ought to perform a certain activity, they are only expressing their attitude. However, as the analysis conducted in this section has shown, it is possible for the notion of moral obligation to arise out of man's cognitive grasp of the human community as related to the given existential state of affairs.

To the notion of man as a "subject," which involved a recognition of him as a being capable of freedom or self-determination, can now be added that of man as a being who is able to know himself as belonging to a certain community of being, and who is able to use this knowledge to evaluate the given state of affairs and its possibilities, enriching the scope of these possibilities with this knowledge of his own nature.

This discussion provides a different perspective on Moore's charge that those who speak of good as the realization of the "true" self are guilty of the naturalistic fallacy because they are maintaining that something is good in that it conforms with some self that actually exists. However, to speak of a true self within the context of the position taken in this section is not necessarily to imply that the self is good because it actually exists. The meaning may be much more complex. The actually existent self may be seen to be open to a variety of different developments. When man is advised to fulfill the true self, he is advised to fulfill that possibility which most conforms with human reason's grasp of the self as a member of the human community. Thus, true in this case does not refer to a simple one-to-one correspondence between the mind and reality. The self is said to be true not in the sense that it corresponds to a self actually existent, but in the sense that it fits into, is coherent with, human reason's grasp of the human community, a community existing as a universal only in the mind although the basis for it is found in man's knowledge of those capacities and functions that are seen to exist only in the life of man. Hence, the ethician who says that the ideal is to be found in the realization of the true self may establish this self as an ideal, not because it actually exists, but because, among the possible selves into which this actually existent self may develop, there is one self that is most consistent with, and "true to" the capacities for human existence that human reason has included in its conception of the human community.

After having explored the difficulties involved in trying to ground moral values in nature, this chapter tried to show that human reason plays an important role in giving man's transactions with his world a moral character. The position defended in this chapter involved the following points. The natural order is not an order of valueless facts. In so far as the beings in this order are agents, i.e., beings possessing an intrinsic principle of activity, they can enter into relationships with other natural beings that may be said to be suitable or unsuitable to one or the other of them. In so far as man is in this world, he is not merely a spectator of such relationships, but is himself engaged in relationships that are either suitable or unsuitable to him. Good is defined in terms of suitability.

Granted all this, the question is not how a moral order can be grounded in a valueless nature, but how such an order can be grounded in a nature full of values. The answer given to this question in this chapter is based on the fact that human reason, which is a factor in man's transactions with his world, does not merely repeat these transactions, but can view them in the light of its conception of the human community, a conception which human reason was able to fashion on the basis of its grasp of the capacities and functions that serve to distinguish men from other natural beings. Possessing this conception, man is able to distinguish between those values that he ought to pursue and those that he ought to avoid on the basis of their suitability or unsuitability to the human community.

It must be admitted that this chapter not only showed how it is possible for a moral standard to arise out of man's transactions with his world, but also showed how the standard of the human community can be fashioned out of these transactions. It is impossible to speak with any degree of precision about the way in which man can discover a standard of morality, without speaking about a particular standard. However, the argument in this chapter was not directed toward proving that the conception of the human community is actually the standard to be used in evaluating man's behavior. This point will be dealt with in the next chapter.

CHAPTER IV

Foundations
of
Ethical Judgments

Whereas the purpose in Chapter III was to try to discover those factors in human experience that make it possible for man to ground his ethical judgments in a rational foundation, the purpose of this chapter is to move beyond the discussion of such a possibility to a defense and a characterization of a specific rational norm for moral judgments. An exposition and evaluation of utilitarianism and deontologism will be useful in fulfilling this purpose, because these positions represent diverse responses found in the philosophical community to the issue concerning the criterion for distinguishing between moral good and evil. The question of the validity of egoism and altruism as possible moral norms will also be considered. Finally, there will be an exploration of the question of whether or not it is possible to establish an unchanging moral norm for man in view of the fact that he lives in a changing world.

1. THE UTILITARIANISM OF JOHN STUART MILL

In order to see the context out of which John Stuart Mill developed his ethical views, it will be necessary to present a brief statement of Jeremy Bentham's version of utilitarianism. Bentham states that his establishment of the principle of utility as the standard of morality is grounded in the recognition that man's activities are governed by the attempt to find pleasure and to avoid pain. Thus, the principle of utility judges the morality of every action, whether the action be that of an individual or a government, in terms of the tendency which that action seems to have to promote or oppose the happiness of the individuals affected by the act.[1] Later, Bentham decided to refer to his standard of morality as the *greatest happiness* or *greatest felicity* principle, rather than as the principle of utility. A major reason for this change was that he thought

[1] Jeremy Bentham, *An Introduction to the Principles of Morals and Legislation* (New York: Hafner Publishing Co., 1948), pp. 1–2.

that the word "utility" did not emphasize the ideas of pleasure and pain as strongly as did the words "happiness" and "felicity." Finally, Bentham also found these latter words preferable to utility because the word "utility" does not emphasize as strongly as those terms the fact that it is the *number* of interests affected by any given act which contributes most to his standard of morality.[2] Hence, when Bentham says an act is to be judged by the happiness it produces, he means it is to be judged by the amount of pleasure it produces among the greatest number of people or by the amount of pain it avoids for the greatest number.

To appreciate the value which Mill finds in Bentham's position, it will be necessary to note his conception of the two basic alternatives confronting moral philosophers from the earliest times to his own day. The first alternative is one which goes by such names as the moral sense theory, the theory of eternal and immutable morality, or the intuitive approach to morality. Briefly, this theory maintains that the distinction between right and wrong is a brute, inexplicable fact of experience. There is some ultimate and naturally given sense, perception, or faculty which grounds this distinction.[3] This doctrine puts the problem of the distinction between moral good and evil outside the pale of rational discussion and investigation. It seems to be linked in Mill's mind with a morality which sanctifies existing opinions and habits, by equating the existing order with the "natural" order and arguing that any innovation of this order is criminal.[4]

The second alternative, and the one which Mill finds acceptable, sees the distinction between moral good and evil not as an inexplicable, ultimate fact that must either be dumbly accepted or be known only through some mysterious intuition, but as flowing from the ordinary properties of human actions which are open to the work of the ordinary human faculties of intellect and sensation.[5] Although Mill's acceptance of Bentham's statement of utilitarianism was by no means a wholly unqualified one, he did think that Bentham made a positive contribution to moral philosophy in that his work served to strengthen the case for this second alternative by making ethicians conscious of the need to attack moral and political problems in an organized, systematic fashion. Mill held that Bentham made the same sort of methodological contributions to man's dealings with the political and moral issues of his world as Francis Bacon did in the area of the natural sciences.[6]

Both the intuitionists and those taking this second approach begin from the

---

[2] *Ibid.*, 1822 note.

[3] John Stuart Mill, "Professor Sedgwick's Discourse on the Studies of the University of Cambridge," in *Dissertations and Discussions: Political, Philosophical, and Historical*, Vol. I (London: John W. Parker and Son, 1859), pp. 122–123.

[4] John Stuart Mill, "Dr. Whewell on Moral Philosophy," in *Dissertations and Discussions*, Vol. II, p. 472.

[5] See footnote 3, pp. 122–123.

[6] John Stuart Mill, "Bentham," in *Dissertations and Discussions*, Vol. I, pp. 337, 346–347. See also footnote 4, p. 462.

same phenomena, namely, that men make moral judgments distinguishing between moral and immoral acts and dispositions, and that there is a feeling of pleasure involved in the contemplation of the morally good acts and dispositions, and a feeling of aversion connected with those judgments of acts and dispositions as immoral.[7] Starting with these phenomena, Mill sets out to establish the validity of utilitarianism. He acknowledges that this is no easy task, because the attempt to establish the principle of utility as the ultimate criterion of morality is an attempt to establish the first principle of moral conduct and the establishment of first principles in any area, whether it be that of knowledge or of conduct, does not admit of proof "in the ordinary acceptance of the term."[8] However, this does not mean that there is absolutely no cognitive way of establishing the truth of first principles. The issue can be decided by man's reason in so far as considerations can be advanced that would be capable of determining the intellect to either reject or accept a given view of the moral standard, and Mill feels that such considerations are equivalent to a proof.[9]

Since the first principles of knowledge are matters of fact, one's acceptance or rejection of them can be based on those human faculties which ground our judgments of fact, namely, our senses and internal consciousness. When we turn to the first principles of human conduct, we are dealing with the issue of what constitutes the end of human activity. For according to Mill, "the end of human action" is "necessarily also the standard of morality."[10] Since this is the case, any defense of a principle as the standard of moral conduct must prove that that principle actually is the end of human conduct. It is in his laying down the ground rules for such a defense that Mill opens himself to the charge of committing the naturalistic fallacy. How are we to prove that anything is an end of human activity?

Mill's oft-quoted answer is as follows:

> The only proof capable of being given that an object is visible, is that people actually see it. The only proof that a sound is audible, is that people hear it. . . . In like manner, I apprehend, the sole evidence it is possible to produce that anything is desirable, is that people do actually desire it.[11]

Mill's position is that the only way to justify the view that X is the end of human conduct, and that it therefore can function as a standard of morality, is to point to the given facts of human experience which show that men actually do desire X. There is no way of giving any sort of syllogistic proof or demonstration that men actually desire X so that the utilitarian position that man desires general happiness could not be justified unless men did actually in

---

[7] See footnote 3, pp. 121–122.
[8] See footnote 8, Chap. III, pp. 51–52.
[9] *Ibid.*, p. 6.
[10] *Ibid.*, p. 17.
[11] *Ibid.*, pp. 51–52.

both theory and practice acknowledge happiness to be their end, i.e., what they desired. However, the utilitarian position is validated by the fact that individual men do desire their own happiness, when they think it is attainable. This fact provides the only "proof" that is possible or required to show that happiness is a good and that an individual's happiness is a good to him, and that general happiness is a good to an aggregate of persons. Mill does not think that this proof is sufficient to ground the contention that happiness is the *only* criterion of morality, because it shows only that happiness is *a* good, but not the *sole* good. Happiness has been established as one of the criteria of morality, but not as the only criterion. In order to establish the latter position, Mill recognizes that happiness must be shown to be not one among many ends, but the only end for man.

There are two closely related difficulties which Mill considers in trying to establish this point. The first is the apparent fact that there are men who continue to lead virtuous lives, even when these lives entail a good deal of unhappiness. This fact would appear to invalidate the view that man seeks only happiness. The second difficulty is that the defense of happiness as the sole criterion of human conduct seems to imply that virtue and morality ought to be practiced only when they can make us happy. This implication appears to justify the view that whenever the virtuous life causes any difficulties or unhappiness one ought to give it up.

With respect to the factual argument, Mill does not deny that many people do *as a matter of fact*, desire virtue in itself. However, he provides a psychological explanation of this fact which shows that it supports rather than destroys the position that man desires only happiness. The explanation is based on the view that things other than happiness are desired either as a means to happiness or as ingredients in the happy life. Turning specifically to virtue, Mill holds that it is similar to money, fame, or power in that it was desired originally not as an end in itself, but as a means to happiness. Unlike music and health, which are not merely means to happiness, but are also ingredients of happiness so that they are desired in themselves, virtue was not originally an ingredient in happiness. However, it is so intimately connected with happiness as a means, that it can and has taken on the character of the end (happiness) toward which it is directed with the result that men have been able to desire and cherish it in itself as constituting a part of their happiness. Once the intimate connection between virtue as a means and happiness as the end has led a man to see virtue as part of his happiness and he becomes confirmed in this view, he will continue in the pursuit of his virtuous purposes even though the happiness that may have once been so intimately related to them is greatly diminished by changes in his character or situation.[12]

The same intimate union of virtue as a means to happiness that allows Mill to accept the fact that men desire virtue as an end without surrendering the

[12] *Ibid.*, pp. 53–57.

view that happiness alone is desired as an end also provides him with a basis for meeting the charge that he advocates the practice of virtue only when such practice does not involve any unpleasantness. Virtue holds a distinctive place among such objects as money, fame, and power which are means to happiness. Whereas the pursuit of these other means are good for society in a rather limited and restricted way, the disinterested pursuit of virtue is *always* such a boon to society that the "utilitarian standard . . . enjoins and requires the cultivation of the love of virtue up to the greatest strength possible, as being above all things important to the general happiness."[13] Hence, although the utilitarian position sees virtue only as being good as a means to something beyond virtue, it advocates the pursuit of virtue as an end in itself, even though, in any individual instance, it may not produce those good consequences which it usually tends to produce.[14]

Once it has been seen that human nature is so constituted that man desires only that which is either a means to or a part of happiness, the essential element of the utilitarian position has been established, namely, that the sole criterion to be used in judging the morality of an act is the tendency of the act either to promote or to destroy happiness.[15] This statement of the utilitarian position stands in need of further specification. Specifically, it is necessary to know something about the character of "happiness" that is to act as a standard of morality. It is not enough to say that an act must be judged in terms of its tendency to produce "happy" consequences.

Mill maintains that a process of self-reflection, together with an observation of the activity of others, will reveal that to desire a thing (which shows that the thing either is a means to or an ingredient of happiness) is identical with finding it pleasant, whereas to dislike a thing is identical with finding it painful. He holds that it is one and the same thing to think a thing pleasant and to desire it so that it is physically and metaphysically impossible to desire anything except in so far as it is pleasant.[16] Hence, Mill states that when an act is said to be right in so far as it tends to produce happiness, and wrong to the extent that it tends to produce unhappiness, "happiness" is understood to mean pleasure and the absence of pain, whereas "unhappiness" refers to pain and the privation of pleasure.[17] Thus, acts are said to be morally good either because they themselves are inherently pleasant or because they are means to the production of pleasure and the prevention of pain.

Mill thinks that the Epicureans and the utilitarians who preceded him have a legitimate answer to those who charge that grounding morality on the promotion of pleasure and the avoidance of pain is tantamount to reducing man to the level of swine. Their answer is that those making this charge are them-

[13] *Ibid.*, p. 56.
[14] *Ibid.*, p. 53.
[15] *Ibid.*, p. 57.
[16] *Ibid.*
[17] *Ibid.*, p. 9.

selves guilty of such a reduction because the charge itself presupposes that man is capable of enjoying only animal pleasures.[18] However, Mill himself does not accept the pleasure-pain basis of morality without adding a qualification to his acceptance. Thus, although he thinks that the utilitarians have proved their case for the superiority of mental over physical pleasures, they have unduly restricted their premises for this case to such factors as "the greater permanency, safety, uncostliness," of the mental pleasures in comparison to the physical pleasures. They have shown the circumstantial rather than the intrinsic advantages of mental over physical pleasures.[19]

He holds that utilitarianism need not restrict itself to these circumstantial or quantitative factors in evaluating the pleasures that lie at the basis of the utilitarian criterion. Utilitarianism can admit that pleasures are *qualitatively* and not simply quantitatively different. "It is better to be a human being dissatisfied than a pig satisfied: better to be Socrates dissatisfied than a fool satisfied. And if the fool, or the pig, are of a different opinion, it is because they only know their own side of the question. The other party to the comparison knows both sides."[20] The view that there is some sort of qualitative hierarchy among pleasure introduces a complication into the utilitarian position. For it requires some sort of principle according to which one can evaluate different kinds of pleasure. In addition to being able to judge the amount of pleasure that an act tends to produce, one must also be able to evaluate the type of pleasure that will be promoted. Mill meets this need by stating that the test for the quality of enjoyments is to be found in the "preference felt by those who in their opportunities of experience, to which must be added their habits of self-consciousness and self-observation, are furnished with the means of comparison."[21] Hence, a given enjoyment is qualitatively better than another if it is preferred by one who has reflected on himself and who has had an opportunity to compare the two pleasures.

The utilitarian view that the morality of acts is to be judged by the pleasurable or painful consequences which they tend to produce would appear to involve the position that the end justifies the means. Mill answers that utilitarianism involves this position as much as any other ethical system and no more. "According to the principle of utility, the end justifies all means necessary to its attainment, except those which are more mischievous than the end is useful; an exception amply sufficient."[22] Thus, utilitarianism weighs both means and ends with a view toward discovering whether the means will cause more pain than the pleasure envisioned in the end. If it does, the end does not justify the means, whereas if it does not cause more pain than the pleasure to be found in the end, then the pleasure of the end justifies the pain found in the means.

[18] *Ibid.*, pp. 10–11.
[19] *Ibid.*, pp. 11–12.
[20] *Ibid.*, p. 14.
[21] *Ibid.*, p. 16.
[22] See footnote 3, pp. 156–157.

Utilitarianism has taken at least two different turns since Mill gave his statement of it. It might be well for us to consider these two different statements which are usually described as act utilitarianism and rule utilitarianism.

2. ACT AND RULE UTILITARIANISM

Although Mill himself did not specifically mention the distinction between act and rule utilitarianism, there are certain features of his statement of utilitarianism which seem to make him a precursor of rule utilitarianism. For example, he presents utilitarianism as advocating that a man love virtue as a thing desirable in itself, even though in a given individual case this love does not produce the desirable consequences which it usually tends to produce.[23] This is rule utilitarianism in that it states that the consequences that ought to be considered in judging the morality of an act are the consequences that generally, or *as a rule*, tend to flow from a certain kind of act.

Perhaps the following statement most clearly places Mill in the camp of rule utilitarianism. Mill is here facing the objection that utilitarianism can offer no arguments against a flattering lie that will make an individual happy, or against the pleasure arising out of illicit sexual relations between individuals that will never come to the attention of the public. Mill answers that if we look at these acts in their solitude both the effects they have on mankind in general and the pleasure accompanying them are so small that it is necessary to consider them not as single acts but as acts multiplied many times over if we are to have an adequate basis for a moral evaluation.

> We must look at them multiplied, and in large masses. The portion of the tendencies of an action which belong to it not individually, but as a violation of a general rule, are as certain and as calculable as any other consequences; only they must be examined not in the individual case, but in classes of cases. Take, for example, the case of murder. There are many persons to kill whom would be to remove men who are a cause of no good to any human being, of cruel physical and moral suffering to several, and whose whole influence tends to increase the mass of unhappiness and vice. Were such a man to be assassinated, the balance of traceable consequences would be greatly in favor of the act. The counter-consideration, on the principle of utility, is, that unless persons were punished for killing and taught not to kill; that if it were thought allowable for any one to put to death at pleasure any human being whom he believes that the world would be well rid of, nobody's life would be safe.[24]

Although Mill does not explicitly refer to a distinction between act and rule utilitarianism here, his statement is a classic presentation of rule utilitarianism. The morality of an individual act is not to be judged simply in terms of the

[23] See footnote 8, Chap. III, p. 53.
[24] See footnote 4, p. 476.

consequences of that act itself. An act of murder considered simply in its given situation may well produce desirable consequences. However, a proper moral evaluation of the act demands that when we consider the consequences of an act, we move beyond a consideration of the act taken singly to the consideration of the act seen as a general rule. Hence, we must ask not what are the consequences of this particular act of murder, but what consequences would flow from the establishment of murder as a general rule of behavior. When we ask this latter question, we find that the acceptance of murder as a general rule of behavior would involve the unpleasant consequence of making everybody's life insecure and unsafe.[25]

J. J. C. Smart, working within the utilitarian position, finds rule utilitarianism unacceptable and would substitute act utilitarianism for it. Act utilitarianism holds that the morality or immorality of a given individual act is to be judged by the consequences, good or bad, that flow from that *particular* act.[26] His rejection of rule utilitarianism is based on the view that it is guilty of "rule-worship," in advocating that a certain action be performed or not be performed, although recognizing that the particular consequences of the performance or nonperformance of that act will be bad.

To say that X, which *in this case* will lead to good results, should not be done in this case, because, *as a general rule*, it usually leads to bad consequences, or because if everyone did X, bad consequences would follow seems to be unreasonable. What is at issue in this particular case is the act of this particular person and these particular good consequences. There is no question of "everybody" performing the act in this case, nor is there any question of the consequences that usually follow from the act. Hence, it is irrelevant to the particular act at issue to say that it should not be performed because bad consequences would follow if "everybody" performed the act or because bad consequences usually follow from it.[27]

The ethical norm espoused by Smart's act utilitarianism suggests that "the rational way to decide what to do is to decide to perform that one of those alternative actions open to us (including the null-action, the doing of nothing) which is likely to bring about the total situation now and in the future which is the best for the happiness or well-being of humanity as a whole, or more accurately, of all sentient beings."[28] There are three points in Smart's exposition of this system which should help us understand its essential features. First of all, recognizing that praise and blame are ways of changing human conduct

---

[25] See also the following statement, "In the case of abstinences indeed—of things which people forbear to do from moral considerations, though the consequences in the particular case might be beneficial—it would be unworthy of an intelligent agent not to be consciously aware that the action is of a class which, if practiced generally, would be generally injurious, and that this is the ground of obligation to abstain from it." See footnote 8, Chap. III, p. 27.

[26] See footnote 10, Chap. I, p. 4.

[27] *Ibid.*, p. 5.

[28] *Ibid.*, pp. 29–30.

and thus either promoting or preventing the existence of certain consequences, Smart holds that we ought to withhold approval of an act which may be right, but the approval of which may have a bad effect. Following this same line of thought, we might also find it useful to praise acts which we do not truthfully approve. Smart uses the following examples to illustrate his point. A combat commander might find it useful to praise the cunning and courage of a captured enemy commander who is fighting for an unjust and inhuman cause because the honor and praise bestowed on the man may influence his own men to try to imitate the enemy's courage, cunning, and efficiency. Similarly, a man coming into a society based on a primitive type of taboo ethics may not criticize this ethics because he recognizes that the weakening of the system of taboos would lead to moral anarchy in the society and that the taboo ethics is better than anarchy.[29]

A second point that will help us to understand Smart's utilitarianism is his description of the type of behavior which it would sanction in the following situation. Let us suppose that there is an electrical power shortage in a community and the people are asked to use a certain restricted amount of power in their homes. If one could be sure that most of the people in the community would comply with the request and that his own use of more than the restricted amount of power would increase his own comfort and that of a few others who agreed with his assessment of the situation, he would be justified, from the point of view of act utilitarianism, in using more than the restricted amount of power. For the excess of power that he and a few others used would not inconvenience those following the request but would increase their own (those who used the excess amount of power) comfort and happiness.

This example presupposes that there are only a few act utilitarians living in society. The problem would be more difficult in a society in which all or the majority were act utilitarians. In such a society, one would face a difficult decision in trying to decide whether or not to follow the request for power curtailment, since he does not know what others will do. In this case the act utilitarian is confronted with three possibilities: (1) comply with the request, (2) not to comply with it, (3) work out a certain mathematical formula in which he could assign himself a small probability of disobeying the request and try to figure out the effect on the whole community if a certain number of others also took advantage of this small probability. Smart concludes that the probability for comfortable noncompliance with the request would be so small that the act utilitarian would tend to go along with the government's request.[30]

This need to go to a mathematical formula of the probable consequences for happiness or unhappiness flowing from a proposed line of action highlights what act utilitarianism needs if its theoretical foundations are to be secure. It needs a method that will enable man to figure out in an approximate way

[29] *Ibid.*, pp. 35–36.
[30] *Ibid.*, pp. 42–44.

at least the numerical probabilities that could be assigned, in theory if not in practice, to the occurrence of imagined events of the future. It needs a method whereby it could compute the probable happiness and unhappiness involved in the probable effects of our actions.[31]

Finally, the way in which Smart answers the objection that his system involves the sacrificing of the present generation to the future sheds further light on the character of his act utilitarian. His first answer to the objection is that one advancing it can be accused of having a limited vision. Smart asks, "Why should not future generations matter as much as present ones? To deny it is to be temporarily parochial."[32] This appears to be a rather weak reply drawing much of its force from its *ad hominem* character in that it meets the objection by characterizing the objector as being parochial and of limited vision. Moreover, in so far as the objection asks why the present should be sacrificed to the future, it does not state, as Smart's question implies, that the future should not count *as much as* the present. A position that wants to sacrifice the present to the future is not holding that the future is of the same value as the present, but that it is of more value. Hence, it is incumbent on one advocating such a sacrifice to answer the question, "Why should not present generations matter as much as the future?"

Smart's second reply has more substance to it. This reply is divided into two parts. First, he makes the point that the problem raised by the question of whether to sacrifice men in the present for the good of future generations raises a factual, not an ethical, question. This means that if one could be sure that, as *a matter of fact*, programs causing the death or misery of "tens of millions" in our own day would result in saving "hundreds of millions" from greater misery and death in the future, and if one knew that only through such a program could the future generation be saved, then the necessary atrocities of the program would be right. Viewed from this perspective, tyrants who cause atrocities for a future Utopia are wrong in their assessment of *facts*, in the way in which they treat future probabilities as if they were certainties, and not in the ethical outlook underlying their behavior. One should have a great deal of certainty about the future before embarking on a program of systematic atrocities in the name of that future, but it should be clear to all by this time that it is impossible to make large-scale predictions concerning the future with such certainty. Smart concludes this part of his discussion with the observation that since the future is such a mystery to man, one would be mad to "sacrifice the present in a big way for the sake of it."[33]

Whereas the first part of his discussion was predicated on the unpredictability of the future in any large-scale way, the second part rests on the hypothesis that the future is clear to man. Granted that man may have a clear vision of the future, it is not very probable that large-scale atrocities in the present would

---

[31] *Ibid.*, pp. 27–29.
[32] *Ibid.*, p. 45.
[33] *Ibid.*, p. 46.

prove very beneficial to this future because of the brutalization of the social order that would necessarily accompany such atrocities. Hence, Smart maintains that the principles of act utilitarianism do permit a condemnation of those committing atrocities in the name of the future, but he emphasizes that the condemnation rests on factual issues, and apparently not on any ethical norm that these atrocities may violate. Large-scale atrocities in the name of the future are wrong first because our knowledge of the future is too limited to justify them, and secondly because the brutalization accompanying such atrocities may well contaminate the future in whose name they were committed. However, these atrocities violate no moral rule so that if we could be sure that atrocities committed against tens of millions today would save hundreds of millions from greater misery in the future, there could be no argument against these atrocities either on ethical or on factual grounds.

3. IMMANUEL KANT'S CRITICISM OF CONSEQUENCES AND HAPPINESS AS STANDARDS OF MORALITY

Whereas Mill and Smart maintain that the morality of an act is to be evaluated by the consequences flowing from that act, Immanuel Kant holds that the worth of a morally good will is neither augmented by whatever utility it may possess nor is it diminished by its uselessness as a means to achieve some end.[34] For example, if I am a witness in a lawfully convened court, there is no need to reflect on the consequences that will result from my testimony in order to know whether or not I am morally obligated to tell the truth. I need look for no end because the end or consequences of this act do not constitute the standard according to which the morality of the act is to be judged. Kant states that if I must look for some ulterior end to convince me to tell the truth, I have shown that I am morally contemptible.[35] Thus, Kant, and others in the deontological tradition of ethics, do not share the utilitarian view that the standard for judging the morality of an act is its consequences or the ends which it achieves.

Mill holds that the principle of utility is a principle which makes human happiness the end and test of morality.[36] He describes his position as one which places, "Utility, or the Greatest Happiness Principle," at the foundation of morality, holding that "actions are right in proportion as they tend to promote happiness, wrong as they tend to produce the reverse of happiness."[37] Again,

[34] See footnote 9, Chap. I, p. 10.

[35] Immanuel Kant, *Religion within the Limits of Reason Alone* translated with an Introduction and notes by Theodore M. Greene and Hoyt H. Hudson (New York: Harper and Brothers, 1960), pp. 3–4.

[36] See footnote 3, pp. 124, 157. See also footnote 8, Chap. III, p. 52.

[37] See footnote 8, Chap. III, p. 9.

Kant and other deontologists are not willing to accept happiness as the standard of morality. He states, "Morals is not really the doctrine of how to make ourselves happy but of how we are to be *worthy* of happiness."[38] The purpose of this section is to explore the arguments which Kant presents in defense of the view that the standard for morality is not identical with the rules one might follow in pursuit of happiness. Although Kant does posit a certain ultimate unity between virtue and happiness in treating the role of God in man's moral life, he holds that this unity is not such that it makes the standard or rules for acquiring happiness identical with the standard of morality.[39]

Kant tends to equate any attempt to use happiness as a standard of morality with an egoistical hedonism, i.e., the view that whatever suits my own individual pleasure is moral. Against the view that morality is to be identified with one's own quest for happiness, Kant points out that common experience contradicts the view that happiness is always proportioned to virtuous behavior.[40]

Kant himself provides a good illustration to sustain the view that working for one's happiness is not the same as acting morally. Let us suppose that someone is recommending a certain man to you as one who could manage all your business affairs and whom you could trust implicitly. In order to inspire your trust in this man, he tells you that the man is very shrewd in looking out after his own interest and that the man is quick to grasp every opportunity to advance this interest. However, he points out that you should not misinterpret the man's self-interest as being a crass type of selfishness. For the proposed business manager's pleasure does not consist in making money, but lies rather in the increase of his own knowledge, in participating in the good conversation of intelligent people, and last but not least in aiding the needy. He is also described as a man who will use any means to advance his own interests. For example, he would not be averse to using another's money and property for his own ends, so long as he could be certain that he would not be apprehended. Similarly, a man who has borne false witness against another in order to secure his own happiness and has been successful at it is certainly not accepted as a paradigm of virtue.[41]

If we accepted these views as representing the sum and substance of Kant's case against happiness as a standard of morality, it would not appear to represent a serious challenge to the utilitarianism of Bentham, Mill, and Smart. For Mill has spoken well for this type of utilitarianism in pointing out that the utilitarian standard "is not the agent's own greatest amount of happiness altogether."[42] However, there is a combination of factors at work in Kant's equation of an ethics based on happiness with an egoistical hedonism that ought to be considered before condemning his position out of hand.

---

[38] Immanuel Kant, *Critique of Practical Reason* in *Critique of Practical Reason and other Writings in Moral Philosophy* translated and edited with an introduction by Lewis White Beck (Chicago: The University of Chicago Press, 1949), p. 232.

[39] *Ibid.*, p. 217.

[40] See footnote 9, Chap. I, p. 61.

[41] See footnote 38, pp. 146–147.

[42] See footnote 8, Chap. III, p. 16.

The heart of Kant's criticism is that those who try to make happiness a stand-ard of morality have constructed a moral system in which human inclinations or appetites, and not reason, function as the ultimate ground of moral distinc-tions. According to Kant, this means that such a moral system can offer only "counsels of prudence," which have a certain necessity connected with them in that they tell us what we *must* do in order to be happy. However, the necessity involved in these counsels is one "that can hold only under a subjectively con-tingent condition, i.e. whether this or that man counts this or that as a part of happiness."[43] Hence, the identification of an ethics based on happiness with egoism is not due to an oversight on Kant's part. It is based on the view that in so far as this ethics is grounded in inclinations, it must be egoistic. For one man's inclinations differ from another's so that morality comes to be equated with what each man finds satisfying to his desires. To those who would argue that not all inclinations are so individualistically oriented and that we find in man a special moral feeling which is of universal scope, Kant answers that the appeal to this special moral feeling is superficial, "since those who cannot think expect help from feeling, even with respect to that which concerns universal laws; they do so even though feelings naturally differ so infinitely in degree that they are incapable of furnishing a uniform standard of the good and bad, and also in spite of the fact that one cannot validly judge for others by means of his own feelings."[44]

Another factor which pushes an ethics based on happiness toward egoism is that the attempt to formulate a rule of happiness usually will involve the frus-tration of some inclinations. Being thus unable to arrive at a conception of hap-piness that would include the satisfaction of all inclinations, it is understandable that man will grasp at the satisfaction of some one inclination which is clear-cut and determinate in what it offers, and which thus can overcome the idea of some indefinite notion of happiness that cannot possibly satisfy all man's needs. For example, a man suffering from gout may decide to accept what he can enjoy here and now, believing that he has therefore not sacrificed the fulfillment of present inclinations to the vague and possibly groundless hope of the good for-tune of a future state of health.[45] Kant seems to be basing his position on the view that once happiness is accepted as the standard of morality, the way is opened for an egoistical concern with fulfilling whatever inclination happens to be most pressing at any given moment. It is not reason that rules in such a moral system, but the inclinations and feelings.

Kant's analysis of the respective roles of good and duty in man's moral life throws further light on his reasons for rejecting happiness as a standard of morality. The problem that leads to this analysis is whether "good" is to be the ultimate standard of morality so that moral duty or obligation is derived from the conception of good, or *vice versa*. It is Kant's contention that if one's con-ception of good is not derived from moral duty, but is itself taken as the norm

[43] See footnote 9, Chap. I, p. 34.
[44] *Ibid.*, p. 61.
[45] *Ibid.*, p. 15.

for such duty, then the only criterion of good is that which is pleasurable. Since good is grounded in inclinations—with that which is immediately connected with the sensation of pleasure being good, and that connected with what is painful being bad—reason's role is reduced to judging the means to that which excites pleasure, and the ways to avoid that which excites pain. Granted Kant's interpretations, it is obvious that reason's role in such an ethical scheme is a secondary one. The feelings of pleasure or pain play the controlling role, with reason standing by to discover what will advance pleasure and avoid pain.[46]

In pursuing this argument further, Kant makes a point which seems to place Mill's utilitarianism in a difficult position. It will be recalled from Chapter III that Mill maintained that a feeling is not necessarily moral in all its promptings simply because it has come from nature. Kant argues that any moral system accepting happiness as a standard of morality accepts nature as the moral lawgiver. Such a system is ultimately grounded in an object, determining man through his natural inclinations. Hence, according to Kant, it is not the man who determines himself to action by his own conception of the proposed action. The stress on happiness as a moral standard leads man to accept as moral whatever objects naturally happen to suit his inclination or taste so that it is not reason, but nature, as found in man's inclinations, that provides the law of morality.[47]

Kant sees man as being confronted with the following alternatives. Either we give reason a primary role in moral life by taking the view that reason a priori provides the rules for moral behavior without any reference to possible objects of the sensuous inclinations, or the faculty of desire is made the ground of morality in which case reason is reduced to a secondary role, and the above-mentioned difficulties must be faced.

Before concluding this section, it ought to be noted that although Kant opposes an ethics which makes good the standard of moral behavior, he does not deny that good has a place in man's moral endeavors. He attempts to clarify the meaning of such terms as "good," and "bad," in order to place them in their proper moral perspective. He agrees that once the conception of good is properly understood, it would be legitimate to say that the man acting out of a sense of duty, i.e. man acting morally, does act for the good. However, this sense of good, as meaning moral good, must be distinguished from good, understood as well-being. The difference between these two meanings lies in the fact that the notion of good as well-being involves "only a relation to our condition of pleasantness, . . . enjoyment," with the object said to be good in this sense being desired "only in so far as it is related to our sensibility and to the feeling of pleasure," whereas good in the moral sense is good as related to the universal law of duty.[48]

[46] See footnote 38, pp. 167–168.
[47] See footnote 7, Chap. I, p. 62.
[48] See footnote 38, p. 169.

Kant's distinction between these two senses of good represents a rather classic statement of the distinction between deontologism and utilitarianism. For a deontologist duty is at the basis of man's moral universe so that moral good is ultimately defined by and grounded in duty. A certain act is morally good because it is my duty to perform it. Kant provides a clear statement of the deontological approach in pointing out that "the concept of the good and evil is not defined prior to the moral law to which, it would seem, the former would have to serve as foundation; rather the concept of good and evil must be defined after and by means of the law."[49] Utilitarianism states that moral duty is grounded in and defined by the good consequences that flow from an act.

The consideration of Kant's criticism of consequences and happiness as standards of morality was undertaken in this section with the hope that it would serve to clarify some of the central issues that seem to establish an opposition between the utilitarian and the deontological approaches to ethics. Kant's deontological approach challenges the central role given to such factors as ends or consequences, happiness, and good in the utilitarian standard of morality, arguing that it is duty that must function as the moral standard. Finally, Kant has pointed out that an ethics which makes happiness its standard also makes human inclinations, rather than human reason, the decisive factors in the distinction between moral and immoral behavior. These are the points that must be considered in judging the adequacy of either the utilitarian or the deontological approach to ethics. However, before undertaking this task, it will be necessary to explore Kant's statement of his duty-centered ethics.

4. THE CATEGORICAL IMPERATIVE: MORALITY AS AUTONOMOUS

{ The purpose of this section is to describe briefly the standard of morality which Kant advances, and the defense of this standard which he presents} Kant's moral system is so intimately interwoven with the rest of his philosophy that there can be no hope of giving a full account of his systematic approach to morality. Therefore, the material for this section will be taken primarily, although not exclusively, from his *Foundations of the Metaphysics of Morals* because, of his mature ethical writings, this work best lends itself to that type of statement of his views which permits one to capture the spirit of his moral position, without becoming directly and explicitly involved with other aspects of his philosophy.

Kant finds support in the common man's moral experience for his contention that the ground for moral obligation is not to be found in some principle such as happiness which is extraneous to this obligation. For example, although we hold that being kind where and when possible constitutes a moral duty, we do

[49] *Ibid.*, p. 171.

not think that a person's kindness is of moral worth if he is so constituted by nature that his act of kindness is caused by, or is grounded in, a feeling of contentment that either follows or accompanies that act.[50]

Such an example has led to the criticism that Kant holds that an act is of moral value, or actually meets man's moral obligations, only when a man finds the act difficult to perform. According to this line of criticism, the fact that a man enjoys performing an act means that the act is of no moral value. However, Kant does not contend that the morality of an act is to be evaluated in terms of its difficulty. His point is that the moral judgments which men make bring out the fact that the moral worth of an act is judged by its motive. It is not the difficulty of an act that leads us to judge it as moral, but the fact that it was done from a sense of duty.[51] Kant thinks that the central role which we give to the motive of duty in judging the morality of acts provides a significant clue pointing to the fact that the character of man's moral duty is such that he is obliged to act morally, not for any extra-moral effect or consequence, but simply for morality's sake. We judge a man to be morally good because he tries to act out of a sense of duty, although he may not have actually accomplished much because of a "particularly unfortunate fate," or " the niggardly provision of stepmotherly nature."[52] In thus emphasizing the central role which the motive of acting for duty plays in man's moral life, Kant does not hold that we can be content to want to act out of a sense of duty, without really trying to carry out this intention. Thus he describes the good will as being not "a mere wish," but "the summoning of all the means in our power."[53]

Working out of the context of the importance that man gives to the sense of duty in evaluating a man's moral condition, Kant sets out to explore the principle that must underlie man's moral life. His notion of "principle," is a rather complex one. However, the attempt to express the principle underlying moral life may be said to correspond roughly to the quest for a moral standard, which is a search not only for the proper basis for man's distinction between moral good and evil, but also for a way to capture this basis in speech, to give expression to it.

a. The Categorical Character of Moral Obligation

Because Kant finds two possible types of obligation, he divides the statements expressing these obligations to correspond to these types, i.e. into hypothetical and categorical imperative. Basically, hypothetical imperatives express that type of obligation that flows from the fact that once someone has chosen to work for a certain end, he is obliged, if he is rational, to use the means that

[50] See footnote 9, Chap. I, p. 141.
[51] *Ibid.*, p. 20.
[52] *Ibid.*, p. 10.
[53] *Ibid.*

will lead to that end. In short, hypothetical imperatives are conditional in the sense that they express an obligation that is binding with respect to means, granted that a certain end has been willed. Such an obligation does not place us under any duty to accept the end. It says, "if you accept such-and-such an end (and you are not duty-bound to accept this end), you *must* reasonably choose the means that will lead you to the end."[54]

Kant describes a categorical imperative as one that declares an action to be objectively necessary in itself without any reference to any other end.[55] When Kant speaks of an action as being objectively necessary, he does not mean that we have absolutely no freedom with regard to it. The action is said to be objectively necessary in the sense that the grounds that are advanced to show that we are to perform this action are rationally valid for all reasonable beings. The difference between a categorical and hypothetical imperative can be seen in the difference between the arguments one might advance to show that someone ought to take an aspirin and that someone ought to be kind. In the case of the aspirin, we would say that one ought to take the aspirin, if one wants to rid himself of a headache. The *moral* defense for being kind rests, according to Kant, on the very character of the kind act itself. Kant does not deny that there may be extra-moral reasons for being kind such as helping to make us more likeable and advancing our economic life. However, the moral defense for the duty of being kind does not look beyond the character of the act itself to some other end. Thus, the imperative to be kind is categorical, whereas the imperative to take an aspirin is hypothetical.

It is clear that the imperatives expressive of man's moral obligation are categorical for Kant. Now the problem is to discover some formula to express the categorical character of man's obligation. Although, as we shall see, Kant expresses the categorical imperative in several ways, he holds that there is only one categorical imperative, with all other statements of this imperative being derived from and contained in this one. The one imperative is: "Act only according to that maxim by which you can at the same time will that it should become a universal law."[56] By "maxim" in this quotation, Kant means "the subjective principle of volition."[57] Maxim is the subjective ground or reason for one's action. To discover the maxim of an action is to discover the factors that an individual considers to be decisive reasons for performing that act. Hence, the categorical imperative states that man should make only those factors decisive in his actions which he could at the same time will to become universal laws, i.e. the factors governing all actions.

It seems to be Kant's contention that this formula of the categorical imperative is implied in the conception of moral duty which we have been exploring. As we have seen, moral obligation is unconditioned in that its value is wholly

[54] *Ibid.*, pp. 31, 34.
[55] *Ibid.*, p. 32.
[56] *Ibid.*, p. 39.
[57] *Ibid.*, p. 17, n. 1.

within itself, and not in any end outside itself which it is to achieve. Kant holds that the categorical imperative presents an action as being objectively binding on an agent by the very character of the act itself and not by an end to be achieved through the act.[58] This means that there are no restrictions on the obligation in the sense that one could say that moral obligation is binding only under the condition that one wanted to achieve a certain end. According to Kant, the unconditional character of moral obligation means that it is universal. Hence, an act is morally binding in so far as the maxim by which that act is performed can at the same time be willed to become a universal law. If the act does not fulfill this requirement, it does not have the unconditional or universal character of moral obligation.[59]

b. The Categorical Imperative Focusing on Man as an End in Himself and on the Community of Ends

Kant states the categorical imperative under several other formulae. However, it will be sufficient for the purpose of this exposition to consider only two of these. These two are important in that they show that Kant's notion of the categorical imperative does include some content so that he is not completely at the mercy of the criticism that we saw Hegel advance against an excessively formalistic ethics, namely that such an ethics cannot be a guide to action because it has no content. The two formulations of the imperative which will be considered in this subsection are: (1) "Act so that you treat humanity, whether in your own person or in that of another, always as an end and never as a means only,"[60] (2) "Every rational being must act as if he, by his maxims, were at all times a legislative member in the universal realm of ends."[61] There is a third formula that mediates between these two which shall be considered in its proper place.

Kant maintains that these formulations are involved or implicated in the universal character of the moral law. Although the universal law already discussed is directed to no end extraneous to itself, Kant asks whether there is some end implicated in the very character of man as a moral being. The fact that Kant raises this issue indicates that he is not as oblivious to ends as one might be led to believe from his attack on an ethics based on happiness and good. The positive role that ends play in Kant's conception of morality will become clear as we work toward the conclusion of this section. He presents the following defense of the need for an end in ethics.

[58] See footnote 34, Chap. III, p. 21.
[59] For this reasoning see footnote 9, Chap. I, pp. 38–39, also pp. 18–19.
[60] Ibid., p. 47.
[61] Ibid., p. 47. For a discussion of each of Kant's expressions of the categorical imperative see H. J. Paton, The Categorical Imperative: A Study in Kant's Moral Philosophy (London: Hutchinson, third ed., 1958).

Ethics provides a *matter* (an object of free choice), an *end* of pure reason which it presents also as an objectively necessary end, i.e. an end which, so far as men are concerned, it is a duty to have. For since the sensuous inclinations tempt us to ends (as the matter of choice) which may be contrary to duty, legislative reason can check their influence only by another end, a moral end set up against the ends of inclination, which must therefore be given *a priori,* independently of the inclinations.[62]

Thus, Kant's rejection of ends in the standard of morality is a rejection of those ends that come out of man's sensuous inclinations. He recognizes the need for some sort of end that arises out of man's moral obligation and out of his reason a priori. Since this end must arise out of man's duty, it must possess the same absolute and intrinsic worth as does moral duty. Kant maintains that man exists as such an end, i.e. a being who is never to be used merely as a means for some end beyond himself. Just as moral duty is not directed toward any end outside itself, so also man is not directed to any end outside himself.

That the unconditioned character of moral obligation requires the reality of rational beings as ends in themselves is seen in the fact that unless there is something of such absolute worth, no absolute principle for reason could be found, since everything would be of conditioned worth. If there is to be a categorical imperative, then there must be an objective end for the will, an end which is itself categorical and not hypothetical. Kant maintains that rational beings are such unconditioned ends. He refers to these beings as "persons" in order to distinguish them from "things," i.e. beings that do not have this absolute worth and are valuable only as means, not as ends.[63]

The obvious question raised by this position is why does Kant maintain that rational beings are objective ends, or beings of categorical and absolute value. Kant's response to this question seems to be grounded in his view that rational beings are distinguished from other beings in that rational natures propose ends to themselves.[64] His point is that a being that is in the position of proposing ends to itself is an end in itself, i.e. the ultimate limiting condition of the ends which it proposes to itself.[65] Whereas the goals of other beings, in so far as they may be said to have goals, are set for them by what they are, by their natures, rational beings can establish goals of their own. In so far as they can do this, it would appear that the rational beings themselves ought to be the limiting condition of the goals which they set for themselves. Put in less technical language, this would mean that man does not exist for the sake of the goals which he sets, but they exist for the sake of man.

Kant pursues this problem further by pointing out that man is seen to be an end in himself by the fitness of his maxims to serve as a universal law.[66] The

[62] See footnote 34, Chap. III, p. 38.
[63] See footnote 9, Chap. I, pp. 46–47.
[64] *Ibid.,* p. 56.
[65] *Ibid.,* p. 49.
[66] *Ibid.,* p. 56.

fact that man, as a rational being, exists under an unconditioned obligation and the fact that he can will that the maxims of his own actions become a universal law show him to be a being whose worth is as categorical as the universal law that he can will, and as unconditioned as the obligation under which he exists. Kant has thus called attention to the being who is capable of existing and acting in a moral context, the being who can exist and act under an unconditioned obligation, and who can grasp this obligation by acting only according to the maxim, which he can at the same time will to become a universal law. A being who is capable of moving and living in a sphere of such unconditioned obligations is itself an unconditioned value.

Perhaps this point can be seen more clearly in Kant's distinction of the two ways in which a will can be said to exist under law. A will can be bound to a law by some interest. In this case, the basis for the law is outside the will so that for this will the obligation is conditional or hypothetical. Here the law states that granted this interest, the will must act in a certain manner. The will can also be considered as giving universal laws, i.e. laws conditioned by no interest extraneous to the will. This is precisely what the rational will does in formulating the categorical imperative, and in doing this, it shows itself to be of unconditioned value, i.e., an end in itself. The very character of the categorical imperative is such that "it can only command that everything be done from the maxims of its will as one which could have as its object only itself considered as giving universal laws. For only in this case are the practical principles and the imperative which the will obeys unconditional, because the will can have no interest as its foundation."[67] Thus, in formulating the categorical imperative, the rational will shows that its value lies not in any object external to it. The rational will that issues the categorical imperative can issue this imperative only in so far as there is no value outside of itself for which it is merely a means, or only in so far as it itself is an end in itself. Kant refers to the fact that the rational will, and not any interest external to it, is the ground for the universal laws issued by that will, as "the principle of autonomy of the will."[68]

This discussion of Kant's reasons for speaking of rational beings as ends in themselves involves another point in Kant's morality which must be explored, if we are to fully understand his defense of rational beings as ends in themselves and if we are to push forward to Kant's expression of the categorical imperative as involving a realm of ends. This point is that rational wills are not only objects of the moral law, but also at the basis of this law. This means that rational beings are legislators as well as subjects of the moral law. They are legislators in the sense that the law which proceeds from them is not conditioned by any self-enclosed interest, but is unconditioned, thus being able to function as a universal law applicable to all rational beings as such. This leads Kant to another formulation of the categorical imperative, i.e. "To act only so

[67] Ibid., pp. 50–51.
[68] Ibid., p. 51.

that the will through its maxims could regard itself at the same time as universally lawgiving."[69]

The notions of rational beings as ends in themselves and as sources of legislation transcending their self-interest lead to Kant's concept of a realm, or as we would say today, a community of ends. By "realm" Kant means, "the systematic union of different rational beings through common laws."[70] Rational beings can form such a realm in so far as they are united by the law that each should treat himself and all others, never simply as a means, but as an end in himself. Hence, according to Kant, the autonomous character of rational beings does not lead to the isolation of these beings from one another. They are autonomous precisely in so far as they are centers of universal moral laws that transcend their pure self-interest and that are inclusive of all other rational beings, thus involving them in a realm or community with all other rational beings. It is this conception of rational beings constituting a realm of ends that is behind Kant's notion of morality as consisting "in the relation of every action to that legislation through which alone a realm of ends is possible."[71]

It is clear from this conception of morality that morality for Kant is not simply the affair of a self-enclosed individual. There is a social thrust found in the very character of the moral enterprise, i.e. a thrust toward the realization of a realm of ends. Kant does not view this realm of ends as an existent state of affairs. Rather, it is a practical ideal, which is useful to give existence to that which does not yet exist, but which can be made existent by our conduct. The realm of ends is an ideal, which can be made real only through the conduct of rational beings.[72]

c. THE RELATIONSHIP BETWEEN DUTY AND ENDS IN MORALITY

It might be well to return to Kant's view of the relationship between ends and duty, with the hope that a discussion of this matter will serve to unify this brief treatment of Kant's position on the principle underlying man's moral life. As we have seen, Kant does not exclude a consideration of ends from man's moral reflections as completely as one might think from reading those texts in which he is concerned with criticizing an ethics centered on happiness as a moral standard. He is very explicit in spelling out the way in which ends come to play a role in man's moral life. He maintains that ethics cannot begin with a consideration of the ends which a man may set for himself and base its conception of moral duty on such considerations.

He advances two arguments to sustain this position, one epistemological, the other psychological. The epistemological argument is grounded in his view that.

---

[69] *Ibid.*, p. 52.
[70] *Ibid.*, p. 51.
[71] *Ibid.*, p. 52.
[72] *Ibid.*, p. 55, note 17.

universality and necessity come not from experience, but from reason a priori. To attempt to ground morality in the ends that men are seen to set for themselves is to attempt to ground it in experience, thus surrendering the universal and absolute character of moral obligation. For moral duty as universal and absolute cannot possibly be derived from experience, which yields only particular and conditioned truths. Moreover, Kant argues that because the ends of man considered apart from duty, have a character of self-seeking, they cannot possibly ground moral obligation.

Kant is concerned with establishing what he considers to be the proper method of approach in relating duties to ends. Thus, having criticized the view that moral duties are to be grounded in a consideration of the ends men set for themselves, he maintains that ends are to be derived from the concept of duty so that the maxims spelling out the ends that we ought to pursue can be established according to valid moral procedures.[73] This is precisely the procedure that we have seen Kant follow in this section. Moving from a consideration of the absolute and unconditional character of moral duty, he discovered the character of rational beings as ends in themselves, and was able to derive from his consideration of duty the ideal of rational beings existing in a community of ends.

Kant becomes more specific in his discussion of the relationship between duties and ends by distinguishing between duties that deal with purely formal issues and those dealing with ends, referring to these latter as duties of virtue. A purely formal duty is not concerned with a certain end, i.e. the object of choice, but is concerned with what is merely formal in that choice. This means that a formal duty obliges a man to act from a sense of duty. It is a duty concerned with the motive for an act, and not with the object that is chosen. There is in Kant's moral system only one formal duty, namely the obligation to act out of a motive of duty. In general, he divides the duties of virtue into two classifications—the duty to work for one's own perfection and the duty to contribute to another's happiness. We cannot simply interchange these duties by saying that it is our duty to work for another's perfection and one's own happiness. We cannot make another's perfection our own end, since one's perfection is precisely that which he alone can achieve by his own efforts. Moreover, it is nonsensical to say that we are morally obligated to pursue our own happiness, since we do so naturally and spontaneously.

Although Kant rejects an ethics that views one's own happiness as the end of one's moral endeavors, he does hold that there is a sense in which man can be said to be obligated to work for his own happiness. However, this obligation makes happiness a means to man's moral life, not the end of this life. This conception of happiness as a means to man's fulfillment of his moral obligations is grounded in Kant's recognition of the fact that a situation in which man lives under the constant pressure of unhappiness and discontent constitutes a threat

---

[73] See footnote 34, Chap. III, p. 40.

to the development of man's moral character, tempting him to renounce his moral duties. For example, although man is not morally obligated to seek prosperity for its own sake, he may pursue it as an "indirect duty," as a means of avoiding poverty which burdens man with serious temptations to transgress his moral duties.[74] In short, the claims of happiness and morality can come together in so far as the overcoming of adversity and dissatisfaction, and the achievement of happiness are seen not as ends in themselves but are recognized as useful means in helping man to develop his moral character and to avoid the temptations to renounce his duty.[75]

5. AN EVALUATION OF PLEASURE AS THE STANDARD OF MORALITY

Before proceeding to an evaluation of utilitarianism and deontologism as described in the preceding sections, it might be well at this point to consider the possibility that pleasure may function as the standard of morality. The fact that this evaluation is being undertaken apart from a consideration of utilitarianism indicates that I do not think that a utilitarian position need necessarily be hedonistic. One may be a utilitarian without accepting the view that it is pleasure that is to ground the notion of utility. However, as a matter of historical fact, the utilitarian position as stated by Mill and Bentham does raise the problem of the validity of pleasure as a moral standard. Hence, this section will be limited to a consideration of this problem alone, leaving the evaluation of utilitarianism to a later section.

Mill is right in pointing out that those who object to pleasure as a standard of morality on the grounds that the acceptance of such a standard reduces man to an animal, are themselves open to this charge because their objection indicates they think that man is capable only of animal pleasures. However, his attempt to draw some sort of qualitative distinction between pleasures so that some are seen to be better than others indicates that there must be some standard at work that is more ultimate than pleasure in that pleasures themselves are to be evaluated by this other standard. For Mill, this other standard is the preference of the reflective man (who has experienced the pleasures to be evaluated) for one of these pleasures.

This position and Mill's emphasis on the qualitative difference among pleasures are very similar to Aristotle's position in Book X of his *Nicomachean Ethics*. For example, Aristotle states that the fact that tyrants, "who have never tasted pure and generous pleasure, find an escape in the pleasures of the body . . . is not sufficient reason for thinking that such pleasures are in fact more

---

[74] *Ibid.*, p. 47.
[75] See footnote 38, pp. 170, 199. See also footnote 9, Chap. I, p. 15.

desirable."[76] Hence, Aristotle holds that those things which are pleasant to the morally good man are to be considered as truly moral pleasures.[77] The point that is significant for us in Mill's and Aristotle's positions is the fact that a philosophy which distinguishes among pleasures, as Mill's does, by holding that some are qualitatively better than others, and thus ought to be preferred over others, does not make pleasure the ultimate standard of moral behavior. It is not pleasure, but that norm according to which we measure pleasures as being either worthy or unworthy of our efforts that actually functions as the moral standard in such a philosophical system. We make this point because we do not think that Mill fully appreciated the implication of his stress on the experienced man with the habits of self-consciousness and observation to his moral system, or, if he did appreciate this implication, he was not sufficiently clear or sufficiently emphatic in noting that this stress makes such a man, and not pleasure, the ultimate standard in his moral philosophy.

Turning from Mill's position itself to the possibility that pleasure may legitimately function as a standard of moral behavior, it seems to us that Aristotle's analysis of the relationship between activity and pleasure provides a valid and decisive argument against such a possibility. He points out that pleasure is a concomitant of activities and that whether or not a man finds a certain activity pleasant will depend on his character or disposition. For example, if one is an avid tennis player, playing a game of tennis will be pleasant to him, whereas playing tennis may be a rather painful experience for one whose character is such that he has neither the inclination nor talent for tennis. Thus pleasure is intimately bound up with that activity which completes or fulfills a certain disposition, power, or nature. Aristotle refers to Heraclitus' observation that an ass finds pleasure in chaff rather than in gold to bring out this point that different kinds of beings take pleasure in different kinds of activities because the activities that are pleasant to these beings are those which accord with the nature or disposition of these beings.[78]

In the case of man, we find that there is a considerable variation in the activities that will be pleasant for different men, indicating the wide variation to be found in the dispositions or characters of men. Whereas the unjust man takes pleasure in "putting something over" on others, i.e. in taking what rightfully belongs to others, the just man is pleased to give to others what is their due. Whereas the sadist takes pleasure in inflicting physical or mental torture on others, the compassionate man is pained by another's suffering and is pleased only when this suffering has been alleviated. A character in one of Albert Camus' novels clearly brings out the point involved in these examples when he

[76] Aristotle, *Nicomachean Ethics*, 1176^b 19–22 trans., with introduction and notes, by Martin Ostwald (New York: The Bobbs-Merrill Company, 1962), p. 287. All page references will be taken from this edition.

[77] *Ibid.*, 1176^a 15–20, p. 285, 1176^b 25, p. 287.

[78] *Ibid.*, 1176^a 5–7, p. 285.

observes, "No man is a hypocrite in his pleasures."[79] In short, those things or activities in which a man finds his pleasure can tell us a great deal about the character of that man.

However, the fact that pleasure can thus function as a sign of one's character hardly qualifies it as a standard of morality. To make pleasure, without any qualification or restrictions, the standard of morality is to say that such moral contraries as justice and injustice, temperance and intemperance, sadism and compassion are all equally "moral." Moreover, the attempt to ground morality in pleasure is open to the charge of committing the naturalistic fallacy. For this position says, in effect, that whatever type of person a man may happen *to be*, is the type that he *ought* to be. It does this in that it tells the man who happens to be unjust that he ought to commit unjust acts, that it is his moral duty to perform these acts, since pleasure is the standard of morality, and his pleasure lies in these acts.

Aristotle has captured the central point of these observations by pointing out that pleasure has no character of its own apart from a given activity. What gives pleasure its determinate character, making it this kind of pleasure rather than that, is the activity with which it is connected. There is no "pleasure in itself," no pleasure apart from some determinate activity. There are the pleasures of eating, of thinking, of doing geometry, of listening to music, to mention only a few. It is the difference between the activities of enjoying music and of doing geometry that accounts for the difference in pleasures that may be connected with these activities. These activities are defined by the capacities used in carrying them out and by the objects toward which they are directed. It is not the pleasure that makes the activity a certain kind of activity. Carrying this analysis into the moral sphere, Aristotle points out that activities also differ in their moral character, some being good, others bad, and others indifferent. Since pleasure is of a certain character because of the character of the activity with which it is connected, it cannot be pleasure that gives to the activity its moral character. For whatever character pleasure has, it receives from the activity from which it arises. This means that there must be some factor other than pleasure that gives to the morally bad act its character as morally bad, and to the good act, its character as good.

6. TOWARD A REFLECTIVE NATURALISM: HUMAN FULFILLMENT AS THE BASIS OF MORAL DUTY

It would appear that the exposition of Mill's and Kant's position provides the following alternative for grounding man's distinction between moral good and evil. This distinction is grounded in either human happiness or moral duty.

[79] Albert Camus, *The Fall*, translated by Justin O'Brien (New York: Vintage Books, 1956), p. 66.

The alternatives can also be stated as involving a choice between an ethics grounded in a consideration of the consequences of human action or an ethics grounded in an attempt to perform one's moral duty, no matter what the consequences may be. [To accept either one of these alternatives to the exclusion of the other is to fail to do justice to the complexity of man's moral life. The purpose of this section is to establish a standard of morality that does a more adequate job in dealing with this complexity than either utilitarianism or deontologism taken separately.] It will be necessary to evaluate certain features of Kant's and Mill's positions in order to situate the standard to be advanced in this section with respect to these positions. A more thorough evaluation of utilitarianism will be undertaken later in this chapter.

Kant has often overstated the autonomy of moral obligation in his attempt to get at the heart of man's moral existence and to see it in its purity apart from extra-moral factors. The following is an example of such an overstatement: "Morality is perfectly able to ignore all ends, and it ought to."[80] Such a statement when coupled with the view that every other motive must give way to duty since duty is "the condition of a will good in itself, whose worth transcends everything,"[81] would seem to imply that duty and morality are more important than man. The emphasis on duty for duty's sake appears to put man in the position of choosing between meeting his moral obligations or working for the betterment of man. Faced with such a choice, it would certainly be reasonable for a man to ask for a rational defense of the view that he ought to meet his moral obligations, no matter what the consequences. Moreover, the question cannot be put off as having its source in a purely selfish motivation which asks, "What's in it for me?" Rather the question may arise out of a concern to avoid sacrificing existing man to a bloodless abstraction called "duty." If man is to work and to sacrifice himself for duty, it is reasonable for him to ask that "duty" present its credentials, or the seal of its exalted office.

The exposition of Kant's position indicates that he does a fine job in handling this problem. In the last analysis, his ethics does not involve the sacrifice of man to duty, although utilitarians undoubtedly would challenge this evaluation. Kant's stress on the fact that moral duty does entail a concern with such ends as one's own perfection, and the happiness of others clearly indicates that he is not asking for the sacrifice of man to moral duty. Moreover, this emphasis is not something foreign to his analysis of man's moral duty. It is not something that he "dragged in," as it were, in order to compensate for an excessively severe and inhuman moral system. [His movement to rational beings as ends in themselves and to the community of ends shows that he does not oppose duty to man. Rather, he argues that man's ability to exist under an unconditional and absolute duty shows the unconditional and absolute worth of man himself.]

My disagreement with Kant is grounded perhaps more in his method of approaching ethics than in his moral conclusions. It would be better to begin with an investigation of the goods of our experience in order to discover a standard for distinguishing between moral and immoral goods than to begin as Kant does, with an analysis of duty and move to a conception of moral good. The value of the former approach lies in the fact that it avoids the danger of making duty itself a value, a position which moves in the direction of fanaticism by accepting obligation as a good simply because it is obligation. To go into the systematic reasons for my differences with Kant on this matter would move us outside the scope of this book into the area of epistemology. It is sufficient to note here that Kant's view that the "ought" could be gathered only in reason a priori, whereas I tried to show in Chapter III that it can arise out of the interaction between man and nature in human experience, is an area of disagreement between myself and Kant that would help account for his opposition to beginning ethics with a reflection on the goods of man's experience, whereas I think ethics can begin with such a reflection.

This position puts me in the camp of the utilitarians, at least with respect to the starting point of ethics, in that we are in agreement in holding that an investigation into the criterion of moral good ought to precede any discussion of moral obligation, since the latter ultimately does require a grounding in the knowledge of the former. However, there are two rather significant points of difference between myself and utilitarianism as expressed by J. S. Mill on this point. First of all, when Mill speaks of man seeking "happiness," I would substitute the word "fulfillment," because in our age the word "happiness" lends itself rather readily to the notion of sensuous, nonintellectual pleasure. Hence, it seems more appropriate to massive evidence of human experience to say that man seeks "fulfillment," this word being more generic and being able to include in its comprehension the types of satisfaction of the many different facets of human existence. Thus using the position taken in Chapter III as background, I think that the quest for a standard of moral good must begin with the fact that man lives in a world full of fulfillments and frustrations. It is one of the major tasks of the ethician to discover and to justify on the basis of his reflections on this world, a standard for distinguishing those fulfillments that are moral from those that are immoral and for being able to evaluate whether or not there are certain moral fulfillments involved in what appear to be simple frustrations.

The second area of disagreement between the position to be taken in this section and Mill's position centers in his contention that what man actually desires is to be accepted as the proof for what is morally desirable, just as the proof that an object is visible is that men actually see it. Mill has failed to recognize the fact that "desirable" differs from "visible," in that desirable means not only "able-to-be desired," as visible means able to be seen, but also means ought to be desired. It is at this point that Mill appears to be guilty of the naturalistic fallacy. For his argument states that something *ought* to be desired because it *is* desired, as a matter of fact. Moreover, since the argument makes what man actually desires the standard of morality, it is guilty of Kant's charge that moral systems based on happiness make desire, rather than reason, the ultimate moral criterion.

It is the conception of reason discussed in Chapter III that further differentiates this position from Mill's in that the implication of his moral position is that reason simply repeats or images the given facts of experience, whereas we tried to show that reason is not simply a repetitive factor in human experience, but enriches this experience, especially by its capacity to deal with reality in a universal manner. More pertinent to the issue at hand, we pointed out that human reason gives man the ability to reflect on himself as a being belonging to a certain community of being, i.e. the human community. It is this point that is behind the position that the standard of morality is "human reason-reflecting-on-man-in-his-world." This standard is presented in quotations and with hyphens in order to emphasize the point that the standard of morality is neither human nature, pure and simple, nor human reason working in splendid isolation and spinning a moral system out of itself.

The position to be taken in this section will be referred to as *reflective naturalism* in order to emphasize that the moral norm comes out of an interplay between reason and nature. The explanation and defense of this position will be conducted under the following three subheadings: a. The Roles of the "World" and of Reason in Reflective Naturalism, b. The Human Community in Reflective Naturalism, and c. The Scope and Limitations of Reflective Naturalism.

a. THE ROLES OF THE "WORLD" AND OF REASON IN REFLECTIVE NATURALISM

The use of the word "world" is meant to emphasize the fact that man's moral decisions cannot be made in a vacuum because his life is not lived in a vacuum. As we saw in Chapter II, man, as a limited being, must live within a context, an environment. We cannot specify exactly what is included in this notion of the "world," except to say that it includes not only the plants, animals, and minerals which are a part of man's environment, but also and especially the religious, political, intellectual, economic, historical, and social factors that make up the context in which man lives. There will be more to say about this point in the discussion of the problem of the relativity of man's moral life.

Turning to the place of reason in this standard, we shall deal first with the problem of specifying *whose* reason is included in this standard. Briefly and bluntly put, the answer is the reason of every man who has reached the level of moral maturity. Does this mean that this standard is "subjective" in that it maintains that every man can do whatever he "feels like doing?" No, it is not "subjective" in this sense. The fact that we have emphasized that reason must function as a tool means precisely that it is not one's "feelings" that must decide moral issues, but that such decisions must be based on what reason discovers in its reflections on man and his world. The standard is "subjective" in that it calls for the morally mature person to use his own reason in dealing with ethical problems.

It is rather strange that when men are told that if they expect to be mathematicians, chemists, or physicists in their own right, they must use their own reason to deal with the problems that arise in these areas, no one maintains that this advice means that a man can take any position that may strike his fancy concerning these problems. It is recognized in these cases that when a man is told to use his own reason, this advice means precisely that the position which he takes must be based on that power which transcends his own feelings and which is open to the questioning and investigation of other men willing to use their reason. Admitting that the issues in the sciences mentioned differ from moral issues and that the precise methodological approaches to these different issues also differ from the approach taken in morals, the fact remains that the advice to use reason in moral issues also means that a man must try to find a basis for his moral decisions that transcends his personal feelings about these matters and that is open to the questioning and probing of others willing to use their reason.

Our next task is to justify the role of reason in a moral standard. A common defense for giving reason a central role in a moral standard is that reason is the "highest" power in man, or the power which distinguishes man from other beings in the natural order. Hence, he should use this distinctively human capacity as a guide for leading a distinctively human life.

Without wishing to quarrel with this position, it seems to me that there are more meaningful grounds on which to base reason's central role in man's moral life. Man's situation in the world is such that any action which he performs has implications and consequences transcending the immediate context in which it is performed. There are times when one would wish that he could isolate a segment of his life from the past and the future. However, the fact is that man is a historically conditioned being, and although, as we tried to show in Chapter II, he can gain a certain freedom under such conditions, the fact remains that he cannot escape such conditions. For example, after putting in a tough four years in high school, a youngster may be "sick and tired" of school and decide not to go on to college. Without trying to defend the indefensible position that everyone should go to college, the fact remains that the youngster should not base his decision on the immediate situation, i.e. his weariness with school work, but should try to consider his decision in the light of future consequences, as well as in the light of his past. He must take into the consideration what type of future will remain open to him, what sort of future will be closed to him as a result of his decision, and he cannot undertake this consideration without looking back to what "he has going for and against him," as a result of his past.

It is because of the fact that human existence is so historically conditioned that human reason must play a role in man's moral life. For it is human reason that is the tool which enables man to consider his present situation in the light of his past and of the possible future arising out of certain alternative lines of behavior] The example we have given is admittedly not of a moral nature, but it does serve to bring out the historical character of human existence, and it would appear to be unreasonable to hold that when moral issues are involved, one can forget about this historical factor. For example, a physician who is "on call" may be attending a party in which everyone is having such a good time that the "spirit" of the occasion may encourage him to enjoy enough alcoholic beverages so as to "get into the swing of things." However, it would appear that he ought to consider the fact that he has made a commitment to care for those who might need his services and the consequences that could result if he were unable to meet this commitment as a result of his excessive drinking.

There is a further factor about the character of human reason and of the human condition that lends support to the central role of reason in morality. Because man is a limited being, all his activities, even those which, on the surface, seem to influence only beings outside of himself, have an influence on him. For example, the man who is hard and cruel in his treatment of animals and who justifies his behavior on the grounds that he is only hurting animals fails to recognize that, as a limited being, he does not stand completely outside of his own activities, even when these are directed toward another. His activities influence not only the being of those toward whom they are directed, but also his own being. This means that it is not only the animals who are affected by the man's cruelty, but he himself is also affected. Cruel actions are not something standing outside of him and resting only in animals toward whom they are directed. These actions take root in the being of the man himself who is performing them. They influence what he is and what he is becoming. This point is true of all man's activities whether they be acts of cruelty or of kindness.

Because man is thus conditioned and influenced by those activities which, on the surface, are directed outside of himself, human reason should be given a central role in evaluating human behavior, because of the reflexive character of reason which provides man with a perspective from which he can weigh the significance of his acts on himself as the agent. No matter how much a man may choose to ignore this aspect of his existence, the fact remains that his activities influence him as an agent, as well as influencing others. Hence, since man's moral life is bound by such a condition, it is only reasonable that man use the capacity which he possesses to take this condition into consideration in judging the morality of his behavior, and this capacity is reason.

b. THE HUMAN COMMUNITY
   IN REFLECTIVE NATURALISM

We have spoken of the importance of reason in judging the implications and consequences of acts. Now we come to the heart of the matter. What is the perspective from which reason can evaluate implications and consequences as being either moral or immoral? The answer to this question lies in human reason's capacity to see the individual human being and his world from the perspective of the human community in which that individual exists. More specifically, the answer lies in human reason's ability to consider whether certain activities and/or their consequences frustrate or contribute to the growth of man as a free agent, or to put it in Kant's terms, to the development of a "realm of ends." Can any rational justification be advanced for this position? Why is it that the morality or immorality of an act depends upon whether the act contributes to or is destructive of the growth of the human community, considered as a realm of ends?

It seems to me that a two-pronged answer can be given to this question. The first part of the response is based on the character of man as a subject. Man's recognition of his own subjectivity, of the fact that he is capable of being a self-conscious originator of activity necessarily implies that man must be treated not as an object for some other thing in nature, but precisely as an end to be served by others.

> Only intellectual creatures operate by themselves in the sense that they are masters of their operations through free choice of their will. . . . Other creatures are involved in operation resulting from the necessity of nature; . . . Therefore, intellectual creatures by their operations are *motivating and regulative* [italics mine], of other creatures.[82]

Man differs from other natural beings in so far as he is a subject, a master of his own operation, and as master he is regulative of other natural beings whose agency results not from free choice, but from natural necessity. Man as a free agent, is the ruler of the natural order so that the moral goodness or evil of activities and things is to be judged in terms of their contribution to or detraction from man as a free agent. In taking this position, we are clearly and squarely in Kant's camp in maintaining that man is always to be treated as an end, never merely as a means.

This brings us to the second part of the defense of the position that reason must view an act in terms of its contribution to or detraction from the development of man as a subject. As we saw in Chapter II, man's freedom is of a limited and conditioned character, as is his existence. In saying that man ought to judge the morality of his acts in light of their contribution to human betterment, we are taking the position that, in the last analysis, man has but two alternatives in trying to reach a decision concerning what to accept as his standard of behavior. Either he makes his being as a member of the human community his standard of behavior or he enslaves himself to some factor or condition of his being, whether that factor be physiological, social, or economic.

If man does not accept his being as a member of the human community as the determining and controlling factor in his life, he will be determined by

<hr>

[82] *ScG* III, 78; see footnote 9, Chap. II, Bk. III, Part I, p. 262.

some other factor in his world.[83] Since man cannot escape the limited and conditioned character of his existence, he must either cultivate those conditions so that they contribute to the development of himself as a member of the human community or he will enslave himself to one or more of these conditions, reducing himself to a means for them. For example, wealth, physical strength, sexual pleasures, food—to mention only a few of the aspects that are a part of man's life and that are the conditions of his existence—can be put to use by man either as a means for the growth of human freedom or as ends to which man will sacrifice himself.

There is no such thing as an "unlimited" freedom for man. His alternatives are a limited freedom developed out of an attempt to see all the values in his world in terms of their contribution to man as a rational agent or to his enslavement to some one or many factors of his environment. Albert Camus brings out this point in rather dramatic fashion in his play *Caligula*. Having gotten the Intendant to admit that the Treasury is of prime importance, Caligula orders him to promulgate the law that anyone having capital, whether large or small, must disinherit his children and will his capital to the State. Moreover, a list of those holding capital will be drawn up and they will be executed as the needs of the Treasury demand. When the Intendant asks him if he realizes what he is doing, Caligula answers: "Now, listen well, you fool! If the Treasury has paramount importance, human life has none. That should be obvious to you. People who think like you are bound to admit the logic of my edict, and since money is the only thing that counts, should set no value on their lives or anyone else's. I have resolved to be logical, and I have the power to enforce my will."[84] Here Camus is pointing out the significance of making something other than man the norm or principle of one's behavior.

c. THE SCOPE AND LIMITATIONS OF REFLECTIVE NATURALISM

The emphasis on evaluating certain activities in terms of their relationship to the growth of human subjectivity in the human community is significant in view of the fact that man is in constant danger of enslaving himself to certain conditions of his environment. Behind this danger lies the fact that man is a being in search of an end to which he can commit himself. Unlike other beings, he is not fitted by "nature" so that he necessarily tends to one end. As we saw in Chapter II, he must either commit himself to certain ends if he is to be free, or he will be a plaything of his environment. Moreover, since man exists in a concrete situation, the end to which he commits himself must take on a con-

[83] See C. S. Lewis, *The Abolition of Man or Reflections on Education with Special Reference to the Teaching of English in the Upper Forms of Schools* (New York: The Macmillan Company, 1947), p. 79.

[84] Albert Camus, "Caligula," *Caligula and Three Other Plays* (New York: Vintage Books, 1962), Act I, pp. 12–13.

crete character. Man must find something particular in his world to work for, whether this something be political power, capitalism, socialism, money. The standard which we have advanced cannot substitute for some particular cause. However, its value lies in the fact that it provides man with a perspective from which to judge these particular causes, a perspective, which calls his attention to the need to consider these causes in the light of man's character as a free being in the human community.

Without the perspective provided by this standard, it is possible that man will become so taken and engrossed by the particular cause to which he has committed himself that he may make the cause a value in itself so that man becomes a means to the cause. For example, economic security can do a great deal to enrich man's life so that a man may well devote himself to acquiring the wealth necessary for such security. However, it is possible for man to become so mesmerized by the process of gaining wealth that he makes of his life a means to this end so that he "works for money," in the most literal sense of this phrase. He thus makes his humanity a means to wealth, not realizing that wealth has no value apart from his humanity. Wealth, sexual pleasure, economic security, technological advances are goods for man in so far as they contribute to the development of Kant's community of ends, but they cease to be goods for him when he literally begins to work *for them*. The standard advanced in this section is meant to help make man aware of this danger and to avoid it when he can.

Perhaps this emphasis on the need to view one's actions from the perspective of their influence on the human community is no more urgently needed than when man undertakes to rectify the injustices of an evil society. This need for such emphasis is the major theme in Albert Camus' study of man in revolt. He criticizes Nazism, Fascism, and Communism for having lost sight of the positive assertion of the value and dignity of man that is inherent in true rebellion.[85] According to Camus, every act of true rebellion is a two-edged sword, with the rebel experiencing simultaneously a revulsion at the infringements of human rights, and a wholehearted commitment to a standard of value that cannot be denied.[86] When rebellion loses sight of, and denies, the positive values which are implied in its revulsion, it ends up negating and denying everything but historical success, thus reducing man to a mere pawn in the march of history to be subjected to a power that acknowledges no limits or checks on itself other than historical expediency.

Against this position, Camus maintains that true rebellion is not nihilistic, for intrinsic to its denial and renunciations of misery and injustice is the affirmation and acceptance of a value.[87]

---

[85] Albert Camus, *The Rebel: An Essay on Man in Revolt,* a revised and complete translation by Anthony Bower (New York: Vintage Books, 1956), p. 294.

[86] *Ibid.,* pp. 13–14.

[87] *Ibid.,* p. 13.

Analysis of rebellion leads at least to the suspicion that, contrary to the postulates of contemporary thought, a human nature does exist, as the Greeks believed. . . . It is for the sake of everyone in the world that the slave asserts himself when he comes to the conclusion that a command has infringed on something in him which does not belong to him alone, but which is common ground, where all men—even the man who insults and oppresses him—have a natural community.[88]

Hence, man's grasp of himself as belonging to a specific community of being underlies man's attempts to alleviate the injustices perpetrated against him as a member of this community, with this same perspective also providing the limits beyond which these attempts cannot go, if they themselves do not want to become guilty of committing injustices against man.

In concluding this section, it might be well to consider the objection that the standard offered by reflective naturalism is too vague and too general to be of any use to man in meeting his concrete moral problems. To the extent that this objection is based on the desire for a moral standard, which would require no further reflection on man's concrete situation, it is asking for a moral standard that cannot be legitimately established. No standard can exhaust all the possible situations in which man may find himself. Being thus unable to know all the existential situations and problems which may confront a man, the ethician cannot provide an answer for problems and situations of which he is unaware. He can only aid personal reflection by indicating the general areas to be considered in attempting to resolve concrete moral issues; he cannot substitute for such reflection.

Not only is it impossible for the ethician to know all the possible existential situations and problems that may confront a man, but it is also impossible for him to give an exhaustive account of the various ways in which the human good may be advanced or of all the factors that may play a role in constituting the complete human good.[89] Without trying to state a full philosophy of history, the fact is that man must find his good in the course of the movement of history. The ethician can provide only a perspective which man can use in trying to evaluate the factors that might either contribute to or detract from the human good in his own time and place. The standard of reflective naturalism is not presented as a cooking recipe that man can follow by simply reading it, without reflecting on what he is doing. It is a call and aid to further reflection, not an end to such reflection.

A more positive response to the objection of the excessive generality of the

[88] *Ibid.*, p. 16.

[89] This point is in keeping with the view expressed by Henri Bergson in the following statement: "How is it possible to ask for a precise definition of liberty and of equality when the future must lie open to all sorts of progress, and especially to the creation of new conditions which are impossible of realization, perhaps of conception, today?" Henri Bergson, *The Two Sources of Morality and Religion*, trans. by R. Ashley Audrce and Claudesley Brereton with the assistance of W. Hersfall Carter (Garden City, N.Y.: Doubleday and Co., 1954), p. 282.

standard offered by reflective naturalism is to be found in the discussion of the relationship of this standard to the possible concrete ends or causes to which man may commit himself. The standard was never meant to function as a concrete end of human activity. Rather, it was advanced as a means to evaluate the possible concrete ends with which man is confronted in his day-to-day life, calling attention to the danger of allowing these ends to become ends-in-themselves, with man being thus reduced to a means to them. Moreover, the discussion of human freedom in Chapter II gives some content to the standard of reflective naturalism. In general, and on a prima facie level, it can be said that actions which obstruct the development of freedom as described in Chapter II are immoral and those which contribute to its growth are moral. The discussion of the scope and limits of human freedom that was conducted in that chapter should prove helpful in specifying what contributes to and what detracts from human freedom.

Kant's work with the categorical imperative can also be used to give content to the standard of reflective naturalism. To treat man as a subject or an end in himself is to treat him as a being who is capable of setting his own ends and who is also capable of taking on the responsibilities of existing under unconditioned obligations—obligations which demand that an act be performed not because of any factors extrinsic to the act, but because of the character of the act itself. To treat man as an end in himself is also to acknowledge that he is a being whose reason enables him to relate himself to other men in terms of obligations that apply to all of them. It is to acknowledge man's capacity to form moral laws, which transcend self-interest and which are inclusive of all other rational beings. These are the dimensions of human existence that are at issue in phrases such as "the growth of human subjectivity," "violation of the character of the human community," "assault on human subjectivity," and other similar phrases that will be used in this book to express judgments on the morality or immorality of certain types of behavior. Finally, the standard that has been defended in this chapter will receive further specification in the discussion of the cardinal virtues in Chapter V.

7. REFLECTIVE NATURALISM AND UTILITARIANISM

The standard advanced in the previous section can now be compared to the utilitarian position. Does this standard imply that consequences are to be ignored in the moral evaluation of human actions? The problem with this question and with the utilitarian position in general resides in the need to specify precisely what is meant by "consequences." Mill tries to meet this problem in one of his essays by specifying two sets of consequences that must be considered in measuring the morality of actions. There are those consequences which he describes as influencing the "outward interests" of the parties involved in the action, including those of the agent himself. There are also consequences affecting the characters of these same parties.

Consequences of the first type are apparently those affecting such things as people's property rights and their physical condition. Mill does not think that there is much difficulty in recognizing these outward interests, at least when the issue is between individuals and not between the State and certain members of society. However, the second set of consequences, which are often essential to judging the morality of an act or situation, are more difficult to judge. These consequences include the influences of an action or rule of action "upon the agent's own mind: upon his susceptibilities of pleasure or pain, upon the general direction of his thoughts, feelings, and imagination, or upon some particular association. Many actions, moreover, produce effects upon the character of persons besides the agent."[90]

Although Mill's distinction is helpful, the need for further precision concerning what is meant by "consequences" remains, as can be seen from Mill's response to the criticism that utilitarianism holds that the end justifies the means. It will be recalled that Mill reponded that utilitarianism holds that the end justifies all means required for its attainment, except those that are "more mischievous than the end is useful." The utilitarian emphasis on the "consequences" of an act would seem to imply that an act has no moral character apart from its consequences. However, Mill's response indicates that a moral evaluation may be required to concern itself with the character of the act that functions as a means, as well as with the end or consequences of this act. This point is brought out in Mill's acknowledgment of the need to ask whether the means to achieve an end are themselves more "mischievous" in their outcome than the utility to be achieved by the end. It is debatable whether concern with means is consistent with the utilitarian stress on consequences as a moral standard.

An example will help bring out the point I have been trying to make. A woman is married to a man whom she and their five children detest. She is in love with another man who is also loved by the children. However, this man does not have much in the way of financial resources, and if she divorced her husband, she would be putting herself, the children, and the man she loved in a difficult economic situation. The present husband carries $100,000 insurance on his life, with his wife designated as sole beneficiary. If she killed her husband, and made his death appear accidental, the "consequences" would be that she, the man she truly loved, and her children would be much happier and more comfortable than they would have been had she remained married or obtained a divorce. Moreover, since the husband had no living relatives other than his wife and children and no close friends, his death would not cause much grief to others. Are we to consider only these consequences, and forget about the character of the act itself that helped bring these consequences into being?

There are not only "consequences" that take place after the act has been completed, but the act itself which may provide an occasion for these later consequences has its own character and "intrinsic" consequences. For example, the killing of a man obviously involves the death af a man. In the case now being considered, are we to ignore this "intrinsic consequence" and consider only the consequence of the happy marriage for which the killing provided an opportunity? Are we to say that this killing is morally significant only when judged in relation to the future consequences to which it contributed? The affirmative answer to this question that seems to be implied in utilitarianism justifies the criticism which we saw W. D. Ross advance against this position in Chapter I.

It will be recalled that Ross criticized utilitarianism for overly simplifying man's moral situation by indicating that only the results of an action are relevant to a moral evaluation. The utilitarian emphasis on consequences does give an excessively *prospective* view of moral issues. Returning to our example, the reflective naturalist would maintain that the killing of a man is not morally justified simply by the fact that, as a consequence of his death, seven people have a better life than they would have enjoyed had he remained alive. Having agreed that the wife and her children and new husband will be happier with the financial security achieved through the killing of the first husband and that presumably only the first husband himself was not too happy about his death, the reflective naturalist would hold that we must turn from a consideration of these consequences to factors that preceded them.

Let it be admitted that the first husband was a failure as a father and as a husband because he failed to make his children and his wife happy and to secure their love and respect. In addition to considering the consequences that can be made to follow on the death of the husband, it is also necessary to ask whether a man's failure as a husband and father gives his wife complete control over his life so that she may dispose of it any way she sees fit. Since a man's failure as a husband and a father does not mean that he is no longer a human subject, the wife has no right to treat him simply as an instrument to the future happiness of herself and her new family. This act of killing the husband was immoral because it was one of the most flagrant and irreparable attacks on the subjectivity of a human person. He was treated in the same way that one treats a piece of furniture that one no longer finds useful by getting "rid of it," for the highest price possible. However, the fact is that a human being is not a piece of furniture or a pet who gets to be a pest and whom no one wants so we "do away with him."

Although I do not know that Smart himself would interpret his philosophic position as justifying the killing of the first husband, it seems to me that this killing would be wholly in accord with the principle of his act utilitarianism.[91]

[91] Since Smart acknowledges that his utilitarianism may in principle permit an innocent man to be punished, it would appear that he would also see nothing immoral about killing a husband under the circumstances described above. For Smart's position on punishing an innocent man see J. J. C. Smart, "The Methods of Ethics and the Methods of Science," *The Journal of Philosophy*, Vol. LXII (June 24, 1965), pp. 347–349.

Smart has suggested that our moral evaluation of possible lines of behavior ought to compare the total consequences which would flow from one line of behavior with the total consequences which would flow from the pursuit of the other line and that we ought to pursue that line of activity which makes as many people as possible happy now and in the future.[92] Since the killing of the husband leads to a future in which seven people are able to enjoy the blessings of a family life that includes love and financial security, whereas if the killing did not occur the best these seven people could hope for would be a second marriage involving love, but lacking the good of financial security, one basing his evaluation on the principles provided by Smart's act utilitarianism would appear to be justified in concluding that there is nothing immoral about this killing.

It is reflective naturalism's emphasis on human subjectivity that separates it from Smart's utilitarianism. His view that there is nothing ethically wrong with sacrificing ten million lives in the present in order to insure the happiness of one hundred million in the future indicates that he has substituted a concern with the number of human beings that can be made happy for a concern with human subjectivity. Against this stress on numbers, I can only point to the analysis of human freedom in Chapter II and the discussion of man as a subject and end in himself in this chapter as evidence that shows that it is not only man in great quantities that is ethically important.

Perhaps Smart's position is grounded in the view that if two men are morally significant, four men must be twice as important. Before accepting this position, it would be well to ask for the factors that render one man morally significant. Reflective naturalism maintains that the significance of man lies not simply in his numbers, but in the character of his existence as a subject, a being who is a member of the human community. This means that there will be times when a reflective naturalist will say that an act is immoral no matter how many people were made happy as a result of that act. Thus, the wife who killed her husband to secure a happier future for herself, her children and her new husband committed an immoral act in treating her first husband as a mere instrument to this happier future.

Smart's contention that tyrants who cause atrocities for a future Utopia are wrong in their assessment of facts, but not in their underlying ethical outlook, indicates that act utilitarianism sees nothing morally wrong with a position that is willing to treat men living in the present as mere instruments for the good of future generations. To accept man as an end in himself is to acknowledge that the promise for a better future, which the pursuit of a certain type of activity may hold out, does not constitute a sufficient ethical justification for that activity. For in so far as men are ends in themselves, they have rights that must be taken into account in any consideration of what is to be done to reach a future Utopia.

[92] See footnote 10, Chap. I, p. 22.

For example, even if Hitler were right in his contention that the human race would come into the glories of the Reich that would last for a thousand years if it were purged of all Jews, he had no moral justification to undertake this purge. Even if one were to grant the truth of Hitler's idiocy that a super race would inhibit the earth once the Jews were destroyed, this fact alone would not give any human being the ethical right to destroy these people. If people are engaged in the day-to-day tasks of trying to earn their daily bread, of reading, of writing, of thinking, of loving, of trying to raise their children to be good human beings, of worshiping God according to their beliefs—in short, if they are merely engaged in the countless tasks that must be a part of every innocent human life—no man has the right to deprive them of their lives, no matter how much better he might think the world would be without them.

When we are dealing with human beings who are thus ends in themselves, the mere fact that they may be standing in the way of progress toward a future that will in the long run prove to be better for more people does not give us a moral justification to kill them. It is necessary to turn from our vision of this future to the question of how these people are obstructing this progress. What precisely are they doing to hold back Utopia? This type of question must be asked because these beings are not mere tools to the future. If it turns out that their obstruction to this future is caused not by any direct assault by them on the lives of their fellow man, if their obstruction consists simply in the fact that they *exist* and that they are directly engaged in the innocent activities that are necessary in all human lives, no man is morally justified in depriving them of their lives. Thus, even if Stalin were correct in his assumption that the reign of terror which he unleashed in the Soviet Union during the 1930's was the only way to bring that nation to a more humane future, his deliberate imprisoning or execution of people whom he knew to be innocent of the charges leveled against them would remain immoral.

It is true that there are considerations in Smart's act utilitarianism for opposing the atrocities of dictators such as Hitler and Stalin. Granted that Smart does advance reasons against these atrocities, is the difference between act utilitarianism and reflective naturalism merely a difference on the level of principle that has no effect at all on a person's reflection on concrete moral problems? It seems to me that this difference in principle will make a difference in one's approach to such problems. Smart's restrictions on what may be done in the name of the future explicitly apply to what he himself terms "large-scale atrocities," and to those atrocities that "would sacrifice the present *in a big way* [Italics mine]."[93] Such phrases lead one to wonder whether this means that his position does allow for small-scale atrocities and/or for acts that sacrifice the present in a small-scale way for a future Utopia. This is an important point because in so far as Smart's case against atrocities rests ultimately and solely on the fact that they will brutalize the future social order and on the fact that

[93] *Ibid.*, p. 46.

our ignorance about the future does not justify large-scale atrocities, he would seem to have no argument against practices that do not come under these restrictions, but that do reduce human individuals to the status of mere means.

This criticism of act utilitarianism's stress on consequences and numbers does not mean that a moral evaluation must completely ignore both these factors in weighing the morality of an act. For example, Smart indicates that there is nothing morally wrong with a battalion commander's sacrificing of a patrol to save a company. Since he gives no other details concerning this specific case, there is no reason to disagree with his judgment. This case is one in which the extrinsic consequences concerning the number of men saved by the commander's decision play a decisive role in the moral evaluation of this decision. The examples used in criticizing act utilitarianism were not presented as offering proof that extrinsic consequences ought never to be considered in evaluating the morality of a given line of behavior. It was not the *inclusion* of these consequences and of numbers in moral evaluations that was being criticized. It was rather the consideration of these factors to the *exclusion of other factors that was being criticized.* More specifically, the examples were used to indicate that there may be times when a certain line of activity which may make more people happy now and in the future ought not be pursued because this happiness is being secured by reducing human beings to the status of mere means.

In so far as Mill sometimes espoused what has come to be called a rule utilitarianism, the criticisms that have been advanced against act utilitarianism do not apply to his position, For example, against the view that utilitarianism would justify a woman's murder of her husband, Mill, speaking as a rule utilitarian, says that, although such an act might be justified by its actual consequences, it ought not to be done, because if everyone were to put to death those whom they despise no one would be safe. Smart's charge of rule worship against this sort of position is valid in so far as the position finds no basis in the particular existential situation for the following of its rule.

If an act is to be morally evaluated solely in terms of its consequences, and if the consequences in the particular situation are good, why not perform the act? To answer that the act should not be performed because if everybody killed those whom they despised and who stood in the way of their happiness, society would be in a sorry mess is to give an irrelevant answer. For the particular case involves only one particular person doing the killing of one particular man. The question is not whether "everybody" should murder those whom they despise, but if this individual woman should kill this individual husband. She is not planning on being discovered, nor is she planning on telling "everyone" to murder. The difficulty with the rule utilitarian position is that it lacks an existential grounding in the given individual case to justify the acceptance of its rule. It says, in effect, in this concrete case there is nothing wrong with this act, nor with the concrete consequences that actually flow from it; indeed, it is willing to admit that the actual consequences that actually do follow from the act are good. However, it holds that the act should not be performed because the consequences *would* be bad, *if* everyone performed the act. The rule is thus totally irrelevant to a situation in which it is not a question of everyone performing the act, but of a single person who intends to keep it secret from everyone.[94]

There are two legitimate conclusions involved in rule utilitarianism, neither one of which is relevant to an act performed by an individual, which would be bad if it *were* performed by many or by everybody. First, people should not be taught that there is nothing immoral about killing a person whom one despises, for such activity should not become a matter of general practice. Secondly, laws should be promulgated informing citizens that certain acts will be punished, again so as to ward off the possibility of these acts becoming a matter of general practice. The moral standard advanced in this section is distinguished from rule utilitarianism in that it points to factors intrinsic to any existential situation that must be considered in judging the morality of an act.

8. THE HUMAN COMMUNITY AND THE ISSUE OF ETHICAL EGOISM AND ALTRUISM

The defense of reflective naturalism in this chapter and the discussion of the relationship between nature and the moral order in Chapter III have placed heavy emphasis on the conceptions of the human community and of human subjectivity as having essential roles to play in man's distinction between moral and immoral acts. The use of both these conceptions in a moral standard requires a consideration of the merits of egoism and altruism as possible moral systems. The emphasis on the notion of community would seem to imply that reflective naturalism does not recognize that there is an individual as well as a social dimension to man's moral life. Balanced against this emphasis is the defense of the morality of aspiration in Chapter II and the emphasis on man as a subject and end in himself, which imply a recognition of the importance of the individual in the resolution of moral issues. The purpose of this section is to clarify matters by bringing out what is implied in reflective naturalism with respect to the question of the merits of egoism and altruism as moral norms.

[94] It must be emphasized that this criticism is restricted to rule utilitarianism and is not directed against every use of the generalization argument in ethics. Thus, Marcus Singer presents the same sort of criticism against rule utilitarianism, although he defends his own conception of the generalization argument in ethics. For Singer's criticism of rule utilitarianism see Marcus Singer, *Generalization in Ethics: An Essay in the Logic of Ethics, with the Rudiment of a System of Moral Philosophy* (New York: Alfred A. Knopf, 1961), pp. 203–216, also pp. 90–95. For a criticism of the logical defense of both rule-utilitarianism and Singer's generalization argument see David Lyons, *Forms and Limits of Utilitarianism* (Oxford: Oxford University Press, 1965).

a. REFLECTIVE NATURALISM AND
A SELF-PERFECTION THEORY OF ETHICS

Ayn Rand sees altruism as identifying moral good with whatever is done for another. This means that anything which a person does for himself is viewed with suspicion, being seen as either amoral, at best, or immoral because such acts are said to be "selfish," with this word being understood in its pejorative sense. Altruism thus places the acting individual in the intolerable situation of not being able to gain any moral satisfaction from doing anything for himself. He is made to think that the only morally justified hope for his own advancement and perfection lies in what other selves will do for him in so far as they will give him what they think he wants or needs.[95] The altruist's social theory holds that an individual's moral duty is "to be the selfless, voiceless, rightless slave of any need, claim or demand asserted by others."[96]

The emphasis on the morality of aspiration clearly indicates that the reflective naturalism advanced in this book does not conform to the type of altruism described by Rand. The ideal of the human community sees the beings in this community as free agents, as ends in themselves. This means that at least a part of the moral task of the beings of this community is to work for their own moral perfection.

The notion that man's moral task includes that of working for his own perfection has come in for criticism in philosophical circles. For example, Marcus Singer holds that an individual's acts take on a moral significance only in so far as they affect the needs or wants of persons other than the individual agent himself. This means that in so far as an agent's acts affect only his own interests, they fall outside a moral universe of discourse.[97] To say that a man has a duty to perform a certain act is to imply that another man has the right to claim the performance of this act. For example, if I have promised my friend that I will help him move his furniture tomorrow, my friend has the right to this help. Granted this correlation between duties and rights, the position that an individual has a duty to himself is seen to imply that he has a right or claim against himself—an implication that Singer sees as nonsensical. The nonsensical character of this implication, if taken literally, is seen when we ask ourselves if an individual can bring suit against himself in a court of law for a sum of money which he owes himself.[98]

Singer also presents what he considers to be a more fundamental argument to sustain his position. He points out that the notion of obligation necessarily

---

[95] Ayn Rand, *The Virtue of Selfishness: A New Concept of Egoism* (New York: The New American Library, 1964), p. viii. See also Ayn Rand, *Atlas Shrugged* (New York: The New American Library, 1957), pp. 956–957.

[96] *The Virtue of Selfishness*, p. 34.

[97] See footnote 94, pp. 303–311.

[98] *Ibid.*, pp. 312–313.

involves the idea that the person who is obliged cannot release himself from his obligation simply because he no longer wants to meet it or has lost interest in it. Of course, an individual can decide not to fulfill his obligation to another, but this does not mean that he has released himself from it. Thus, I can decide to break my promise, but I cannot relieve myself of the obligation I incurred in making it. However, the friend to whom I made the promise can release me from this obligation. If a man had a duty to himself, this would not only mean that he had a right to himself, which we have already seen to be nonsense, but that he exists under an obligation from which he can release himself at will. It is this latter implication that is self-contradictory. A so-called duty from which one could release himself whenever he so desired can not in any literal sense be said to be a duty at all.[99] For example, I might promise myself that I will read the first volume of Tolkien's *The Lord of the Rings* over the weekend. I may also have promised to help my friend complete some of his work over this same weekend. It is clear that if I failed to read Tolkien, I have not really done anything immoral, whereas if l fail to help my friend, I have been immoral.

Two sides of the problem connected with the question of an individual's moral responsibility to himself are now before us. On the one hand, Rand has pointed out that if morality is restricted to what an individual does for or to another, the individual is deprived of any moral satisfaction in having accomplished things for himself. On the other hand, Singer points out that there can be no literal meaning given to the notion that one has a moral responsibility to oneself.

There is danger of interpreting a moral theory which restrict's man's moral duties to his social life, to mean that an individual has totally unrestricted license to do anything and everything in those activities that directly influence only himself. This would be a naïve and simplistic interpretation based on the misconception that there is a neat and complete compartmentalization in a man's life between the social and individual aspects of his existence. Singer's more sophisticated view is able to take into account the close interrelations between these two aspects and the fact that an individual's responsibilities to others places an obligation on him to make himself the type of person who is able to meet these responsibilities. If a man is morally obliged to act in certain ways in his dealings with others, he must also be obliged to make himself the type of agent who can and will perform these acts. This means that an individual must ask himself whether certain acts, which directly influence only himself, are likely to make it more difficult, if not impossible, to meet his moral responsibilities to others. Thus, even if a parent were to accept the view that his moral duties are restricted only to his dealings with others, he could not argue that there is no moral significance in the issue of whether he is becoming an alcoholic.

Singer's distinction between duties seen as self-regarding and as owed to

[99] *Ibid.,* p. 313.

others provides a principle which enables us to bring such behavior into the moral sphere.[100] Although a parent may be spending his own money and may be drinking the liquor himself, he does have a duty to avoid alcoholism. Using Singer's distinction, one could say that this duty is self-regarding in that it concerns what the parent does to himself, but that it is not a duty which he owes to himself. Rather, it is a duty which he owes to his family. Thus, basing ourselves on Singer's work, we can say that there are times when what an individual does to or for himself may come within the scope of moral obligation because it does influence the lives of others in a morally significant way.

If one could show that whatever an individual does to himself has morally significant repercussions on others, it could be argued that there is no significant difference between a moral theory that restricts man's moral duties to what influences others and a moral theory that speaks of man as having responsibilities to himself. However, it is possible to conceive of cases in which an individual's acts with respect to himself have no such repercussions. For example, a man who is very wealthy and has no relatives may not harm any other person by his alcoholism. Similarly, a man who has no friends or relatives may harm no other person by taking his own life. If one were to accept the view that a man's acts are morally significant only if they influence others, he would conclude that there was nothing moral or immoral about this killing. However, one who held that in principle an individual's act may be morally significant even though it may influence no one but the agent who performed it, would want to ask whether the taking of one's own life is immoral. Finally, aside from such rather striking cases, it seems clear that one's perspective on one's own life will be different depending on whether one accepts Singer's view or the view that what an individual does with himself is morally significant. Those moments in life when one is alone with his thoughts will have a different character, depending on which view one accepts.

It is now necessary to deal with Singer's position more directly. Basically his opposition to the notion of an individual's duty to himself is grounded in two considerations: (1) a duty implies the existence of a right by another person, (2) an individual could release himself from a duty to himself, but such a possibility contradicts the very nature of duty. If one restricts the notion of duty to the legal order, Singer's case is sustained. The idea of an individual suing himself in court for money which he owes himself is indeed ridiculous. However, before concluding from this that no literal significance can be attached to the idea of an individual's moral responsibility to himself, it should be recalled that in Chapter II we attempted to show that the legal and moral orders are not to be identified. If the distinction between these orders is accepted, the fact that an individual cannot be said to have an obligation to himself in the legal order cannot be taken as excluding the possibility of such an obligation in the moral order. One may admit that a legal obligation implies

---

[100] *Ibid.*, pp. 316–317.

the existence of a right by another person, but may ask for the premise or premises which lead to the conclusion that moral obligation must conform to the character of legal obligation.

This question leads to the more fundamental basis of Singer's position, namely, the view that an individual could release himself at will from an obligation to himself and that such a possibility is wholly incompatible with the notion of duty. The example of a man promising himself that he will read a certain book over a given period of time certainly serves to advance Singer's position. However, it is necessary to be careful about accepting examples as decisive evidence for the establishment of a conclusion that is of universal scope. It may be true that there are some areas in an individual's dealings with himself which are morally neutral, just as there may be areas in his dealings with others that are morally neutral. It is possible that I may take one of these morally neutral areas as a basis for the conclusion that no acts in this area are morally significant. Thus, if I take my wife's problem as to whether or not my son should wear a blue or a red tie on his first day of school as an example of man's relationships to others, I might erroneously conclude that all these relationships are morally neutral. Hence before concluding that man has moral responsibilities only in those areas of his life that influence others, we should look for the basis of these responsibilities in this area. We might then be in a better position to judge whether or not an individual has moral obligations to meet in those activities which influence only his own life.

As was indicated in the evaluation of Kant's position, reflective naturalism holds that moral obligation is grounded in moral goodness. Hence, if we are to discover what we ought to do in our relations with others, we must try to discover what is in keeping with their character as beings capable of freedom. If my obligation to another is thus grounded in his character as a being capable of freedom, it is difficult to see any justification for the view that what I do to myself falls outside of the sphere of moral obligation. If I ought not to contribute to making another person an alcoholic or a dope addict because these ways of life hinder this person's growth as a free being, I ought to avoid becoming a dope addict myself for the same reason. The point is that I have moral obligations to others not because they are distinct from me, but because they are beings capable of freedom. Since I also am such a being, my moral responsibilities must include what I do to myself.

Although I have indicated that the example of a man breaking a promise to himself cannot be validly used to prove that a man never has moral obligations in those areas of his life that concern himself only, there is an insight into the character of moral obligation in this example that must be considered at this point. There is a certain "binding" element involved in the notion of duty or of obligation. Singer is clearly correct in holding that a so-called obligation is not truly an obligation if it is grounded in the individual's own will or desire. If it turns out that my "obligation" to read a book over the weekend is grounded only in my wish to read it, I am not really obliged in this case. Since my wish was the basis of this so-called obligation, a later wish not to perform the act is sufficient to free me from the "obligation." Hence, the question that must now be faced: Is there any factor involved in that sphere of activity in which an individual influences only himself that binds him whether he wishes to be bound or not?

The response to this question demands that we ask ourselves what accounts for the binding character of moral obligation in any sphere of man's life. I shall try to make a case for the position that man's reason which enables him to know himself as a member of the human community can ground the presence of moral obligation in his life. His knowledge of the capacities which he possesses to advance the good of this community is sufficient to place a demand on him. Reason which makes an individual man aware of himself as a member of the human community liberates him from the self-enclosed individuality, making him aware of the resources which he himself has at hand to realize certain possibilities for the good of this community. He sees these valuable possibilities as goods he *ought* to realize. The character of "oughtness" or obligation is grounded in man's awareness that his choice when confronted with such possibilities is a limited one. He can either be a man who works for the realization of these goods (and hence a morally good man) or a man who frustrates their realization (and hence a morally evil man). There is thus an inescapable quality connected with specifically moral duties in that man has no third alternative between being a good or a bad man. A man is "stuck" with being a man. He can be "a man-who-acts-like-a-pig," but he cannot be a pig.

This view of the grounding of moral obligation in human experience fits in with the position taken in Chapter II and in Section 5 of this chapter concerning the grounding of man's knowledge of moral values. The same interplay between human reason as a creative factor in nature and the given particuluar facts of human experience grounds both man's knowledge of moral values and his recognition of himself as a being who has obligations and responsibilities. The immediately preceding paragraph has simply emphasized that aspect of this interplay which grounds moral obligation in human existence. An individual's knowledge of the capacities which he possesses to advance the good of human subjectivity is sufficient to place a demand on him whether he is dealing with other human beings or with his own growth as a human subject. The ideal of the good of human subjectivity in the human community does not magically pass from the moral individual's mind when he is considering activities that may affect only himself, nor does the recognition that he can be either a human subject whose acts accord with this ideal or one whose acts are incompatible with it. He can no more release himself from what he knows to be the possibilities for human good and the demand which these possibilities place on him, when he is following a line of activity that will influence only himself, than he can, when his activity influences the lives of others. Finally, the fact that an individual is free to act contrary to his moral responsibilities in his personal life no more releases him from these responsibilities than does the same freedom in his social life release him from his social responsibilities.

This view of the basis of moral obligation in man's life appears to be in keeping with the character of man as a being who is capable of exercising moral agency. Moral obligation is not something imposed upon man by some force or power external to him. It arises rather out of the use of his own rational resources. Man is a being capable of being morally responsible and of existing under moral obligation because he can know himself as a human subject and as a member of the human community, he can gain some knowledge of the possibilities for the fulfillment of himself as such a subject and as a member of this community, and he can recognize the demand which such knowledge places on him. Granted all this, there seems to be no justification for restricting the scope of man's moral obligations to his social affairs.

Singer may be right in pointing out that the term "duty" is usually used to refer to a situation in which an individual owes something to another person who has a claim over him. In view of this linguistic usage, it might be well to avoid speaking of an individual's duty to himself. However, this point does not detract from the validity of the argument advanced to show that an individual's moral responsibilities and obligations extend to his private as well as to his social life. We shall return to a consideration of moral obligation in the course of probing the issues connected with the relationship between God and man's moral life in Chapter IX.

The position taken in this section can be described as a "self-perfection" theory of ethics. Basically this theory maintains that an individual is morally responsible for cultivating the elements of his life's process that come under his control in such a way that they will contribute to his growth as a free being.

R.N.

b. THE SOCIAL DIMENSIONS
OF REFLECTIVE NATURALISM

Although the self-perfection theory of ethics agrees with Rand's egoism in so far as it maintains that an individual's moral responsibilities include the task of working for his own moral perfection, there is a fundamental disagreement between both theories with respect to the scope of an individual's moral responsibilities to others. Any discussion of the scope of an individual's moral responsibilities must begin with the realization that he does not live in a sin-tight compartment which completely isolates him from other human individuals who are also subjects. He enters into and influences their lives, just as they enter into and influence his life. If a moral theory is to be true to the complexity of human existence, it must not only avoid reducing the acting human individual to a selfless, voiceless slave of any need asserted by others, but it must also avoid reducing others to a mere means for one's own interests. Rand's ethics of rational self-interest fail to do justice to the fact that an individual finds himself interacting with other beings that are also ends themselves.

Although Rand accepts the view that every living man is an end in himself, she holds that a man should decide whether or not to help another man by consulting his own rational self-interest, asking himself if the effort which he exerts in helping the other is proportionate to the contribution that the other makes to his own happiness.[101] This means that there is no moral obligation placed on an individual by the fact that another man needs his help.[102] Thus, an individual has the moral duty to help another man who is suffering only if he finds selfish pleasure in some value that the suffering man is able to offer. The mere fact that a man is suffering is not a value and therefore this fact alone can place no moral demand on another individual. To accept another's suffering as such, his faults, or his need as making moral claims on us is to expend our efforts for things that are valueless.[103] Suffering and need cannot make a moral claim on the man of rational self-interest because they are not values and thus can offer such a man nothing in return for his expenditure.

This view of an individual's responsibilities to his fellow man is not in keeping with the notion of man as an end in himself. If I say that I need consider only what another person has to offer to my own happiness in deciding whether I am morally obligated to him, I am saying that he has a claim on me only in so far as he is instrumental to my happiness. This means that the fact that man is said to be an end in himself is not a relevant consideration in an individual's examination of the moral claims which other men may make on him. In considering such claims, I can forget about the other man's character as an end in himself, and restrict myself to asking, "What good is he for me? What does he have to offer me?" To restrict oneself to such questions is to imply that others are valuable *only in so far as they contribute to his good.*

Kant's recognition of the fact that the conception of man as an end in himself applies both to himself as an individual and to his fellow man is behind his view that man is obligated to work for his own perfection and for the happiness of his fellow man. The difference between Kant's and Rand's positions can be seen in Kant's contention that the duties of respect and of beneficence must be included in man's duty to work for the happiness of others. The duty to respect our fellow man is not a duty that obligates one to have a certain feeling for others. Rather, it is a duty that obligates an individual "to acknowledge, in a practical way, the dignity of humanity in every other man."[104] The duty of respect requires that an individual acknowledge in his practical dealings with his fellow man that he himself does not exhaust the value of man as an end in himself. His actions must be such that they are in keeping with his status as one among many ends in themselves. In so far as this duty of respect is grounded in the character of others as subjects, it applies to all men whether they be moral or immoral. The fact that a man is immoral does not mean that I can treat him as a mere means, that I can do anything I desire with him or to

---

[101] For the view that man is an end in himself, see *The Virtue of Selfishness*, p. 27. See also p. 45.

[102] See *Atlas Shrugged*, p. 937.

[103] *Ibid.*, p. 984.

[104] See footnote 34, Chap. III, p. 132.

him. For example, it means that the punishment that one would inflict on an immoral man must always be limited by the recognition that he is an end in himself. Hence, Kant states that the duty of respect rules out such punishments as having a man quartered or torn by dogs.[105] We shall return to this matter in Chapter VIII in considering the morality of capital punishment.

It is conceivable that Rand's morality of self-interest may be able to include what Kant refers to as man's duty of respect to his fellow man, since this duty is primarily of a negative type in that it obligates an individual to keep his activities within certain limits so as not to detract from the worth of others as ends in themselves.[106] Rand does say that man ought not impose his own will on another through the use of physical force. However, it is doubtful that she would emphasize as strongly as Kant does, the fact that a man simply because he is a man is a being of value, and thus cannot be considered a zero simply because he is incompetent or immoral. Be that as it may, the obvious point of difference between Kant and Rand is to be found in Kant's conception of the duty of beneficence.

The duty of beneficence requires every man "to promote according to his means, the happiness of others who are in need, and this without hope of gaining anything by it."[107] This position is consistent with the recognition of all men as ends in themselves. I acknowledge that another is an end in himself when I help him *because he is in need,* and not because I happen to find him useful for some interest of my own. As Kant correctly points out, we do not treat another as an end in himself by simply avoiding treating him as a mere means, for such avoidance is compatible with complete indifference.[108]

In fulfilling the duty of beneficence, an individual must realize that he is dealing with free beings and that therefore (except in the case of the insane and children) he must try to offer aid that conforms not to his own conception of good, but to that of the one being helped.[109] This position is also in keeping with the acknowledgment that the man whom I am helping is an end in himself. Kant qualifies this duty of beneficence in such a way that he is not guilty of the charge of having reduced the acting individual to the selfless, voiceless slave of any need asserted by others. He holds that the man who makes himself useful for the good of others must do so only in a way that is not in conflict with his own being as a person and an end in himself.[110] This means that in so far as I am a moral agent, I am not obliged by the duty of beneficence to fulfill another's need if I think that the fulfillment of such a need requires that

---

[105] *Ibid.,* p. 133.
[106] *Ibid.,* pp. 116–117.
[107] *Ibid.,* p. 120.
[108] *Ibid.,* p. 56.
[109] *Ibid.,* p. 122.
[110] See Immanuel Kant, *Lectures on Ethics,* trans. by Louis Infield (New York: Harper Torchbooks, 1963), p. 120. This book is a reconstruction of Kant's class lectures on Ethics taken from student's notebooks.

I do something that I consider to be immoral, or that directly contributes to the immoral behavior of the one whom I am helping. Thus, although I am obliged to help another in need, I am not obliged to keep an alcoholic supplied with as much wine as he desires.[111]

The outcome of this section is that a moral philosophy that is either exclusively egoistical or exclusively altruistic in orientation does not do justice to the complexity of man's situation in the world. Since a human individual is a person existing in a community of persons, he is not to reduce others to a mere means to his own interests, nor is he to reduce himself to a mere means to the happiness of others. This position does not deny that conflicts actually do arise between individuals or between individuals and a given social order. However, it maintains that a moral philosophy is deficient if its emphasis on the value of the human individual is such that it gives the impression that all conflicts between an individual and society are to be resolved in an a priori fashion in favor of the individual. Similarly a moral philosophy is deficient if its emphasis on the value of society leads one to conclude that all conflicts between an individual and society are to be resolved in an a priori way in favor of society.

The conflicts that do arise between individuals and a society can be resolved only through a reflection on the concrete facts of each particular conflict in order to see whether the individual is overstepping his moral limits or failing to meet his moral responsibilities or whether those asserting the rights of society are losing sight of the subjectivity of the individual. One must ask himself whether a proposed resolution corresponds to the ideal which sees a human individual as a member of a community of ends. The problem discussed in this section is relevant to the consideration of the nature of justice to be taken up in Chapter V and to the evaluation of the morality of socialism and capitalism to be considered in Chapter VII.

9. REFLECTIVE MORALITY AND MAN AS A SOCIAL AND HISTORIC BEING

This section will be subdivided under the following headings: (a) Reflective Morality and Customary Morality, and (b) Reflective Morality and Man's Changing World.

a. REFLECTIVE MORALITY AND CUSTOMARY MORALITY

This subsection will examine the view that the distinction between moral good and evil is grounded in custom rather than in reason. Two pieces of evidence advanced in defense of this view will be considered. That the moral

---

[111] See footnote 34, Chap. III, p. 153, also p. 47.

values which a man holds are a matter of custom, and not of reason, is obvious in view of the fact that his knowledge or morality is grounded in those values which he was taught by the society in which he was educated, a society personified by his parents, religious authorities, and any other influential figures in his life.

There can be no doubt that a child is dependent on the society in which he lives for his education in moral matters. Man is not born with an innate knowledge of morality, just as he is not born with an innate knowledge of speculative truths. He is dependent on the mature members of the community for the development of his intellectual capacities in both these areas. This fact is simply one of the factors involved in the social character of human existence. The development of man's knowledge, whether it be in the area of speculative or of moral truths, can occur only within a social context. Since there is this dependence on society in the development of all areas of human knowledge, it seems that there is no justification for the view that a man's knowledge of morality is, and can only be, a matter of custom, whereas his knowledge of physics, chemistry, or mathematics is objective. Since a man is dependent on the education which he receives from society for the beginning of his knowledge in all areas, all knowledge must be customary, if by "customary" is meant that one learns from the members of one's society.

The problem is to discover what distinguishes customary knowledge from objective knowledge. The distinction obviously does not lie in whether or not one's knowledge was originally learned from other human beings. It must lie rather in the manner in which any individual man develops what he has learned. Knowledge in any area of speculation can be merely customary. For example, the physics student who says that a body in motion tends to stay in motion, but who, when pressed for the basis of his statement, admits that he accepts it as true because he "read it in a book," or because his physics teacher "said so," possesses a customary knowledge of this law of physics, in that his knowledge is simply an unreflected repetition of what he has read or heard. He attains the level of "objective" knowledge in this area, as he puts his own mind to work on the evidence for the law so that this knowledge is no longer grounded in what others have told him, but arises also out of his own reflective inquiry.

Similarly, one who holds that socialism is immoral, and who has not actually employed his own reason to reflect on the basis for his position, but who simply repeats the view popular in his society is said to have a customary rather than a reflective grasp of this point, with this distinction meaning that the basis of his knowledge lies entirely in the society of which he is a member and not in his own reflections. Thus, the line between customary and reflective knowledge is not simply identical with the distinction between knowledge of moral values and knowledge in other areas. The distinction depends on the mind from which such knowledge has proceeded, and the work which that mind has put into such knowledge.

In every area of intellectual endeavor, man must acquire a certain amount of knowledge before he can be in a position to attempt to move to a reflective knowledge of a given area. Thus, in order to be a physicist, one must spend some time studying and acquiring the funded knowledge available in the community of physicists of his day, and during this time there will be certain stages in his development when his knowledge is predominantly, if not exclusively, of the customary variety. The same can be said of one's moral knowledge. One must pass through a customary stage in this area also. Furthermore, it is undoubtedly true that no man ever reaches the stage of possessing a fully reflective knowledge of all factors in any area of human investigation. This means that any man's knowledge of physics or of morals will always be a mixture of the customary and the reflective. For example, a physicist working in a specialized area will accept as true certain facts outside of his area because he knows that these facts are acceptable in the community of physicists, although he himself has not considered the evidence for these facts. Similarly, one who has spent a good deal of time exploring questions of business ethics, and has achieved a high degree of reflective knowledge in this area, may have little more than a customary knowledge of the ethical issues connected with marital life.

Another reason advanced for the view that there is no rational basis for distinguishing between moral good and evil is the fact that practices considered moral in one age and in one society are viewed as immoral in another age and in a different society. Some societies have sanctioned polygamy, whereas others reject it as immoral. The Greeks seemed to have seen nothing wrong with homosexuality, whereas the practice is generally considered immoral in our own day. The diversity and contradictions in the moral practices of men in different societies and ages are too well known to need any listing here. The *fact* of such diversity and contradictions cannot be denied. However, the interpretations of these facts deserve consideration.

Brand Blandshard makes an excellent point with respect to the problem of interpreting these facts.

Why not account for the diversity by the very simple hypothesis that some men are stupid in moral matters and others more discerning? Indeed if agreement is to be made out in science itself, it would seem to be only by taking advantage of this sort of explanation; we tacitly rule out the dissenting votes of savages on mathematics and chemistry as not worth including in our poll. If we did include them, we should have a diversity very similar to that in ethics. But it is clear how we should go about it to deal with that diversity. No one would question a judgment of Newton on the ground that some Andaman Islander shook his head over it. We should say that if the Islander failed to see, that was not because Newton's insight was false, or indeed anything less than self-evident to a mind qualified to judge, but because the Islander was stupid or untrained. And if we are entitled to say that in science, why not in ethics? The civilized man sees clearly, or thinks he does, that to rob a stranger is wrong, and that to deprive a man of rights because he is of another colour or country is unjust. To most savages such views are absurd. Does this show that fairness is really not better than unfairness? Is it not far more sensible to say that fairness really is better, but that the savage has not reached the point where he can see it?[112]

Blandshard's statement represents a very sound objection against the view that there can be no rational basis for moral judgments because of the great diversity of moral beliefs. If unanimity of all people of all ages were the basis upon which to decide whether a position could be rationally resolved, it is doubtful that the heliocentric view of the universe could be said to be rationally defensible against the geocentric theory. It would appear to be rather safe to say that most men, before being exposed to the rudiments of science, would tend to hold that the sun moves around the earth, rather than vice versa. Moreover, it is doubtful that most men would accept Einstein's theory of relativity. Indeed, the acceptance of this theory by the majority of people even in the most sophisticated societies is perhaps based more on an act of faith in science than in any intellectual grasp of the issues involved in the theory.

The point of all this is not to engage in a diatribe against science, but to point out that just as there is no need to conclude from the diversity of views held by men through the ages concerning the physical, chemical, or biological features of their environment that there is no possibility of reaching any rationally grounded positions on these matters, so also there would seem to be no necessity to conclude from the diversity of views concerning moral issues that there is no possibility to work toward a rational resolution concerning these views.

Having made this point, it must be admitted that the issues with which the ethician deals do not lend themselves to the same sort of clear-cut mathematical treatment as do the problems in physics. Moreover, ethical issues cannot be easily isolated from other issues such as the problem of human freedom, the role of God in human knowledge, the character of man's natural environment—to mention only some of the major points that enter into the ethical universe of discourse. However, unless one is committed to the view that only those issues susceptible of mathematical treatment can be dealt with on a rational plane, the fact that moral issues are complex, touching many areas of human existence, need not mean that they cannot be treated in a rational way or that one moral position is as valid as another since there is no rational basis for either.

b. Reflective Morality
   and Man's Changing World

[The purpose of this subsection is to try to show that the acceptance of the possibility of a reflective morality need not involve the conclusion that human morality is wholly immutable so that what is moral today, must have been moral in the past, and will be moral in the future and forever more.] The issue of the mutability or immutability of moral values is a complex one that is not open

---

[112] See footnote 33, Chap. I, pp. 118, 119.

to a simple solution. There is a sense in which moral values are changeable and a sense in which they are enduring.

There are factors inherent in the standard of reflective naturalism that make this standard open to certain changes. In so far as human reason plays a central role in this standard, there is built into the standard itself a possibility for changes in man's moral perspectives. For the human reason deciding moral issues is not different from or isolated from the human reason dealing with other facets of man and his world, so that the knowledge developed in other areas may influence his moral views. For example, before Louis Pasteur's work with bacteria, there was perhaps no moral responsibility on a surgeon's part to be as certain as possible that the instruments to be used in performing an operation be completely sterilized. However, once the knowledge that unsterilized instruments would introduce debilitating or fatal bacteria into the patient had been firmly established, the sterilization of the surgeon's instruments did become a moral matter.

Perhaps a more striking example is to be found in the 1954 Supreme Court decision concerning the doctrine of separate, but equal schools for Negro and Caucasian students. On paper, such a doctrine may conceivably have appeared to involve no moral difficulties in the late nineteenth and early twentieth centuries. However, the experience gained by putting the doctrine into practice showed that such a separation based on racial considerations alone was harmful to the human good of both Negroes and Caucasians, contributing to a deep-seated feeling of inferiority and hopelessness in the Negro and an exaggerated feeling of superiority on the part of Caucasians with respect to Negroes. Whereas the Negro was made to feel that the mere fact of his race militated against the possibility of his making a significant contribution to the human community or of being accepted as a full-fledged member of this community, Caucasians were led to feel that the mere fact of their race made them superior to the Negroes. In short, the doctrine of separate, but equal schools was seen to introduce not a healthy diversity in the community of ends, but a fragmentation of this community in which the mere fact that one was a Negro meant that one was not "quite as much" an end in himself as was a Caucasian.

The other two aspects of the reflective standard, "man-in-the-world," also lend themselves to the possibility of change and development in man's moral values. As man fills his world with new objects, he is required to rethink his ethical positions in view of the addition of these objects to his life. For example, the introduction of atomic and hydrogen bombs into the world would appear to call into question the moral justification of war which was based on the conception of a war that spares the lives of noncombatants. Man must now consider the justification of a war which uses these new weapons. For the explosion of these weapons introduces factors into the atmosphere that threaten the lives and well-being not only of the noncombatants living during the period of hostilities, but also of future generations. This point will also be more fully discussed in Chapter VIII.

Another example of how changes in the objects of man's world require re-thinking of his moral stands is to be seen in the introduction of pills which have helped women exercise control over their periods of ovulation by preventing such ovulation. Whether or not these pills will lead to any change of views on the part of those who see birth control by artificial means to be immoral, the fact remains that the pills introduce a new element in the moral situation that must be taken into consideration in dealing with this question.

The fact that "man-in-the-world," has been dealt with as one unit in this discussion was not purely accidental. For the changes in man's world which include changes in such areas as his political, economic, and educational institutions, influence the very being of man himself. To take any other position would presuppose that man exists in himself somehow cut off from and unaffected by the world in which he exists. As was pointed out in Chapter II, if this were true, it would mean that a great deal of time, energy, and concern has been wasted in man's attempt to improve his environment since environmental changes would have absolutely no influence on the being of man. The view that changes in man's world introduce changes in man's being does not mean that—as long as human life persists—man will cease to be a being who is capable of reasoning, of loving the pleasurable good, of either giving in to the most pressing needs of the moment or of trying to regulate them for a more inclusive good, and a being who is in search of solitude and society. However, the position taken here does mean that the conditions that will either frustrate or fulfill these dimensions of human existence do not remain the same from age to age, and that part of the reason for this lies in the fact that the way in which these human dimensions can be fulfilled or frustrated depends on the type of environment in which man lives.

A specific example may serve to illustrate this point. One must consider the social milieu in order to decide what constitutes a just economic system. Thus, during the age of feudalism, it may have been sufficient to supply a serf with a roof over his head and a piece of land so that he could put food on his family's table. Since institutions of higher education were not so numerous as they are today and since the conditions of employment were not such that it was necessary for a man to insure that his children had at least the equivalent of a high school education as a preparation to meet the responsibilities of adulthood, it was not necessary to take these factors into consideration in deciding what would constitute a morally just economic system. However, man's social situation has changed so that a wage which provides a man with only enough to provide food and lodging for his family is no longer morally justified. He must also be provided with the economic resources that will give him a reasonable opportunity to meet the costs of that education that his children will need if they are to have the opportunity to become responsible and self-supporting members in tomorrow's community. An economic system that may have contributed to true human fulfillment as such fulfillment was possible in a past age may today fall short of contributing to the fulfillment that is generally open to man, and thus may be immoral today. This discussion was used simply to exemplify the fact that changes in man's world will change the factors that may be considered as contributing to human fulfillment.

A final point that ought to be mentioned with respect to the possibility for changes in man's moral life centers in the need to consider the history and customs of a society and how deeply ingrained these customs have become in the lives of the people in order to judge how a better system can be introduced into this society. For an ideal that might work in a society with different customs and a different historical background might produce conditions in *this* society with *its* customs that are more immoral and inhuman than those presently existing in the society. Unfortunately, those who have profited from the miseries of others have used, or, we should say, abused this point as an excuse to avoid any change whatsoever. However, the legitimate conclusion to be drawn from the need to consider the customs of a people is not that one must stand by and do nothing in the face of flagrantly immoral conditions, but that these customs must be taken into consideration in inaugurating a program to improve these conditions, realizing that it may take more time to bring about these changes in this confused, confusing, and imperfect world than it would in the best of all possible worlds.

Having thus seen some of the factors involved in human existence that contribute to the relativity of moral values, it is now necessary to explore the possibility that there may be certain enduring factors in man's moral situation. Thomas Aquinas provides an excellent beginning in dealing with this issue. He states that justice and moral goodness can be considered in two ways—*formally* in which case they are always and everywhere the same, and *materially* in which case they are not the same in all circumstances, but must be determined in accord with the situation. As an example of a *formal* character of justice which is always and everywhere the same, Aquinas states that the transaction involved in buying and selling must always be accomplished in an equal way so that the buyer does not give more than the object is worth, nor does the seller receive less than the worth of the object. However, considered *materially* justice is not always and everywhere the same, so that whereas in one place and at one time it may be just to pay a certain amount for a given measure of grain, in another place and at another time, it may be just to pay either more or less than was paid in the first case.[113]

In a more contemporary setting, John Dewey expresses the same insight by pointing to three "enduring values," which he considers to be at the heart of the liberal tradition, the values being "liberty, the development of the inherent capacities of individuals made possible through liberty, and the central role of intelligence in inquiry, discussion, and expression."[114] These values might well

---

[113] *De Malo*, q.2, a.4, ad.13.

[114] John Dewey, *Liberalism and Social Action* (New York: Capricorn Books, 1963), p. 32.

be part of that "framework of moral conceptions" that he describes in another book as being "as permanent as human life itself."[115] Dewey maintains that it is man's task to make these values relevant to the situation in which he lives. He brings out this point very well in the following statement concerning the need to give specific content to what might be called, using Aquinas' language, the formal conception of liberty.

> If we employ the conception of historic relativity, nothing is clearer than that the conception of liberty is always relative to forces that at a given time and place are increasingly felt to be oppressive. Liberty in the concrete signifies release from the impact of particular oppressive forces; emancipation from something once taken as a normal part of human life but now experienced as bondage. At one time, liberty signified liberation from chattel slavery; at another time, release from serf-dom. During the late seventeenth and early eighteenth centuries it meant libera-tion from despotic dynastic rule. A century later it meant release of industrialists from inherited legal customs that hampered the rise of new forces of production. Today, it signifies liberation from material insecurity and from the coercions and repressions that prevent multitudes from participation in the vast cultural resources that are at hand.[116]

This statement provides a good example of the valid insight behind Aquinas' distinction between moral values *formally* and *materially* considered. There are certain moral values that are "absolute," in the sense that these values must play a part in a society or in the life of an individual man, if that society or indi-vidual is to be said to be moral.

Using Dewey's statement, liberty is seen to be one of these absolutes, or en-during values as Dewey prefers to refer to them. Considered formally, liberty is release from oppressive forces. It is man's task to introduce this value into his own society, if he is to contribute to the moral development of this society. The introduction of this value into a particular society requires that this value be materially considered. In order to discover the concrete and particular meaning of liberty in today's society, this society must be examined so as to discover those particular oppressive forces which may once have been unavoidable fac-tors in the human condition, but which now have become an unnecessary bond-age for man. Whereas at one time man may have been said to enjoy liberty in so far as he was not held in chattel slavery, the fact that a man is not held in such slavery today does not mean that he enjoys the value of liberty because human society has reached a stage of development in which man can reasonably be released from other oppressive forces, a release which in ancient times was beyond the power of man to achieve.

Thus, there are absolute moral values, i.e. values which must enter any

---

[115] John Dewey, *The Theory of the Moral Life* (New York: Rinehart, Winston, 1960), p. 176.
[116] See footnote 114, p. 48.

human life or society, if that life or society is to be moral. Chapter V will be devoted to an exploration of some of these enduring values in their purely formal character, i.e. the cardinal virtues of practical wisdom, justice, temperance, and fortitude.

CHAPTER V

Habituation and Moral Judgment

John Stuart Mill has pointed to the need for building a system of "secondary or middle principles," on the foundation of one's ultimate moral standard: "Without such middle principles, a universal principle, either in science or in morals, serves for little but a thesaurus of commonplaces for the discussion of questions, instead of a means for deciding them."[1] Mill's observations apply to the standard defended in Chapter IV. For it may be well and good to speak of "reason-reflecting-on-man-in-his-world," as the moral norm, but it is also necessary to try to fashion some secondary principles that will spell out the *type* of acts or the character that acts must possess, if they are to be seen as conforming to this norm. An examination of the character of what have been called the cardinal virtues—practical wisdom, temperance, fortitude, and justice—provides a knowledge of the *type* of acts that contribute to the establishment of the human community and to the growth of human subjectivity. Hence, this chapter will inquire into the meaning and character of these virtues. Because virtues will be described as good moral habits, it will be necessary to explore certain basic issues concerning the nature and growth of habits.

Furthermore, a major factor that will be brought out in the course of this discussion of the virtues is the importance of the role that the appetitive dimensions of human existence play in the moral life of man. My disagreement with

---

[1] See footnote 4, Chap. 4, p. 461.

[2] See Vernon J. Bourke, *Ethics: A Textbook in Moral Philosophy* (New York: The Macmillan Co., 1951), p. 139. The phrase "practical wisdom" is used to refer to the type of moral knowledge that is discussed as "prudence" in some circles. This phrase is used instead of the word "prudence," because this word is sometimes understood as referring to a man's ability to know what will work for his own benefit, apart from any moral considerations. For example, Kant speaks of "the maxim of self-love (prudence)." *Critique of Practical Reason*, p. 148. According to Kant, the prudent man possesses technical rather than moral knowledge in that he knows how to achieve whatever ends he may happen to pursue, although these ends are not necessarily moral. *The Doctrine of Virtues*, pp. 43–44, 123. See also footnote 9, Chap. I, pp. 31–33, 35 note 5.

For a contemporary discussion of the meaning of "prudence" that follows the general lines of Kant's usage see Singer, pp. 302–311.

emotivism, along with my emphasis on the role of reason in morals, may have led some to conclude that, despite protestations to the contrary, I have seen the appetites as playing no significant role in human morality. However, the discussion of temperance, fortitude, and justice will serve to show that I am in substantial agreement with the following observations made by C. S. Lewis.

> I had sooner play cards against a man who was quite sceptical about ethics, but bred to believe that 'a gentleman does not cheat,' than against an irreproachable moral philosopher who had been brought up among sharpers. In battle it is not syllogisms that will keep the reluctant nerves and muscles to their post in the third hour of the bombardment. . . . Magnanimity—Sentiment—these are the indispensable liaison officers between cerebral man and visceral man.[3]

Lewis has made a legitimate point. When we get down to "brass tacks," to the concrete situation in which a man is under great stress, a man's appetites play a decisive role in the course of action which he pursues. I have never intended to deny that the appetites are springs of human action. However, the issue is not whether a man's moral life is either a matter of reason alone or of the appetites. To give reason a central role in judging the morality or immorality of an act, is not necessarily to commit oneself to the Stoic view that the appetites are to be eradicated so that human reason alone will hold sway in man's life.

What I am advancing is a view in which there is an interplay between the appetitive side of human life and human reason, an interplay such that reason may play the role of molding, rather than of destroying, man's appetites so that in times of stress, a man's character (which includes his appetites) "will keep the reluctant nerves and muscles to their post in the third hour of bombardment." Here, again, there are only two alternatives. Either man's character is so formed that human appetites can respond easily, consistently, and with pleasure for the good of man, or his character is so formed that they are determined by some factor that will, in all probability, put them to work for some object outside of man such as money, alcohol, or for one facet of human existence such as sexual or physical prowess to the exclusion of all else. Hence, far from denying that appetites do play a role in man's activities, I maintain that the role they do play is too important to be left to chance and that man must work to mold them so that they will respond to the demands of reason, easily, consistently, and with pleasure.

Finally, the discussion of practical wisdom will raise the issue of the relation between the general moral principles established by the ethician's reflections and the knowledge that a man must acquire if he is to resolve his concrete moral problems. This discussion will require an exposition and evaluation of what has come to be called "Situation Ethics."

[3] See footnote 83, Chap. 4, p. 34.

1. DISADVANTAGES AND ADVANTAGES IN AN ANALYTIC APPROACH TO MORAL CHARACTER

Before proceeding to a discussion of the virtues, some consideration must be given to the analytic approach that will be taken in this discussion. John Dewey brings out certain factors that should be considered by anyone intending to treat moral virtues in an analytic way. He points out that the very idea of cataloguing virtues commits one to the view that "virtues may be kept apart, pigeon-holed in water-tight compartments."[4] Such a view loses sight of the fact that man's task is the development of a unified and integrated moral character. The virtuous man is not a hodgepodge of different things called "virtues." He is the man who acts with what is called "courage," when met with a situation that calls for "persistence and endurance in the face of obstacles."[5] In a different time and in a different situation, it is impartiality and equity that are morally required, and the man who can meet these requirements is said to be just. In another situation, man finds it necessary to subordinate a pressing desire for an immediate good to the need to work for a more comprehensive good, if he is to be moral, in which case the man who meets this need is said to be temperate. The difference between temperance, justice, and courage is only a difference in emphasis,[6] with this difference in emphasis being determined by what is the most pressing moral issue facing the virtuous man in any given situation.

An analytic approach to the virtues leads man to try to cultivate each virtue in itself, instead of trying to develop a "rounded and positive character."[7] Thus, the tendency to isolate virtues in watertight compartments not only distorts one's understanding of man's moral life, but also involves disastrous practical consequences. When such a tendency is acted upon, morality begins to appear to be a negative and restrictive matter. For example, when temperance is seen as existing in itself rather than as one dimension of a fully integrated moral character, it becomes "mere inhibition, a sour constraint."[8] Dewey's point is that the cataloguing of virtues involves a tendency to turn one or other of these virtues into a "fetish." When we lose sight of the fact that a virtue is a virtue only in so far as it plays a role in, and contributes to, the development of an integrated and unified human person, this virtue takes on a life of its own, and it is this "virtue" in itself that is the important thing. Morality is no longer seen in the positive light of developing a fully integrated human person.

Finally, Dewey brings up another point that is worth considering in any

[4] See footnote 115, Chap. 4, p. 115.
[5] *Ibid.*
[6] *Ibid.*
[7] *Ibid.*, p. 117.
[8] *Ibid.*, p. 116.

treatment of virtues, whether or not this treatment involves a cataloguing of virtues. We must be careful not to be so concrete in our definition of a virtue that we tend to equate the very character of that virtue with the institutions or objects found in our own society.[9] For example, we should be careful not to equate just economic arrangements with the particular type of economic institutions under which we presently live. This does not mean that they are not just, but it does mean that there may be other economic arrangements that may be equally as just or that may more fully meet the demands of justice.

Dewey has made a strong case against an analytic approach to the virtues. It is true that the philosopher is always prone to committing what Alfred North Whitehead has termed the "Fallacy of Misplaced Concreteness," i.e., the fallacy of substituting one's abstractions for the concrete situation.[10] This fallacy could be committed in an analysis of the virtues, if one were led by this analysis to conclude that in the existential situation these virtues are completely cut off from one another. The fact of the matter is that the virtues, which are rather easily separated in discussion, are by no means cut off from one another *in fact*. Hence, anyone who says that he is going to be just without worrying about being temperate or courageous is only fooling himself. For example, the man who is intemperate in his sexual desires will find it extremely difficult, if not impossible, to be just to his wife by refusing to engage in adulterous liaison when the opportunity presents itself. Indeed, he would probably tend to seek out such opportunities. Similarly, there are times when the demands of justice may require a man to face up to real difficulties. If he has not developed the virtue of fortitude, he will be unable to fulfill these demands, because he will be unable to withstand the difficulties involved in fulfilling them. Hence, Dewey is right in pointing out that man's task is to develop a rounded and positive character rather than to cultivate any one virtue in itself.

Although I am in agreement with Dewey's exposition of the difficulties connected with an analytic approach to the virtues, I do not think that it is necessary to abandon this approach. For I think that so long as one is aware of these difficulties, he need not necessarily be led astray by the analysis. Moreover, there are three advantages connected with such an approach.[11]

(1) This approach brings out the fact that when man is confronted with a moral problem, there are usually four basic factors that he must take into consideration in trying to come to grips with this problem. The four factors to be taken into consideration are as follows: First, there is need for knowledge concerning the pertinent moral factors involved in *this* concrete situation. For example, there is need to consider the character of the particular alternatives open to man in the given situation and the possible consequences that would flow from following one of these to the exclusion of others. This need for

---

[9] *Ibid.*, pp. 112–113.

[10] Alfred North Whitehead, *Science and the Modern World* (New York: The Free Press, 1967), p. 51.

[11] These three advantages are discussed in Bourke, *Ethics,* pp. 263–266.

knowledge, and the type of knowledge that is needed, will be explored in the discussion of practical wisdom. A second factor to be considered is the effect of one's action on the good of others. It is perhaps "natural" for a man to view a situation from the perspective of the good that possible lines of action will bring to him. However, the fact is that his actions may influence other human beings, as well as himself. This aspect of the moral situation will be considered in the discussion of justice. A third problem involved in man's attempt to perform the right act is that there is need for him to moderate and regulate his desire for pleasurable goods. This desire if not moderated, may blind man to the demands of his relationships to others or may lead him to enslave his being to some given pleasure or object. This aspect of the moral situation will be investigated in this discussion of temperance.

A fourth area that may cause moral difficulties and may be a constituent feature of a man's moral problem is that concerned with the fact that the goods that man ought to pursue are not always easily attainable, so that there is need for persistence and endurance in the pursuit of such goods. Included under this sort of difficulty is also the fact that man must try to find a balance between the goods pursued and the dangers involved: i.e., there are not only certain dangers that ought to be met in the pursuit of certain goods, but there are also dangers that ought to be avoided because whatever good may be connected with the facing of these dangers is not valuable enough to justify the confrontation of the dangers in question. This area of moral difficulty will be discussed in the consideration of fortitude or courage. Thus an analytic discussion of the cardinal virtues is worthwhile because it fulfills a major task of moral philosophy, viz., that of helping man solve his own moral problems by clarifying these problems and by pointing out the major areas of difficulty to be considered in meeting these problems.

(2) Another advantage of this analytic approach is that it calls to man's attention those dimensions of his being which must be cultivated if he is to be equipped to meet these moral problems. If man is to meet the moral challenge of his existence, he must sharpen and develop his intellectual capacity to grasp the concrete moral significance of a situation and to arrive at a proper judgment of this situation (the virtue of practical wisdom). He must also develop the appetitive dimensions of his existence so that he can respond with ease, consistency, and pleasure to the good of others, and can with the same ease, consistency, and pleasure respond in a proper way toward pleasurable and difficult goods. For it is true that unless a man's appetitive capacities in these areas are properly developed, his knowledge of moral philosophy is not likely to make much difference in his life. At best, it may only make him feel uneasy in the knowledge that he is not living up to the ideals which he knows to be right. What is more likely in such a case is that he will be so controlled by his vices as to shrug off such knowledge as being simply irrelevant to him. Hence, the task of building a moral character, of becoming moral, is a task for the *whole* man, requiring all the resources he can bring to bear on this task. It is thus a

task requiring the cultivation of the appetitive, as well as of the cognitive, dimensions of man's existence.

There is another facet to this second justification of an analytic approach to virtues that ought to be mentioned. Aristotle has indicated that if one wants to distinguish between moral and immoral pleasures, he ought to look to the good man, for those things in which the good man finds his pleasures are morally good. The discussion of the various capacities that man must develop if he is to meet his moral problems, and of the character of such development, represents an attempt to sketch a *general* outline of those factors that constitute the "good man." The key word in the preceding sentence was "general." It is beyond our scope and our capacity to depict the "good man" in his full existential complexity, "in the flesh," as it were, for there is no one definition of the "good man." All that moral philosophy can hope to do is to point to the different facets of the human person that play a major role in his moral life, and the general type of development of these facets that will equip him to act morally. The accomplishment of this task represents a step toward the establishment of those secondary principles that Mill found to be essential if moral philosophy is to help man solve his moral problems.

(3) Finally, this analytic approach is valuable because it serves to make us aware of the full complexity of any human act that is said to be truly virtuous. Although the four cardinal virtues do not exhaust the full range of virtues open to man, they are all implicated, to some degree, in every virtuous act that a man performs. Any morally virtuous act must arise out of a proper consideration of the concrete demands of a situation (practical wisdom); it must be properly ordered with respect to the goods of others (justice); it must be moderated and regulated with respect to goods as pleasurable (temperance); finally, it must be done with the proper firmness and persistence in the pursuit of difficult goods (fortitude or courage). It would undoubtedly be better, if man were able to talk about the complexity of a single, virtuous act, all at once, without going through the process of discussing first this feature and then that feature of the one act. However, the fact of the matter is that man must go through this process if he is to get any clarity in his speaking, writing, or thinking about virtue.

In conclusion, because I see these advantages in an analytic treatment of the virtues and because I think that the dangers which Dewey has pointed out as being involved in this approach are avoidable, I shall proceed to an analytic consideration of the virtues, always keeping in mind the danger of being misled by this analysis to view the virtues as existing in "watertight compartments."

2. THE NATURE AND GROWTH OF HUMAN HABITS

In his famous treatment of habits, William James placed habits outside the arena of human consciousness, pointing out that *"habit diminishes the con-*

scious attention with which our acts are performed."[12] Thus, a man learning to swim or to skate must pay close attention to what he is doing. However, once these activities have become habitual, man performs them without thinking. "The marksman sees the bird, and, before he knows it, he has aimed and shot."[13] In short, habitual acts are simply a reflex response to a given "cue," occurring without the intervention of thought or volition.[14] James points out that the more activities man can relegate to the area of habitual behavior, the better will his life be—provided, of course, that these activities are beneficial to man. For the higher powers of his mind will become more free to concern themselves with their own proper work as more of his actions become purely automatic.[15] Thus, the major thrust of James's treatment of habits is to place them in an *infra*-conscious area of behavior.

If this identification of habitual acts with purely reflex acts were accepted without qualification, a case could be made against the development of habits in the moral sphere of human action. For, if we were to apply James's conception of habits to the man of "good moral habits," we would be saying in effect that this man had become a "moral automaton," which is a contradiction in terms. For, as was seen in Chapter II, a man is a moral agent only in so far as he acts freely, which means that he acts with a conscious awareness of what he is about. Using James's conception of habit, it would be necessary to say that precisely in so far as a man has developed habits of dealing justly with his fellow man, or of being moderate in his enjoyments of pleasures, he has ceased being a moral agent in these areas—a being whose acts proceed from his intellect and will. As habitual, these acts have become automatic, occurring as a reflex response to a certain cue without the intervention of cognition or volition.

It might be held that a man is responsible for the development of the habit of dealing justly with others. Granted this point, the fact remains that James's conception of habit leads to the conclusion that as a man develops moral habits, he becomes less conscious of those areas in which those habits have been developed, and hence, is stunting his growth as a moral agent. The man who has developed the habit of justice is less aware of the demands of justice in a given situation than the man who never spent a day in his life trying to be just. If the development of habits in a certain sphere diminishes our conscious awareness of that sphere, it follows that the more habits man forms in his moral life, the more blind, the more unaware he becomes of the moral dimensions of his existence. James himself did not draw out this implication of his position. However, the fact is that the position does carry this implication.

The difficulty this position raises in the moral area is not the only reason for questioning the opposition between habit and consciousness. What are we to

[12] William James, *The Principles of Psychology* (New York: Dover, 1950), Vol. I, p. 114.
[13] *Ibid.*
[14] *Ibid.*, pp. 114–116.
[15] *Ibid.*, p. 122.

say about mathematicians, physicists, biologists? It would seem that these men can also be said to have developed habits in that after working and studying in certain areas, they have been changed so that they can now deal more easily and consistently with problems in their respective areas than before. The mathematician is not said to become less conscious of what is involved in mathematics as he becomes more habituated to dealing with mathematical issues. Indeed, he is "more alive to," more conscious of, the issues, problems, and possibilities involved in a mathematical universe of discourse than is the man who has not become habituated to thinking mathematically.

It is clear that habit cannot be unqualifiedly identified with a diminishing of one's consciousness of the area in which a habit has been developed. If the conception of habit is to be grounded in the facts of human existence, it must be admitted that not all the habits which man acquires involve a diminishing of of his awareness. James's conception of habit must be broadened to include those habits which serve to heighten man's awareness of the area in which a habit has been developed.

An indication of the need for such a broadening is found in James's treatment of habit. In speaking of the role of habit in the education of youth, he points out that the youth who keeps to his studies will one day note that "between all the details of his business, the *power of judging* in all that class of matter [the subject matter in which the student invested the time and effort that goes with mastering a field] will have built itself up within him."[16] However, James's formal treatment of the character of habits is so emphatic in identifying them with reflex acts that it does not seem to leave any room for the type of habit that builds up the power of judging.

George Klubertanz's treatment of habits explicitly allows for those habits that involve a diminishing of awareness and those that involve a heightening of consciousness. He distinguishes between "mastery habits," and "automatism habits." Automatism habits are those that are not necessarily dependent on the function of intellectual awareness or volition for either their acquisition or use. Although a certain minimal amount of intellectual awareness may be required to acquire these habits and may also be involved in their use, such an awareness is not an *essential* constituent in the habit itself. It is possible that such a habit may become so separated from intellectual awareness and volition that the introduction of such an awareness into a situation in which this habit might function would serve to frustrate the habit. Unlike automatism habits, mastery habits cannot possibly be acquired or used apart from human intellection and volition. The work of intellect and will is an *essential* factor in both the acquisition and use of mastery habits.[17]

The distinction between mastery and automatism habits may be clarified by examples. Dancing is an example of an automatism habit. One need have no

[16] *Ibid.*, p. 127.

[17] George P. Klubertanz, *Habits and Virtues* (New York: Appleton-Century-Crofts, 1965), pp. 95–96.

intellectual knowledge of the laws of rhythm or of the laws relating to bodily movements. Hence, it is clear that a minimal amount of intellection, if any, is necessary to acquire this skill. Moreover, it is important to keep intellectual awareness out of the use of this habit as can be seen by the fact that if one begins to think about which step follows another or which movement follows another, he only confuses himself and destroys the fluid movement that is essential to the dance. The dancer must have so developed certain capacities that he takes his "cue" from the music, reacting without the intervention or intrusion of thought to the beat and rhythm of the music.

A story told concerning the famous New York Yankee catcher Yogi Berra may also serve to exemplify habits that are automatisms. Berra was a notorious "bad ball" hitter, swinging at balls that were not even close to the strike zone. With the hope of making him a better hitter, someone advised him to think before he swung at a ball. He tried this, and failed to match his previous success as a batter. The experience led him to conclude that it is impossible to think and hit at the same time. He was right. Thinking of where the ball is, or of the movement of one's feet in the course of a swing is destructive of the quick reflexes, timing, and coordination necessary to being a good hitter. These examples, and many more, could be advanced to show that man acquires certain habits that fit the Jamesian conception of habitual acts as automatic or reflex responses to a certain "cue," or stimulus.[18]

However, the fact that men can become mathematicians, physicists, or philosophers indicates that not all the habits acquired by man are automatism habits. Although all of these disciplines call into play capacities other than the human intellect—capacities such as the imagination—the fact remains that they are primarily intellectual undertakings so that if one is to become proficient in those areas it is absolutely essential that his intellect be so developed as to make his thinking in these areas easy, consistent, and pleasant. For example, the habit of doing mathematics can be neither acquired nor used apart from the intellect. A mathematician is not one who accidentally happens to guess the right answer to a problem without knowing why the answer is right or how certain axioms or premises lead to that answer. As Klubertanz points out, a person dealing with a problem in a scientific way need not say to himself that he is going to think in terms of the rules of scientific thought. However, if he is to think scientifically, he must actually be thinking, and his thinking must be using the canons of the particular science at issue.[19] Whereas one can acquire the habit of swimming without being aware of the principles of water displacement that underlie this activity or of why certain movements of the arms and feet keep him afloat, he cannot acquire the habit of thinking mathematically or philosophically without being aware of the principles and relationships involved in such thinking.

Klubertanz points out that it is possible to go through a process of reasoning

[18] *Ibid.*, pp. 83–88.
[19] *Ibid.*, p. 90.

without really understanding the reasoning involved, with the results of such a procedure being as follows:

> Nothing happens except that one understands each proposition separately. A student may understand a proof sentence by sentence; he may go over the proof hundreds of times as a series of propositions which *de facto* follow one another in such a series. From such repetition he will never learn the proof; the connections are mechanical, external, and not reasoned. We cannot simply go through the motions to acquire an intellectual habit. Intellectual habits are not acquired unless there is in the process an awareness of what is being done, an awareness of the process itself.[20]

This statement is important to the purpose of this chapter because it can be used to differentiate the morally virtuous man from the "moral automaton," if we may be allowed to use such a contradictory phrase. Just as the man who merely "parrots" the reasoning and the conclusions of the mathematician is not himself a mathematician, so also the moral automaton, whose life is lived in a mechanical and external fashion—simply following the customs of his society with no awareness of the basis of these customs or of their moral implications— is not the morally virtuous man. Although the virtues of temperance, fortitude, and justice are primarily modifications of the appetitive dimensions of human existence, they are mastery habits in that an intellectual awareness of the moral factors of a situation is an essential ingredient in these virtues.

One of the factors that may account for the tendency to confuse mastery habits with automatism habits lies in the fact that one, who has acquired a mastery habit in mathematics, for example, may be able to solve a mathematical problem so easily and quickly that his solution seems to be a purely reflex act. We marvel at the speed and ease with which the mathematician has handled a problem. We are tempted to say that he has solved the problem "without thinking." The truth of the matter is that he did think and that his intellect has become so attuned to mathematical issues that he can see connections immediately. His acquisition of the habit of thinking mathematically has not narrowed his intellectual awareness of mathematical issues, but has broadened this awareness, thus enabling him to see at a glance principles and connections in a problem that could be seen by the mathematical neophyte only with a great deal of difficulty, if at all.

At this point, it will be well to try to tie this discussion together by giving a definition of the nature of habits and by exploring the role of habits in human life. Basically, a habit, whether it be a mastery or automatism habit, is a qualitative determination of a capacity or group of capacities within a being enabling that being to act with ease, consistency, and pleasure.[21] When a baby is born into the world there is not much that he can do very well. Given the opportu-

[20] *Ibid.*, p. 91.
[21] *Ibid.*, p. 101.

nity and sound physical and neurological characteristics, he will develop such motor skills as walking and running. Provided with a proper educational environment, he will gain some acquaintance with various facets of his environment. The importance of the development of good habits in man's life lies in the fact that habits are perfective of man, strengthening the resources that are available in his own being so that he can use these resources to exercise a mastery over himself and his world. For example, the development of the habit of physics has enabled men to extend mankind's control over the physical forces of nature.

Moreover, through the development of habits, man can take advantage of the historical character of his existence in that the habits he has developed in the past will help him to meet the problems and difficulties of his present and of future situations with an ease that would be impossible had he not developed certain habits. Indeed, there may be certain problems which are simply beyond the capacities of a man who has not perfected these capacities through habits. For example, there are certain problems in physics that the untrained layman cannot begin to understand, whereas the physicist not only understands the problem, but is also aware of a number of possible solutions.

The development of habits is important to man because the capacities with which he is born are not adequate to dealing with the complexities of life, unless these capacities have been nurtured, strengthened, and determined through the development of habits. This point was illustrated by the example of man dealing with issues in physics, but it is applicable to all areas of human endeavor, including the moral area. Just as man is not born a physicist or a philosopher, so also he is not born a moral agent. If a man is to gain any depth as a moral agent, if he is to begin to be aware of the complexities and possibilities inherent in the moral dimensions of his existence, if he is to be able to take effective moral action in the face of these complexities, he must develop habits in those areas that are involved in these dimensions. Unless a man works to develop habits relating to the moral issues of life, he will be as unprepared to deal with the complexities of these issues as the layman in physics is unprepared to meet the deeper problems of physics.

This discussion of the nature of habits and of their value to human life leads to the question of the way in which habits are acquired. Since the virtues are mastery habits, the consideration of this problem will be restricted to the way these habits are acquired. This restriction is important, because, as Klubertanz points out, not all habits are developed in *exactly* the same way, although, generally speaking, there are certain factors common to the development of all habits.[22] Aristotle emphasizes one of the factors that is essential to the development of all habits, whether they be mastery or automatism habits.

The things which we have to learn before we can do them we learn by doing: men become builders by building houses, and harpists by playing the harp. Simi-

[22] *Ibid.*, p. 131.

larly, we become just by the practice of just actions, self-controlled by exercising self-control . . . In a word, characteristics develop from corresponding activities.[23]

A man does not become temperate by merely thinking about temperance, just as a man does not become a biologist by merely thinking about how nice it would be to be a biologist. If man is to develop a habit, if he is to become a certain type of person, he must actually engage in those activities that will exercise and call into play those dimensions of his existence that are pertinent to the habit in question or to the type of person that he is to become.

This position seems to involve a vicious circle in that it seems to be saying both that a man must perform certain activities in order to acquire habits and that he cannot perform these activities unless he has acquired these habits. Aristotle states the problem very well.

> The question may be raised what we mean by saying that men become just by performing just actions and self-controlled by practicing self-control. For if they perform just actions and exercise self-control, they are already just and self-controlled.[24]

It is true that if an act is to be said to be just in the most proper sense, it must proceed from a character that is just. It is possible to consider an act *in abstraction* from the concrete agent from whom it proceeds so that we may speak of the act *abstractly considered* as just.

An act that proceeds from an agent who is not just, but which happens to give to another his due, is not as completely and fully just as one that proceeds from an agent in whom the habit of justice is deeply ingrained. In short, the full existential character of an act in the moral sphere is determined by the character of the agent from whom it proceeds as well as by its effects or outcome. Hence, existentially considered, an act is most properly just when it gives another his due and when it proceeds from an agent in whom the habit of acting justly has taken root. This point does not invalidate the view that a man becomes just or builds a certain moral character by performing acts that are just or that conform to that character. It is true that while he is in the process of becoming just, the acts that he performs will not be done with the same ease, consistency, and pleasure that will characterize his just acts once he has acquired the habit of justice. However, these acts can be said to be "just" in the sense that they do give to others their due.

The man who is trying to be just by performing just acts is reaching beyond himself either to some ideal or to some man that he is trying to imitate. However, *to the extent that a man acquires the habit of justice,* his just acts will be more firmly rooted in his own existence in that they will arise out of his own being rather than out of his imitation of others or out of an ideal grasped by

---

[23] See footnote 76, Chap. IV, 1103ª 35, 1103ᵇ 21, p. 34.
[24] *Ibid.,* 1105ª 18–20, pp. 38–39.

his intellect, but which has not taken hold of him as an appetitive as well as an intellectual being. Any individual act of justice thus is more properly said to be just in so far as it proceeds from a being in whom the habit of justice has more firmly taken root. Of course, this does not mean that any man is the fullness of justice, but it does mean that a man can succeed, more or less, in making himself just so that his acts of justice proceed from the fullness of his being.

The emphasis up to this point has been on the performing of acts in order to acquire and develop habits. However, a purely mechanical performance or repetition of acts, merely "going through the motions," will not suffice for the growth and develpment of mastery habits. The *way* in which the acts are performed will have an important bearing on whether or not they will add a new dimension to one's existence in the form of a habit. James has emphasized this point in stating that in attempting to acquire a habit, "we must take care to *launch ourselves with as strong and decided an initiative as possible.*"[25]

Klubertanz points out that if the performance of acts is to lead to the development of a habit, this performance must be marked by what he terms a certain "intensity." A man must be wholeheartedly engaged or involved in an activity if it is to become habitual. It is important to note that such a wholehearted involvement is not identical with overcoming great difficulties. Thus, it is not necessary to place oneself in a situation in which the practice of temperance would be very difficult in order to perform temperate acts with intensity. Such situations may offer the *occasion* for these acts, but they do not necessarily *cause* them. Temperate acts may or may not be performed in difficult situations. Hence, the intensity of an act is determined not by the character of the external circumstances surrounding it, but by the degree of involvement in the act by the person performing it. Finally, it ought to be noted that the intensity of an act is not equated with strain and effort. An act is said to be intense in so far as it occupies a prominent role in the agent's consciousness, becoming the center of his attention.[26]

This section has dealt with the nature of habits, their contribution to human life, and the way in which mastery habits can be acquired and developed.

3. THE APPETITIVE CARDINAL VIRTUES: TEMPERANCE, FORTITUDE, AND JUSTICE

This section will be devoted to a consideration of certain habits that modify the appetitive character of human existence in such a way that man will be able to perform morally good acts with ease, pleasure, and consistency. Habits that bear directly on the moral dimensions of human existence are

[25] See footnote 12, Vol. I, p. 123.
[26] See footnote 17, pp. 135–142 on which this discussion of the intensity of acts was primarily based.

referred to as either *virtues* or *vices,* depending on whether they contribute to man's moral betterment or debasement. Those habits are said to be virtues which enable a man to act morally with ease, consistency, and pleasure, whereas those habits are termed vices which enable a man to act immorally with ease, consistency, and pleasure.

The distinction between virtues and vices, between habits that are good or bad, viewed from a moral perspective, indicates that not all habits make a positive contribution to human life. The discussion in the previous section concerning the role of habits in human life was restricted to a consideration of "good" habits. It is clear that if a man develops a bad habit in a certain area of endeavor, he will find it very difficult to act properly in this area. The man who forms a bad habit in a certain area will be able to perform wrong acts in that area with a certain ease, consistency, and pleasure.

For example, it is easy for the sadist to perform sadistic acts, and these acts give him "pleasure" in so far as pleasure is understood, according to the disussion in Chapter IV, as that which complements an activity, which is in keeping with the character of the agent performing the act. The vicious man is the one who performs vicious acts easily, consistently, and with pleasure. It is because vicious acts have become so much a part of him that he can perform them with ease and pleasure. These acts complement and fulfill his vicious character. It is also because such acts have taken root in his being that the vicious man finds it difficult to change his ways, even when he may come to realize either that he is enslaving himself to some object or pleasure or that he is reducing his fellow man to an object. Having realized the error of his ways, he may try to act differently, but he will find that his vicious ways have become so much a part of him that his existential resources all tend toward the vicious acts. He will be in the position of the man who is described by Spinoza as being "often forced to follow the worse, although he sees the better before him."[27]

The task of the remainder of this section will be to explore the character of those virtues that determine man to act morally with respect to biological and pleasurable goods (temperance), the difficult good (fortitude), and the good of others (justice). Basically these virtues are modifications of the appetitive dimensions of human existence. They modify man's appetitive responses to the goods of his world. However, it would be a mistake to think that the work of the human intellect is completely isolated from these virtues. Man does not live in isolated compartments, one intellectual, the other appetitive. All virtues are mastery habits and hence cannot be separated from human intellection. One who has no idea of what he is doing, who is unaware of the

---

[27] See footnote 4, Chap. II, Part IV, p. 282. Consistency has been given as a third characteristic of habitual action. This characteristic is meant to emphasize the fact that an act is not said to be habitual simply because a man happened to perform it once or twice. The successful performance of an act in one instance does not mean that the agent performing the act has been so modified that he can perform this same type of act in other situations with ease and with the same success.

moral features of his activities cannot be said to be temperate. Granted that the intellect must thus be involved in every virtuous act, the fact remains that man responds to his concrete moral problems appetitively as well as intellectually. Hence, it is necessary to cultivate human appetites so that these will respond properly and morally to the various goods that are part of the human condition. Just as man is not born with a knowledge of what is morally good, but must work to develop his intellect in order to be able to gain this knowledge, so also he is not born with the proper appetitive responses to moral good, he must also work to develop these responses. In short, the task of building a moral character is a task involving the whole man, man in both his appetitive and intellectual dimensions.

This section will be devoted to exploring some of the factors involved in the appetitive side of this task. It is hoped that treating each of these virtues in its turn, will shed some light both on their respective roles in the formation of man's moral character and, in a general way, on how man must try to relate himself to the goods of his world.

a. TEMPERANCE

"Common-sense" discussions of moral problems tend to view them as involving a choice between good and evil. This is an overly simplified view of man's moral condition. If man were faced with deciding between a course of action that is wholly and simply good and one that is wholly and simply evil, it would be impossible to account for the difficulties that confront him when he wants to make the right decision, and for the uncertainty that such a man often feels both before and after making such a decision. The fact of the matter is that in any serious and significant moral problem, the issue is often between two goods and man is in the position of trying to discover which of these two goods is moral, i.e. in conformity with reason's grasp of the human community and human subjectivity in that community, and which is immoral.

For example, if there were no good at all connected with an adulterous union, adultery would not be a moral problem for man. However, the fact is that such a union involves at least the good of the immediate and pleasurable gratification of sexual intercourse so that man must weigh this good against the good of being faithful to his spouse, or against what may be a wider, more inclusive and significant human good, which is grasped by reason's reflection on the human community and the place of sexual intercourse in the community. Finally, although this conflict may be a purely intellectual matter in the reflective atmosphere of the class room, it is by no means an exclusively intellectual matter in the concrete situation. The adulterous union does fulfill a real human appetite for sexual gratification.

Basically, temperance is the virtue which modifies man's appetitive response to what may be termed the "biological" goods of the world: food, drink, and sex. The use of the word "biological" does not mean that these objects are bad, nor does it mean that they may not also serve dimensions of human existence other than the biological. Without reducing the satisfaction of psychological needs to the biological, the fact is that these needs are fulfilled through engaging in such acts as eating, drinking, and sexual intercourse which are biological activities in the sense that man must use certain bodily functions in performing these acts. The virtue of temperance so modifies and determines man's appetite for the goods connected with these activities that the appetites respond to these goods according to the demands of reason, which places them in their proper role in the life of a human subject as a member of the human community.

The temperate person is not one who is engaged in the foolish process of trying to destroy his appetite for these goods, or to act as though such an appetite were nonexistent. Temperance involves the _moderation_ and _control_ of man's appetition for such goods in the sense that this appetition is determined to play a positive role in human life, contributing to the growth of human subjectivity in the human community so that these goods do not control this life in such a way that man is reduced to a being mastered by pleasures offered by these goods. The temperate man so responds to the goods involving such pleasures that, in effect, he asserts that the human subject does not exist _for_ these goods, but that they exist for him as a subject in the human community. He has so habituated himself that he comes to feel an aversion toward the immoral use of biological goods and an attraction toward the morally suitable use of these goods. Such aversion and attraction are constitutive factors in the virtue of temperance.[28]

In order to specify further the character of temperance, it might be well to distinguish the temperate man from the man who may be described as the "continent" man. Both men may be said to be virtuous. However, whereas the temperate man has so determined his appetite for food, drink, and sex that it responds with ease, consistency, and pleasure to the proper use of these goods, the continent man has not so habituated his appetitive response, with the result being that he can control and moderate his response to these goods only with great difficulty and by the "force of his will," as it were.[29] For example, whereas the continent man is in a constant turmoil in trying to behave morally with respect to the good of sexual intercourse, although he is consistently able to overcome this turmoil and to do the right thing, the temperate man has so modified his appetite for sexual pleasure that he can more easily respond to such pleasure in a moral manner.

This distinction does not mean that the temperate man is apathetic to the goods of food, drink, and sex. Rather the difference lies in the fact that the temperate man has achieved an internal unity and harmony of being in accordance with man's character as a subject in the human community that is lacking to the continent man, who is at "odds with himself," in trying to react morally

[28] See _S.T._ II–II, Q. 143, a.1.
[29] _Ibid._, Q. 155, a.1–4.

to these goods. This unity and self-possession in the face of pleasurable goods is the essential feature of temperance.[30] It is preferable to the division and inner turmoil of the continent man not simply because the temperate man has an easier time of it, but especially because such unity and self-possession provide a firm foundation for the growth and development of man's moral character in other areas of moral endeavor, e.g., those concerned with discovering what is the concrete moral good in any particular situation, and those concerned with introducing a moral order in the relations among men. The man who must constantly struggle to bring himself under control will have difficulty in deepening and expanding the area of his moral growth. Finally, it should be noted that since no man ever achieves the full perfection of temperance, just as no man ever achieves the full perfection of any of the other virtues, there will always be a certain amount of effort and difficulty in his life as he tries to grow in temperance and the other virtues, a process of growth that will be open to the continent man only after he has become temperate.

There are, of course, goods other than those of food, drink, and sex that threaten the self-possession and inner harmony of man. For example, there is the good of achieving a place of status and honor in one's society for undertaking and completing a certain type of honorable task. It is certainly obvious that man should do the best he can in pursuing a task that will call on, develop, and perfect whatever capacities he may possess. However, there is a danger to human subjectivity in the attraction of honorable vocations or pre-eminent goods. This danger lies in the fact that although a man may be fully aware of his inability to engage in a certain vocation, he may be so attracted to it that he cannot pursue the vocation which is most suited to his talents. Man is in danger of becoming victimized and enslaved by such goods in that his attraction to them is such that he cannot perfect the capacities that are in him for some other good because he is so taken by the good that is beyond his reach. He knows very well that the good is beyond him; yet, he is so appetitively drawn to it that he cannot put his resources to work for the task that is within his reach. The virtue of humility regulates and moderates man's appetitive response to pre-eminent and honorable goods in such a way that the response accords with one's awareness of the individual's capacities to deal with such goods.[31]

Humility, as here understood, is not a stupid unwillingness to acknowledge and to use to the fullest those capacities which a man possesses. It involves rather a modification of one's appetitive response to pre-eminent goods that prevents those among these goods which one knows to be beyond one's capacities from so disrupting the unity of the self that he becomes unable to perform those tasks that lie within the scope of his resources. Just as temperance develops the unity and self-possession of a man in the face of biological goods, so also

[30] Joseph Pieper, *Fortitude and Temperance*, trans. by Daniel F. Coogan (New York: Pantheon Books, 1954), pp. 47–53.
[31] *Ibid.*, pp. 98–102. *S.T.* II–II, Q. 161, a.1–6.

humility develops this same unity and self-possession in the face of pre-eminent goods.

In concluding this discussion of temperance and the related virtue humility, it will be well to point out how they are related to the growth of human subjectivity in the human community. The need for these virtues flows from the limited and conditioned character of human existence. This means that man's pursuit of pleasurable and pre-eminent goods will be conditioned by some factor or factors. There is no escaping this fact. The only question is whether man will be conditioned by these goods themselves or whether he will make himself as a human subject the factor that conditions these goods. In dealing with pleasurable or pre-eminent goods, man can decide whether to make himself as a subject in the human community the principle underlying his conditioned existence so that these goods are made to exist for him, or to make the goods themselves the determining principle with the result that he exists for them.

b. FORTITUDE

Man's world is not simply and exclusively a world of pleasurable and pre-eminent goods. It is also a world of difficulties and dangers. It would be very convenient, if human existence were "compartmentalized" in such a way that the goods of this world existed in one section, and the dangers and difficulties in another. However, such is not the case. This means that man often finds himself in the position of being able to attain certain goods only if he is willing and able to face up to the dangers and difficulties of his world. Thus, man's moral project is not limited to regulating and moderating his appetitive response to pleasurable and pre-eminent goods, but must be expanded to include the task of strengthening his appetitive response to the difficulties and dangers that may be involved in fulfilling his moral responsibilities.

We are now dealing with that area of man's moral life which requires the cultivation of the virtue of *fortitude*. It is not enough that man know that there are dangers and difficulties involved in the realization of moral values. If he is to actually realize these values, his appetitive response to the dangers that he must face in working for them must be such that these dangers do not turn him away from his moral task. Fortitude does not blind a man to the dangers inherent in any given attempt to realize moral values, nor does it make him "fearless," if this term is taken to mean that he feels no fear in a fearful situation. It must be emphasized that there is an intimate connection between fortitude and moral goods in the sense that it is a virtue enabling a man to face the dangers necessary to achieve these goods. Thus, a man who puts himself in danger of death for no moral good is said to be foolhardy, not courageous.

Both Aristotle and Thomas Aquinas maintain that the virtue of fortitude, most properly and strictly understood, refers to the strengthening of man's appetitive response to the danger of death, which is the greatest danger that he might be called to face in his attempts to meet his moral responsibilities.[32] However, the word can be extended to apply to other dangers that man must face. Fortitude involves the ability to *endure* the dangers connected with achieving or sustaining moral values, as well as the ability to take the initiative, to *attack* in the face of those dangers threatening the realization of moral values.[33]

Since man is a limited being, there may be times when he must endure certain difficulties because he may not then and there possess the wherewithal to overcome these difficulties and sorrows. As a limited being, man is open to physical, economic, political influences, to mention only a few, which are beyond his control. There are times when these influences on him are such as to cause him sorrow and when he cannot escape these sorrows in a moral manner. In short, man must be *patient* in his pursuit of moral values, which means that he must not allow himself to be so overcome by the present difficulties under which he lives and the sorrows that they cause as to surrender his moral responsibilities and the whole moral enterprise.[34]

It is undoubtedly true that in many societies, those living off the sufferings and misfortunes of others have abused the notion of patience, using it as a type of opiate to stultify the moral awareness of those enduring the evils of an unjust political or economic system. However, the abuse of this notion does not mean that there is no place for endurance in human existence. As a limited being, man cannot make all the sufferings and difficulties of a given situation disappear simply by a wave of the hand. He is not always in the position of being able to change those factors of his existence that cause him sorrow.

Having made this point, it must be emphasized that the endurance involved in being patient is not a wholly inactive and passive matter. The patient man is engaged in achieving an inner unity and self-possession that is necessary to him if he is to continue to pursue his moral responsibilities in a world of suffering. He endures sufferings and difficulties for a moral purpose, i.e., to so control and assert himself in the midst of such suffering that he does not lose sight of his moral responsibilities and of the moral ways to work toward the eventual alleviation of such suffering. This means that there is nothing to prevent the patient man from rising up against injustices when he thinks that such an attack can be accomplished in a moral way.[35] Patience does not involve the enduring of suffering when there are moral ways and means to overcome such suffering.

There is another factor of human existence that requires the cultivation of a virtue similar to that of fortitude if man is to accomplish his moral task. Man is an historical being, a being who must grow and develop through time if he is to achieve his moral perfection. He cannot always fulfill his moral responsibilities in an instant. The length of time that may be required for the fulfill-

---

[32] See footnote 76, Chap. IV, 1115 a.30–35, pp. 69–70. S.T. II–II, Q. 123, a.4.
[33] See footnote 30, pp. 24–33.
[34] See S.T. II–II, Q. 136.
[35] Ibid., Q. 136, a.4, ad.3.

ment of a moral task very often makes the accomplishment of that task difficult. One may *know* that a task is good, and may *know* that it will take time to accomplish, but may be lacking the "drive" necessary to bring the task to its completion. Man must therefore develop the virtue of perseverance in order to meet this difficulty involved in his striving for moral good.[36] For the man who perseveres, time becomes an ally, not an enemy in his moral undertakings in the sense that he is not overcome by the length of time connected with achieving a moral goal, but simply uses whatever time necessary for this achievement.

c. JUSTICE

The virtue of justice is directly concerned with the moral ordering of relations among men. The present discussion will limit itself to a consideration of three conceptions of justice: the equalitarian, meritarian, and welfare conceptions. The equalitarian conception holds that all men are to be treated equally. The meritarian conception holds that all men are to be treated in accordance with their merit. There is some room for differences within this conception, depending on what one considers to be the merit that ought to be taken into account in attempts to decide what is due to a man in justice. For example, one might say that a man's merit is determined by the quantity and/or quality of his work, whereas another might hold that his merit is determined by the quality of his moral character. When we speak of the meritarian conception of justice we shall mean the justice that is determined by a man's work, by what he produces. The welfare conception of justice holds that a man ought to be treated in accordance with his needs.

No claim is made that the above list exhausts all the possible meanings of justice. However, the list does include those meanings that are most central to the discussions of justice in our culture. The mere listing of these meanings helps clarify, but certainly does not resolve, the question concerning the meaning of justice. The Belgian philosopher Chaim Perelman does a fine job in pointing out what is involved in this question. He points out that there are three possible approaches that one might take when confronted with diverse conceptions of justice. One might hold that the conceptions are simply diverse and that there is no underlying common conceptual bond that might unite them. Another approach might argue that only one of the conceptions is the true conception of justice and that the others are to be rejected as being false conceptions. Finally, one might try to discover what is the common bond underlying these various conceptions.[37] Perelman himself takes this last approach. It will be well for us to follow him in this approach, since it is only after working through this approach that one might have an adequate ground for taking one of the other two positions.

[36] *Ibid.*, Q. 137.
[37] Chaim Perelman, *The Idea of Justice and the Problem of Argument*, trans. from the French by John Petrie (New York: The Humanities Press, 1963), pp. 10–11.

Perelman searches for a conception of justice that is more abstract and more general than the three previously mentioned—one that could include these three in that it could be specified first by one characteristic and then by another, and thus could be made to fit first the meritarian conception and then the welfare conception.[38] He finds that the notion of equality is involved in the various conceptions of justice. The presence of this notion is obvious in the equalitarian conception. It is found also in the meritarian conception in that this conception involves the view that those doing the same sort of work ought to receive the same compensation. It is also present in the welfare view of justice in that this view holds that men having the same need should receive the same treatment. Hence, it would appear that a more abstract and more inclusive conception of justice than the three described would define justice as a principle of action which demands that beings belonging to one and the same category be treated in the same way.[39]

Perelman is rightly not satisfied with this definition. He points out that it may be well and good to say that beings of the same essential category ought to be treated in the same way. However, this position does not help decide the important issue concerning the factors that are to be considered in placing beings in the same essential category. Whereas the welfare conception of justice makes needs the decisive factor in determining what constitutes essential categories, the meritarian conception makes the quality or the quantity of one's work the decisive factor.

Perelman points out that the equalitarian notion that is at the basis of this purely abstract and formal definition of justice is itself open to question. He asks for the basis of the demand that all those belonging to one and the same essential category be accorded equal treatment. He sees this demand as flowing from the fact that having treated a being belonging to a certain category in a certain way, we can establish a rule that all other beings belonging to this category be similarly treated. Hence, the notion of equality that seemed to provide a formal basis for the various conceptions of justice is itself rooted in a more ultimate basis—the decision to act according to some rule. The various conceptions of justice are formally united not by the notion of equality, but by the commitment to apply a rule to all members of an essential category. Equality of treatment is thus itself seen to be a logical consequence of following a rule. The various conceptions of justice differ in that they would insist on the following of different rules, but they agree in presenting justice as the application of a rule.[40]

Although Perelman's purely abstract and formal consideration of justice does not tell us which conceptions of justice are to be accepted and which rejected, it is valuable in specifying what is at issue in the ethician's reflections on the nature of justice. Since the various conceptions of justice involve the following

[38] *Ibid.*, p. 15.
[39] *Ibid.*, p. 16.
[40] *Ibid.*, pp. 40–41.

of certain rules, it is necessary to ask ourselves whether these rules can be incorporated into a single value system. This problem will be dealt with by first considering the values that are being established by the meritarian, equalitarian, and welfare rules taken singly.

As a dependent being, man finds that many factors in his world are useful in helping him to keep alive and to develop his capacities for freedom. For example, plants and animals help him in that they provide him with food, with materials which he can use to clothe himself, and, in general, help make his life more pleasant, contributing to his health and well-being. He also finds the objects of technology useful to him. Automobiles and airplanes help him to get where he wants to go; refrigerators help preserve his foods until he is ready to use them. What is important with regard to the place of meritarian justice in human life is that it is not only nonhuman things that are useful to man. As a social being, he also finds the work and achievements of other men useful to him.

A man is not said to owe anything in justice to his automobile, which transported him to a distant city, although he is said to be indebted to the service station attendant, who provided him with gasoline and who helped him find the right road when he was lost. The difference between one's relationships to nonhuman things that are useful to him and to human beings, who are also useful, lies in the fact that human beings are beings capable of freedom and of self-possession. In so far as they possess this capacity, they do not exist solely for the benefit of others. When another man performs a service for me, I acknowledge that he is an end in himself and not simply an instrument for me by admitting that I owe him something in return for services rendered.

This discussion serves to bring out the point that meritarian justice is grounded in the character of man as a being who is an end in himself and who is also able to be of use to his fellow man. The value which underlies the meritarian rule is the realization of the community of ends. This rule is directed toward ordering the social relations among men in a way that contributes to the realization of this community. Granted the validity of this position, it is now necessary to see whether the equalitarian and welfare conceptions of justice can fit into this value system.

One can make short work of the equalitarian conception of justice by interpreting it as denying the moral significance of the diversity of human talents, needs, and interests. Such an interpretation loses sight of that feature of this conception which makes it a morally significant rule. The equalitarian conception of justice informs an individual that he and his loved ones—his family and friends—are not alone in being capable of freedom and self-possession. There are others in this world who also have this capacity and thus who also have the right to be treated as ends in themselves. The equalitarian rule does not say that it is unjust for a person to show special affection to those especially close to him, but it does condemn as unjust any activity or practice which manifests this affection by using some other human being as a mere instrument for the good of loved ones. Thus, a mother who wants to help her child overcome his lack of self-confidence is morally limited in what she can do in that she cannot build her child's confidence at the expense of the psychological health and well-being of a stranger's child. She is being unjust if she purposely places the children in situations in which her own child's self-confidence is being established by the introduction of a deep-seated inferiority complex in the other child. The fact that she cares very deeply for her own child does not mean that he has more of a right to psychological health than does the stranger's child.

The equalitarian rule is also morally useful because it serves to make man aware that although men of unusual talent are useful in improving man's situation in the world, we ought not to treat men solely in terms of their usefulness to society. This rule emphasizes that the ultimate value of a man lies not in any unique talents he may possess, but simply in his capacity for freedom and self-possession. It rejects as unjust any position that holds that because only men of outstanding intellectual ability can make significant contributions to improving the lot of mankind, there is no need to concern ourselves with providing the means for the human growth of those whom tests have shown not to possess outstanding intellectual abilities. This rejection is based on the view that a man's talents as a physicist, musician, business executive, politician, or philosopher do not give him or others representing him the right to treat other men as if they were mere instruments to be considered only in light of what they can or cannot contribute to society or to the lives of these talented men. Men who do not possess talents that are of significant social value also have a capacity for freedom and a right to be treated as ends in themselves and not simply as instruments for the advancement of other men.

Equalitarian justice as presented here is similar to meritarian justice in that it also is a rule meant to contribute to the realization and development of a community of ends among men. The moral significance of equalitarianism lies not in a reductionist denial of differences in talents, needs, and interests among men, but in an emphasis on the existence of many different centers of free agency and on an individual's moral responsibility to acknowledge the subjectivity of all those who come under the influence of his power. This emphasis means that the equalitarian rule is not calling for identical treatment simply for the sake of identical treatment. It does not require that a physician prescribe the same medication for a diabetic and for one suffering from pneumonia. Such a stupid requirement would show a greater concern with similarity for similarity's sake than for the good of the two patients. However, the equalitarian rule is concerned with making the physician aware that the diabetic has as much right to his physical health as does the pneumonia patient, who also happens to be a very influential member of the community. Hence, in so far as the physician's use of different medication is grounded in his commitment to work for the physical well-being of both patients, he is not acting contrary to the demands of equalitarian justice.

If one accepts the conclusion that meritarian and equalitarian justice are morally valuable because they are ways of social interaction that are in keeping with the character of man as an end in himself, he must expand the notion of justice to include the welfare conception of justice. This conception concerns what a man owes another man simply because of the latter's character as a member of the human community. More specifically, whereas the meritarian conception of justice makes me aware of what I owe to another because of what the person has given to or done for me, this conception makes me aware that I may be obliged to another simply because he is a human being in serious need, and because I have the means to help alleviate this need without seriously endangering my own subjectivity.

For example, I have a moral obligation to help a man who is drowning, if I know that I have the swimming ability to reach him and to return him to shore without endangering my own life. If there are factors in the situation that make it impossible for me to help him—if, for example, I am a poor swimmer and would seriously endanger my own life in trying to help him—I am not obligated in justice to try to swim out to him. I would still be obligated to look for other ways to help him.

This conception of justice is similar to the other two in that it flows from the recognition of man as an end in himself. As a result of circumstances, the good of a man who is in direct and immediate danger of death or of suffering serious bodily harm may be wholly dependent on me. If I simply ignore his need, or if I limit my thinking to the question of what use this man was or would be to me if I decided to save him, I am taking the position that since his good is wholly within my hands, I need consider only my own desires or my own good in deciding what I ought to do. The man is thus reduced merely to an object of my own desire or of what I consider to be my own good. However, because he is a being capable of freedom, the fact that his good is wholly dependent on me does not lessen my responsibility in justice to him, but rather increases my responsibility. I must consider his good as well as my own.

There is an unavoidable ambiguity in the notion of "serious need," a notion that is essential to the welfare rule of justice. A need is said to be serious in so far as its fulfillment is necessary in order to preserve a person's life and physical health, and/or to preserve and develop those capacities that are essential to his character as a free being. Hence, a man is not obliged in justice to try to satisfy every passing whim of his fellow man. I am not obliged to meet the need of a gourmet who has plenty of food available, but who is satisfied only if he has caviar as an hors d'oeuvre.

A possible objection to the welfare rule is that it is guilty of simply identifying two things which are admittedly good, but which also are different. Both love and justice are human goods. However, it may be argued that it is wrong to make them identical, as the welfare rule seems to do. Is it not love or benevolence rather than justice that prompts a man to give to others according to their needs? In answer to this question, it should be noted that in so far as love can be described as an appetitive response either to one's own good (self-love) or to the good of another, the just man's voluntary movement toward the good of another may be said to involve a type of love.

However, the love that is involved in justice is different from what we usually term love or benevolence in three significant respects. First, the man who acts out of benevolence is so committed to the good of the other that he is willing to place himself in serious danger in order to achieve that which is good for the other. The welfare rule does not require one to place his own life in serious danger in order to help another man. If I knowingly place my life in such danger in order to save another man, I am acting out of benevolence and not simply out of justice. Secondly, the man who acts out of a love that transcends justice will try to fill the nonessential, as well as the essential, needs of the loved one. Thus, although I may not be obliged in justice to supply the gourmet with his caviar, I may do so out of love. Finally, the lover's relationship to the loved one involves a commitment to the individual in his or her uniqueness that is different from the just man's relationship to his fellow human being in need.

The man who saves the drowning man because of his responsibility to him in justice may truthfully say that he would have done the same for any man who was in the same or a similar predicament. For his commitment to the man in need is simply a commitment to him as a member of the human community. However, the man who loves his wife is not committed to her good simply in so far as she is one among many members of the human community. He strives for her good because he is committed to her as this unique individual. He is willing to bear burdens for her good that he would not bear for any other individual and that he is not required in justice to bear for any other person.

The preceding discussion has indicated that there is a unity underlying the meritarian, equalitarian, and welfare rules of justice in so far as each is seen to be a way of so ordering the social relations among men that all those involved in these relations are treated as ends in themselves and not simply as means. It is now necessary to ask whether this unity is not illusory. Are not these rules mutually exclusive in the sense that if one tries to meet the demands of the meritarian rule, he must surrender the possibility of acting in accord with the requirements of the equalitarian and welfare rules? Before attempting to respond to this specific question, we shall deal with the problem of the relationship between the equalitarian and welfare dimensions of justice.

It is of utmost importance to begin a discussion of this problem with the awareness that man is morally responsible only for that which comes within the scope of his power. This point is important because there may be times when our lack of power leads us to draw the erroneous conclusion that there is an essential incompatibility among the three conceptions of justice that have been discussed. However, the fact that a man finds himself in a situation in which his resources are such that he can help only one of two men who are in serious need does not prove that there is such an incompatibility between the equalitarian and welfare rules. Since he lacks the resources to help the two men he is not bound in justice to help both of them.

The admission that there may be situations in which a man finds that it is existentially impossible for him to meet the demands of both the welfare and equalitarian rules may lead the realist to smile knowingly, since this admission confirms his belief that the moralist is not to be taken seriously, dealing as he does with a "dream world" rather than with the real world. If it can be shown that the incompatibility between the welfare and equalitarian rules is only a factual and not a logical incompatibility, we can leave the realist to his pleasure, while we look for ways to reconstruct the world so that it becomes possible to meet the multidimensional demands of justice. However, since men differ in their needs, it would appear that there is more than a factual incompatibility between the welfare and equalitarian rules and that the attempt to do justice to the essential needs of all those influenced by a practice will conflict with the attempt to treat these same people according to the demands of equalitarian rules.

The basis for the response to this problem has already been given in so far as it was pointed out that the equalitarian rule does not demand similarity of treatment merely for similarity's sake. The fact that a physician may spend more time caring for a child suffering from a serious and sometimes fatal lung disorder than he does caring for a nine-year-old child who is suffering from a common case of the mumps does not mean that he is acting contrary to the demands of equalitarian justice. The difference in treatment meets the demands of both welfare and equalitarian rules in so far as it is determined by what each patient needs and in so far as it acknowledges that the physical health of one patient is as important as that of the other. The physician's behavior is in keeping with the welfare rule, which emphasizes the possible claim that another man's serious need may place on me, and the equalitarian rule, which emphasizes that I must acknowledge the subjectivity of all those who come under my influence. Doing justice to the serious needs of all those whom I can help is thus not only not in conflict with the equalitarian rule, but it is a way of meeting the demand of this rule to acknowledge the subjectivity of all those who come under my influence.

Those denying the possibility of placing the three conceptions of justice under a single ideal roof would rightly rest the bulk of their case on the impossibility of finding any compatibility between the demands of meritarian rules on the one hand, and those of equalitarian and welfare rules, on the other hand. The answer to this difficulty will begin by noting that if there is a scarcity of goods and services necessary to human growth, the meritarian rule ought to prevail in the distribution of such goods and services. It is beyond our power to meet the demands of the equalitarian and welfare rules in such a situation. To try to make these latter rules effective in this situation is to embark on the practice of robbing Peter to pay Paul. The goods which some have been able to acquire through their labor are as necessary to their growth as they are to the growth of those who have not been quite so successful in their labors. Hence, neither equalitarian nor welfare rules would justify taking the goods from those who have been successful. The claim over these goods, which they have established through their work, must be respected.

It is now necessary to consider situations in which there is no scarcity of essential goods—situations in which it is possible to provide at least some of these goods to all. In such situations, the equalitarian and welfare rules must function as limiting principles with regard to what a man can be said to deserve as a result of his work. This position is simply a restatement of a point made earlier. The fact that a man may not have the talents to make a contribution to the good of society does not mean that he no longer has any rights as a human subject to that which is essential to his preservation and growth as such a subject. Without denying the justice of the meritarian demand that a man's contribution to society be recognized, this position states that this recognition ought not be of such a nature as to deny the rights of those who may not have made a contribution to society, to that which is essential to their existence as human subjects. For example, if the resources are available to provide necessary medical care both to the man whose work has contributed much to society and to one who has not been successful at any job, we cannot deny the care to the latter on the grounds that he has done nothing to merit it.

In conclusion, justice has been seen to be a tridimensional virtue. This means that whenever we are considering the justice of a practice affecting many lives we ought to examine it from the perspective of the meritarian, equalitarian, and welfare rules. We may not always have the resources to meet all three of these demands, but when we do have the resources, we ought to try to use them in such a way that the following of the meritarian rule will not conflict with the demands of the welfare and equalitarian rules.

4. PRACTICAL WISDOM

The discussion in the previous section emphasized that all virtues must proceed from a man's cognitive grasp of a situation. The purpose of this section is to explore the character of that type of knowledge of the individual moral situation that is essential to living a virtuous life. As was indicated in the discussion of the relativity of moral values, it is necessary to discover what is the moral thing to do *at this time,* and *under these particular circumstances*. It is the virtue of practical wisdom that perfects and modifies man's cognitive capacities so as to enable him to make such discoveries with ease, pleasure, and consistency.

Up to this point, such an emphasis has been placed on the essential role that knowledge must play in the virtues that one might be led to conclude that virtues such as temperance, fortitude, and justice are dependent on the virtue of practical wisdom, but that this latter virtue is in no way dependent on them. Actually, man's moral life is a more complex affair, with there being an interdependence between the appetitive and cognitive dimensions of human existence. Indeed, just as it can be said that there can be no temperance, fortitude, or justice without practical wisdom, it can also be said that there can be no practical wisdom without these virtues. As was pointed out in Chapter IV, the standard of morality as universal cannot provide man with the concrete moral ends for which he ought to work. Hence, he cannot resolve a concrete moral issue by simply deducing such ends from the moral standard or from an understanding of the general character of justice, temperance, or fortitude.

It is with regard to this matter of concrete ends that the proper development of man's appetitive life becomes important. The particular possibilities that will appeal to a man as possible ends for him—that will attract him as goods to which he ought to commit himself—will be those that accord with the character that he has formed. Thus, it is the just man that is attracted to this concrete just act, whereas this act will hold little or no attraction for the unjust man. The knowledge that an unjust man may have of the standard of moral behavior will not be sufficient or adequate to move him to perform *this* just act. Since this particular act holds no interest for him, he will be able to shrug off the standard of morality or the knowledge of the general character of justice as being "too abstract" to have any cogency for or relevance to this concrete situation. If practical wisdom is seen as involving the right decision as to what I ought to do in this concrete case, it is clear that the unjust man will be unable to come to such a decision. For this decision involves the individual's commitment to certain concrete ends, and the unjust individual will not commit himself to just ends because these do not attract him.

Realizing that the man of practical wisdom cannot depend solely on a knowledge of moral principles grasped in their universal character in trying to reach his decision as to what he ought to do in any given case, Thomas Aquinas states that such a man must depend on the concrete ends provided him by his appetitive responses as modified by such virtues as temperance, fortitude, and justice. These ends function as the particular principles necessary to his reasoning if he is to come to a decision concerning the particular course of action he is to follow in this case. For granted a particular end, the man of practical wisdom can proceed to his task of discovering what particular means are available to the achievement of this end and which among those possible means are morally appropriate in *this* case and with respect to *this* end.[41] Thus, the interplay between the appetitive and cognitive dimensions of human existence in the resolution of concrete moral issues is essential to such a resolution. Basically, this interplay is such that practical wisdom is directed to discovering the concrete moral means to achieve the moral ends determined by human appetition as modified by such virtues as temperance, fortitude, and justice. It is possible that his reflections on the means to achieve a concrete end may lead the man of practical wisdom to surrender this end. For he may discover either

[41] See *S.T.* II–II, Q. 58, a.5.

that the end is achievable only through immoral means or that the means will frustrate a good that is morally more valuable than the original end.

An act of practical wisdom can be described as involving a deliberative process and a preceptive judgment that results from this deliberation. The need for deliberation arises from the fact that in any particular case, there is usually no simple, "cut-and-dried," moral way of achieving a given end. Hence, man must stop and think—must take counsel with himself—in order to discover the means, which in a given case, are most likely to be morally appropriate to the achievement of the end. The use of the phrase "most likely," in the preceding sentence is no accident. It is meant to emphasize the lack of certainty that is involved in man's dealing with individual existential issues; he can never be absolutely certain that his deliberations have exhausted all the possibilities open to him. The full character of the concrete existential situation cannot be fully encompassed by human intellection. Having deliberated concerning what is to be done, the man of practical wisdom uses this deliberation as a basis for the judgment that this particular means ought to be employed in this particular case.

This judgment was described as perceptive in order to emphasize that it is immediately directed to action that ought to be done or avoided here and now. Practical wisdom is not simply a knowledge of the moral factors involved in a concrete situation. Ultimately, this knowledge leads to a conclusion directing the individual to perform or not to perform a certain act. This concluding judgment is not that of a spectator standing outside the situation which he is judging. It is the judgment of one very much involved and implicated in what he is judging. This personal involvement serves to reinforce the position taken earlier in this section, namely, that practical wisdom is impossible apart from the moral development of the appetitive factors of human existence.

There are two factors involved in the knowledge and commitment of the man of practical wisdom that ought to be mentioned here to complete certain positions taken earlier in this book. The man of practical wisdom is *docile* in the sense that he is able to learn from others. Docility, as used here, involves an openness of the individual's mind to the mind of another whom he knows to be competent in the moral area. There is nothing slavish or blind about this openness. Such openness is not the passive reception of another's thoughts. Rather, the man of practical wisdom puts his own mind to work on the advice of others, and it is only by doing this that he is able to profit from the advice, whether he ultimately accepts or rejects it.

This feature of practical wisdom ought to be taken as complementing the position advanced in Chapter IV, which stated that each man must use his own reason in making moral decisions. There is no incompatibility between using one's own reason and being open to advice from others. Just as the individual physicist does not ignore the work and positions of other respected physicists in conducting his own experiments, so also an individual ought not to ignore the advice of those in the community who are respected for their moral perspicacity and achievements. To say that one ought not to ignore the advice of others, or put more positively, that one ought to be open to the advice of others is not to say that one ought always follow such advice. The point is that one ought to be open to advice in such a way that, whether one accepts or rejects it, he has enriched his own moral awareness and is able to bring the advice to bear on the resolution of his own concrete moral problems.

The man of practical wisdom is also able to relate universal and/or general moral principles to concrete moral problems. The discussion of this matter may help to meet a possible objection to the way in which the virtues have been discussed up to this point. For example, one might point out that it is well and good to describe temperance as a virtue, which helps man to respond properly to pleasurable goods, but that this description is not sufficient or adequate to resolve a concrete moral difficulty, unless what is meant by "properly," be spelled out in greater detail. This same criticism can be made with respect to the discussions of all the virtues treated in this chapter. One of the points that Dewey made earlier in this chapter is relevant to meeting this criticism. It will be recalled that he cautioned against the attempt to be so concrete in the definition of a virtue that the very character of that virtue becomes equated with the institutions or objects found in one's own society or age. The ethician who thinks that he can be specific in his description of the character of the virtues is under the misapprehension that his intellect has been able to comprehend every existential situation in which man may ever find himself. As a matter of fact, what he does is freeze man's world into the mould of his own society or situation, by equating the very character of a virtue with the way in which that virtue may be realized in his own time and place.

It is the task of the man of practical wisdom to discover precisely and concretely what it means to be temperate or just in any given situation. He does not make these discoveries by simply deducing what is the temperate or just thing to do here and now from his knowledge of the nature of justice. Rather he can "relate," the knowledge of what it means to be temperate to a concrete situation only through a careful reflection on the existential situation in which he finds himself. For example, what is meant by a "proper" amount of food is determined by such factors as one's physical condition, by what one needs to preserve his physical and mental well-being and to perform whatever tasks may be required of him in his particular situation and station of life. Moreover, considerations of justice may also enter into deciding what is a "proper" amount of food, if one finds himself in a society in which food is in short supply.

5. SITUATION ETHICS: IS LOVE ENOUGH?

This section will be devoted to a brief exposition and evaluation of Joseph Fletcher's statement of "situation ethics," with the hope that this undertaking will give more precision to the discussion of practical wisdom. There are certain areas of agreement between Fletcher's situation ethics and the reflective naturalism defended in this book. There is agreement with respect to the views that a moral agent must make his own decisions concerning the morality or immorality of the concrete alternatives open to him and that this decision must be based on a consideration of the concrete situation in which he finds himself. The discussion of the morality of aspiration in Chapter I, the emphasis on the fact that the moral standard defended in Chapter IV is not a substitute for further moral reflection, but a call and an aid to such reflection, and the view that man must reflect on his concrete situation if he is to give existential substance to such values as justice and liberty—all show that I share Fletcher's opposition to a "prefabricated, pretailored morality."[42] Finally, there is no disagreement between us in so far as what he calls "personalism" involves an acceptance both of Kant's view that persons are always to be treated as ends and never merely as means and of the position, "human welfare and happiness (but not, necessarily pleasure)," are "the *summum bonum* or first order value."[43]

The exposition and evaluation of Fletcher's position will center in the following points: (1) the nature of love and its role in the moral situation, (2) the influence of this first point on the role of reason in morality, (3) the problem of the internal consistency of a position that makes love the only norm and that also accepts utilitarianism as a norm, and (4) the question of the task of moral philosophy. In dealing with these issues I shall prescind from Fletcher's theological orientation.

Fletcher maintains that love is the norm according to which the morality of any action is to be evaluated.[44] Love, and "nothing else," is said to be the "ruling norm of Christian decision."[45] This emphasis on love as the sole norm of morality is also seen in the title of Chapter VI of Fletcher's book in which love is said to be "the Only Norm."[46] This love "will not share its power," being an "imperious law unto itself."[47] Since love is given such a central role in Fletcher's ethics, it is important to discover precisely what he means by love.

He points out that the love that grounds ethics is indefinable in terms of something else, because it is similar to realities such as blue or sour which simply are what they are.[48] He thinks that it is best described as being the type of love which in Greek is referred to as *agape*, and which is distinguished from friendship (*philia*) and romantic love (*eros*). Whereas these two latter loves, which certainly have a legitimate function in human life, are selective and exclusive, the love (*agape*) grounding situation ethics includes all men within its scope,

[42] Joseph Fletcher, *Situation Ethics: The New Morality* (Philadelphia: The Westminster Press, 1966), p. 134.

[43] Joseph Fletcher, "Love is the Only Measure," *Commonweal*, Vol. 83 (January 14, 1966), p. 429.

[44] See footnote 42, p. 43.

[45] *Ibid.*, p. 86.

[46] *Ibid.*, p. 69.

[47] *Ibid.*, p. 85.

[48] *Ibid.*, p. 47.

even enemies. Although Fletcher is somewhat unhappy with the rather weak meaning "benevolence" may have in contemporary society, he further describes *agape* as "benevolence, literally, Goodwill."[49] This description is acceptable to him because it involves the idea of a love that goes out to others neither for the sake of the lover nor the loved one, but for God's sake.

Acknowledging that moral choices require intelligence and sound information as much as good will and a good disposition, Fletcher maintains that situation ethics meets this requirement, because the love upon which it is based is a "matter of intelligence, not sentiment."[50] Explicitly separating himself from those who think that love is nonrational, he identifies love as *agape* with what he terms "prudence," which is comparable to what has been discussed in the previous section as practical wisdom.[51] This identification of love with prudence is open to question. It may well be true that unless one has some concern (love) for his fellow man, he will not undertake the type of reflective inquiry required to come to a decision concerning what is the moral thing to do in any given situation. This means that a certain type of interest is a prerequisite for practical wisdom, just as a certain type of interest is a prerequisite for scientific knowledge. However, the interest is not the knowledge. The "will-to-know," whether the knowledge be of a scientific or prudential character, is essential to disposing one to do the thinking necessary for the achievement of such knowledge, but this "will-to-know," is not the knowing itself. Thus, I would agree with Fletcher if he means that unless a man has some concern with being moral, he will not do the thinking necessary to discover what he ought to do. However, he seems to be saying something other than this in speaking of love as the only norm for evaluating the morality of an act.

Perhaps, his treatment of what he considers to be "THE ROCK-BOTTOM issue in all ethics," will help clarify his position.[52] This issue concerns the existential locus of values. Is the moral character of an act as good or bad intrinsic to the act itself or is it extrinsic to the act, and thus dependent for this character on factors other than the act itself to which the act is related? Fletcher describes himself as a nominalist in answering this question. This means that he holds things to be extrinsically right or wrong. More specifically, he holds that nothing is good or evil in itself or inherently, "except love (personal concern) and its opposite, indifference or actual malice."[53] He contends that values do not exist, but that there are only material or immaterial things that "happen to be valued by persons."[54] Hence, anything becomes a value either because it happens to help a person, or because it hurts persons.[55]

---

[49] *Ibid.*, p. 105.

[50] *Ibid.*, p. 114.

[51] *Ibid.*, p. 87.

[52] *Ibid.*, p. 57.

[53] See footnote 43, p. 430.

[54] See footnote 42, p. 58.

[55] *Ibid.*, pp. 59–60.

I agree with Fletcher that one of the factors which makes an act morally good or bad is whether the act helps or hurts human beings. However, Fletcher must make a choice in his interpretation of this position. For there is a difference between saying that things are valuable because they happen *to be valued by persons* and that they are valuable because they happen to help a person. It is certainly conceivable that an act may help a person, although it may not be valued by him, or conversely, that it may hurt him, although he values it. In so far as Fletcher grants that an act has value because it helps or hurts persons, it is difficult to see his justification for a nominalistic conception of values. Values are as real as the frustrations and fulfillments that are a part of the human condition. There is nothing "nominal" about them. Acts are performed which *really* do reduce the human person to a mere means or which really are destructive of human subjectivity. In order to proceed further with this evaluation, it will be necessary to consider the other half of his nominalistic conception of values, viz., the view that only love and its opposite, indifference and malice, are inherently good and evil respectively.

This view of love and malice, together with the nominalistic conception of all other values, grounds Fletcher's conclusion that whatever is done lovingly is right and whatever is done without love or indifferently is wrong.[56] Is it moral or immoral to lie? If the lie is told lovingly, it is right; if told unlovingly, it is evil.[57] Would it be moral for an unmarried couple to decide to engage in premarital intercourse so as to have the girl become pregnant, and thus force a selfish parent to surrender his overbearing opposition to the marriage? The answer is affirmative if the couple act out of a loving concern, but negative if they act out of some sort of "liking."[58] Is prostitution always immoral? Fletcher finds it difficult to answer this question. A whore could be doing something good, if her act is for love's sake. Paid sex might be moral depending on the situation, for women have engaged in it to feed their families, to pay their debts, or in the service of their country as counterespionage agents. Hence, one cannot say that paid sex is always immoral.[59]

Fletcher lists four factors that must be considered in judging the morality of any act, viz., the end, the means, the motive, and the consequences.[60] However, it appears that these four factors are somewhat similar to the "three guesses," someone is given to answer an obvious question. He has three guesses, but the first two do not count. Similarly, Fletcher seems to be saying that there are four factors to be considered in evaluating the morality of an act, but only one counts, viz., love (*agape*). "Nothing can justify an act except a loving purpose."[61]

[56] *Ibid.*, p. 64.
[57] *Ibid.*, p. 65.
[58] *Ibid.*, p. 104.
[59] *Ibid.*, p. 146.
[60] *Ibid.*, pp. 127–128, 154.
[61] *Ibid.*, p. 125.

According to Fletcher, a common objection to situation ethics is that it requires a critical intelligence and factual information that exceed the capacity of most people.[62] I certainly see no justification for such an objection. Indeed, a more appropriate objection is that his ethics requires hardly any intelligence or information beyond the knowledge that one is acting out of a loving purpose, *agape*. It is true that he has stressed the need for intelligence, discernment, and calculation in moral matters. However, his nominalistic view of values, his view that love alone is the norm and is inherently good, and the examples which he uses to illustrate his position lead to the conclusion that one need examine only his own attitude in evaluating the morality of his acts. It is true that Fletcher places a great deal of emphasis on love as *concern*. However, having evacuated the world of all values but love and having taken the view that nothing but love can justify an act, he has situated the loving person in a world in which he has nothing about which to be concerned, except to be certain that he is concerned.

Moreover, the view that no act is immoral if done with a loving purpose leads to a reactionary type of social policy. For example, if a woman is a prostitute because this profession is the only way in which she can feed her family, and if she is engaging in this profession out of a loving concern for her family, situation ethics provides no moral basis for criticizing a society that puts a woman in such a situation. There would appear to be no *moral reason* to try to change such a social system, since the woman is not doing anything immoral. To argue that prostitution is moral only if one is forced to choose between it and the starvation of one's family is to admit that there is something immoral about prostitution in itself and that, granted that one is in such a difficult situation, one must choose the lesser of two evils.

However, a fundamental feature of Fletcher's nominalism is that a person has not done the lesser of two evils when he performs an act lovingly. He criticizes the "lesser evil" doctrine for taking the stand that acts are immoral, no matter how lovingly they are performed.[63] To deny that the woman who has chosen a life of prostitution rather than the starvation of her children has chosen what may be the lesser of two evils, is to take the stand that prostitution in itself is not a moral evil. This position implies that even when one's alternatives are wider than prostitution and the starvation of one's children, there is no moral basis not to choose prostitution. For example, there would be no moral grounds for a girl to reject prostitution in favor of being a physician. I am back to my earlier criticism. If it is true that the loving man lives in a universe in which every act, except love or its opposite malice and/or indifference, is evacuated of any moral significance, then that man has no moral issue about which to be concerned except love or its opposite. If Fletcher wants to be consistent in maintaining this position, it would seem that he would be forced to conclude

[62] *Ibid.*, p. 81.
[63] *Ibid.*, p. 65.

that there is no *moral* difference between being a physician or a prostitute. Hence, the only morally relevant factor to be considered in trying to decide between these two careers is whether one can be more loving in one rather than in the other.

The conclusion that Fletcher's situation ethics involves the view that one need be concerned only with whether or not one *is* concerned is further strengthened by his criticism of the position that an act can be both loving and wrong on the grounds that such a position is guilty of "an obvious contradiction."[64] This criticism amounts to making the loving man infallible in his moral decisions, and again gives him no reason to reflect on anything but his own love. For the criticism indicates that an act that is loving is *ipso facto* right. It thus misses one of the most agonizing facts of human existence, viz., that no matter how deeply we may love someone or how concerned we may be with advancing our neighbor's good, our action toward him may be harmful to his good as a person and may thus be the type of action that is immoral in so far as it causes such harm or is not in keeping with his being as an end in himself.

The criticism of Fletcher's position advanced up to this point is based on the assumption that his situation ethics holds consistently to the nominalistic view of values and to the position that love is the only norm. This criticism may be validly turned aside by an appeal to Fletcher's statement that there is no rivalry between his situation ethics and Mill's utilitarianism.[65] However, I do not think that Fletcher can consistently hold both a utilitarian norm of moral judgments and the view that love is the only norm. Either consequences are decisive in giving an act its moral character, in which case there would be no contradiction in saying that an act can be both loving and wrong; or love is truly the only norm and it is contradictory to hold that an act can be both loving and wrong, in which case there would appear to be no reason to consider consequences. I have already pointed to positions taken by Fletcher, which seem to indicate that he accepts the latter alternative. When stressing the utilitarian side of his position, Fletcher states that the situationist prefers to serve the neighbor with the greater need, and to serve more rather than fewer neighbors.[66] This indicates an acceptance of our first alternative, and thus involves the possibility that an act can be performed lovingly and with a great deal of good will, and yet be immoral in that it actually has served fewer rather than more neighbors.

It is possible to conceive of an ethical position that would require that both consequences and one's motivation be considered in evaluating the morality of acts. One can say that the consequences of our acts show the depth of our love, in which case these consequences function as an ultimate norm in that they provide a basis for judging whether or not one has *agape*. One might also appeal to some standard other than love or consequences, such as the growth of human

[64] *Ibid.*
[65] *Ibid.*, p. 115.
[66] *Ibid.*, p. 113.

subjectivity in the human community. Such a standard would replace both love and consequences as the ultimate moral norm, but it would require that they be considered in so far as they might either contribute to, or detract from the good involved in this standard. However, Fletcher accepts neither of these possibilities, and is left with what appears to me to be the inconsistent position of saying that love is the only norm and also that there is no conflict between this norm and the utilitarian position, which makes consequences the norm of morality.

In working out his situation ethics, Fletcher seems to be concerned with the problem of passing moral judgments on people. For example, he points out that "technical virgins" are not to be praised for their morality. He asks, "Is the girl who gives her chastity for her country's sake any less approvable than the boy who gives his leg or his life? No!"[67] It may be true that if the ethician were to concern himself with judging the moral character of another man he would in the last analysis, rest his judgment on the man's desire to do the right thing and on his use of every resource available to him not only to discover what act he ought to perform but also to actually perform that act.

However, it is not the task of an ethician or of any man to judge the moral character of another human being. This position is not taken as a matter of choice. It is grounded in the fact that it is impossible for one man to possess the knowledge of another's motives, of his outlook, and of his problems that would be necessary for an evaluation of the other's moral character. It is the task of moral philosophy to try to discover those dimensions of a human act that render it moral or immoral. It may well be that a certain kind of act may be immoral, although the person performing the act may have been moral because his motives were good and his knowledge of his situation and of what was required of him may have led him to conclude that the act was moral. For example, as an ethician, I may conclude that it is immoral to deliberately abort a human fetus who may be born deformed, although I would be unable to pass judgment on the moral character of the individuals who engage in such activities. Hence, it is clear that there is no need to reduce the whole moral enterprise to a matter of love in order to justify the distinction between judging the morality of acts and of persons.

6. PARTICULAR EXISTENTIAL SITUATIONS AND THE HUMAN COMMUNITY

Perhaps, it might be argued that the consideration of Fletcher's situation ethics up to this point has not proceeded to the heart of the issue raised by this position. Since every existential situation is *unique*, how can one hope to come up with moral principles that are binding in all situations? This question points to what appears to be an unbridgeable gap between the uniqueness of the

[67] See footnote 43, p. 431.

existential situations in which human individuals actually find and try to resolve their moral problems, and the commonness of moral principles which purport to be morally significant in all human situations.

There can be no denying that no two existential situations are ever exactly alike. For example, contemporary man lives in a world whose history includes two world wars, a factor that makes his situation different from that of man existing in the Middle Ages. There are, of course, other factors separating today's man from those who went before him. He exists in a world that includes psychoanalysis, Marxism-Leninism, evolutionary theory, poll-taking and statistical analysis, birth-control pills, knowledge of the female ovulation cycle, abortion techniques that are very safe for the pregnant woman, motion pictures, television, automobiles, space flights, large industrial complexes, and nuclear weapons—to mention only some of the factors that differentiate today's world from that of the Middle Ages and of the Greece of Socrates, Plato, and Aristotle.

Up to this point, I have been speaking about the differences among eras. When we move to the level of individuals, the differences are perhaps more striking. The milieu in which a Rockefeller moves and lives is certainly different from that of a poor Negro in Harlem. Even in the life of one individual there are differences in the situations in which he finds himself. Each classroom situation is different for the college professor, because he has changed as a result of his past experiences and his students have changed because of their past experiences. A mother cannot have exactly the same relationship with two of her children, because the fact that she had one some time before the other is a new factor in her relationship to the second child, not to mention the influence that differences between the children themselves will make in her relations to each.

The acknowledgment of the uniqueness of the situations in which man finds himself should not blind one to the fact that in so far as these situations involve moral problems, they involve issues that relate to man as a subject in the human community. The uniqueness of a man's situation does not mean that he ceases to be a man, to be a member of the human community. A man may decide to "act like a pig," but he can never "be" a pig. He remains a "man-who-acts-like-a-pig." The point of all this is that the uniqueness of a man's situation and his individuality do not place him outside the human community. Hence, his character as a member of the human community is at issue in all these situations.

I think the observations of the American Idealist Josiah Royce and of Immanuel Kant can shed some light on this issue. Royce points out that the man who gives up his life in fighting against those who would deprive man of freedom calls our attention to the fact that the given situation in which he finds himself is not wholly self-enclosed. Royce puts the matter as follows: "Liberty was no individual man, and no mere heap of individual men. Liberty was a cause, a certain superhuman unity of the ideal life of a free community."[68]

[68] Josiah Royce, The Philosophy of Loyalty (New York: The Macmillan Co., 1908), p. 392.

Although I do not accept the idealistic overtones to Royce's use of the term "superhuman," I think that his account of the man who gives up his life for freedom highlights the fact that there are values at issue in an individual human situation that are relevant to the human community and to a man's knowledge of his place in that community. The man who willingly and knowingly gives up his life in the cause of liberty sees that what is at issue in this situation in which he finds himself is a matter that is relevant to himself as member of the human community. He sees in this given situation a challenge to human freedom, a challenge to "the ideal life of a free community." It is in light of this factor—a factor which opens the situation to issues that have a significance beyond it—that he makes his decision to meet this challenge even to the point of death.

Kant's statements of the categorical imperative are also useful in making us aware of the fact that the situations in which men work out their moral problems are open-ended affairs, requiring a resolution that takes into account man's character as a legislative member of the community of ends. This point is perhaps most clearly brought out in the following statement of the categorical imperative: "Every rational being must act as if he, by his maxims, were at all times a legislative member in the universal realm of ends."[69] A morally valid resolution of a concrete moral issue is one that takes into consideration the effect of this resolution on the realization of a community of ends. Kant makes us aware of the fact that no matter how unique our situations may be, we carry with us in these situations the burden and responsibilities of our humanity. Without denying a man's individuality or the uniqueness of situations in which men may find themselves, this position emphasizes that there are human values to be realized, protected, or preserved in these situations.

Granted that the uniqueness of one's situation does not place him outside the human community—does not relieve him of the burden and responsibilities of being a member of this community—these situations are not completely closed off from the demands of those principles which have captured something of the general character of what it means to be a member of the human community and of how one ought to act to live up to this membership. For example, the virtues discussed in this chapter can be said to be moral principles in that they provide us with an understanding of the *type* of behavior that is demanded of one who is a member of the human community. No matter how unique one's situation may be, if he is to act morally, he must meet the demands of justice, temperance, or fortitude.

Unlike Fletcher who speaks of moral principles as "illuminators," but not "directors," I maintain that such principles as justice, temperance, and fortitude are not only helpful as illuminating the areas that man must consider in resolving moral problems, but are also directors in the sense that once man discovers, for example, that this is the just thing to do in this situation, he is morally

---

[69] See footnote 9, Chap. I, p. 47.

obligated to perform that act.[70] Hence, the uniqueness of a man's situation does not "get him off the hook," as it were, with respect to the task of meeting his moral obligations.

Fletcher seems to have had other principles in mind, such as "Lying is always wrong," "Suicide is immoral," "Murder is immoral." There are three questions raised by principles of this type. First, it is necessary to describe what is meant by these words. What is the character of the activity which these words are meant to convey? Am I telling a lie when I fail to give a straightforward answer to a man who is probing into my private life merely out of curiosity? Is all killing murder? If not what distinguishes murder from other acts of killing human beings? Can a man be said to have committed suicide, because he refused to cooperate with a totalitarian regime even though he knew such a refusal would mean that he would be killed?

Secondly, supposing that we are able to come up with a description that would comprehend the character of such acts, can we show that this character is such that the performance of the act is always destructive of human subjectivity or of the realization of the human community? What is it about the character of lying that makes it always wrong, if it is always wrong? If it is not always wrong, what is it about its character that makes it wrong sometimes and right at other times, and, in a general way, what sort of circumstances make it right and what sort make it wrong?

Thirdly, and now we begin to move into the area of practical wisdom, is this particular act that I am about to perform here and now actually an act of murder, lying, or suicide? This question may appear to some to be merely a repetition of the first question. However, the nuances of a concrete situation are often such that it is difficult to tell whether *this particular act* is an act of murder, suicide, or lying. In the case of lying, for example, can we say that a salesman is lying because he has told a prospective customer about the good features of the product that he is trying to sell, but he has not told him that the product of his competitor is even better, although he knows this to be the case? In short, how much of what one knows to be true with respect to a particular issue is he bound to tell another, if he wants to avoid being a liar?

Murder provides what is perhaps the best example of the need to discover whether *this* act in *this* circumstance is an act of murder. This is a particularly difficult matter for one who holds that not every act of killing another human being is murder. One might hold that to kill a man who is a direct and immediate threat to my life is not murder, but self-defense. Does the man walking behind me on a dark and deserted street constitute a "direct and immediate" threat to my life? Is he "following" me, or he is simply walking behind me? If a man merely says that he is going to kill me, does this constitute a direct and immediate threat to my life? Must I wait until the man actually shows a weapon and points it at me before I can say that I can attempt to kill

---

[70] See footnote 42, p. 31.

him and that this attempt is an attempt to defend myself, and should not be classified as an attempted murder? Was the attempt to kill Adolph Hitler an attempted murder, or a justifiable act of war?

Thomas Aquinas provides a listing that is helpful in pointing out the circumstances that should be considered in trying to determine the morality of a given act. These circumstances can be divided under three headings—circumstances relating to the causal factors involved in the situation, circumstances relating to the effect of the action, and circumstances that have a bearing on the action itself.[71]

Taking the causal factors first, it is obvious that the morality of an act will be influenced by the agent who is performing an act. For example, an act proceeding from an elephant has no moral character about it. Thus, one of the factors to be considered in deciding *whether* an act possesses a moral character and *what* this character is, is the cause of the act, or the agent performing the act. It will also be necessary to consider both the *final* and *material* causes involved in a given situation. The final cause answers the question *why* did the agent perform the act, and the material cause, the question, on whom or what was the act performed. Another causal consideration that might be relevant to the morality of an act in a given situation is the *instrumental cause,* i.e. the instrument that the agent used in performing the act.

It is also necessary to consider the effect of an act in judging its morality. Finally, the factors relating to the act itself must be considered. These factors include the *way* or *manner* in which an act was performed, and the *time* and *place* of its performance.[72] All these factors are to be considered in the light of their contribution to or detraction from the growth of human subjectivity or of the human community. More specifically, they can be considered in terms of whether or not they meet the demands of justice, temperance, fortitude, or prudence, since all morally problematic situations will involve one or more of these virtues.

There is certainly no shortage of examples to show how these factors can influence the morality of an act. Let us take the case of a parent (the agent) disciplining his child (the material cause), and doing so for the child's own good (the final cause or purpose). All this seems to be perfectly in keeping with the respective roles of both parent and child in the human community. However, if we add that this disciplining is done with a baseball bat (the instrumental cause) applied to the child's head, our evaluation of the morality of the act changes, since the instrumental cause used endangers the physical health and well-being which is necessary to the child's growth as a mature human subject. The act would also take on an immoral character if the parent struck the child with his hand with such force (the manner in which the act is performed) that the child suffered a concussion.

---

[71] S.T. I–II, Q. 7, a.3; see footnote 36, Chap. I, Vol. II, p. 243.
[72] See *Ibid.*

Granted that we know what lying or suicide is, a consideration of these circumstances should help us decide whether this particular act is a lie or a suicide. Moreover, if an act is morally neutral considered in the *abstract*—e.g. walking, talking, or reading—a consideration of how the circumstances in which the act is concretely placed affect the good of man as a subject in the human community will help evaluate the morality of the act.

I have tried to make two points in this section. First, the unique character of existential situations does not entail the conclusion that general moral principles have no significance for these situations. These situations do involve issues relating to the growth of human subjectivity. In so far as we can achieve a general knowledge of the factors that contribute to this growth, as in the case of the virtues, such knowledge is relevant to the unique situation. Secondly, I have tried to point to the problematic areas that must be dealt with in the attempt to establish moral principles and to relate these principles to concrete situations. It was emphasized that the "relating" of these principles to these situations requires a reflection on the facts of the situation itself. Hence, there is no disagreement here with situation ethics in so far as it insists that man cannot expect to resolve all his moral difficulties in an ethics classroom. At best the work of moral philosophy can be only an aid to further reflection on the various situations in which a man will find himself in the course of his life; it cannot substitute for such reflection.

7. MORAL EXISTENCE AND MORAL PHILOSOPHY

Two points ought to be emphasized in concluding this chapter. First, it should be clear that moral existence is not reducible to moral philosophy. One does not become moral by simply reading books on moral philosophy. A man develops his moral character by actually meeting the concrete problems and issues that confront him in his day-to-day existence. Such meetings will involve appetitive movements toward or away from the concrete goods or evils of these various situations. The man, who is thus engaged in meeting the problems and challenges of his existential situation, is in the process of making his own moral personality and also of contributing to the shaping of the world in so far as his acts move beyond himself as they inevitably must. The stress on appetition *— desire* does not mean that there is no place for knowledge in this process. Moral growth is not achieved through blind appetition or commitment. There is certainly a need for that type of moral knowledge referred to in this chapter as practical wisdom. Man must work to gain a cognitive grasp of his concrete situation before actually undertaking a certain line of activity in pursuit of a good or to avoid an evil.

However, this cognitive grasp will never be so complete as to do away with the uncertainty that is involved in a man's pursuit of a concrete line of activity. As John Dewey points out,

> The distinctive characteristic of practical activity, one which is so inherent that it cannot be eliminated, is the uncertainty which attends it. Of it we are compelled to say: Act, but act at your peril. Judgment and belief regarding actions to be performed can never attain more than a precarious probability.[73]

A man's activity in the world will inevitably involve a movement into the unknown. Human reason can never ensnare in its nets the fullness and complexity of a concrete existential situation and the future toward which that situation is moving. This state of affairs does not mean that there is no need for practical wisdom. Granted that human reason is fallible and granted that it cannot grasp the full complexity of a given existential situation, it remains the best resource available to man to see a given act in light of its various relations and possibilities.

We come now to the second point in this section. This discussion, together with the whole tenor of this chapter, might raise the question of the value of moral philosophy to man's moral growth. To say that moral development is not reducible to the study of moral philosophy is not to say that this study is totally irrelevant to such development. Although moral philosophy as understood in this book cannot substitute for reflection on concrete issues, it can contribute to a man's moral development by broadening and deepening his intellectual awareness of the various factors that underlie this growth. The material in this chapter, the discussion of the standards of morality in Chapter IV, the exploration of the character of moral good and its relation to human reason and nature, the discussion of freedom as essential to the moral enterprise, and the discussion of emotivism were all directed to such a broadening and deepening process. Thus, it must be obvious that the discussion of the virtues in this chapter was not pursued under the misconception that a knowledge of the general character of the cardinal virtues would resolve concrete moral issues. However, the attempt to point out those aspects of human existence that make these virtues valuable for man was undertaken with the hope that it would serve to give intellectual substance to the words that signify these values.

Those who would shrug off a philosophical discussion of these values on the grounds that they are interested in the concrete existential order and not in dealing with meaningless abstractions must show that their interest in changing the existential order is not simply a blind striking out against conditions that they do not happen to like. Is there any intellectual substance behind their activity, or is it all mere sound and fury signifying nothing but their own idiosyncrasies? Such enduring values as freedom, justice, and fortitude will indeed be only bloodless abstractions, if man does not try to grasp their formal meaning, and,

---

[73] John Dewey, *The Quest for Certainty: A Study of the Relation of Knowledge and Action* (New York: Capricorn Books, 1960), p. 6.

in the light of this meaning, and, after an examination of his concrete condition, try to discover the meaning that they may have in his own time and the way in which they can be introduced either into his own life or the life of the community in which he lives.

John Dewey has made an excellent case for the practical significance to man's moral life of a philosophical reflection on the character of moral values. He points out that most people agree in voicing their respect for the Golden Rule. However, if this or any other moral value or rule is not subject to reflective inquiry and criticism, it will degenerate into a meaningless command that has no relevance to man's situation in the world. Dewey states this point very well.

> That it [the Golden Rule], or any other rule, may be a workable tool, that it may really give aid in a specific case, it must have life and spirit. What can give it the life and spirit necessary to make it other than a cramped and cramping petrification except the continued free play of intelligence upon it?[74]

Thus, the work of moral theory is not something cut off from man's moral existence. The reflective work of moral theory can help transform moral rules and values from the status of mere empty verbiage to that of meaningful working tools that can help man in his dealings with concrete situations.

Perhaps there is a disillusionment in our own day with the type of moral inquiry undertaken in this book because every conflicting ideology from communism to fascism has claimed that it represents justice, freedom, and the good of man. These words have been put into the service of so many diverse and conflicting ideologies that there is a temptation to ignore them. "Everybody is in favor of 'justice' so let us not ask anybody precisely what he means by the term." To acknowledge that words such as "justice" have become the instruments of propagandists is not to hold that they should be left in the hands of such people. The values that are represented by such words are too important to human existence to be ignored by a systematic and organized inquiry into the conditions of man's moral existence.

[74] John Dewey, "Moral Theory and Practice," *International Journal of Ethics*, Vol. I (January, 1891), p. 195.

CHAPTER VI

Morality
and
Human Sexuality

This chapter will explore the moral issues surrounding the questions of premarital coition and of induced abortions. The discussion of these questions brings us to a level of moral discourse that stands midway between the rather general problems that have been treated in this book up to this point and the concrete problems that face an individual as he tries to come to a personal decision concerning the particular line of action he ought to follow here and now. It is important to note that although the problems of premarital coition and induced abortion are not quite as general as the issues that have been discussed up to this point, we shall treat them as problems in moral philosophy. This means that the positions to be taken with respect to them are meant to be aids to further personal reflection and not substitutes for such reflection.

1. THE CASE FOR PREMARITAL COITION

When we speak of premarital sexual intercourse or coition in the discussion that follows, we mean a heterosexual union between unmarried persons. Unless it is explicitly stated that those engaging in such activities are committed to marry each other at some future date, the phrase should be understood to refer to unions in which no such commitments have been made. Such unions are said to be premarital in the sense that those involved in them may intend to marry in the future, although not necessarily to each other. They may not be certain that they have found the right person as yet.

There are three arguments that are commonly advanced in defense of the view that there need be nothing immoral about premarital sexual intercourse. The first argument is one that accuses those who hold that premarital sexual relations are immoral of committing what the British philosopher John Wilson describes as the "fallacy of discrimination." This fallacy moves from the position that some activity is of great human value to the view that discrimination ought to be practiced in the exercise of this activity, and finally to the conclusion that this activity ought to be practiced only under the restriction of certain rules or ideals in order to preserve it from becoming trivial, meaningless, or even positively evil. That this fallacy exercises a very significant influence on our view of sex is seen by the fact that anyone who holds that sexual intercourse should be engaged in mostly for pleasure is accused of being insensitive and incapable of engaging in deep relations.[1]

In opposition to the fallacy, Wilson points out that we need not conclude, as the fallacy would seem to imply, that because a certain activity may have a significant value under certain conditions, it is cheap, degraded, and despicable under different conditions. For example, it may be true that a dinner including pheasant under glass and a rare French champagne reaches the heights of gastronomical achievement, but the great value of such a meal is certainly no reason to condemn a snack of a hamburger and soda pop as being degrading and despicable. Similarly, it may be true that a casual sex affair does not have the same value as the sexual relations between people who have made a lifelong commitment to each other, but this difference in value is hardly reason to condemn the casual affair as degrading and immoral. Just as it is fallacious to condemn the snack of hamburger and soda pop for not being the dinner of pheasant under glass and rare champagne, so also it is fallacious to condemn casual sex affairs because they are not married love.[2]

Wilson's point has been stated in a different way by another British philosopher Ronald Atkinson. Atkinson holds that those who characterize premarital sexual relations as immoral are guilty of confusing morality with their personal preferences or ideals. So long as the parties engaged in such activities are clear-sighted about what they are doing and are honest with each other, there seems to be nothing immoral about their activities. They are harming no one and are guilty of no injustice. Hence, although premarital sexual relations may not be in accord with one's personal ideals, he has no basis for condemning them as immoral.[3]

The psychiatrist Eustace Chesser who shares Atkinson's position seems to ground it in the view that man's sexual urge is a simple fact of nature and is neither good nor bad in itself. It is the way in which man gives expression to this urge that determines whether his sexual activity is moral or immoral. If a girl knows and accepts the fact that a boy is interested only in gaining sexual experience and if they take the proper contraceptive precautions, there appears to be nothing immoral in their activity. They have injured no innocent third party, and neither feels any remorse. So long as two people are honest in their premarital sexual activity and so long as there is mutual respect between them, there is nothing immoral about their relations. Finally, since the social and

---

[1] John Wilson, *Logic and Sexual Morality* (Baltimore, Md.: Penguin Books, 1965), p. 59.

[2] *Ibid.*, pp. 60, 72–73.

[3] Ronald Atkinson, *Sexual Morality* (New York: Harcourt, Brace and World, 1965), pp. 102–103.

psychological consequences of such sex play may be no more serious than if the two had gone to a movie, there is no reason to raise a moral issue about it.[4]

Those who are guilty of the fallacy of discrimination with regard to premarital sexual intercourse sometimes try to defend their position on the grounds that anyone who becomes involved in premarital affairs will be unable later in his life to treat his wife as an end in herself or to form a deep and abiding relationship with her. Wilson responds to this argument by pointing out that it is psychologically possible for man to treat women in different ways at different times. The fact that a man has treated a woman as a "body to take to bed," does not mean that he will be unable to treat his wife as a goddess. Moreover, he indicates that those who are unable to treat women as a goddess at one time, a companion another time, and as a body to be enjoyed at some other time are psychologically narrow and impoverished.[5]

The second line of argument in defense of premarital coition is based on the belief that it can be helpful to people in their choice of a marriage partner. Those who have not engaged in sexual intercourse before marriage may well be unable to distinguish mere sexual attraction from the type of love that grounds a strong marriage. If two people feel a strong sexual attraction for each other, and if they think that it is wrong to satisfy their mutual desires except in marriage, they will enter into a marriage that is grounded in the flimsy foundation of mere sexual attraction. When this attraction dies, as it inevitably must, the sad day will dawn when the partners realize that they have nothing in common.[6]

Bertrand Russell holds that it is important that one's first experience with sexual intercourse not be put off until one has already contracted legal marriage. Since man does not have instinctive knowledge as to how to engage properly in sexual intercourse, it is important for him to gain experience in this area before embarking on the serious venture of raising a family. Moreover, the difficulties encountered by a young man in his attempts to be chaste will probably make him timid and inhibited with the result that when he finally marries he will find it extremely difficult to break through his inhibitions, or he may be able to overcome his timidity only in a sudden and brutal way. Finally, aside from considerations such as those that have been mentioned, it is absurd for two people to make a lifelong commitment to each other without being certain that they are sexually compatible. We do not prohibit a man from inspecting the inside of a house until he has already completed the purchase, why then do we place a prohibition on sexual experimentation by people contemplating marriage?[7]

---

[4] Eustace Chesser, *Unmarried Love* (New York: Pocket Books, 1965), pp. 28, 35–36, 66, 68.

[5] See footnote 1, pp. 62–63.

[6] See footnote 4, p. 38.

[7] Bertrand Russell, *Marriage and Morals* (New York: Bantam Books, 1959), pp. 112–113, 190.

Russell maintains that one way for people to avoid the difficulties connected with trying to be chaste and to prepare themselves for the serious task of rearing children is to contract temporary marriages. Such marriages would be characterized by an understanding between the couple that they would take the necessary contraceptive precautions to avoid having children. For it is Russell's contention that it is only the task of rearing children that requires that marriage entail a long-range commitment between partners. Temporary marriages will help those people who find it difficult to contract a stable relationship with one person without having had previous experiences with a variety of other persons. Moreover, such marriages would help university students in their work in that it would provide them with a means to avoid the present obsession with sexual matters that interferes with their work. These marriages will also help them acquire sexual experience that will be of great value to them when they take on the responsibility of rearing children. Finally, they will be able to acquire this experience without the dread of contracting venereal disease and without the necessity for deceit and concealment that presently mar youthful adventures.[8]

A third tack taken by those who defend the morality of premarital coition is to ask how a marriage certificate can transform sexual intercourse from an immoral to a moral act.[9] Young people who defend the morality of their premarital coition on the grounds that they love each other clearly have a stronger case than those who would make the possession of a piece of paper the determining factor in the moral evaluation of the sexual relations between people. The important question that must be asked by those contemplating sexual intercourse is not whether the intercourse takes place before marriage, but whether their love and regard for each other is sufficient to include coition as part of their total relationship.[10]

The position that grounds the morality of sexual intercourse in a marriage certificate or ceremony fails to acknowledge that there is no necessary connection between marriage and satisfying and constructive sexual relations. Sexual relations that occur within the framework of a legalized marriage may be destructive of the good of the couple, whereas those occurring outside of such a framework may work for the benefit of both partners. The traditional view of the necessary relationship between sexual intercourse and marriage often obscures this point and is guilty of giving unexperienced youths the mistaken idea that full and satisfying sexual relations are absolutely guaranteed by the process of the wedding ceremony. The fact of the matter is that the ability to establish satisfying sexual relations between people may often take time and may be achieved only through what may be at times a rocky learning process.[11]

[8] Ibid., p. 190.

[9] Ibid., p. 27.

[10] Hans Hofman, Sex Incorporated: A Positive View of the Sexual Revolution (Boston: Beacon Press, 1967), pp. 75–76, 82.

[11] Ibid., pp. 84–85.

2. HUMAN SEXUALITY AND THE MORALITY OF ASPIRATION

Disagreements concerning the morality of premarital intercourse are often grounded in differing conceptions of the character of man's moral task. For example, Chesser sees no moral issue raised by a situation in which two consenting individuals, without pressure from either side, engage in an activity which leads to no social consequences. Thus, because two people can engage in premarital sexual intercourse without causing any social consequence such as the birth of a child, there is no moral issue concerning such activity.[12] Working out of the context of the discussion of the relationship between law and morality that was conducted in Chapter II, I would say that Chesser has confused the legal and the moral orders. The fact that two consenting adults may fornicate without harming others may indicate that there should be no laws against fornication, but it does not prove that fornication raises no moral issue. If morality is understood as the morality of aspiration in which man tries to live up to what he finds to be best in himself or to be most in keeping with his character as a human subject, an argument that shows that a certain type of activity need not be a matter of legal concern will not be accepted as proof that this activity is moral.

Wilson's use of the fallacy of discrimination also requires that thought be given to clarifying one's conception of the nature of the moral venture. This fallacy can be legitimately applied to certain positions taken with respect to what we may term aesthetic matters, e.g. matters concerning one's personal tastes in music, food, clothing, or furniture. It can also apply to moral matters if we presuppose that there is no difference between a situation in which a man is confronted with a moral decision and one in which he is confronted with an aesthetic decision. I shall try to show that there is a difference between the two situations and that the character of this difference is such that the fallacy of discrimination is not applicable with respect to moral matters.

The difference between aesthetic and moral matters may be gathered from the following examples. A man looking over a menu may say to himself: "Let me see, should I order pheasant under glass or a hamburger. I know that pheasant under glass is considered to be better than hamburger, but I simply don't feel like having such an elegant dinner. Besides, I've had a great many elegant dinners lately; so, for a change, I think I'll order hamburger." It certainly would be fallacious to accuse this man of being insensitive and despicable simply because he did not choose the meal that is considered to be of greater gastronomical value.

Are we prepared to say the same thing about a life guard at a beach who

[12] See footnote 4, p. 28.

goes through the same process of reasoning in trying to decide whether he ought to try to save a drowning child? Can we pass the same sort of neutral judgment on the behavior of the life guard who reaches his decision through the following line of thought? "Let me see, I saved a child from drowning a few days ago. I know that the just thing for me to do is to save this child, but I think that I'd prefer a change from justice today, so I'll watch this child drown." It seems clear that a prima-facie view of both decisions indicates that there is a significant difference between them—a difference of sufficient magnitude to call into question the validity of applying Wilson's fallacy of discrimination to any and all types of human decisions.

This same sort of question can be raised with respect to Wilson's charge that those who cannot treat a woman as a goddess one time, a companion another time, and simply a body to take to bed another time are psychologically narrow and impoverished. Are we to say that a man who can only try to help alleviate the suffering of others, but who cannot take pleasure in watching them suffer is also psychologically impoverished and narrow? If this latter inability, together with such inabilities as the inability to cheat another man of his life's savings and the inability to surrender one's commitment to a worthwhile task the minute the smallest obstacle is placed in one's way, make a man guilty of being psychologically narrow and impoverished, then let us acknowledge that a good part of man's moral task consists in making himself psychologically narrow and impoverished.

However, in making this acknowledgment, we should note that the use of the pejorative words are justified only if one takes a purely quantitative view of human life. Seen from this perspective, Adolf Hitler's life was richer and more expanded than a man who could not bring himself to order the systematic extermination of innocent human beings. The discussion of the virtues in Chapter V indicated that a major part of man's moral task consists in trying to develop a character who can act in certain ways with ease, pleasure, and consistency. The fact that a man has worked to develop his character so that he cannot with ease and pleasure be unjust to another man does not constitute a shortcoming in his person, if we are considering his person from a moral point of view. The moral richness of a human person is to be judged not solely and exclusively by the number of different acts he is able to perform, but by the kind of person he is and by the types of acts he is able to perform with ease, pleasure, and consistency. Hence, if there is nothing morally wrong with treating a woman as a mere body to be enjoyed in bed, a man who is unable to treat women in this way might well be accused of not being sufficiently diversified in his approaches to women.

If, however, such behavior is immoral, Wilson's charge of psychological narrowness and impoverishment has no more significance than the taunt "Chicken!" which boys level at a companion who refuses to participate in the "mugging" and robbery of a man enjoying an evening's stroll through the park. Man's moral task is not simply to try to do anything and everything indiscriminately, but to try to pursue those activities that contribute to his growth as a subject in a community of ends and to avoid those activities that are contrary to his being as a member of this community.

These criticisms of Wilson's position on premarital sexual unions have been directed to showing that his arguments are valid only on the presupposition that sexual unions precisely in so far as they are premarital are morally neutral or are matters of aesthetic, rather than moral, significance. The criticisms certainly are not sufficient in and of themselves to justify the position that such unions are immoral, but they point to the task that faces one who would disagree with Wilson. It is necessary to specify that which differentiates moral issues from aesthetic issues and try to point to the character of human sexual unions that makes them matters of moral significance. The first task will be taken up in the remainder of this section, and the second task in the following section.

Moral issues differ from aesthetic issues in that the man confronted with a moral decision is not a spectator judging the relative merits of something wholly external to himself such as hamburgers and pheasants seen from the perspective of their gastronomical or nutritional value. It is the character of his own being as a human subject that is at issue in moral decisions. He is faced with deciding what sort of person he will be. The question of justice that confronted the life guard in the example given above was not a question concerning the value of some thing that was wholly external to him. His behavior toward another human being in need would determine whether or not he would accept the responsibility of making himself a just person. Wilson's fallacy of discrimination applies if an activity is being condemned in the name of a value that is neutral to the question of the assertion or denial of one's own human subjectivity or that of another. Thus, if a casual sexual affair is condemned in the name of a value that is neutral in this sense, Wilson is right in holding that the failure of such an affair to live up to such a value does not mean that the affair is immoral.

This discussion is also helpful in distinguishing between moral matters and matters relating to what Atkinson refers to as personal preferences or ideals. Whether or not one considers an activity a matter of personal preference or of moral significance will depend ultimately on the standard of morality with which he is working and the relationship between the activity in question and that standard. For example, working out of the context of reflective naturalism, I may personally be disgusted with a man who slurps his soup, but such a personal feeling does not constitute a sufficient basis for condemning the activity as immoral. Such behavior can be said to be immoral from the point of view of reflective naturalism only if reasons can be advanced showing it to be destructive of human freedom or not in keeping with the character of human subjectivity. Because such behavior does not appear to play a very significant role in the character of man as a subject, it is seen as a matter of personal preference and not of moral significance by a reflective naturalist. It is thus clear that one's judgment concerning whether or not premarital sexual unions are matters of moral significance will depend on the moral standard with which one examines the issue. If one is a utilitarian, one might very properly conclude that there is no moral issue involved in premarital coition so long as one could be reasonably sure that such activity will not result in such bad consequences as the birth of a child out of wedlock, the contraction of a serious venereal disease, or the suffering of psychological damage such as pangs of guilt or remorse.

In keeping with the standard of reflective naturalism and the criticism of utilitarianism advanced in Chapter IV, the following section will base its evaluation of the morality of premarital unions not simply on a consideration of their possible extrinsic consequences, but also on an evaluation of the character of these unions in the light of our knowledge of man as a subject and end in himself. I shall not press the utilitarian considerations, admitting that it may be possible for people to engage in premarital sexual experiences without being afflicted with physical disease or much psychological discomfort. This admission should not be taken to mean that I think that in most cases people come out of such unions completely unscathed. I think that in our culture it is probable that premarital sexual unions may extract a rather high psychological price from many people. However, I know no way of proving this.

What I shall be concerned with is the compatibility between premarital sexual intercourse and human subjectivity. If it can be shown that such unions involve the reduction of human subjects to the status of objects, the immorality of the unions has been established. The fact that people can engage in immoral unions without suffering any harm simply shows that it is possible for people to get away with immorality in this world. That two people can impoverish the quality of human existence without suffering physical disease or conscious psychological difficulties simply illustrates a fact that should be well known to any mature person, namely people may be immoral and happy. The same stepmotherly nature that through disease or economic disaster can make the moral man unhappy can contribute to the happiness of the immoral man.

The confusion of morality with wealth was once rather commonly held in the United States. It seemed obvious to many that the poverty of the poor man was to be accounted for by his immorality. Hopefully we have put this bit of nonsense aside, but I wonder if we have not fallen victim of another confusion in equating morality with physical and/or psychological health. In calling attention to this possible confusion, I am not denying that physical and psychological well-being are human goods—goods for which we ought to strive—but I am pointing out that the mere fact that one comes out of a certain situation physically and psychologically healthy, according to present standards of psychological health, does not mean that one acted morally in that situation. Thus, the embezzler may be a perfect specimen of physical health and may be so secure in his technique and having such a good time spending other peoples' money that he enjoys better psychological health than his fellow worker who is trying to make financial ends meet with the wages he has honestly earned.

G. E. Moore's open question argument also serves to bring out this point. The fact that I know a man is honest, just, and courageous tells me nothing about his physical health (he may be a diabetic or have a poor heart condition), or about his psychological well-being (he may be suffering from an anxiety neurosis whose roots reach back to his childhood). Similarly, the knowledge that a person is healthy tells me nothing about his moral character. Hence, if we grant that premarital intercourse is not harmful to the couple's physical or psychological well-being, we may still ask whether it is morally good.

There is a similar difficulty in the defense of the morality of premarital coition in so far as this defense is grounded in the view that such activity is not immoral so long as neither partner suffers guilt or remorse. The knowledge that a person either does or does not feel guilt with respect to a certain line of behavior may tell something about his character, but not about the morality of the type of behavior in question. For example, the fact that many Nazis felt no guilt about their role in the extermination of six million Jews certainly does not prove that such behavior was or is moral. To move from the fact that an individual or group of individuals felt no guilt after performing a certain activity to the conclusion that this activity is thus proved to be moral is to commit the naturalistic fallacy. For whether or not a man feels guilt about something will often depend on such factors as an individual's character, his outlook on life, or the type of society in which he lives. Thus, granted a sadistic character or granted that an individual sees nothing wrong with sadism, there will be no guilt connected with sadistic behavior. Hence, we are moving from what is the case—for example, a given sadistic character—to what ought to be the case. Once we realize that whether or not we feel guilty concerning certain activities is largely determined by the existential state of our character or of the culture in which we live, we come to see that the task of building one's moral character includes that of trying to become a person who feels guilt concerning those immoral acts for which he ought to feel guilt and who does not feel guilt concerning acts that are either morally good or morally neutral.

Having indicated the possible pitfalls that may confuse our moral judgments, it is now necessary to indicate the possible stance which reflective naturalism may take with respect to the issue of the morality of premarital sexual unions. It is clear that premarital intercourse need not deprive man of his freedom, but there is a further point that deserves consideration in dealing with this issue. Man in his freedom is in the process of deciding the way in which human subjectivity is to be realized in the world. He determines the existential character of his own subjectivity and he contributes to the existential character of the subjectivity of others. Hence, he must ask himself what is he making of himself and of his partners in premarital unions. This question moves the issue of premarital intercourse beyond the narrow and negative confines of asking whether I can engage in premarital coition without harming anybody. The moral vision of man will certainly not ignore this type of question, but neither will it be mesmerized by it to the exclusion of all other aspects of man's moral venture.

As a moral being, man is the being in the world who decides whether values such as loyalty, courage, and justice will be mere words or will be as real as is his life in the world in that his lived response to his world will be in terms of such values. For example, it may be possible for a married man to engage in extramarital affairs without harming anyone because his wife will never know about the affairs and because he is able to find women who are willing to be his sex partners, despite the fact that they know that he is married. However, a moral evaluation of this situation requires one to look beyond this possibility to the fact that the man is confronted with the decision of whether or not in his response to this situation, he is going to give a standing in the world to faithfulness and adherence to a promise. He must decide whether he will use his freedom to make faithfulness a mere word or a living reality. Similarly, the man, who would prefer not to meet his responsibilities and who knows that others will meet them for him without any trouble, cannot say that he has met his moral obligations because his irresponsibility harmed no one. He has failed in the moral task of giving existence in his person to man as a being capable of taking on and meeting responsibilities.

If one sees man's moral task as being simply that of not harming anyone, that is if one sees this task in purely negative terms, he will certainly not accept the argument to be presented in the following section. However, if one accepts the notion of the morality of aspiration, if one accepts the view that man's moral task involves the positive attempt to live up to what is best in man, to give reality to what he sees to be the perfection of himself as a human subject, the argument may be acceptable.

3. SEXUALITY AND THE HUMAN SUBJECT

The discussion of Wilson's fallacy of discrimination and of Atkinson's distinction between moral matters and matters of personal preference has left us with the question as to whether sexual intercourse is a type of activity that is similar to choosing a dinner from a menu. This question is of utmost significance in that one's view of the morality of premarital intercourse seems to depend on the significance that one gives to the sexual encounter in human life. Those such as Wilson and Chesser who see nothing immoral about the premarital character of sexual intercourse seem to see sexual intercourse as being no different from myriad of other purely aesthetic matters. This point is seen in Chesser's questioning of the reason for demanding permanence in the relationship of sexual partners when we do not see such permanence as being important to other human relationships.[13] It is also seen in his asking why we raise a moral issue about premarital coition when two people may engage in it, with the resulting social and psychological consequences being no different than if they had gone to a movie.[14]

---

[13] *Ibid.*, p. 29.
[14] *Ibid.*, pp. 35–36, see also p. 66.

Wilson most explicitly makes a case for the view that sexual intercourse does not differ significantly from other human activities. He holds that people think that there is a logical difference between the question "Will you engage in sexual intercourse with me?" and the question, "Will you play tennis with me?" only because they are influenced by the acquisitive character of contemporary society.[15] Granted that the two questions may be identical from the purely formal perspective of logic, the ethician must move beyond this perspective to a consideration of their content. Men and women find themselves involved in many different relationships: for example, as buyer-seller, employer-employee, teacher-student, lawyer-client, and partners or competitors in certain games such as tennis or bridge. Is there any morally significant difference between these relationships and sexual intercourse? We cannot examine all the possible relationships into which a man and woman can enter, but we will consider the employer-employee relationship in order to get some perspective on the distinctive character of the sexual relationship.

A man pays a woman to act as his secretary. What rights does he have over her in such a situation? The woman agrees to work a certain number of hours during the day taking dictation, typing letters, filing reports, arranging appointments and flight schedules, and greeting clients and competitors. In short, we can say that the man has rights to certain of the woman's services or skills. The use of the word "services" may lead some to conclude that this relationship is not significantly different from the relationship between a prostitute and her client in that the prostitute also offers her "services."

It is true that we sometimes speak euphemistically of a prostitute offering her services to a man for a sum of money, but if we are serious about our quest for the difference between the sexual encounter and other types of human relationships, it is necessary to drop euphemisms and face the issue directly. The man and woman who engage in sexual intercourse are giving their bodies, the most intimate physical expression of themselves, over to the other. Unlike the man who plays tennis with a woman, the man who has sexual relations with her has literally entered her. A man and woman engaging in sexual intercourse have united themselves as intimately and as totally as is physically possible for two human beings. Their union is not simply a union of organs, but is as intimate and as total a physical union of two selves as is possible of achievement. Granted the character of this union, it seems strange to imply that there is no need for a man and woman to give any more thought to the question of whether they should engage in sexual intercourse than to the question of whether they should play tennis.

In opposition to Wilson, I think that it is the acquisitive character of our society that has blinded us to the distinction between the two activities. Wilson's and Chesser's positions seem to imply that exactly the same moral considerations ought to apply to a situation in which a housewife is bartering with a butcher for a few pounds of pork chops and the situation in which two human beings

[15] See footnote 1, p. 67.

are deciding whether sexual intercourse ought to be an ingredient of their relationship. So long as the butcher does not put his thumb on the scale in the weighing process, so long as he is truthful in stating that the meat is actually pork, so long as the woman pays the proper amount with the proper currency, the trade is perfectly moral. Reflecting on sexual intercourse from the same sort of economic perspective, one can say that so long as the sexual partners are truthful in reporting their freedom from contagious venereal diseases and so long as they are truthful in reporting that they are interested in the activity for the mere pleasure of it or to try out their sexual techniques, there is nothing immoral about such activity. That in the one case pork chops are being exchanged for money whereas in the other the decision concerns the most complete and intimate merging of one's self with another makes no difference to the moral evaluation of the respective cases.

It is not surprising that such a reductionistic outlook should pervade our thinking on sexual matters, since in our society sexuality is used to sell everything from shave cream to underarm deodorants, to soap, to mouthwash, to cigarettes, and to automobiles. Sexuality has come to play so large a role in our commercial lives that it is not surprising that our sexuality should itself come to be treated as a commodity governed by the same moral rules that govern any other economic transaction.

Once sexuality is taken out of this commercial framework, once the character of the sexual encounter is faced directly and squarely, we will come to see that Doctor Mary Calderone has brought out the type of questions that ought to be asked by those contemplating the introduction of sexual intercourse into their relationships: "How many times, and how casually, are you willing to invest a portion of your total self, and to be the custodian of a like investment from the other person, without the sureness of knowing that these investments are being made for keeps?"[16] These questions come out of the recognition that the sexual encounter is a definitive experience, one in which the physical intimacy and merging involves also a merging of the nonphysical dimensions of the partners. With these questions, man moves beyond the negative concern with avoiding his or another's physical and psychological harm to the question of what he is making of himself and what he is contributing to the existential formation of his partner as a human subject.

If we are to make a start toward responding to Calderone's questions we must cease talking about human selfhood in abstraction. The human self is an historical as well as a physical being. He is a being who is capable of making at least a portion of his past an object of his consciousness and thus is able to make this past play a conscious role in his present and in his looking toward the future. He is also a being who looks to the future, who faces tomorrow with plans, ideals, hopes, and fears. The very being of a human self involves his past

---

[16] Mary Steichen Calderone, "The Case for Chastity," *Sex in America,* ed. by Henry Anatole Grunwald (New York: Bantam Books, 1964), p. 147.

and his movement toward the future. Moreover, the human self is not completely shut off in his own past and future. Men and women are capable of consciously and purposively uniting themselves in a common career and venture. They can commit themselves to sharing the future with another, sharing it in all its aspects—in its fortunes and misfortunes, in its times of happiness and times of tragedy. Within the lives of those who have so committed themselves to each other, sexual intercourse is a way of asserting and confirming the fullness and totality of their mutual commitment.

Unlike those who have made such a commitment and who come together in the sexual act in the fullness of their selfhood, those who engage in premarital sexual unions and who have made no such commitment act as though they can amputate their bodily existence and the most intimate physical expression of their selfhood from their existence as historical beings. Granting that there may be honesty on the verbal level in that two people engaging in premarital intercourse openly state that they are interested only in the pleasure of the activity, the fact remains that such unions are morally deficient because they lack existential integrity in that there is a total merging and union on a physical level, on the one hand, and a conscious decision not to unite any other dimension of themselves, on the other hand. Their sexual union thus involves a "depersonalization" of their bodily existence, an attempt to cut off the most intimate physical expression of their respective selves from their very selfhood. The mutual agreement of premarital sex partners is an agreement to merge with the other not as a self, but as a body which one takes unto oneself, which one possesses in a most intimate and total fashion for one's own pleasure or designs, allowing the other to treat oneself in the same way. It may be true that no physical or psychological harm may result from such unions, but such partners have failed to existentially incorporate human sexuality, which is at the very least the most intimate physical expression of the human self, into the character of this selfhood.

In so far as premarital sexual unions separate the intimate and total physical union that is sexual intercourse from any commitment to the self in his historicity, human sexuality, and consequently the human body, have been fashioned into external things or objects to be handed over totally to someone else, whenever one feels that he can get possession of another's body, which he can use for his own purposes.[17] The human body has thus been treated no differently from the pork chops spoken of previously or from any other object or commodity, which human beings exchange and haggle over in their day-to-day transactions. One hesitates to use the word that might be used to capture the moral value that has been sacrificed in premarital unions because in our day the word has taken on a completely negative meaning at best, and, at worst, it has

[17] The psychoanalyst Rollo May makes an excellent point in calling attention to the tendency in contemporary society to exploit the human body as if it were only a machine. Rollo May, "The New Puritanism," *Sex in America*, pp. 161–164.

become a word used by "sophisticates" to mock or deride certain attitudes toward human sexuality. However, because the word "chastity" has been thus abused is no reason to leave it in the hands of those who have misrepresented the human value to which it gives expression.

The chaste person has often been described as one intent on denying his sexuality. The value of chastity as conceived in this section is in direct opposition to this description. It is the unchaste person who is separating himself from his sexuality, who is willing to exchange human bodies as one would exchange money for tickets to a baseball game—honestly and with no commitment of self to self. Against this alienation of one's sexuality from one's self, an alienation that makes ones' sexuality an object, which is to be given to another in exchange for his objectified sexuality, chastity affirms the integrity of the self in his bodily and historical existence. The sexuality of man is seen as an integral part of his subjectivity. Hence, the chaste man rejects depersonalized sexual relations as a reduction of man in his most intimate physical being to the status of an object or pure instrument for another. He asserts that man is a subject and end in himself, not in some trans-temporal, nonphysical world, but in the historical-physical world in which he carries on his moral task and where he finds his fellow man. He will not freely make of himself in his bodily existence a thing to be handed over to another's possession, nor will he ask that another treat his own body in this way. The total physical intimacy of sexual intercourse will be an expression of total union with the other self on all levels of their beings. Seen from this perespective, chastity is one aspect of man's attempt to attain existential integrity, to accept his body as a dimension of his total personality.

In concluding this section, it should be noted that I have tried to make a case against the morality of premarital sexual intercourse even in those cases in which the partners are completely honest with each other. There is reason to question whether the complete honesty, to which those who see nothing immoral in such unions refer, is as a matter of fact actually found very often among premarital sex partners. We may well have been dealing with textbook cases which present these unions in their best light. One may be pardoned for wondering whether sexual intercourse often occurs under the following conditions: "Hello, my name is Josiah. I am interested in having a sexual experience with you. I can assure you that I am good at it and that I have no communicable disease. If it sounds good to you and if you have taken the proper contraceptive precautions, we might have a go at it. Of course, I want to make it clear to you that I am interested only in the sexual experience and that I have no intention of making any long-range commitment to you." If those, who defend the morality of premarital sexual unions so long as they are honestly entered into, think that I have misrepresented what they mean by honesty, then they must specify what they mean by an honest premarital union.

My point in raising this issue is that matters sound so easy when one says, as Chesser does, that there is nothing wrong with premarital intercourse so long as both partners are honest with each other and so long as there is no pressure from either side. I have tried to discuss the issues granting that there actually is honesty and no pressure from either side. However, it seems necessary to ask whether or not these conditions are actually fulfilled in the majority of pre-marital encounters. For example, Lester Kirkendall, who interviewed 200 college-level males and gathered the case histories of 668 premarital intercourse experiences, states that he believes that the great bulk of premarital intercourse appears to be of an exploitive and advantage-taking character.[18] Among the cases he presents is one in which a boy, who, recognizing that a girl was afraid of losing him, worked to heighten this fear and to use it as a leverage to secure the girl's agreement to engage in sexual intercourse. He also points out that many of the seventy-seven men, who had premarital intercourse with dating partners for whom they had considerable emotional attachments, simply drifted into sexual intercourse, being carried away by prolonged petting and repeated stimulation.[19] When sexual intercourse occurs under such conditions, it is simply ludicrous to talk about an honest decision to engage in premarital intercourse.

It may well be that beneath the exploitation that seems to characterize a good number, if not a majority, of premarital sexual unions, there may be more pro-found, unexpressed human factors at work. David Riesman may have made a valid point in reflecting on the motivation that may lead young people to engage in premarital intercourse. "It seems to me that young people are increasingly preoccupied with their capacity to love as well as to be loved. And I have the impression that sexual relations themselves when they do occur come about less frequently from a desire on the part of boys to present trophies to their own male vanity than to secure themselves against the anxiety that they may not be truly and deeply loved, or capable of love."[20] This analysis moves the issue of human sexuality from what appears to me to be the rather empty fantasy world in which the sexual encounter is seen as being analogous to playing tennis or going to the movies with a member of the opposite sex, to the character of human love and its relationship to human sexuality.

To ask the question, "Is one's capacity to love or to be loved truly and deeply to be simply identified with engaging in sexual intercourse?" is to answer it. Prostitutes, rapists, intoxicated adolescents, Don Juans, nymphomaniacs—all can and do engage in sexual intercourse. The mere fact of engaging in sexual intercourse does not of itself manifest a capacity to love or to be loved. Sexual intercourse can be a manifestation and expression of a deep human love, but human beings are clearly capable of engaging in sexual intercourse without any love existing between them. If the purpose of this section has been achieved, and if love is seen as involving a respect for the selfhood of another, it is clear

[18] Lester Kirkendall, " 'Interpersonal' Morality," *Sex in America*, p. 118.

[19] Lester Kirkendall, *Premarital Intercourse and Interpersonal Relationships* (New York: Gramercy Publishing Co., 1956), p. 134.

[20] David Riesman, "Permissiveness and Sex Roles," *Marriage and Family Living*, Vol. XXI (August, 1959), p. 213.

that to engage in sexual intercourse with another under certain conditions is to manifest a lack of such respect and that this point is true even if the other is agreeable to engaging in the activity.

4. MARRIAGE AS A TOTAL HUMAN COMMITMENT

The preceding argument against the morality of premarital sexual unions was not based on the view that the moral character of marriage rests on a legal certificate or on a legal or religious ceremony. The argument was not directed against "preceremonial" intercourse, but against premarital intercourse. Morally speaking, a man and woman are married when they make the mutual and total commitment to share the problems and prospects of their historical existence in the world. Although marriages are not to be identified with ceremonies, the words used in marriage ceremonies have captured the character of marriage in the promise which the partners make to each other to join their lives "for better, for worse, for richer, for poorer, in sickness and in health, till death do us part." Granted this conception of marriage, Hofman is right in saying that those contemplating sexual intercourse must ask themselves whether their love and regard for each other is sufficient to include sexual intercourse as part of their total union.

If one is going to hold that people who have a sufficient love and regard for each other are not being immoral in engaging in sexual intercourse, it is necessary for him to specify in a general fashion, at least, what is involved in his notions of "love" and "regard." Unless such an attempt is made, the words are so empty as to be meaningless. Atkinson has struck the proper note with regard to this point in his criticism of the view that sexual intercourse that is the result of "emotional sincerity" is moral. He points out that one can give no value to this criterion apart from a knowledge of the type of behavior it would entail.[21]

The description of the meaning of commitment which was given above tries to meet this type of difficulty. The commitment that constitutes marriage is a total commitment of one person to another person of the opposite sex. To understand the character of such commitment, it is necessary to know something about the being of those involved in the commitment; for if it is to be truly total, the commitment must be as rich as the being of those who have made it. It is at this point that the historical character of the human self's existence becomes important. A total commitment to another means a commitment to him in his historical existence. Such a commitment is not simply a matter of words or of feelings, however strong. It involves a full existential sharing on the part of two beings of the burdens, opportunities, and challenges of their historical existence.

Granted the importance that the character of their commitment to each other

[21] See footnote 3, p. 81.

plays in determining the moral quality of a couple's sexual encounter, it is clear that there may be nothing immoral in the behavior of couples who engage in sexual intercourse before participating in the marriage ceremony. For example, it is foolish to say that two people who are totally committed to each other and who have made all the arrangements to live this commitment are immoral if they engage in sexual intercourse the night before the marriage ceremony. Admittedly this position can be abused by those who have made a purely verbal commitment, a commitment, which will be carried out in some vague and ill-defined future. At some time or other, they will unite their two lives totally by setting up house together and by actually undertaking the task of meeting the economic, social, legal, medical responsibilities that are involved in living this commitment. Apart from the reference to a vague and amorphous future time when they will share the full responsibility for each other, their commitment presently realizes itself in going to dances, sharing a box of popcorn at Saturday night movies, and sharing their bodies whenever they can do so without taking too great a risk of having the girl become pregnant.

Having acknowledged that the position advanced in this section can be abused by those who would use the word "commitment" to rationalize what is an interest only in the body of the other person, it must be pointed out that neither the ethician nor any other human being can tell two people whether they actually have made the commitment that is marriage or are mistaking a "warm glow" for such a commitment. There comes a time when this issue falls out of the area of moral philosophy and into the area of practical wisdom. It is hoped that the discussion of the issues in this chapter can provide guidelines for the decisions of those faced with the question of whether they are ready to make sexual intercourse a part of their relationship, but it must be emphasized that the discussion was never meant to substitute for such personal reflection and decision.

The characterization of marriage as a total commitment between two human beings may lead some to conclude that the marriage ceremony is a wholly superfluous affair. It must be admitted that people may be morally married without having engaged in a marriage ceremony. However, to conclude from this point that the ceremony is totally meaningless is to lose sight of the social character of human beings. The couple contemplating marriage do not exist in a vacuum, although there may be times when they think they do. Their existences reach out beyond their union to include other human beings. By making their commitment a matter of public record, by solemnly expressing it before the law and in the presence of their respective families and friends and, if they are religious people, in the presence of God and one of his ministers, they sink the roots of their commitment more deeply and extensively in the world in which they live, thus taking steps to provide for the future growth of their commitment to each other. The public expression of this commitment makes it more fully and more explicitly a part of a couple's lives and of the world in which they live.

The ethician must acknowledge that there may be times when the mutual commitment binding engaged couples is so strong that they may be married from a moral point of view. However, circumstances may be such that they must postpone for a year or so the full existential sharing of their lives that this commitment involves. May they not morally engage in sexual intercourse during this period? It is conceivable that under such conditions, there would be nothing immoral about their sexual relations.

However, there are practical issues that ought to be taken into consideration by those who are trying to reach a concrete decision in such situations. These issues center around the question of whether sexual intercourse under these conditions will serve to strengthen and nourish the bond that unites them or weaken and possibly destroy that bond. For since they have agreed to embark on a lifelong union, they must consider the effects of their actions on this union. Viewing the question from this perspective, there are two considerations that ought to give pause to those who intend to make sexual intercourse a part of their relations over an extended period of time preceding the full-scale task of living together.

First, they ought to ask themselves whether they are beginning the difficult and challenging task of marriage in the best way by trying to find ways to keep their families and friends from knowing the full extent and depth of their actual involvement in each other's lives. Is their union best served by the fact that they must sneak off to some lovers' lane and have sexual intercourse in an automobile, hoping that they will not be spotted by patrolling policemen? Is their union best served by the stories they must frabricate to keep their families and friends from knowing that they spent the weekend together in a motel registered under assumed names? Will these practices contribute to the establishment of a sense of trust between them? Such a situation seems to engender an atmosphere of deceit and hypocrisy that would appear to be a weak foundation for a marriage. This point has been raised not with the idea that it would be absolutely impossible for two people to avoid such an atmosphere, but simply to indicate a possible source of difficulty that ought to be seriously considered by engaged couples.

The second possible difficulty is that the engaged couple may be expecting sexual intercourse to bear an excessively heavy burden in their union.[22] When sexual intercourse occurs within the lives of those who have actually begun to live the lives of two thoroughly united persons, it alone does not have to carry the full burden of strengthening their union. There is a multidimensional character to the union of two people who have set up house together. They are sharing financial burdens, planning for entertaining guests, decorating of their home or apartment, caring for the other when he or she is tired or perhaps physically ill, planning vacations, discussing issues of the day when they are

---

[22] Peter A. Bertocci, *Sex, Love, and the Person* (New York: Sheed and Ward, 1967), pp. 106–134.

alone in the quiet of the evening, becoming fully integrated in a new community. Sexuality is only one feature of this very complex union of two lives. However, when people engage in sexual intercourse before uniting their lives in such complex ways, there is the danger that their commitment to each other may in time be reduced simply to that of going to bed with each other.

Their union may become too simple an affair with the result that if any problem arises in their sex lives, they may be tempted to conclude that all is lost for them. As a matter of fact, they may have truly loved one another, but they have not provided this love with a rich enough soil in which to grow and mature. They have not provided themselves with a context that would allow the full resources of their personalities to play a role in the growth and maturation of their love. The intimacy that love needs to grow and to deepen is not simply the intimacy of sexual intercourse; it requires the intimacy involved in the day-to-day shared living that is found in a household.

This position is not based on the erroneous notion that no problems will arise in such shared living whereas they will arise in the lives of engaged couples. The point is that there are more human resources available to those who live together to help them meet their problems than are available to those who will set up house sometime in the future, but who now are expressing their love in acts of sexual intercourse. Involved in this point is the possibility that the couple may lose their perspective on the proper role of sexual intercourse in the lives of married people. Instead of seeing it as one aspect of their lives, they may begin to treat it as the whole story. When the sexual encounter begins to lose something of its edge, as it almost inevitably must if it is taken to be the sole essential feature in the lives of two people, the couple will be tempted to lose faith in their love for each other. For this love has come to be identified with the sexual encounter. Such a possibility may hardly seem to be a probability in the nonemotional atmosphere of the classroom. However, it seems to me that it could represent a real danger to the love that the engaged couple have for each other in the actual context of their lived experiences.

5. CRITICISM OF DEFENSE OF PREMARITAL COITION AS AN AID TO MARRIAGE

Having emphasized that marriage is a total commitment between two persons and having pointed to a possible danger of placing oneself in a situation that might lead him to treat sexual intercourse as the whole of marriage, it does not appear to me that the argument presented in this chapter against premarital intercourse is guilty of leading people to take on the burdens, responsibilities, and challenges of married life simply because they feel a sexual attraction to each other. If any position is guilty of implying this misleading conclusion, it would appear to be Russell's position, which states that a man and woman should test their sexual compatibility before embarking on the serious business of marriage. People working out of the context of an acceptance of this position would certainly not be acting illogically if, after a few pleasurable sexual encounters, they decided to be married.

Those who see sexual intercourse before marriage as helpful to the establishment of a good marital union would perhaps agree with the following position taken by John Wilson: "The amount that can be learned about people via sex is of course immense: a few hours in bed are often worth weeks of verbal communication."[23] If this position is to be accepted as a valid defense of the usefulness of sexual intercourse to a future marriage, it will be necessary to point out what can be learned in bed about the significant issues of married life. The response to this challenge may be that the couple can learn whether they are "sexually compatible."

The basic flaw in this position is its failure to note that the quality of any given sexual encounter is a matter inextricably bound up with the very particular conditions under which it occurs. For example, the novelty of sexual intercourse may make the experience a matter of great satisfaction for some, or it may cause problems for others. A woman who knows that her performance in this sexual experience will determine whether or not a man will marry her may either become so tense that she may not be able to respond properly, or she may rise to the occasion, although once the commitment of marriage is made, her response may become halfhearted. Moreover, its character as forbidden fruit may give to premarital sexual experiences a satisfying quality which will be lost when the couple is married. For many it is the element of the "chase" that makes the sexual encounter outside of marriage very pleasurable. Once this element is gone, once the marriage has become a part of their lives, the sexual encounter may lose its pleasure for them, at least as the encounter relates to the other partner.[24] Finally, for persons who truly love each other, it may happen that sexual intercourse gains a depth of satisfaction as it gains in meaning by becoming incorporated into the total sharing of all aspects of their lives that is involved in marriage. These complexities were noted in order to call attention to the fact that premarital intercourse is not a reliable test for anything that will occur over the long haul in a marriage, not even for the quality of a couple's future sexual experiences.

The choice of a marriage partner would indeed appear to be a comparatively easy matter if the fact that one had an unspecified number of pleasurable sexual encounters with a person of the opposite sex could be taken as evidence that their future union would not crack under the strains of economic hardships, of the loss of a child, of the birth of a retarded child, of the loss of physical beauty and/or health, not to mention the less serious stresses and strains that are inevitably a part of shared human living. This criticism is meant to point to the

[23] See footnote 1, p. 64.
[24] Ignace Lepp, *The Psychology of Loving* (New York: The New American Library, 1965), pp. 165–166.

type of questions that must be considered by persons wondering if they ought to make a lifelong commitment to each other.

Because marriage involves a union of persons, those contemplating marriage must try to come to an awareness of their own personality, as well as of the personality of the possible marriage partner. What things are important to you, what values do you cherish? What values are important to the other person? What do you think of the other person's values and what does he or she think of yours? What role does religion play in your respective lives? What differences separate you and how deeply engrained are these differences? What are your views on the place of money in human life? What forms of entertainment do you enjoy? Questions of this type are to be considered not with the idea that one's future partner should be identical with oneself. Indeed, if one thinks that he finds a complete identity between himself and his future partner, he had better look again. For the other person is different from himself, and in time and under the stress and strain of life, these differences will certainly come out. One must remember that one is marrying another person, not a mere image of oneself. If one is looking for such an image, one is perhaps not ready for marriage.

Once the types of issues that must be decided by those contemplating marriage are noted, it is difficult to see the justification for the view that sexual intercourse is necessary or even helpful before marriage as a way of establishing a better marriage. If two people have not reached an understanding of themselves with respect to the type of issues that have been mentioned through conversations, through the sharing of pleasant times and of difficult times, through the misunderstandings that may occur in their courtship, through the showing of affection that is appropriate to their courtship, they will make no great discovery of the other person's character through sexual intercourse. It is presumptuous to promise that abstinence from premarital coition will guarantee a happy marriage, but it is no less presumptuous to make such a promise to those who engage in premarital intercourse.

Russell's argument against chastity before marriage is based on a parody of the nature of chastity. It will be recalled that the argument maintained that the difficulties encountered by a young man trying to be chaste would probably cause him to be timid and inhibited and that such a man would be able to overcome these inhibitions either with extreme difficulty or in a sudden and brutal manner. This position fails to draw an important distinction between the factors that may underlie a young man's decision not to engage in premarital intercourse. If the decision is based on a view of human sexuality as being something inherently evil, or if it is based exclusively on a fear of contracting venereal disease, or if it is the result of a deep-seated psychosis, the young man may find himself in the predicament described by Russell. However, the situation changes radically if the man tries to be chaste because he thinks that he ought to engage in sexual intercourse only with a woman with whom he could share his whole self. Such a man does not see sexual intercourse as an evil in itself. He sees it as a moral good under certain conditions and as a moral evil under other conditions. He does not avoid it out of fear or disgust, but out of a positive concern to assert what he sees to be its proper place in human life. It is his respect for his own subjectivity and for that of others that is behind his abstinence. There is no reason to suppose that such a man will find it difficult to engage in sexual intercourse with the woman whom he loves or that he will lose his concern and tenderness for her in the act of sexual intercourse.

Russell's account of the possible harmful effects of abstaining from premarital intercourse fits in with an attitude that seems to be prevalent in some circles which holds that any frustration of man's sexual desires is bad. It should be noted that this position is far from being universally accepted in psychological circles. For example, the psychoanalyst Erich Fromm states, "The obvious clinical facts demonstrate that men—and women—who devote their lives to unrestricted sexual satisfaction do not attain happiness and very often suffer from severe neurotic conflicts or symptoms. The complete satisfaction of all instinctual needs is not only not a basis for happiness, it does not even guarantee sanity."[25] A similar point is made by the psychoanalyst Ernest Van Den Haag who points out, "It can be as healthy to frustrate as it is to gratify one's desires."[26] Although the position which I have taken with respect to sexual morality did not promise health, it seems clear that it cannot be accused of calling for a line of behavior that is destructive of human health simply because it counsels abstinence from sexual intercourse apart from the total commitment of the partners to each other.

Moreover, the view that we ought not to frustrate our sexual desires because they are "natural" is involved in all the problems raised by John Stuart Mill and by Moore's naturalistic fallacy which were discussed in Chapter III. Although Russell, at one point, seems to see the thwarting of natural impulses as bad, he states that he does not advocate a morality that tells people they ought to follow their impulses and do whatever they please.[27] He sees a need for self-control in human life: "There has to be continuous effort directed to ends that are not immediately beneficial and not at every moment attractive; there has to be consideration for others; and there should be certain standards of rectitude. I should not, however, regard self-control as an end in itself."[28] Once one acknowledges the need for self-control in man's moral life, as I think everyone must who is aware of the fact that man does not come from the hand of nature as a morally perfect being and that he must shape his natural impulses into a moral character—once this acknowledgment is made, it is necessary to acknowledge also that there are certain frustrations and difficulties that a man ought to accept freely as a part of his life because he can meet his moral obligations only through such an acceptance. Admitting then that abstinence from premarital unions will involve difficulties, I have tried to show that such difficulties ought

[25] Erich Fromm, *The Art of Loving* (New York: Bantam Books, 1963), pp. 77–78.
[26] Ernest Van Den Haag, "Love or Marriage," *Sex in America,* p. 198.
[27] See footnote 7, p. 198.
[28] *Ibid.,* p. 209.

to be borne, if man is to avoid relationships in which the parties involved alienate themselves from their bodies, treating them as objects or commodities to be exchanged.

There are two issues involved in Russell's notion of trial marriages, a moral and a legal one. Having already taken the stand that sexual relationships outside of a total commitment to the other are immoral, I have presented my argument with respect to the moral issue. I have no moral opposition to offer against the passage of a law that would allow for trial marriages, because the law could be made to apply to mature adults and because there is no moral justification for the law intervening in such cases. However, there are pragmatic considerations which lead me to conclude that the law would not deliver as much in practice as it seems to promise on paper.

We now have some experience with these types of relationships in the United States in which a young lad going into his last year or two of college or beginning his graduate or medical studies marries a girl who will finance him through school, keep house for him during this period, and provide him with a bed companion. After completing his studies, the man finds that his wife is not his type and leaves her for a more sophisticated girl. At present, this sort of thing seems to happen accidentally, without either the man or the woman planning it this way. If Russell's plan were to be implemented, the girl would go into the relationship with an explicit understanding that she might be left when a better catch comes along. Aside from the morality of the situation, one must say that any girl who knowingly becomes involved in such a relationship manifests a lack of intelligence; but the law cannot protect adults from their stupidities.

It might be pointed out that I am painting too gloomy a picture for the girl, since she will be aware of the temporary character of the marriage. She would thus be as free to be on the lookout for good possibilities for future alliances as would her husband. This is certainly true, but it does not appear to be a very pleasant way for two people to live together. The intimacy of marriage is difficult enough when both partners share common goals. When the intimacy occurs in a context in which each of the partners feels that he must protect his or her own interest against the day when the other partner will find something better, the situation does not appear to contribute to a harmonious union.

Finally, it would be necessary for the law to state what action could be taken by the state in the event the couple had children. There would be no problem if both partners agreed to have children, since neither would press charges. What would the punishment be if the wife decided that she could make the union permanent by simply not taking her contraceptive pills? Would the husband have the right to call the police who would take the woman to the hospital and force her to undergo an abortion? How could the husband prove that he did not agree with the wife's decision to bear a child? Would the state force the couple to remain married to each other?

Some might respond that the state would not handle the issue any differently than is now the practice in various states, when married people who have children decide on a divorce. Moreover, it might also be pointed out that the difficulties that I have outlined are to be found in the present state of affairs. If one were to agree with both these points, he would then be required to show what significant change for the better would occur if the state were to recognize trial marriages. For my point has been precisely that the legalization of trial marriages will not introduce any significant improvements with respect to the current legal status of marriage.

6. THE CASE FOR LESS RESTRICTIVE ABORTION LAWS

The purpose of this section is to present some of the major arguments offered by those who hold that the laws governing abortion in most states of the United States are too restrictive and must therefore be changed. There are two matters that must be clarified before we can proceed to this task. First, the meaning of the term "abortion" must be specified. As the word is used in today's medical circles, it refers to the expulsion of the embryo or fetus from the uterus before it is capable of living outside of the uterus. Thus, the present medical use of the term includes what layman commonly refer to as a "miscarriage." For purposes of the discussion that follows, it will be well to distinguish between induced abortions and spontaneous abortions. Spontaneous abortions are those abortions that are caused by factors other than the voluntary intervention of man. This phrase covers those abortions that laymen refer to as miscarriages. Induced abortions are abortions that are brought about by the voluntary intervention of man in the growth process of the embryo or fetus. Induced abortions are the ones that will be at issue in the following discussion.

The second point that must be considered is the type of laws that will be under criticism in this section. Because the states differ in their statement of the laws, we shall simply indicate the type of law that is at issue. The proponents of a more liberalized abortion law are opposed to those laws that allow abortion only in cases where the mother's life is in danger.[29] The precise extent of the proposed liberalization will become apparent as we proceed. The arguments for liberalization will be treated under the following headings: (a) Problems with Presently Existing Laws, (b) Abortion Laws and the Confusion of Law and Morality, and (c) The Question of the Human Condition of the Fetus.

[29] For a summary statement of the abortion laws of the various states of the United States as of 1958 see Abortion in the United States, ed. by Mary Steichen Calderone (New York: Hoeber and Harper Book, 1958), pp. 187–192. Colorado, North Carolina, and California have recently liberalized their abortion statutes. See Paul G. Reiter, "Trends in Abortion Legislation," Saint Louis University Law Journal, Vol. 12 (Winter, 1967), p. 260.

a. PROBLEMS WITH PRESENTLY EXISTING LAWS

Those arguing for liberalized abortion laws often emphasize that restrictive abortion laws are motivated by a desire to punish women who have engaged in extramarital sexual intercourse by forcing them to bear the children resulting from such unions. These restricted laws are grounded in the view that women who have had illicit sexual unions should bear the consequences of such unions, and hence the possibility of abortion should not be open to them.[30]

A further difficulty with restrictive abortion laws is brought out by noting the estimated number of illegal abortions conducted in the United States annually and by contrasting the safety of abortions performed by competent doctors under proper hospital conditions with the dangers involved in criminal abortions. Estimates of abortions performed in the United States range from 200,000 yearly to 1,500,000, with figures 800,000 to 1,000,000 being cited most often by those favoring a liberalized abortion policy.[31] These figures are shocking when we realize that most of the abortions are performed illegally. It is intolerable that women should submit to the dangers of illegal abortions when abortions performed under hospital conditions are no more dangerous than a tonsillectomy, are rather inexpensive (with costs being estimated between $100 and $500), and result in sterilization only in comparatively rare instances.[32] One proponent of liberalized abortion laws states that the *Encyclopedia of Criminology* estimates that 10,000 women die yearly as a result of criminal abortions, whereas an editorial in *Time*, which also advocates a liberalized abortion policy, thinks that the death toll from such abortions is probably 1,000.[33]

These figures are relevant to the problem because it is argued that once outmoded abortion laws are changed, women will be able to obtain safe abortions in hospitals instead of placing their lives in the hands of incompetent criminal abortionists.

The question of the effect of abortions on the health of the women who undergo them also extends to their psychological well-being. The biologist Garrett Hardin who favors a liberalized abortion policy acknowledges that the data may be somewhat inconclusive with respect to this issue. He mentions a Swiss survey that showed that 50 per cent of those who had undergone an

[30] For examples of such characterization see the following. Lawrence Lader, *Abortion* (New York: The Bobbs-Merrill Co., 1966), p. 7. Garrett Hardin, "A Scientist's Case for Abortion," *Redbook* (May, 1967), p. 123. William B. Ober, "We Should Legalize Abortion," *The Saturday Evening Post* (October 8, 1966), p. 14.

[31] See footnote 30. Lader, p. 2. Ober, p. 14. Hardin, p. 63. "Decision . . . In the Wrong Hands," *St. Louis County Medical Society Bulletin* (October 21, 1966), p. 10. Carlson Wade, *Sex and Abortion* (Hollywood, California: The Gennell Corp., 1964), p. 19.

[32] See footnote 30. Lader, pp. 17–20. Hardin, p. 123.

[33] Wade, 19, "The Desperate Dilemma of Abortion," *Time* (October 13, 1967), p. 32.

abortion reported that they suffered some psychological disturbances. However, he also notes that a Norwegian survey contradicts the Swiss findings in that only 2 per cent of the women interviewed in this survey suffered any psychological difficulties. Hardin offers an explanation for the difference between the surveys. The difference is accounted for by the different climate of opinion pervading in each country. There is a moralistic climate in Switzerland which is still dominated by the puritanical teachings of John Calvin, and it is this climate, and not the abortion, that accounts for the women's guilt feelings.[34]

b. ABORTION LAWS AND THE CONFUSION OF LAW AND MORALITY

Those favoring restrictive abortion legislation are accused of confusing law and morals in that they are trying to legislate the moral behavior of others. People who think that abortion is immoral should realize that the liberalization of abortion laws will not force them to undergo abortions against their will. However, the restrictive laws, which they defend, actually force others to bear children against their will or to face the dangers and unpleasantness of a criminal abortion.[35] Acknowledging that every religious faith has the right to use moral suasion in trying to convince its own members and the general public not to engage in practices that it considers sinful, Lawrence Lader, a proponent of a liberalized abortion policy, points out that this right does not extend to the use of the force of the law as an instrument to impose one's views on others.[36] Since Roman Catholics are the chief culprits in regard to the abortion issue, Lader cites a position that states that Roman Catholics have no more right to force their beliefs on others than the Jews have to legislate against the use of pork for all or than Jehovah Witnesses have to legislate against blood transfusions for all.[37]

We are now at what seems to be the basis of the argument for a liberal abortion policy. No woman should be forced to bear a child she does not want. Human sexual activity practiced by consenting adults and the reproductive consequences of such activity are outside the legitimate scope of the state's activity. No church and no state has the right to tell a woman what she can or cannot do concerning her own pregnancy.[38] A woman ought to have the type of control over her own procreativity that is involved in the decision of whether or not to undergo an abortion. Women cannot be truly said to have rights, unless they are acknowledged to have the right to determine the number of children they will bear. In the final analysis, this reasoning leads to the con-

---

[34] See footnote 30. Hardin, p. 123. See also Lader, pp. 21–22.
[35] See footnote 30. Ober, pp. 14, 20.
[36] See footnote 30. Lader, p. 93.
[37] *Ibid.*, pp. 148–149.
[38] See footnote 30. Ober, p. 14.

clusion that any woman should have the right to an abortion whenever she wants one and without being required to give reasons to justify her desires.[39]

Up to this point, the presentation of the arguments for the liberalization of abortion laws has been vague in that it has not given a precise description of what is to be the nature and scope of the proposed liberalization. The reason for this vagueness is that there appears to be a number of different views taken with respect to this issue. The immediately preceding paragraph gives the basic reasoning behind one position. This position states that a woman should have an abortion whenever she wants one. It holds that the decision concerning an abortion should be a purely medical matter to be decided by the woman and her doctor without any need to justify their decision to any judge or hospital committee.

It is sometimes difficult to be sure that other suggestions for liberalizing present abortion laws are significantly different from this position. For example, Lader quotes a statement issued by the 1963 General Assembly of the Unitarian-Universalists, which states that abortions should be permitted if a pregnancy constitutes a grave danger to the mother's physical or mental health, if there are indications that the child may suffer from serious physical or mental defects, if the pregnancy is the result of rape or incest, and finally if there is "some compelling reason, physical, psychological, mental, spiritual, or economic."[40] Is this any different from the position that advocates abortion on demand? Perhaps those who take this type of position would help clarify their stand by giving some indication of the conditions, if any, under which they think abortion ought *not* be permitted.

The American Law Institute included in its 1962 Model Penal Code suggestions for a revision of abortion laws that presently restrict abortion to those cases in which the mother's life is in danger.

> A licensed physician is justified in terminating a pregnancy, if he believes that there is substantial risk that continuance of the pregnancy would gravely impair the physical or mental health of the mother or that the child would be born with grave physical or mental defects, or that the pregnancy resulted from rape, incest or other felonious intercourse. . . . No abortion shall be performed unless two physicians, one of whom may be the person performing the abortion, shall have certified in writing the circumstances which they believe to justify the abortion.[41]

The last condition concerning the need for certification differentiates this position from that which calls for abortion on demand. The use of the words "believes" and "believe" raises the question as to how it would be possible to prove that the physician or physicians did not believe what they certified.

[39] See footnote 30. Lader, pp. 2, 126, 169.
[40] *Ibid.,* p. 100.
[41] *The American Law Institute: Model Penal Code* (July 30, 1962), Section 230.2 (2), (3), pp. 189–190.

Moreover, although the Code is not as specific as the General Assembly of the Unitarian-Universalists in stating the conditions under which abortions are to be made legitimate, it might be argued that practically speaking there would be no difference between the two suggestions since the concern with the mother's physical and mental health could be taken as a shorthand expression for the conditions that were explicitly stated by the Unitarian-Universalists. For example, if a woman states that she has too many children and that she is not emotionally ready to take on the responsibility of another child, would a physician be right in accepting her statement as a basis for his belief that an abortion in her case is called for? Would it also be possible for a newly married woman pregnant with her first child to receive a legitimate abortion on the grounds that the birth of the child at this stage in her marriage would impair her mental health in that she would find it difficult to make the psychological adjustment to the marriage and to the child so soon in her marriage? Would the fact that a woman simply cannot stand the idea of bearing a child, whether it is her first or her fifth pregnancy, and that this pregnancy is making her very nervous and apprehensive constitute a legitimate ground for abortion? These questions are not offered in criticism of the Law Institute's proposal. They are raised simply to indicate that there may not be any significant difference in the last analysis between this proposal and the proposal that abortion be granted on demand.

c. THE QUESTION OF THE HUMAN CONDITION OF THE FETUS

This subsection will present three different answers given to this question by proponents of a liberalized abortion law. One answer is given by the Protestant theologian John C. Bennett who holds that those opposing the liberalization of abortion laws on the grounds that any direct killing of the fetus is murder are guilty of being so concerned with the humanity of the fetus that they fail to take into consideration other factors that have a bearing on the morality of abortion. He characterizes such a position as a "harsh and unconvincing form of legalism" in that it bases its conclusion on a single principle without any regard to other human factors in the concrete situation.[42] For example, to stress that the direct killing of a fetus is murder and to fail to note that the fetus in question may be born as a deformed child or to fail to consider the future human situation that may be brought into existence if the fetus is not aborted is to take a "blindly one-sided" view of morality.[43]

This overly simplified approach to the problem gives those who want strict abortion laws an advantage in presenting their case. They can be very precise

[42] John C. Bennett, "The Abortion Debate," *Christianity and Crisis*, Vol. XXVII (March 20, 1967), p. 47.
[43] *Ibid.*, p. 48.

in condemning the killing of the fetus as an act of murder. Unfortunately no word has been developed in our language to characterize the callousness of people who are willing to endanger a mother's health or sanity and to allow a child to be born knowing that there can be no hope that the child will achieve any fulfillment as a person.[44] Moreover, to characterize abortion as murder is to fail to acknowledge the importance of the distinction between potential personality and actual personality.[45] Lader may also have this distinction in mind in taking the position that a mother's life is far more valuable for what she actually is than fetal tissue for what it may become.[46]

Lader challenges those who oppose a liberalized abortion policy in the name of the "sanctity of human life" to specify what they mean by this high-sounding phrase. Does the phrase mean that "an inch-long piece of fetal tissue" possesses the sanctity of human life? Can a fetal tissue possess any more sanctity than an appendix or any other part of the mother's body which is usually surgically removed if it threatens her health? In short, if talk about the sanctity of human life is to have any significance with respect to the abortion tissue, it is necessary for those employing such talk to tell us how much fetal tissue marks the start of human personality.[47]

Lader moves to a scientific approach by pointing out that the doctrine of immediate animation must now depend entirely on faith and that it comes into conflict with the scientific knowledge of the natural wastage that occurs in the process of embryonic development. It is now biologically known that at least one in three of all fertilized human eggs do not develop correctly and die in the uterus, leading either to a spontaneous abortion or reabsorption.[48]

The biologist Garrett Hardin presents a more thorough scientific defense of abortion by making use of comparatively recent discoveries concerning the role which the chemical deoxyribonucleic acid (DNA) plays in the development of living things. A study of the DNA of a fertilized egg will tell us whether a man or monkey will be produced. This chemical also determines the color of hair a man will have, whether his blood cells will be normal or deformed, and a variety of other things about him. Hardin points out that the DNA enclosed in the neucleus of a fertilized egg contains almost all the information needed for the production of an adult man or woman. The significance of the discovery of DNA to the question of whether abortion is murder can be grasped by comparing the zygote to a blueprint for a $50,000 house. If a practical joker destroys such a blueprint, one could not ask him to pay $50,000 to compensate for the destruction of the blueprint, because a blueprint for a house clearly is not the house itself. Hardin thinks that the principle underlying our thinking about the blueprint applies precisely to the moral issue concerning abortion. The

[44] *Ibid.*
[45] *Ibid.*
[46] See footnote 30. Lader, p. 102.
[47] *Ibid.*
[48] *Ibid.*, p. 101.

zygote with its DNA information for the determination of a human being is itself not human and is thus "almost valueless."[49] To substantiate this position, he points out that at least 38 per cent of all zygotes are spontaneously aborted. There is very nearly no loss connected with such abortions, even when the zygote has developed to the fetal stage. Moreover, there is actually a gain, since the fetuses that are aborted are usually defective. Even in those cases in which the fetus might not be defective, there would not be much of a human loss since very little human effort has gone into the development of an individual fetus.

Hardin does acknowledge that his comparison between a zygote and a blueprint is deficient on two counts. First, the DNA chemical of a human being is incorporated in every cell of the human body and is constantly being reproduced. However, there is certainly no moral obligation to preserve DNA. If there were, it would be immoral for man to brush his teeth and gums, since such brushing destroys DNA. The second difference is that a zygote is a unique information system, whereas a blueprint is not unique. However, Hardin sees no moral significance in this difference.

Those who see abortion as being immoral often try to make use of such uniqueness by pointing out that if Beethoven's mother had undergone an abortion, there would be no way of replacing him. Hardin does not consider this observation relevant to the problem at issue, because one could also say that if Hitler's mother had undergone an abortion there would be no way of replacing him. The relevant point is that although each zygote is unique, the potential value that one could have expected from an aborted fetus is exactly the value found in the average child born. This is a mathematical fact. It is thus meaningless to speak of a loss to humanity when a particular fetus is aborted. For example, knowing that the human female has about thirty thousand eggs in her ovaries at birth, we would not say that mankind has suffered the loss of 29,997 fruitless eggs because a woman has borne only three children during her lifetime.[50]

A philosophical defense for the morality of abortion is based on the view that an individual achieves true human personality when he is able to make himself an object of his own consciousness. Such self-awareness can be achieved only through an individual's communication with other human beings. The major part of this communication is verbal, but there may be nonverbal elements involved. For the purposes of the present discussion, it is sufficient to note that, according to this view, an individual achieves human personality not on a purely biological or organic level of existence, but only on a sociocultural level. This means that a truly human life cannot begin before birth because such a life requires the interaction with other human beings that is found on the sociocultural level of existence. Because the fetus is restricted to an organic

---

[49] See footnote 30. Hardin, p. 124.
[50] *Ibid.*

or biological level of existence while it is in the womb, it is not a human person. Hence, those defending restrictive abortion laws "would do well to drop the unnecessarily emotional charge that abortion is murder."[51]

7. STATISTICAL DATA CONCERNING ABORTIONS: THEIR ACCURACY AND SIGNIFICANCE

The purpose of this section is to evaluate the statistical data presented in defense of a less restrictive abortion policy. This evaluation will concentrate on two points. First, it will be necessary to ask whether the statistical data provide an accurate picture concerning such matters as the number of illegal abortions performed annually in the United States and the psychological sequelae of abortions. Secondly, it will be necessary to consider the question of the legal and moral significance of the data.

Commenting on a 1957 report that placed the yearly incidence of induced abortions in the United States between 200,000 and 1,000,000, Dr. Mary Calderone, Medical Director of Planned Parenthood Federation of America, Inc., stated that no way had as yet been found for obtaining reliable statistics concerning the number of induced abortions occurring annually with respect to the total population of the United States.[52] Moreover, the report which mentions the figures 200,000 to 1,000,000 abortions is based on three studies which it acknowledges are inadequate to provide accurate figures that would apply to the total population of the United States.[53] Dr. Allen Guttmacher who is certainly no opponent of liberalized abortion laws, referring to a study of abortions made in 1936 and which seems to provide the basis for the current figure of 1,000,000 illegal abortions in the United States, states that the study is based on formulae that could have offered different figures if different values were substituted for those used in the study.[54] The estimate of 10,000 women dying annually in the United States as a result of illegal abortions has also been challenged. Dr. Andre Hellegers of the Georgetown University Medical School has stated that it is known "for certain" that 247 deaths occurred as a result of abortions in 1964 and he estimates that this figure might be moved up to about 500 to cover unreported deaths.[55]

It would seem that at this time both those who uphold and those who oppose

[51] Martin J. Buss, "The Beginnings of Human Life as an Ethical Problem," *The Journal of Religion*, Vol. 47 (July, 1967), p. 250.

[52] See footnote 29, p. 180.

[53] *Ibid.*, p. 179.

[54] *Ibid.*, p. 50, see also p. 18. Reporting on a national conference on abortion held in September, 1967, a Roman Catholic newspaper states that nobody was able to say whether the estimates of between 200,000 to 1,000,000 illegal abortions were accurate. *St. Louis Review* (Friday, September 15, 1967), pp. 1, 12.

[55] *Ibid.*, p. 1.

a liberalized abortion policy ought to admit that they can only guess at the number of illegal induced abortions performed and the number of women who die yearly as a result of submitting to such abortions. The lack of reliable statistical data certainly does not destroy the case for liberalizing present abortion laws, but it does weaken the argument, which states that present restrictive laws ought to be changed because so many women are forced to go to incompetent private abortionists.[56]

The argument that a liberalization of abortion laws will reduce the number of women going to abortionists working outside of the medical community suffers from evidence that seems to indicate that the liberalization of abortion laws in other countries has not produced a significant reduction of the number of abortions occurring under improper medical conditions. For example, a report on abortions in Sweden indicates that studies conducted thus far have failed to provide "any clear-cut evidence" that there has been a "noteworthy" reduction in the number of abortions occurring under improper medical conditions in Sweden, although that country allows abortions for medical, humanitarian, and eugenic reasons.[57]

Another report on the result of the liberalization of abortion laws in Denmark cites a study that offers the tentative figure of a 77 per cent increase in the number of criminal abortions occurring in Denmark in the period 1940 to 1950, noting that Denmark's permissive abortion laws went into effect in 1939.[58] One can only conjecture about the factors that are behind the failure of liberalized abortion policies to reduce the number of abortions performed by unauthorized personnel. The failure may be accounted for by the fact that women who seek an induced abortion prefer the anonymity offered by unauthorized abortionists.

Although these data raise questions concerning the claim that a liberalized abortion policy will substantially reduce the number of abortions performed by unauthorized personnel under unauthorized conditions, they certainly do not constitute an insuperable difficulty for the proponents of a liberalized abortion policy. There is nothing immutable about the figure quoted from the Denmark experience. For example, once a liberalized abortion policy is accepted by a nation, it may be possible for that nation to engage in a massive advertising campaign that would make having an abortion as respectable as having a baby, if not more respectable as a way of solving population difficulties. It may also be possible to launch an advertising campaign informing the women of the dangers involved in submitting to an abortion under improper medical conditions and of the safety of the same abortion under the proper conditions.

It is now necessary to turn to the question of the legal and moral significance of the statistical data concerning the number of criminal abortions occurring annually in the United States. We shall consider the legal issue first. For pur-

[56] See footnote 30. Lader, p. 3.

[57] *Pregnancy, Birth and Abortion*, ed. by Paul H. Gebhard, Wardell B. Pomeroy, *et al.* (New York: Paul B. Hoeber, Inc., 1958), p. 224.

[58] *Ibid.*, pp. 228. See also footnote 29, pp. 173–174.

poses of discussion let it be granted that the figures 200,000 to 1,000,000 represent a rather rough approximation of the actual state of affairs in the United States. These figures will have different meanings for people depending on the different views that they take of abortion. If one comes to a consideration of the abortion laws now in effect with the idea that abortion is a rather neutral type of activity, which harms no one or which involves a potential danger only for the woman who freely submits to it, he would rightly conclude that the restrictive laws ought to be changed. However, if he comes to a consideration of the abortion laws holding that abortion involves two human lives, the mother's and the embryo's, he would come to a different conclusion. For he would hold that there must be some way of protecting the life of the embryo from unjustified attacks. This point is made to indicate that the statistics on the number of illegal abortions performed in the United States is not the decisive factor in the problem concerning the type of abortion laws that ought to be established.

An example taken from another area of human life may serve to illustrate this point. A few years ago there was a good deal of discussion in the United States concerning the fact that a substantial number of people were pilfering whatever they could whenever they could from supermarkets and large department stores. The fact that many people engaged in such activities was not used as a basis for the argument that there should be no laws against pilferage and that the present laws should either be liberalized so as to make pilfering easier or simply abolished. Rather the stores put up mirrors in strategic spots that would enable employees to see all parts of the store, signs were posted warning that shoplifters would be prosecuted, and merchandise, which because of its small size could easily be pocketed, was either packaged in a way that made it a bigger object and more difficult to hide or put near the cash register where it would always be under the eyes of the cashier.

I am not advocating a similar "get-tough" policy with respect to criminal abortions, but I used the example to indicate that one's response to the fact that many people are breaking a law need not be limited to abolishing the law. If it is true that a very large number of women pay for the services of criminal abortionists, we may try to make them aware of the dangers to their life and well-being, which they face, when they submit to such abortionists. We may also try to make them more conscious of the fact that they are taking another human life, if we think that this is the case.

Turning to the question of the moral significance of the figures on the annual number of criminal abortions in the United States, it is clear that the mere fact that many people undergo abortions does not make such abortions morally good, unless one is willing to argue that an act is morally good because a great many people perform it. Such a position would clearly be guilty of committing the naturalistic fallacy in equating moral good, i.e. that which people ought to do, with the existential fact that a certain number of people act in a certain way.

Finally, the observations made concerning the moral significance of the fact that people may engage in premarital intercourse without guilt feelings apply with equal force to the question of whether or not women have felt guilty about undergoing an abortion. Hardin's handling of the difference between the Swiss survey, which showed that women did suffer psychological difficulties, and the Norwegian survey, which showed only a small percentage of the women suffering these disturbances, is a good example of the fact that a group of people's feelings of guilt or lack of such feelings cannot be used to tell us anything about the moral character of the activity in question. As Hardin interpreted the Swiss findings, they revealed not the moral or immoral character of abortion, but the type of moral standard that he thinks is prevalent in Switzerland, a standard that he does not accept.

8. THE LEGAL AND MORAL DIMENSIONS OF THE ABORTION CONTROVERSY

If the only justification for restrictive abortion laws is the desire of self-righteous people to punish women who have engaged in premarital intercourse by forcing them to bear the children conceived in such unions, it is clear that all reasonable men must favor the liberalization of these laws. The withholding of needed medical attention is rightly not accepted as a legitimate form of punishment in our society. However, I shall try to show in this section that the legal issue concerning abortion is not simply resolved into an issue between those who want women to suffer for their indescretions and those who want to help them.

The proponents of a more liberalized abortion policy have raised a more fruitful issue in charging that those favoring a restricted abortion policy are guilty of trying to impose their morals on others. As should be clear from the discussion of the relationship between law and morals in Chapter II, I am in agreement with the need to distinguish between the legal and moral orders. It is true that those who think abortion immoral will not be forced to undergo abortions if the abortion laws are liberalized or removed from the books entirely. Seen from this point of view, they have no reason to oppose such changes.

What complicates this rather simple situation is the problem of the human character of the fetus. If it can be shown that the fetus is not human, the charge that abortion laws constitute an infringement in the area of private morality is sustained. However, if the fetus is human, then abortion laws can be defended as fulfilling the task of law, which is to regulate the external relations among men, a task that includes protecting the lives of those who cannot protect themselves. For example, although there is no justification for laws against homosexuality in so far as such behavior is practiced in private by consenting adults, there would be a justification for laws against homosexuality involving an adult and a child, because the child may not have the resources to protect himself or to know what he is doing. Similarly, it might be true that a law permitting slavery may not force those who think that slavery is immoral to become slaveholders. However, it seems to me that one would have the right to oppose such a law on the grounds that it concerns the relationships among men and that it fails to acknowledge the character of the slave as an end in himself.

It is necessary to clarify what is meant when one says that the state ought not have the right to determine how many children a woman should bear and that the state ought not have the right to force a woman to bear a child against her will. It is certainly true that the state cannot force a woman to engage in sexual intercourse in order that she may bear a certain number of children. It would seem to be in keeping with this position to point out that no state has the right to force a woman to undergo sterilization after she has had a certain number of children. This last point ought to be a matter of concern for the defenders of women's freedom because it is a distinct possibility. For example, for a time it seemed as though the government of India was going to pass a law that would require that a woman be sterilized after bearing her third child. Hence, there are ways of interpreting the view that a woman ought to have a right over her procreative functions with which I can agree.

Once the woman has engaged in sexual intercourse, and once a fetus begins to grow in her, ought she have an unlimited right to do whatever she desires with respect to the life of that being? Again, it seems that the answer to this question depends on whether or not one considers the fetus to be human. If the fetus is no different from some other type of growth such as a wart, it is clear that the woman ought to have as absolute a right over the disposal of the fetus as she does over her wart. If the fetus is different from other growths, if this being does have a standing in the human community, the issue becomes more complex. The state certainly does and ought to place a limit on a woman's right over the infant that she brings home from the hospital. If the infant's crying gets on her nerves and she decides to kill him, she is liable to arrest, trial, and some form of punishment if proven guilty and sane.

The outcome of the evaluation of the case for a liberalized abortion policy up to this point has been that the significance of the statistical data, of the presence or absence of guilt feelings in women who have undergone abortions, and of the distinction between law and morals depends on whether or not the fetus is human. This outcome must be emphasized because much of the current discussion of abortion is so centered in statistical issues and in questions of the effect of abortions on women that the question of the human character of the fetus becomes a purely side issue.

The stress on the importance of the human character of the fetus opens this position to Bennett's charge that such an emphasis fails to give due consideration to other factors that have a bearing on the morality of abortion. Bennett is right in emphasizing that factors other than the humanity of the fetus also must be considered. The problem is to indicate what those other factors are and the relative significance that must be given to these factors and to the human character of the fetus, if this point can be established, in weighing the morality of induced abortion. Bennett's emphasis on the importance of considering the future human situation indicates that he espouses a utilitarian approach to the problem of abortion. As has been indicated in Chapter IV, the difficulty with utilitarianism is that its concern with consequences leads it to treat those in the present situation as mere objects for the future good. If the fetus can be shown to be human, it will be necessary for us to balance our concern for the future with a concern for the character of the fetus as an end in himself. More specifically, we may be forced to conclude that although we have the medical capability to bring into existence what we consider to be a better future, we ought not to use this capability because its use would involve treating the fetus as a mere object or instrument.

9. THE HISTORICAL CHARACTER OF HUMAN EXISTENCE AND THE HUMANITY OF THE EMBRYO

This discussion of the problem of whether or not the fetus can be said to be human will prescind entirely from theological issues. This means that we shall not be interested in whether or not a Pope at a given time allowed abortion or whether the Shinto religion considers the fetus to be human, unless these positions present us with philosophical or scientific evidence to justify their views. If we are to decide about the humanity of the fetus or embryo, it is necessary for us to be clear on what we mean by man. There is of course no hope of giving an exhaustive definition, but we can describe man as a being capable of freedom. This aspect of human existence has been of utmost importance to the ethical stand taken in this book. There is a further feature of human existence that was dealt with in the discussion of premarital sex and in the discussion of human freedom, namely, man is a historical being. As we noted in Chapter II, man's freedom is developed in time. This is an important point because it means that we cannot take a static view of man or of his freedom. Thus, to be a man is not reducible to being a forty-year-old man at the height of his intellectual powers; rather, to be human is to be embarked on a certain type of historical venture.

There are certain facts about man's growth in freedom that are known to all of us. We know that every mature man, whether he be Albert Einstein or Clark Gable, must have passed through periods of infancy, childhood, and adolescence. Moreover, we have also come to realize that the human being undergoes certain physical and psychological changes as he passes through these stages. The facts that an infant cannot sit up by itself, that it cannot speak, that the myelin sheath that covers and insulates his nerve fibers has not yet been fully developed are not used as a basis for questioning whether he is human. We know that he is embarked on the human venture and that he is passing through one of the necessary stages involved in this venture.

What reason do we have for excluding the embryonic and fetal stages as part and parcel of these various stages that we now know to be essential ingredients in the life of a man? It seems to me that this exclusion can be justified only if one continues to treat the question of the humanity of the fetus in a way that presupposes that we have not moved beyond Aristotle's treatment of this question. To treat the problem in this way makes as much sense as to deal with problems of space travel in terms of Aristotle's doctrine of natural place. One working out of Aristotle's biology might hold that the being developing in the mother's uterus passes through the vegetative and animal stages of existence before becoming human.

This position is no longer scientifically acceptable.[59] For example, the embryologist George W. Corner whose book *Ourselves Unborn* emphasizes the continuity between man and other living things, opposes the view that the human embryo passes through an ascending scale of animal life. Acknowledging that there are resemblances among all vertebrate embryos, he states that amid all these resemblances are differences that distinguish these embryos.[60] What may look like gills in the month-old embryo actually are not openings and lack gill fronds. What looks like gills are actually five folds of tissue that are piled up at the base of the head and that provide the raw material for the development of the chin, cheeks, jaw, and external ear.[61] Moreover, we now know that the human fertilized egg possesses the full human complement of forty-six chromosomes.[62] Finally, we know that the fertilized egg is embarked on a human career by the specific composition of DNA that functions as the instructions or blueprint for the further development of this egg.[63]

It is difficult to see how one can oppose including the embryo and fetus as parts of that historical process that is human life in view of the fact that we now know that there is a continuity between the child's life in the womb and the rest of his life from infancy to the time he dies. For example, an account of human growth that is based on an exhibit developed by the University of Illinois in collaboration with Chicago's Museum of Science and Industry returns time and again to the point that the process of human growth is a continuous one beginning with the fertilized egg. A new life is said to begin when the sperm and ovum are merged, and from that moment on, "the physical growth and change is persisted in without halt until the moment of death."[64] The embryologist Corner makes the following comment about his description of the

[59] See Leslie Brainerd Arey, *Developmental Anatomy: A Textbook and Laboratory Manual of Embryology* (Philadelphia: W. B. Saunders Co., 1965), pp. 7–8.

[60] George W. Corner, *Ourselves Unborn: An Embryologist's Essay on Man* (New Haven: Yale University Press, 1944), pp. 8, 67.

[61] Geraldine Lux Flanagan, *The First Nine Months of Life* (New York: Pocket Books, Inc., 1965), p. 53.

[62] Arnold Sundgaard, *The Miracle of Growth* (Chicago: University of Illinois Press, 1967), p. 34.

[63] See footnote 61, pp. 30–32. For a good introductory discussion of the role of DNA in the life process see George and Muriel Beadle, *The Language of Life: An Introduction to the Science of Genetics* (New York: Anchor Books, 1967), pp. 160–216.

[64] See footnote 62, p. 8; also pp. 1, 11, 13, 15–16. See also Benjamin F. Miller and Ruth Goode, *Man and His Body: The Wonders of the Human Mechanism* (New York: Simon and Schuster, 1960), p. 216.

development of the human zygote in the first few weeks of life: "This is your history I am telling and mine, and that of my own child and of yours."[65] This outlook indicates that there is no valid reason for excluding the zygote from one of the stages of human growth. We can now say that to be human in time includes the zygote, the embryonic, and the fetal stages as well as the stages that were mentioned above.

Some might wish to reduce this emphasis on the developmental character of human existence to a *reductio ad absurdum* by pointing out that it seems to imply that all human sperm and ova should be treated as ends in themselves since the argument advanced above must include these as part of the continuity that is the human career. This criticism implies that my position cannot draw any morally significant distinction between the zygote or embryo, on the one hand, and the sperm and ovum, on the other. However, there is a basis in present knowledge of the biological facts to draw such a distinction. There was a time in the history of biology when there was a conflict between the ovists who maintained that minute, perfectly formed babies were in every woman and that the sperm gave these babies the impetus to grow, and the homunculists who said that the fully formed baby was in the sperm and that the mother was simply an incubator for this baby.[66]

So long as this conflict was viable, there may have been reason to hold that either the sperm or ovum ought to be treated as an end in itself. The fact is that we have moved beyond this conflict. We now know that neither the sperm nor the ovum alone is the baby. The forty-six chromosomes of the human adult are found not in the sperm alone nor in the ovum alone, but in that union of them which forms the human zygote. When we put this knowledge alongside the known fact that no human life begins from a sperm exclusively or from an ovum exclusively, we have the evidence necessary to distinguish between the human embryo that is actually embarked on the human venture and the sperm and ovum that have the potentiality for human existence if they are united under the proper conditions, but which separately are not actually human. It is now necessary to weigh this position against those who maintain that the embryo is not human.

It is difficult to see the validity of Lader's and Hardin's reasoning that moves from the premise that approximately one in three embryos may be spontaneously aborted to the conclusion that the embryo is not human. The premise simply indicates that the embryonic stage of life is a particularly vulnerable stage, but seems to say nothing about whether the being existing in this stage is human. I would imagine that the same ratio of one in three would apply to elderly people, perhaps those in their midseventies or eighties, but this ratio certainly could not be accepted as evidence that the people in this age group are not human. Finally, when we recall the high mortality rate among infants, who

[65] See footnote 60, p. 36.
[66] See footnote 61, pp. 6–9.

lived before the twentieth century in the Western world, we realize that a ratio of the type mentioned by Hardin and Lader tells us more about the limits of man's medical capabilities in a given age than about the human or nonhuman character of beings involved in the ratio.

The difference between Hardin's position and the position taken in this section shows how people may accept the same facts and interpret them differently. Hardin's comparison between a blueprint and the human zygote fails to take into account a point of difference between these two that is of utmost significance to the abortion issue. There is no continuity between the blueprint and the house. It does not grow and develop into the house, as the zygote grows and develops. The blueprint can be said to be the exemplar cause of the house in so far as a human builder uses the blueprint as his model in building the house. However, the zygote is not the exemplar cause which somebody else uses to build the infant and the mature human being. It is that human being in the process of developing, whereas the blueprint is one thing and the house is another thing. There is not the living continuity between blueprint and house that is found between zygote and child, or between child and adult.

Hardin's position that there is nothing immoral in destroying DNA because we always destroy DNA in brushing our teeth fails to take into account the difference between destroying a chemical when it is essential to the preservation of life and destroying that same chemical when one's life is not dependent on it. There is nothing immoral about destroying insulin. However, if this insulin was necessary to preserve the life of a diabetic, the destruction of insulin would be immoral. Similarly, the loss or destruction of DNA that is not essential to human life does not present a moral problem, but the destruction of a human embryo is not simply the destruction of a chemical. It is the destruction of a being embarked on a human career.

Hardin's point that the potential value of any aborted fetus is exactly the value found in the average child born is relevant to the abortion issue only if one claims that the fetus' right to life is based on the fact that he is better than any other man. However, just as the right to life of an infant, an adolescent, or a mature person is based not on his character as a genius or as another Beethoven, but simply on his character as a human being, so also the right to life of the embryo or fetus is based on this character.

There seems to be a difference between Hardin's view of the value of human life and the view of man as an end in himself that has been taken in this book. This difference has an important role to play in determining the stand which one will take with respect to the morality of abortion. Hardin seems to take an instrumental view of the value of human life in that he speaks of the value of the zygote in terms of what that being can offer to humanity. He also sees no loss in spontaneous abortions because very little human effort has gone into these beings. In saying that man is an end in himself, I have tried to show that his value lies not only in what he can do for others, but in his character as a being capable of setting his own ends and capable of exercising some sort of self-determination over his life. Thus, the fact that one could expect from any one fetus only the value found in the average child born does not mean that this fetus has no right to life for the view of man taken by reflective naturalism, whereas Hardin seems to see this fact as denying that the fetus does have a right to life.

It is clear that I have no quarrel with the view that a mark, if not the chief mark, of human personality lies in man's ability to come to self-awareness. It will be recalled that in Chapter III man was distinguished from other beings by his ability to know himself as a member of a certain community of being. The point of difference between the position taken in this section and the philosophical justification for abortion given above lies in my contention that the human person is not some disembodied spirit cut off from his historical-biological origins. It is true that the embryo or fetus may not have as yet achieved self-awareness, but we know that he is a being moving toward such an achievement. In short, we are confronted in this world of process not only with human personality that has been more or less formed, but also with human personality in the making. It is difficult to see how one can say that human personality is the ultimate moral value in this world and proceed to justify the direct and deliberate killing of an innocent human fetus. Unless we are talking about some disembodied nonhistorical human person, a respect for the human person's right to life is a respect for this life as it moves through time, i.e. as it develops and as it grows old.

Buss' position seems to offer no moral objection to the deliberate killing of an infant at the moment of birth. For example, a family that owns a cat often drowns a certain number of kittens after they have been born. Could not the physician be told to drown a female infant by parents who already have three girls and wanted a boy or nothing? Since the infant has not been exposed to the sociocultural level of existence, it would seem to have no rights as a human being. Finally, it would appear that Buss has no moral basis for holding that the infant ought to be given the advantages of the sociocultural level of existence. Since before the infant has been integrated into this level he has no rights, can one say to the parents that they are obliged to provide him with whatever sociocultural advantages they have at their disposal? These dialectical difficulties with Buss's position are secondary to the major difficulty that was presented in the preceding paragraph.

10. THERAPEUTIC ABORTION: A PROBLEM IN EQUALITARIAN JUSTICE

Therapeutic abortions are abortions performed to save the life of the mother. The purpose of this section is to explore the general conditions under which therapeutic abortions may be morally and legally justified. Once it is acknowledged that the embryo is human, the problem of abortion is seen to center in the equalitarian rule of justice, with the issue being whether a proposed abortion does justice to both the mother's and the embryo's right to life. This issue is a particularly difficult one because the lives of mother and of embryo are so closely united. All men as limited beings require an environment in which to live. In the case of the human fetus, the mother's womb is the sole environment in which he can live at least up to approximately the twenty-sixth and perhaps more realistically the twenty-eighth week of pregnancy. There may come a time when medical technology may be able to provide an alternate environment at an earlier stage of fetal life. Such an advance would represent a major step in reducing the moral difficulties present in the abortion issue. However, until that time comes, we must work with the situation as it presently exists.

Unfortunately, as matters now stand, there are times when we cannot save the life of both mother and child. As we saw in Chapter V, when it is simply beyond our power to save two or more people who are in danger, we cannot be held morally responsible for failing to save those whom we simply could not save. For example, if we have one pill and are able to provide it only to one of two people who need it for the preservation of their lives, we cannot be held morally responsible for the death of the person who did not receive the pill. A similar problem may arise in the course of a woman's pregnancy. She may develop carcinoma of the uterus. If the uterus is not removed, the woman will die. If the uterus is removed, the fetus will die. The environmental conditions that are necessary for the fetus's life represent a direct threat to the woman's life. In this case, it is morally permissible to operate on the cancer, although it is known that such an operation will result in the death of the child.

It will be well at this point to return to the example of the two people who needed a certain pill to preserve their lives in order to bring out the factors that underlie morally permissible abortions and that serve to distinguish such abortions from immoral abortions. There is a significant moral difference between a person who gives the only lifesaving pill he possesses to one of two people who are in need of it and the person who tries to save the life of a person with a failing heart by rendering a perfectly healthy person unconscious and transplanting his heart into the body of the man with the failing heart. In the first case, one is not saving the life of the person in need by directly attacking the life of the other. In the case of the heart transplant, the action is immoral because the life of the heart patient is saved by a direct attack on the life of the person with the healthy heart, thus making his life a mere instrument to the life of the heart patient.

It is now necessary to try to fashion some general working principles from these examples that will be helpful in dealing with situations in which the meeting of the demands of equalitarian justice leads to a mixture of good and bad results. It seems to me that the traditional principle of double effect serves this function very well. This principle indicates that there are four factors to be considered in these situations. First, the action that leads to the mixed results must itself be either morally good or neutral, e.g., giving a man a pill that saves his life or operating on a cancerous uterus that is threatening a woman's life.

Secondly, the good effect must not flow from the evil result. The saving of the heart patient's life was immoral because it was achieved by means of the killing of the healthy man, whereas the saving of the pregnant woman's life was moral because it was achieved by the removal of the cancerous growth. It is true that the removal of the cancerous growth also resulted in the death of the fetus. However, this does not make the death of the fetus the means to saving the mother's life. The fact that the removal of the cancerous uterus resulted at one and the same time in the death of the fetus and the preservation of the mother's life no more makes the death of the fetus a means to the protection of the mother's life than does the fact that the person who did not receive the lifesaving pill died, make his death a means to the preservation of the life of the person who received the pill. It is the removal of the uterus itself and not the presence of the embryo in that uterus that is instrumental in saving the mother's life. The presence of the embryo in the uterus is not at all an essential means to saving the life of a woman who has uterine cancer in that the removal of the uterus may work to save her life even if no fetus were present in the uterus.

Thirdly, there must be a reasonable proportion between the value preserved or gained in the good result and the value lost or destroyed in the evil result. This demand is met in the removal of a cancerous uterus in that the loss of the fetus's life is accompanied by the preservation of the mother's life. These three points relate to the moral character of the act apart from any consideration of the agent performing the act. A fourth factor in the principle states that the agent performing the act must not be motivated by a desire for the evil result itself. This requirement does not mean that the surgeon performing the operation on the cancerous uterus is expected to fool himself and make believe that the fetus will not die as a result of the operation. It simply means that he ought to view the evil result as something that he would prefer to avoid, but that he cannot if he is to save the life of the mother.

In general, the use of the principle of double effect permits the physician to take whatever steps to save the life of a woman that he would take if the woman were not pregnant. For example, if a pregnant woman's life is endangered by an appendicitis attack, by a serious gall bladder disorder, by a ruptured uterus, or by a seriously scarred uterus that is in danger of rupturing, these organs may be surgically removed even though the removal may or will involve the abortion of the fetus. The point is that the principle of double effect does not prevent a physician from saving a woman's life by attacking the problem or disorder where it exists. Of course, he is expected to use practical wisdom in dealing with these issues. This means that he will not attack a disorder in a way that he knows will involve the abortion of the fetus if he thinks that he can preserve the life of both the mother and the fetus by taking less drastic measures.

What the use of the principle prohibits is the direct attack on the life of the fetus undertaken as a means to alleviate such physical disorders as severe cardiac disease or pulmonary tuberculosis. It prohibits practices in which it is not the disorder itself that is attacked, but the life of the fetus, which is thus treated as an instrument to the life of the woman. It should be noted that present medical knowledge and technology has found ways of dealing with such cases without resorting to abortions. Any further discussion of the morality of abortion in cases in which there is a danger to the mother's continued existence would require the consideration of technical medical points that are beyond the scope of this book and the competence of the author.

The present discussion concerning abortion laws does not revolve around questions concerned with the preservation of the mother's life, because all the states have laws that will allow for such abortions and that are stated in a sufficiently general way to allow the physician to use his discretion in individual cases. The discussion concerns the advisability of allowing for abortions in situations in which there is no question of the mother being in danger of death. The remainder of this section will be concerned with the possible liberalizations of the law that were discussed earlier in this chapter.

Granted that the fetus is human, it seems clear that the law ought not to permit abortion on demand. Such a law would give a woman an absolute and unlimited right over the life of another human being, stating in effect that she can do with him what she wills. Parents are rightly given a good deal of freedom under law in dealing with their own children, but this freedom is also rightly limited so that a parent is not acknowledged to have the right to put his or her child to death or to inflict serious bodily harm on the child.

The human character of the fetus would also militate against laws that would allow abortions to be performed because the pregnancy constitutes a threat to the mother's psychological well-being. There are two points to be noted with respect to this issue. First, the period of pregnancy often places a temporary strain on a woman's psychological resources. There appears to be a lack of proportion in the decision to kill one human being in order to rid another human being of a temporary difficulty. It might be well to provide those women who suffer psychological difficulties with psychological aid during the period of the difficulties. Certainly this suggestion would be more in keeping with the claims of equalitarian justice, which demand that we treat all those influenced by our activity as ends in themselves, than is the suggestion that the killing of one of the human beings in such a situation should be legalized.

Secondly, it is unfortunately true that there is an abrasive quality in the relationships among human beings. It is not only the fetus that causes psychological difficulties for other human beings. The children that have been born to a woman as well as her husband, may also cause her psychological difficulties, but it is clear that the remedy for these difficulties is not to give the woman the legal right to kill these people. A woman may be so filled with hatred for her divorced husband that the fact that he is now happily married to another woman causes her to suffer from severe states of depression, but in doing all we can to help her, we acknowledge that there is a limit to what we can do in a moral way to help. We cannot kill the husband for her, or destroy the happiness of his second marriage. Since the fetus is a human being, the same limits ought to apply to situations in which his existence is involved in a woman's psychological difficulties.

The argument that abortion should be allowed in rape cases because the fetus is an aggressor appears to be as unreasonable as the practice of stigmatizing a child who is born out of wedlock. To take the life of the fetus is to punish one human being for the crime of another. It makes the fetus a scapegoat. Since the semen of the rapist is not a human being, steps such as curettage or the use of germicidal powder can be used to kill the sperm that have been introduced into the body of the woman, thus reducing the possibility of pregnancy occurring as a result of the rape. However, once a new human life begins to grow in the woman there is a moral limit to what can be done to help her. This limit which denies that a man has the moral right to take the life of a fetus because this fetus is the result of a rape is not imposed in the name of some abstract principle. It is a limit imposed to protect the life of a human being. Moreover, this limit is not grounded in a denial of the humanity of the woman, but in a recognition that there are two lives to be considered in such cases and that we cannot directly take the life of one of these human beings to help the other.

Again, one way of helping the woman that would do justice to the humanity of both beings involved in such a tragic situation is to provide the woman with psychiatric help that would see her through this difficult period and that might alleviate to some extent at least, the permanent scars of having been subjected to the horrible ordeal of a rape, which appears to me to be the real problem in this situation and not the birth of a child. One might well investigate the possibility of having legislation passed that would require the state to provide the financial means necessary for such psychiatric aid in cases of women who have become pregnant as a result of rape.

The eugenic argument for abortion also appears to lose its validity if the humanity of the fetus is established. The fact that a human being is blind, or is missing a limb or limbs, or is mentally retarded does not give us a right to kill him. Experience has certainly taught us that man can overcome many serious physical handicaps without being reduced to a "human vegetable," a phrase that seems to come rather easily to those arguing for the legalization of eugenic abortions. The life of Helen Keller who, in early infancy suffered the loss of two of the most crucial senses in the life of man, i.e., the sense of sight and of hearing, is living proof of what man can achieve in the face of serious physical handicaps. She does not stand alone. There have been countless human beings who have led meaningful lives despite serious physical disabilities.

In taking this position, I am not trying to advance a myth that all physically handicapped people are supremely happy and perfect specimens of all that is good in humanity. There have undoubtedly been many handicapped human beings who have led miserable and tragic lives, but certainly the same can be said about people who came into this world as perfect physical specimens. Indeed, one thing can be said with certainty about most, if not all, human beings born into this world—their lives will involve frustrations, disappointments, and tragedies. This certainty makes it easy for those arguing for abortion on eugenic grounds to paint a bleak picture of the future of those fetuses whom they think should be killed. However, if the treating of man as an end in himself is to have any concrete existential meaning for us, it must involve a respect not for our own idealized image of a superman, but for man as we actually find him in history, man with his weaknesses as well as his strengths, man with his tragedies as well as his strokes of good fortune.

Perhaps the right to life of a fetus that may be born mentally retarded is most difficult to justify on purely philosophic grounds. For it might be argued that such a being is not embarked on the human venture since he will never be able to attain the perfection of human freedom. There are three points to be made with respect to this issue. First, if abortion were legalized to cover situations such as those in which a woman contracts rubella (German measles) during the first three months of pregnancy, we could not be certain before the abortion that any given fetus was actually defective. Since there appears to be approximately a fifty-fifty chance that the fetus in such cases will be defective, we would be killing as many healthy children as defective ones. Secondly, since the law develops in terms of precedents, we must consider the precedent that such a law would establish for future lawmakers. If the law sanctions the killing of a human fetus *on the chance* that it *may be* mentally defective, would future legislators who gave legal sanction to the killing of human beings who *are known to be* mentally retarded be acting contrary to, or in keeping with, the rationale of an abortion law which permitted abortions on eugenic grounds?

It is on the third point that I want to rest the bulk of my case against the morality of abortions performed because the child may be mentally retarded. Work presently being done in the field of mental retardation indicates that with proper training and care mentally retarded children can achieve a level of self-consciousness and self-possession that we would not have thought possible twenty or thirty years ago. It is true that such children may never scale the intellectual heights of an Einstein or a Kant, but how many men actually do achieve the intellectual greatness of such men? It is true that many of these children will be unable to progress beyond the intellectual achievements of an eight year old, but the fact remains that they are able to achieve some level of human consciousness.

We are back again to the point concerning physical disabilities. If we accept the conception of man as an end in himself, we must avoid the temptation to substitute a commitment to our own idealized conception of a perfect man for the commitment to man as we actually find him in the existential world. All the men we find in our experience fall short of the full realization and actualization of human perfection. No man, whether he be the President of the United States or the most outstanding scientist of his time, exists without imperfections and deficiencies in his character as a human subject. When we take this point into consideration, the mentally retarded are not seen as beings wholly foreign to a human community that includes only fully perfected human beings, but are seen as imperfect human beings existing in a community that includes nothing but other imperfect human beings.

Granted this state of affairs, our task is not to kill human beings whose intellectual level of achievement is not up to a standard established by our society, but to build a world in which all human beings can find a measure of human fulfillment within the context of their imperfections, and to work toward overcoming whatever factors in this world stunt the growth of human subjectivity, whether these factors be of an institutionalized variety—e.g., economic or political factors—or of the chemical, metabolic, or physiological variety that may cause mental retardation. That there are people in our day calling for a law that would sanction the killing of those who are suspected of being mentally retarded is rather paradoxical because it is precisely in our day that man has begun to take serious steps toward conquering or alleviating the effects of mental retardation and has met with some success, as can be seen in his ability to overcome one form of retardation by controlling an infant's diet.[67]

The defense of abortion on eugenic grounds may be motivated by a highly laudatory concern with the fact that most families may not have the resources necessary for the proper care and training of mentally retarded children. I share this concern, but I have tried to show that the moral answer to this problem does not lie in killing those whom we suspect of being mentally retarded. It seems to me that the way to combat this problem in a nation as affluent as the United States is to try to bring into existence a program in which the states would play a more meaningful and effective role than they presently do in helping parents cope with the problem of mental retardation.

I have dealt with the right to life of the physically handicapped and of the mentally retarded on the general level that is appropriate to moral philosophy. It must be acknowledged that anyone accepting the position on this level may be confronted with some very difficult problems on the level of practical wisdom. For example, one can imagine a situation in which a person has suffered rather extensive brain damage as a result of an accident or a cerebral hemorrhage. If it is known with a good degree of certainty that medical technology can do nothing for the person except keep him alive in a comatose state, one may well decide

---

[67] I am referring to the treatment for phenylketonuria (PKU). Since this inborn error of metabolism may not occur very often, one might scoff at this research advance, but such an advance indicates that we are making progress in conquering birth defects. See *Children's Bureau Activities in Mental Retardation* (U.S. Department of Health, Education, and Welfare, 1966), p. 5. We also appear to be far along in the development of an effective vaccine against rubella. "Latest Advances in Medicine—New Drugs, New Techniques," *U.S. News and World Report* (May 6, 1968), p. 89. Such a vaccine would be a major advance in the battle against birth defects, since rubella is a major source of some of the most serious forms of birth defects.

that he is not morally obligated to take the steps necessary to preserve life in this form. For in such a situation, it might be literally true that we would be keeping the person alive merely as a vegetable, with no hope of ever bringing him to any level of human awareness. My difficulty with the defenders of eugenic abortion is that they appear to be too free and easy in their characterization of physically or mentally defective people as "vegetables." A child that is born without limbs is not a vegetable; a child who has an I.Q. of sixty-five is not a vegetable. Such beings are capable of achieving a certain level of human awareness. They may not be as perfect and complete as we would like them to be, but we ought not allow our disappointment to blind us to the fact that with our help they may achieve a level of human awareness and fulfillment.

In concluding this section, it should be noted that the opposition to current demands for a liberalized abortion policy was not based on any desire to punish women who engage in premarital intercourse. I have seen no defense of a restricted abortion policy based on any such vindictive motive; nor have I seen any evidence brought forward by the proponents of a liberalized abortion policy to justify this characterization of those who disagree with them. The issue is not between people with bad motives and those with good motives. It is between those who see the human fetus as a being, who has a right to life, and those who maintain that the fetus is not human. Moreover, I have tried to present evidence for the humanity of the fetus that is not dependent on the prior acceptance of the beliefs of any religious institution. It is only this type of evidence that can be appealed to in deciding the type of law that ought to be established in a pluralistic society.

This discussion of the legal aspects of abortion may well become obsolete in a rather short time if a pill can be developed which might not only help regulate a woman's menstrual cycle, or prevent conception, but also might abort a fertilized egg. If the pill could be made to serve more than the function of abortion, there could be no justification for an argument against its distribution under a certified physician's guidance. For it would be similar to many other drugs presently on the market in that it could work for human health or human destruction depending on the conditions under which it is used. The legal issue would thus disappear, but, if the position defended in this chapter is accepted, the moral issue would remain.

CHAPTER VII

Morality
and
the Socio-Economic
Order

The need to clarify the language of moral discourse is strikingly evident in moral evaluations of capitalism and socialism. In certain circles and countries, the word "capitalism" means an economic system in which a rapacious, avaricious few enjoy all the material comforts of life at the expense of millions of dehumanized workers who are permitted by the ruling capitalists to eke out a bare subsistence level of existence. In other circles and countries, capitalism is seen as an economic system that is in keeping with the dignity of man and that allows for the fullest use of human freedom and initiative, with the word "socialism" being used to describe a bureaucratic, totalitarian system that reduces the majority of the population to automatons.[1] Those who conceive socialism in this manner have tended to view social welfare legislation with grave doubts and suspicions because such legislation is seen as a movement which will inevitably lead to all the evils of socialism.

If any advance is to be made in evaluating the moral character of these systems, it is essential to begin such an evaluation by taking the words "capitalism," "socialism," and "welfare state," in their descriptive meanings. Capitalism describes an economic system in which the means of production are owned by private citizens, whereas socialism refers to a system of government ownership and control of the major means of production. A welfare state is one in which the government assumes the responsibility for the economic well-being of its citizens. Using this descriptive account as its starting-point, the purpose of this chapter is to explore the major moral issues involved in weighing the respective merits of these systems.

[1] For a brief discussion of the misunderstandings that surround the words 'capitalism' and 'socialism' see Ralph K. White, " 'Socialism' and 'Capitalism': An International Misunderstanding," Foreign Affairs, Vol. XLIV (January, 1966), pp. 216–228.

1. CAPITALISM AS A BASIS OF HUMAN FREEDOM AND PROGRESS

The purpose of this section is to outline the major features of F. A. Hayek's defense of capitalism in so far as this defense revolves around issues that are pertinent to the concerns of moral philosophy. This task will be pursued under the following subheadings: (a) Criticism of Socialistic Quest for "Justice" and "Equality," and (b) The Capitalistic Market and a Rule of Law As Essential to Human Freedom and Progress.

a. CRITICISM OF SOCIALISTIC QUEST FOR "JUSTICE" AND "EQUALITY"

This section will concentrate on Hayek's criticism of the view that government must take on the responsibility of controlling the economy in order to meet somebody's standard of justice. Having accepted this responsibility, a government will find itself confronted with questions such as the following:

> By what principles will it or ought it to be guided? Is there a definite answer to the innumerable questions of relative merits that will arise and that will have to be solved deliberately? Is there a scale of values, on which reasonable people can be expected to agree, which would justify a new hierarchical order of society and is likely to satisfy the demands for justice?[2]

All that the socialists can offer as a response to these questions is a principle that calls for total and absolute equality of all individuals in all those areas of their lives which are subject to human control. Because such a principle is too naive to be accepted by people today, it is replaced by the more ambiguous demand for "greater equality." This latter demand is about as vague as such general phrases as the "common good," or "social welfare." Hence, because it is empty and without much content, it cannot provide rational guidance for a government in its day-to-day task of directing the economy.[3]

Even if we were able to enunciate a scale of values on which reasonable people could agree, the fact remains that we would be unable to reward men according to some standard of justice, because no man knows enough about another man to pass judgment on his moral merit. In order to pass moral judgment on another man's work, it would be necessary for one to know conclusively the other's capacities and the amount of effort he put into trying to make the best use of these capacities. No man or group of men possess this sort of knowledge of another human being. There is no way of knowing with any degree of certi-

[2] F. A. Hayek, *The Road to Serfdom* (Chicago: University of Chicago Press, 1944), p. 109.
[3] *Ibid.*, pp. 109–110.

tude that the man who did a masterful job of laying these bricks worked to the full extent of his capacities, and that the man whose results were not quite so masterful was not really trying. For all we know, the one who did the poorer job may have been truly interested in his work and may have put all his abilities into it, whereas the one who achieved the more successful results was blessed with a certain knack for laying bricks and never found it necessary to work too hard at the task. Because our ignorance prevents us from judging the moral merit of our fellow man, we can pay each man only according to the objective results of his work.[4]

Furthermore, Hayek calls attention to the need to consider the possibility that the attempt to realize someone's standard of justice may cause more discontent than is caused by the free play of the market.[5] This greater discontent arises from the fact that difficulties are more easily borne when they are seen to be the result of impersonal forces than when they are seen as the results of someone's conscious decision. It is no affront to a person's dignity in a capitalistic society when he is told that a particular firm cannot use his services, for the decision is dictated by the impersonal workings of the market and thus is not to be taken as a judgment of his personal worth.

In a socialistic society, one's standing in the society is determined by the conscious decision of another person who must decide not only whether there is any need for a person in a particular job, but also whether this person is of any use at all, and the extent of his usefulness.[6] A society in which one's economic status is presumed to be determined by one's moral merit would place the economically unsuccessful in a much more unbearable condition than they would be in a capitalistic society in which it is clearly recognized that there is no necessary connection between moral merit and economic success.[7] Because economic success is not presumed to be based on one's moral character in a capitalistic society, the economically unsuccessful man can find some solace in the thought that he is morally upright. Such solace is not open to a man in a socialistic economy that claims to distribute economic rewards according to moral merit.

Hayek also criticizes the socialistic defense for an equal distribution of the wealth, which maintains that one's citizenship in a certain state entitles him to a certain level of material well-being, with this level being determined by the general wealth of the community. Two of the points that he presents in opposition to this position are pertinent to this study. One cannot say that an individual has morally merited a certain standard of living simply because he happens to have been born into a certain community; nor can one say that the mere fact of birth in a community entitles one in justice to a certain standard of living. The lack of moral justification for this demand brings Hayek to his second point. The

[4] F. A. Hayek, *The Constitution of Liberty* (Chicago: The University of Chicago Press, 1960), pp. 88, 94–95.
[5] See footnote 2, p. 99.
[6] *Ibid.*, pp. 106–107.
[7] See footnote 4, p. 98.

only justification for the position is that the government has the power to expro-priate the goods of the wealthy. Such a justification sets no limits to the power of government. It might try to give this dependence on power alone a "democratic" form by holding that so long as the majority demands a sharing of the wealth such a sharing is justified. There apparently are no limits to what can be done in the name of the majority.[8]

In advancing their case for an equal distribution of the wealth, socialists often distinguish between those differences among men caused by nature and those caused by nurture, emphasizing that they intend to abolish the difference caused by nurture. Hayek indicates that there is no more moral justification for depriv-ing a man of the advantages that he has achieved by having been fortunate enough to have been born in a wealthy family than there is for trying to abolish the artistic advantages that one man may have over another because of natural talent. For no moral merit accrues to an individual either for having had the good fortune to be born with certain desirable qualities or for having the good fortune to have been born into a wealthy family.[9] Hence, one could not say that there is a moral justification for depriving an individual of the advantages of having been born in a good family, but no justification for depriving him of the advantages of having been born with certain desirable characteristics.

Hayek holds that egalitarians are inconsistent in acknowledging the social values of certain qualities if they happen to be the result of the interaction be-tween an individual's native talents and conditions that are the same for all, but denying the value of these very same qualities if they happen to be the results of a healthy and well-balanced home life. Moreover, many socially desirable results of a good family background require more than a single generation in order to finally come to fruition in some one individual. It is unreasonable to oppose an accumulation simply because it is wealth that is being accumulated, and at the same time to praise an accumulation if it happens to involve a de-velopment in taste, morals, and knowledge. There is no difference in justice between the fact that some children are born to wealthy parents and others to intelligent parents. Furthermore, if we are to allow for the growth of taste, morals, and knowledge, we must allow for the continuity of external environ-ment, of material goods, because such continuity is essential to the transmission of the immaterial values.[10]

An excessive concern with trying to achieve some fanciful state of equality blinds men to the values that are found in a society as a result of the unequal distribution of wealth. The existence of very wealthy individuals within a society contributes to its material and nonmaterial well-being and advancement. These individuals contribute to the material order both as consumers and as owners. Many of the material comforts, which a great many people presently enjoy, were once the luxuries of the few. The conveniences now enjoyed by many in

[8] Ibid., pp. 100–102.
[9] Ibid., p. 89.
[10] Ibid., pp. 89–90.

such areas as transportation, communication, and household utilities could at first be produced only in small quantities and at great expense. The wealthy, who were willing and able to pay for these conveniences when they were first produced, actually contributed to the experimentation that led to the possibility of producing these conveniences on a mass scale and at a price that most people are able to pay. They have not only financed experimentation with goods already known to man, but they have pioneered in creating demands for new goods. Their experimentation with new styles of living has laid the ground work which would enable the less fortunate to enjoy similar styles of living later on.[11]

Admitting that his position is open to ridicule, Hayek states that the successful use of leisure requires its pioneers and that many wealthy playboys filled this role so that many of the toys and much of the sporting equipment that the less fortunate presently use in their leisure were first developed for the playboy. It cannot be denied that many of the idle rich will abuse their position of financial independence and that the public conscience will be shocked by their conspicuous waste. It is also true that those enjoying the advantages of wealth may not have gained their position through any merit of their own. However, unless we allow for the existence of such people, we shall stifle the proliferation of material goods, as well as the growth of nonmaterial values, which will be discussed later. By preventing some from being the first to enjoy certain advantages, we shall be preventing ourselves and others from ever enjoying them.[12]

An obvious way in which the existence of financially independent individuals contribute to the well-being of the less fortunate is by providing them with many different alternatives for employment from which they can choose. Such individuals also give a creative impetus to the economic life of the nation. The man of independent wealth who is able to bear risks keeps corporate structures from stagnating by taking the risks of launching into new ventures.[13] Of course, if we expect these men to undertake these risks, it is necessary that we make it worth their while. Unless those who are successful in meeting the challenges of breaking new ground are allowed to reap all the credit and gain that a free market will give to such success, we cannot expect to attract the most highly qualified men to these endeavors. This observation serves to strengthen Hayek's case against attempts to frustrate the inequalities fostered by the market. For if everyone receives the same remuneration whether he has been successful in his undertaking or not, there will be no especial reason for the most highly qualified men to strive to achieve success.[14]

Having pointed to the importance of the man of independent means to the economic life of the community, Hayek holds that his importance may be even greater in the areas of thought and opinion, of the arts and of tastes. Being financially secure, these men need not direct their energies to economic consider-

[11] Ibid., pp. 43–45.
[12] Ibid., p. 130.
[13] Ibid., p. 124.
[14] Ibid., p. 95.

ations. They are able to support and to initiate causes in such areas as politics, art, morals, and education, which may seem strange to the present majority and which consequently would not get an adequate hearing if it were not for the man of independent means. The majority tend to support only those ideals that have already been accepted. Hence, the independently wealthy man plays the part of a pioneer in the area of ideals, as well as in the area of the market. He is able to move a civilization beyond what is already accepted, to new ideals and new horizons so that these may have a chance to be accepted by the majority.[15] The independently wealthy man can play this role because he is free from the need to devote himself to economic considerations, thus having more time to work with the noneconomic factors of existence, and also because his wealth serves to provide the security that can act as a buffer against opposition.

Moreover, the fact that many men in our society have gained a position of financial independence through inheritance helps to prepare them for a position of leadership in nonmaterial values. For leaving aside the probability of inherited ability, these men will have been educated for a position of leadership, and because the material advantages of wealth have become commonplace with them, they will find their main source of satisfaction not in the pursuit of these values, but rather in pursuit of nonmaterial goods.[16] In taking this position, Hayek explicitly opposes any view which would restrict members of the wealthy class to purely economic concerns. He argues that we should not demand that all concern themselves with aims that are governed by economic considerations, simply because most of us must earn our incomes. Society needs men whose freedom from economic concerns allows them to pursue goals that have not as yet won general favor.[17]

b. THE CAPITALISTIC MARKET AND A RULE OF LAW AS ESSENTIAL TO HUMAN FREEDOM AND PROGRESS

Hayek's defense of capitalism and his rejection of socialism are not grounded merely in the difficulties and inconsistencies that he finds in attempts to make the government responsible for a just distribution of the wealth, nor in the social values that he finds in an unequal distribution of wealth. The philosophical heart of his position involves the following three points: (1) an emphasis on the limits of human reason, (2) a conception of human freedom as the absence of coercion, and (3) the necessity of a rule of law to a free society. This section will be devoted to an exposition of these three facets of Hayek's position.

Hayek holds that a capitalistic economy allows for more novelty and creativity

---

[15] *Ibid.*, pp. 125–126. See also F. A. Hayek, *Individualism and Economic Order* (Chicago: University of Chicago Press, 1948), p. 118.

[16] See footnote 4, p. 127.

[17] *Ibid.*

than does an economy governed by a single plan. The spirit behind this position is perhaps best expressed in Shakespeare's *Hamlet*, "There are more things in heaven and earth, Horatio, Than are dreamt of in your philosophy." Socialism's case for a planned economy is grounded in an exaggerated rationalism, which sees all human achievements as the direct result of a plan consciously worked out by the reason of an individual human being. A more realistic view of human reason must acknowledge that individual human reason is a very limited and imperfect tool and that much of what man has achieved has not come out of the plan of an individual's reason, but has been achieved as the result of the workings of impersonal social processes that were beyond the power of individual reason.[18]

The difference between the socialist's view and Hayek's position, which he terms "true individualism," is as follows:

> While the design theories necessarily lead to the conclusion that social processes can be made to serve human ends only if they are subjected to the control of individual human reason, and thus lead directly to socialism, true individualism believes on the contrary that, if left free, men will often achieve more than human reason could design or foresee.[19]

To limit man's economic pursuits to what can be encapsuled in a single plan is to place a lid on the possibilities for novelty and development inherent in the interplay of social processes. No one plan can encompass all the possibilities for human improvement inherent in man's existential situation.

It is paradoxical that the excessive intellectualism of those defending a centrally planned economy leads to an economic system that is destructive of the growth of human knowledge. This results from the fact that this intellectualism views human reason as if it were something standing outside of nature and were possessed of knowledge independently of man's interactions with his environment. However, the fact of the matter is that human reason grows and develops only in so far as it tries to come to grips with new problems raised by man's changing environment. Thus, in so far as a socialistic economy limits the possibilities for changes in man's environment that result from his economic pursuits, it limits the conditions that contribute to the possibility for the development of new knowledge, values, and ends.[20]

If man were to limit himself to acting only in the light of the commonly accepted knowledge of a given period, if he were to prohibit the asking of any questions and the performing of any experiments that did not seem to be significant from the perspective of ruling opinion, and if he were not allowed to engage in any activity that seemed wasteful to this opinion, he might very well find himself living in a world in which everything was controlled by his reason,

[18] See footnote 15, p. 8.
[19] *Ibid.*, p. 10, 11. See also footnote 4, pp. 33, 41.
[20] *Ibid.*, pp. 23–24.

since he had restricted himself to doing only what was wholly predictable. However, it ought to be noted that the comfort of such a world is purchased at the price of making further human advances impossible. Man will have succeeded in bringing civilization to a standstill,

> not because the possibilities for further growth had been exhausted, but because man had succeeded in so completely subjecting all his actions and his immediate surroundings to his existing state of knowledge that there would be no occasion for new knowledge to appear.[21]

Against the excessive rationalism that underlies the demand for a controlled economy, Hayek points out that the growth of civilization as we know it was made possible through man's submission to the forces of the market in the past, and that it is by this type of submission that man is every day contributing to the building of a society that is greater than any one of us can fully grasp through reason.[22]

The concern with leaving open the possibility for novelty and creativity in human society is also seen in Hayek's interest in preserving individual freedom. Because both the defenders of socialism and of capitalism claim that their respective systems are compatible with human freedom, and because Hayek himself contends that the private property system is the most important guarantee of the freedom of both property owners and those who own no property, he very wisely tries to determine the character of human freedom.[23] He distinguishes between freedom understood as a man's freedom from coercion or from the arbitrary will of other men and freedom understood as a man's freedom from the restrictions of circumstances or of impersonal forces.[24] This second conception of freedom is seen as involving a confusion between freedom and power. It is the type of freedom that men picture in dreams when they are under the illusion that they are not bound by gravity and thus can fly like a bird. Freedom understood in this sense is identified with omnipotence. Socialists use this identification of freedom with power to justify their demand for an equal distribution of wealth, arguing that it is wealth that makes men free, i.e. gives man the power to overcome the restraints of his environment.[25]

This identification fails to see the difference between a man who is master of himself and who is able to pursue his own choices, and a man who has a great deal of power or enjoys the fruits of great wealth. For example, the director of a construction project, who has the power to give orders to many men, may be less free than a poor farmer because he himself must do the bidding of others whereas the farmer need follow no will but his own. Similarly, a member of a

[21] *Ibid.*, pp. 37–38.
[22] See footnote 2, p. 204.
[23] *Ibid.*, pp. 103–104.
[24] *Ibid.*, p. 25.
[25] See footnote 4, pp. 16–17. See also footnote 2, p. 26.

wealthy movie star's entourage may be living in a very posh environment, but
may not be as free as a grocer living in a slum because the former is always at
the beck and call of the movie star, doing his will, whereas the grocer is able to
live his life according to his own choices.[26] Thus, although having power and
being wealthy are good things, just as freedom is a good thing, wealth and power
are not identical with freedom.

Freedom, understood as absence of coercion, avoids the evil of coercion that
consists in reducing one man to the status of a mere object or tool to be used by
another to fulfill the aims and purposes of this order. Coercion is thus destructive
of man as an agent who is able to set his own ends. Hayek acknowledges that
this conception of freedom is negative. However, he points out that it is the basis
for all positive value in that it leaves the individual with the option of deciding
what use he will make of his freedom in whatever particular circumstances he
may find himself.[27] There are two factors implied in Hayek's conception of
coercion. It implies both the threat of doing some sort of harm and the intention
of using this threat to bring another to act in a certain way.[28]

The intention to bring about a certain type of behavior is absolutely essential
to this conception of coercion. For example, according to Hayek, a man who
finds that he must take a very low-paying job from the only man that is willing
to employ him in order to avoid his own starvation or that of his family, is not
coerced. So long as the act which put this man in this predicament was not
aimed at making him work for that given employer, so long as the intent of the
employer's offer was not to make the man serve his (the employer's) ends, the
effect of this sort of situation on the man's freedom is no different from any
natural calamity, such as a fire or flood that destroys a person's home.[29] The fact
that a man must make a difficult decision does not mean that he is coerced.
Coercion requires that one man or a group of men deliberately and intentionally
put another man or men in a situation in which they must either do the will
of these men or suffer very serious consequences, e.g., the loss of their lives or
of something essential to their own lives or the lives of loved ones. In short, we
can say that the conditions for coercion are present when one has the sole and
exclusive control of certain goods and/or services that are indispensable to the
lives of others and uses this control by deliberately and intentionally placing
another in a situation in which he must do exactly what the one in power desires
or suffer the loss of this indispensable good or service.

In so far as a capitalistic economy functions according to the impersonal forces
of the market rather than under the control of any human agent, it lessens the
chance that man may lose his freedom. For the man who has suffered a very
serious financial loss as a result of the impersonal forces of the market and now
faces very difficult decisions as to his future standard of living has no more lost

---

[26] See footnote 4, p. 17.
[27] Ibid., pp. 19, 21.
[28] Ibid., p. 134.
[29] Ibid., p. 137.

his freedom, that is, been coerced, than the man who has suffered the loss of his home in a tornado and who also faces difficult decisions. Because freedom is the absence of coercion and because coercion can result only from the intention of one man to use his power so as to get another to do his will, it is reasonable to conclude that an economy that is not in the hands of any central planner, but functions according to the impersonal forces of the market, is more conducive to freedom than is one that is controlled by some human agent.

The conception of freedom as the absence of coercion underlies Hayek's contention that an economy cannot provide for freedom and at the same time satisfy everybody's sense of justice. An economy provides for freedom by meeting two very closely related conditions. First, the remunerations that an individual can expect to receive for the way in which he uses his resources and abilities will correspond to the relative utility for others of what he has done. Secondly, these remunerations will be determined by the *objective* results of an individual's labor and not by his *subjective* merits. This second condition means that the reward, which an individual receives, will not be determined by the goodness or badness of his intentions, but by the market value of his results for others. Although our sense of justice may revolt against the second condition, the fact is that the preservation of freedom requires both conditions.[30]

The link between the objective results of one's labor as registered in the market and human freedom is essential to human freedom because it enables man to lead his own life according to his own knowledge of the market. If human individuals are to choose their own types of lives, if each man is to be able to judge for himself what he ought to do, there must be some readily intelligible standard that can be used to evaluate the social significance of different occupations. Unless a man were able to see that one occupation offered more advantages to him because it was more useful to society than another, he would be unable to use his own knowledge to decide which occupation he ought to pursue.[31] A man is able to achieve such knowledge in the competitive economy of capitalism, because the remunerations offered in a free market serve to inform him of the value that his achievements have for other people, and, therefore, help him to decide whether certain activities are worth the effort required of him. If this system were destroyed, he would be dependent on somebody in authority who controlled the economy to tell him what would constitute the best use of his abilities, the worth of certain activities, and what his obligations and remunerations would be.[32]

Because a worker's remuneration in a planned economy is no longer objectively determined by the impersonal forces of the market, but depends on human authority, a man must turn his attention from studying the workings of the market to trying to win the favor of those who control his remunerations.[33] In

[30] See footnote 15, pp. 21–22.
[31] See footnote 2, pp. 124–125.
[32] See footnote 4, p. 96, also pp. 356–357.
[33] See footnote 2, p. 107.

so far as the value of one's work is consciously determined by some central authority, his life is in the hands of this authority. What a person will make of himself is no longer determined by his own knowledge of the functioning of the market and by his ability to put this knowledge to use to achieve whatever aims he himself thinks he is capable of achieving. It is another person who will decide whether he is a success or a failure.[34]

When these considerations are put alongside the fact that a socialistic economy places all the means of production in a single hand, the socialistic threat to human freedom becomes more obvious. Because the means of production in a capitalistic economy are controlled by many different people acting independently, no one person has enough control over economic resources to control completely the life of another individual. The existence of different centers of control provides the individual with possible alternatives that he may pursue to avoid being wholly controlled by another person. This situation is in marked contrast to a socialist economy in which all the means of production are under a single authority who thus has the power to control the whole life of an individual.[35]

The protection of human freedom in a society is grounded not only in the functioning of a free market, but also in the institution of a rule of law. In order to see the role that a rule of law plays in the protection of freedom, it will be necessary to examine Hayek's conception of a true law. A true law must be of general application, must be known and certain, and must apply to all equally. Because the second characteristic is perhaps most obvious, it will be discussed first. The law must be so stated and so promulgated that men will be able to know, in the great majority of situations and without too much difficulty, which acts are allowed by the law and which are not permitted.[36]

The requirement of generality means that a true law must be a general abstract rule. This requirement points to the fact that a law is directed toward insuring an individual's sphere of freedom. As an abstract, general rule, a law does not spell out in concrete and complete detail how a man is to act in any given individual case. A law thus establishes a general framework for action, with the individual being free to decide the particular course of action that he will pursue within this framework. Thus, a law differs from a command, which is directed toward telling *this* individual that he must act in this one way at this given time and in this given place. The individual living under a rule of law is not coerced by the law because the law does not establish specific aims for him. The general character of law also serves human freedom in that it does not single out any specific individuals or class of individuals. Because it applies to all men irrespective of their individual differences, it allows them to use their individuality in any way they see fit within the limitations of the very general framework.[37]

The requirement that law be of a general character does not exclude the pos-

---

[34] See footnote 4, pp. 80–82.
[35] See footnote 2, pp. 103–104, 145–146.
[36] See footnote 4, pp. 208–209.
[37] *Ibid.*, pp. 148–154.

sibility that laws may be made applicable to certain classes of people if these classes happen to possess qualities not possessed by others. For example, certain laws may apply only to women, or to blind persons, or to persons in a certain age group. However, in most cases of this type, it is not necessary to spell out the class to which the law applies; it is clear that only women can be raped or bear children. Hayek indicates that we can guard against the possibility that such laws may be arbitrary by seeing whether the law is acknowledged to be justified both by those in the group singled out and those who are outside this group. This test does not mean that there must be complete unanimity. The fact that a majority both inside and outside the group find the law satisfactory is certainly sufficient to justify the presumption that the law will serve the ends of both groups. Such a test serves to insure that the law does not discriminate against one of the groups and grant a privilege to the other.[38]

Hayek has some difficulty in distinguishing the third characteristic of law, equality, from its abstract and general character. This third characteristic requires that all be treated equally before the law. This characteristic must be stated because Hayek thinks that it is possible that a law, which is stated in general and abstract terms, may nonetheless be discriminatory. The notion of the equality of all before the law serves to emphasize the requirement that a law not single out any individual or group and that it neither discriminate against anyone nor grant special privileges to anyone. Hayek does not think that any satisfactory criterion has yet been discovered to test whether or not a certain law does allow for the equality of all before the law. He thinks that the demand that the law not make irrelevant distinctions or that it not discriminate between persons on grounds that are not connected with the purpose of the law evade rather than help clarify the issue. The criterion used to test the generality of the law can also prove useful to test whether this law treats all equally. Another way of testing equality before the law is to ask whether one can or cannot foresee how the law will influence particular people. For the ideal of equality before the law is directed toward equally improving the opportunities of persons yet unknown and is not compatible with benefiting or injuring known persons in a predictable way.[39]

Socialism is incompatible with a rule of law because government planners are required to move beyond the framework of abstract general laws in which individuals are free to choose their own ends. A socialistic government has accepted responsibilities that cannot be resolved by the formation of formal rules applying indiscriminately to all, but that demand it make concrete choices between individuals, deciding that this individual is more worthy of this job and of this salary than is that individual. A government that tries to meet the responsibilities of deciding such issues as the number of pigs to be raised, the number of buses to be run, and the price for which shoes are to be sold cannot deduce decisions

[38] *Ibid.*, p. 154.
[39] *Ibid.*, pp. 209–210.

concerning these issues from formal principles applicable to all. These decisions inevitably lead a government to take into account particular circumstances and to evaluate the interests of competing groups, deciding which interests are more important or more valuable. Such evaluations will result in the establishment of laws which will favor certain groups over other groups.[40]

The same factors, which make socialism incompatible with a rule of law, also make it incompatible with democracy. The fact that a socialistic government must engage in a great number of activities and must be able to control these activities down to the last detail inevitably means that this government must surrender the democratic process, no matter what its intentions may have been when it embarked on the path of socialism. Because the planning required for the effective management of a socialistic economy must cover every facet of a nation's economy down to the most particular details, such an economy can function properly in a democracy only if there exists an almost total agreement by the great majority of the citizens on every facet of life. Citizens in a democratic society may be expected to come to agreement in the establishment of a rule of law, because they need only agree on certain general principles. However, it is unrealistic to expect this same agreement when the matters to be decided are as extensive and detailed as they must be in planning a country's economy. Because it will be impossible to reach the necessary agreements through democratic processes, the people will inevitably become dissatisfied with these processes, and the conviction will grow that the economy will function more efficiently if it is removed from the political arena and placed under the total control of a certain group of experts whose decisions will be wholly independent of the democratic process.[41] Thus, socialism is seen to be not the "Road to Freedom," but the "High Road to Servitude."[42] Hayek also states that the totalitarianism of the Soviet Union is the necessary result of the systematic implementation of traditional socialism.[43]

He warns that the erosion of human freedom and of the institutional safeguards of this freedom present in a rule of law and in democratic procedures may also result from the "hodge-podge of ill-assembled and often inconsistent ideals," that' are included under the banner of the welfare state.[44] This position does not commit Hayek to an unqualified rejection of every form of state activity in the economic order. His opposition to certain types of welfare programs is directed not to the aims of these programs, but to the manner in which these aims are pursued. In evaluating welfare programs, it is necessary to guard against the danger of thinking that because the aim of a certain program is not contrary to

[40] See footnote 2, p. 74, see also p. 73.

[41] *Ibid.*, pp. 62–64.

[42] *Ibid.*, p. 27. Hayek summarizes his position in this book as arguing that "the unforeseen but inevitable consequences of socialist planning create a state of affairs in which, if the policy is to be pursued, totalitarian forces will get the upper hand." P. xvii.

[43] See footnote 4, p. 255.

[44] See footnote 2, p. ix.

the legitimate function of government, any means may be employed to achieve this goal.[45]

Hayek is opposed in principle to any type of welfare legislation that can be achieved only if the state no longer acts under a rule of law. No matter how laudable its aim may be, a welfare program must be rejected, if, in order to achieve this aim, government must decide issues in a discriminatory fashion based on nothing more than some vague standard of justice from which the conclusion is drawn that a certain segment of society "deserves" certain goods or services that are to be paid for by another segment. Seen in this light, the welfare program is simply another way of pursuing the socialist's aim of redistributing income and services at the expense of a rule of law and thus also at the expense of individual freedom.[46] Hence, the same arguments that applied against socialism also apply against programs of this nature.

The importance that Hayek attaches to the method used to achieve welfare aims is seen in his insistence that a means test is essential to insuring that the state's legitimate function is not to degenerate into a way of redistributing income that is destructive of a rule of law. A system of social insurance must distinguish clearly between the benefits to which an individual has a moral and legal claim, because he has fully paid for them, and benefits, which he receives because he is in need, in which case he must show proof of such need.[47] Unless the needy are required to submit to a means test, they will come to believe that the assistance, which they have received, is the "product of their own effort or merit."[48]

Welfare programs are compatible with a free society so long as the needy are required to prove that they actually are in need and so long as an individual does not receive any benefit for which he has not personally paid without the establishment of such proof. A welfare program that ignores these restrictions is not carrying out the state's proper function of providing a minimum level of welfare for the needy, but is performing the socialistic task of redistributing income according to some vague and preconceived notion of justice.[49] Programs that do not include a means test are directed not to providing "security against severe physical privation, the assurance of a given minimum of sustenance for all," something that can be accomplished under a rule of law, but to providing "assurance of a given standard of life, which is determined by comparing the standard enjoyed by a person or group with that of others."[50] Such assurance can be provided only by ignoring the rule of law and by placing a man's life in the hands of other men who must try to decide what he "deserves."[51]

[45] See footnote 4, p. 260, see also pp. 221–222.
[46] *Ibid.*, pp. 289, 302.
[47] *Ibid.*, p. 293.
[48] *Ibid.*, p. 303.
[49] *Ibid.*, pp. 289, 302.
[50] *Ibid.*, pp. 259–260.
[51] See footnote 2, pp. 122, 124–125.

2. MORAL RESPONSIBILITY
IN AN ECONOMY OF ABUNDANCE

Although this section will take a position that is opposed to Hayek's moral rejection of socialism, it will not try to prove that socialism is the only morally acceptable economic system, but only that socialism must be included among the morally viable alternatives open to man. The primary purpose of this section is to establish the validity of certain moral principles as a foundation for further reflections on the morality of economic institutions rather than to defend any particular institutional arrangement as the only moral one. More specifically, I shall try to develop the notions of freedom and justice discussed in Chapters II and V and to present considerations that relate to such issues as the rule of law and man's knowledge of the future in a way that will provide a different moral perspective on man's economic situation from that provided by Hayek. It is hoped that the points established in this section will function as intellectual tools that will be helpful to individuals dealing with the moral issues involved in concrete questions concerning specific types of welfare legislation or other forms of government involvement in the economic sphere.

The task of trying to decide the specific type of institutional framework that best fits the demands of the moral principles to be developed in this section is best left to the man of practical wisdom, who is in a position to relate these demands to the concrete problems and possibilities that he finds in his own society at a given time in history. However, it would be misleading to give the impression that the principles to be developed in this section are compatible with any and every type of economic arrangement. They are not compatible with any type of institutional framework in which a significant segment of an affluent society must depend on the charity of others for goods and services that are essential to their well-being as human subjects.

I shall argue that welfare legislation in an affluent society is not a charitable action, if "charitable" is understood to refer to action that is not morally demanded in justice, but that is performed out of a sense of benevolence that leads the more fortunate members of society to share their good fortune with those in need, even though the latter have no moral claim to such a sharing. If man has the ingenuity to meet the demands of justice without placing the direct control of the major means of production in the hands of the state, well and good. However, as I shall try to show, socialism is a morally viable alternative, if it happens that these demands can be met only in a socialistic economy.

The attempt to show that a socialistic economy need not involve the dire moral consequences that Hayek sees should be distinguished from an attempt to defend socialism as a utopia, totally free of all problems. A socialistic economy may not be able to produce the same diversity of goods as does a capitalistic economy. For example, it may not be able to produce as many different types of automobiles or as many different brands of cigarettes, of soaps, and of tooth paste.

It may also suffer from a rather cumbersome bureaucracy. However, difficulties of this type do not provide a moral basis for rejecting socialism. It may be that a nation must work with these difficulties if the citizens of that nation are to meet their moral responsibilities to their fellow citizens. If one argues that despite my protestations to the contrary, the principles that I shall be defending necessarily lead to socialism, then I can only respond, "So much the better for socialism."

The ultimate basis for the position to be taken in this section is a view of man's relationship to nature that is shared by Karl Marx and Thomas Aquinas, two thinkers who would appear to have absolutely nothing in common. Both recognize that the limited material character of human existence means that man must use the subhuman beings of his environment for his continued existence and for his growth and development as a free being. Marx expresses this view by referring to nature as "man's *inorganic body*," meaning by this that the air, animals, and plants of nature are as necessary to human life and human activity as is what we usually refer to as man's body.[52] Nature functions as man's inorganic body both in so far as it is "(1) his direct means of life, and (2) the material, the object, and the instrument of his life activity."[53] The conception of nature as the direct means of human life refers to the fact that man's continued physical existence requires the air, the sunlight, the rain, and the food provided by nature. That nature is the material, the object, and the instrument of man's life activity refers to the fact that man cannot produce out of nothing. He needs given objects on which to work. He also needs instruments with which to work, and he finds his instruments in the powers of nature. For example, animals, steam, electricity, and now atomic power have played an instrumental role in man's productive activities.

Any evaluation of the morality of an economic system based on the conception of man as an end in himself must not lose sight of man's dependence on nature for his continued physical existence and well-being. Thomas Aquinas seems to have recognized this point in holding that man's right to use the subhuman things of this earth is morally prior to his right to own them. This moral priority means that the right to own things is limited by the right to use them. Thus, if there is ever a conflict between the two rights, if, for example, it can be shown that a man's possession of a surplus food supply deprives another man of the food necessary for his continued existence, the right of the deprived man to the use of the food necessary for his existence takes precedence over the other man's right to ownership.[54] A moral evaluation of any economic system must ask

---

[52] See footnote 42, Chap. III, p. 112.

[53] *Ibid.*

[54] See *S.T.* II–II, Q. 66, aa.1–9. See also *ScG.* III, 127–135; see footnote 9, Chap. II, Bk. III, Part II, pp. 156–190. This brief summary of Aquinas' thought should not be taken to mean that he is a socialist. For a discussion of this point in Aquinas, see Vernon J. Bourke, "Material Possession And Thomism," *Ethics in Crisis* (Milwaukee: The Bruce Publishing Co., 1966), pp. 178–192.

whether or not the things upon which man is dependent for his continued earthly existence and for his growth as a free being are distributed in such a way that as many men as morally possible are able to use these things.

Although a consideration of man's right to use the material things of nature must be involved in any moral evaluation of economic institutions, it cannot be the sole consideration especially when dealing with the complicated economic situations of our own day. Hayek's case for capitalism has pointed to such factors as individual freedom and the rule of law that must be considered in any moral evaluation of contemporary economic institutions. These topics will be considered under the following headings: (a) Justice in an Affluent Society, (b) The Market, Human Freedom, and the Rule of Law in an Affluent Society, and (c) Human Reason and Man's Future.

a. JUSTICE IN AN AFFLUENT SOCIETY

Hayek has made a valid point in arguing that a government ought not to try to distribute goods and services to its citizens on the basis of their individual moral goodness because it cannot have the type of knowledge necessary to evaluate the moral character of individuals. However, his argument against a socialistic economy is open to question in so far as it seems to be based on the view that there should be no attempt to secure justice in the economic order because there appears to be no scale of values on which reasonable people can be expected to agree that will satisfy the demands for justice. Hayek has provided himself with an easy mark by presenting a socialistic government that is trying to impose an order on a people who share no common moral principles. Any government, whether it be working within a capitalistic or socialistic framework, would find itself in serious difficulty if it were trying to impose an order on a people who did not share a certain consensus concerning general moral principles, who were not united by commonly held moral beliefs. Granted a moral community, the principles that are to guide a government in its task are given.

Because a democratic form of government allows those representing different interests to play a role in the political process, a democratic statesman will not surrender a program simply because he finds that there are others who will oppose this program. He expects such opposition. If we grant that a people are in general agreement concerning the general direction a nation ought to take, they will be able to live with the differences that inevitably separate men when they begin to deal with concrete issues. My point may be brought out by a consideration of the development of law and programs in the United States. If we take the statement that all men are created equal, which is found in the Declaration of Independence of the thirteen American colonies, and the commitment in the Preamble of the Constitution of the United States to "establish Justice" and to "promote the general Welfare" as expressing certain features of the general moral outlook shared by the citizens of this country, the task of these citizens at any given point in history is to see whether there are any values captured in the words that are worth keeping and to see what concrete institutional expression can be given to these values at any time in the nation's history. They must ask whether the values expressed in these words have matured in a way that indicates the direction in which that nation ought to move and whether the resources are available to pursue this direction.

The Civil Rights and the Medicare legislation that have passed in this country in recent years provide excellent examples of the way in which a nation tries to give concrete meaning to the shared principles that make it a moral community. Admittedly, there will be difficulties as a nation tries to come to a more concrete realization of its commitment to justice among its people, but it seems to me that these are difficulties that must be faced if a government is to avoid imposing an order that is unjust on its citizens.

A further point of difference between Hayek's position and the position to be taken in this section is the difference between our respective notions of equalitarian justice. Although Hayek undertakes no explicit treatment of the nature of justice, it is clear that he conceives of the equalitarian rule as an attempt to abolish differences among men. For example, he depicts the socialists as being concerned with doing away with the differences in nurture among men. It is important to recall that the defense of an equalitarian rule of justice offered in Chapter V explicitly stated that the moral significance of this rule did not lie in any attempt to establish similarity merely for the sake of similarity. Thus, one working with this rule would not conclude that there has been a breach of justice simply because one man has a better car, more expensive clothes, and a more responsible job than another man.

I can bring out the differences between Hayek's view and the position that I shall try to defend by criticizing Hayek's opposition to the view that one's citizenship in a certain country entitles him to a certain level of material well-being, with the level being determined by the general wealth of the community. In a book first published in 1935, John Dewey pointed to a factor in modern man's economic situation that provides a basis for questioning Hayek's position. Dewey pointed out that, as a result of scientific and technological advances, man has within his grasp the productive potential that will enable him to overcome the state of scarcity that has plagued man for most of his history. It was Dewey's contention that man's failure to rid himself of the affective and intellectual outlooks that were bred in ages of scarcity has prevented him from taking full advantage of the age of abundance that is in his grasp.[55]

As was pointed out in Chapter I, an increase in man's power over nature

---

[55] See footnote 114, Chap. IV, pp. 57–59. This same point has been made in more recent times by economists such as John Kenneth Galbraith and Robert Theobold. See John Kenneth Galbraith, *The Affluent Society* (New York: Mentor Books, 1958), pp. 13–14, 29. The main point of this book is that the affluent character of the American economy demands that we change those views on economic issues which may have been adequate in ages of scarcity, but which are not in keeping with this affluence. See also Robert Theobold, *Free Men and Free Markets* (Garden City, New York: Doubleday Anchor Books, 1965), pp. xiv, 4, 9–10.

means an increase in the scope of his moral responsibility. Seen in the context of the present discussion, this means that the scope of a community's responsibilities in justice to those who are lacking certain essential material resources increases as that community moves from an age of scarcity to one of abundance. It may well be true that in an age of scarcity, a man has moral claim to certain benefits only if he has fully paid for them. During such an age, man's ability to control these benefits may be so limited that the community would be wholly unable to make them available to all. Attempts to make these benefits available to all in such an age might result in seriously jeopardizing the material well-being of those who were able to acquire them through their work. Because man's control of material resources would be so limited that he would be unable to help one group of people without seriously endangering the well-being of another group, the distribution of certain goods to the needy would be a matter of charity rather than of justice. However, in a period of material abundance, there can be a sharing of goods, which does not jeopardize the material well-being of the more fortunate members of the community. Hence, the position taken in this section is that a community that has achieved a state of affluence has the moral responsibility in justice of discovering ways and means to insure that no member of this community is prevented from developing into a free being for lack of financial resources.

The type of situation envisioned by this position can be summarized under the following points. First, a community's scientific, industrial, and technological resources are such that it can produce an abundance of goods and services. Secondly, there are many in the community who cannot take advantage of the medical, educational, or cultural opportunities available in the community and essential to their growth as free agents simply because they lack financial resources. Thirdly, these opportunities can be made available to these people without so impoverishing the more fortunate members of the community that they are no longer able to take advantage of these opportunities. This third consideration means that the subjectivity of neither the fortunate members nor unfortunate members of the community is being denied.

Hayek's contention that an individual cannot be said to have a moral claim to a certain standard of living simply because he happened to be born in a certain community is grounded in an excessively narrow conception of justice. He saw equalitarianism as being concerned only with the establishing of similarities among men for the sake of similarity, and rightly rejected such a conception. Although he does not give a formal and explicit statement of his own conception of justice, his handling of what a community owes its members and of welfare legislation indicates that he is working out of an exclusively meritarian conception of justice, which holds that a man has a moral claim in justice to certain benefits only because he himself has provided benefits to others either in the form of money or of labor. Thus, the issue between the stand taken by Hayek and the view defended in this section hinges on the defense of the equalitarian and welfare rules of justice presented in Chapter V.

It is true that a society cannot make a man free, but it can provide certain resources that he needs in order to achieve his full moral development. If the equalitarian and welfare conceptions of justice presented in Chapter V are accepted, it follows that the affluent society, which can provide these resources to members without depriving others of the same resources, is morally obliged in justice to find a way to make them available to all. The man in such a society, who is suffering from a brain disorder that impairs the exercise of his intelligence, deserves the medical attention necessary to alleviate the disorder whether he can pay for it or not. A man's inability to pay for these services in an affluent society does not make him a charity case. If that society treats him as a charity case, it is failing in its moral responsibility to make available to its members those resources that are at hand and that are essential to the moral growth of these members.

The existential situation in which an affluent society may find itself at any given moment in history may be such that because of certain factors, it may be unable to meet its responsibilities. For example, the citizens of such a society may not have had the time to reconstruct their institutions in a way that permits them to meet their new responsibilities. The acknowledgement of such a possibility should not lead that society to lose sight of its responsibility and of the need to begin moving toward the meeting of this responsibility.

Hayek's description of the social value of the man of independent means can be used to show that an affluent society that uses its affluence to render the lives of its members economically secure and provides them with the material resources necessary to their physical and moral well-being is not only meeting its moral responsibility, but is also securing practical advantages for the whole community. The man of independent means was depicted as a creative force in the introduction of new values into society. "It is only natural that the development of the art of living and of the nonmaterialistic values should have profited from the activities of those who had no material worries."[56] Taking the material benefits of wealth for granted, Hayek's man of independent means finds his satisfaction in the pursuit of nonmaterial goods—for example, in the arts, in politics, and in working for the more humane treatment of the insane. Mankind has had the good fortune to reap the harvest of these pursuits. If the financial independence and security of a few is so great a boon to the advancement of a society, it is nonsensical to deny similar independence and security to a greater number in the society, if not to the majority, when society has the resources to effect the necessary distribution.

In making his case for the man of independent means, Hayek uses the life of the great British economist Lord Keynes to exemplify his position. He points out that Keynes felt that he had a message to deliver to society, but realized that he had to gain a position of financial independence in order to deliver it.[57] Fortunately, Keynes had the financial acumen to gain his financial independence, and hence was able to make his contribution to the science of economics.

[56] See footnote 4, p. 130.
[57] *Ibid.*, p. 447, note 7.

In a society in which man's basic economic resources are in short supply, it may be necessary to require that every man or every family secure its own economic resources before that man or certain individuals in the family undertake the development of whatever scientific, artistic, or political talents they believe themselves to possess. However, in a society in which the basic economic needs of its members can be more adequately met, there seems to be little justification for making economic success a prerequisite for all other human undertakings. Certainly the fact that a youth's parents have not been economically successful, or that the youth himself has been unable to achieve financial independence does not mean that he has no talents to be a great physician, statesman, or scientist. Who knows how much human talent has never come to fruition because individuals lacked the financial resources to cultivate their talents and because they were forced to put time and energy into securing these resources—time and energy that would have been more valuable to society had it been put into the cultivation of their real talents.

The requirement that men first be economically successful or be born into an economically successful family before engaging in other socially valuable human pursuits is certainly not sustained by the following defense which Hayek makes of the wealthy man's pursuit of nonmaterial values: "It is doubtful whether a wealthy class whose ethos requires that at least every male member prove his usefulness by making more money can adequately justify its existence."[58] The position being advanced in this section argues that it is doubtful that an affluent society whose ethos requires that at least every male member prove his usefulness by making more money can adequately justify its existence.

What good is the economic progress of a society, of what value is its abundance, if it continues to require that a significant number of its members, if not the majority, give the same primacy to economic considerations in planning their lives as those who went before them were required to do in an age of scarcity? If a significant number of individuals in an affluent society continue to suffer from economic insecurity and continue to be frustrated in the development of socially valuable talents because of a lack of economic resources, there would appear to be no justification for the existence of an affluent society, unless one were willing to defend the indefensible thesis that the production of material abundance is an end in itself.

This discussion has not been directed toward denying the social value of economic pursuits. The men who are directly and immediately involved in the production and distribution of material goods provide a valuable and indispensable service for society. To interpret the foregoing discussion as a jeremiad directed against business or economic pursuits is to miss the point completely. The point is that just as it is nonsensical to make success in philosophy a prerequisite for success in other areas of human endeavor, so also is it nonsensical in an affluent society to require that an individual's family or he himself be

[58] *Ibid.*, p. 128.

successful in the market place as a prerequisite to the pursuit of other socially valuable tasks.

Having tried to indicate both the moral and utilitarian justification for the view that one's citizenship in an affluent state entitles him to a certain level of material well-being, with this level being determined by the general wealth of the community, it is now necessary to consider two difficulties that Hayek thinks will confront a society that tries to achieve a just distribution of its wealth and resources. First, he maintained that a society planning for justice will generate more discontent among the economically unfortunate and make their lives more unbearable than would be the case if matters were left to the impersonal forces of the market. This position is justified if the planning tries to use the moral character of an individual as its criterion of what he deserves. However, because there is no necessity that economic planning use such a criterion, this dimension of Hayek's position cannot be held as a valid objection against all forms of economic planning.

Moreover, the general contention that a planned society will generate more discontent among the economically unfortunate than a market economy cannot be sustained with respect to an affluent society. Granted the advances that man has made in bringing more and more of the impersonal forces of nature under his control and granted the general affluence of the community that has resulted from such control, it is not likely that those who find that they are not sharing in this affluence will be content with an explanation that accounts for their difficulties in terms of the impersonal forces of the market. The explanation will be taken as meaning that those who enjoy the blessings of affluence are not willing to use the power that they possess to aid the economically deprived sector of the community. It does not seem too unreasonable for those in this sector to demand that the same effort be put into controlling the impersonal forces of the market as is put into building more and more efficient weapons of mass destruction or into getting a man to the moon.

Hayek has also maintained that the attempt to establish a just distribution of material resources in a community will destroy the incentive of the most highly qualified members of that society to use their talents. The economists Robert Theobold and John Galbraith point to certain features in our present economic situation that indicate that the connection between human incentive and economic insecurity is not as necessary as this position might lead one to believe. For example, Robert Theobold, arguing for a guaranteed annual income, points out that such an income will allow an individual to take the same sort of risks to develop his own talents for his own benefit and that of society's as those risks that corporations were able to take under the protection of the laws of limited liability.[59] Whether or not a guaranteed income is the particular mechanism whereby the affluent society is to achieve justice is not at issue here. The point is that Theobold has indicated that the economic security engendered in the

[59] See footnote 55, *Free Men and Free Markets*, p. xii.

laws of limited liability may have been a contributing factor to corporate creative risk-taking.

Galbraith argues that a part of the increased productivity of American farmers in the period since the 1930's may well have resulted from the fact that price-support legislation, which reduced uncertainties of price and income, may have enabled farmers to invest in new technological developments with a greater sense of confidence. He also cites figures, which indicate that labor productivity measured in terms of national income per man-hour shows a greater increase in the ten years following the thirties (a period when the United States government began to take serious steps to lessen the fear of economic insecurity) than in the years between 1900 and 1929. Whereas in the latter period the total increase was 23.7 cents, the increase in the ten years following the thirties was 47.7.[60] Admittedly, the use of statistics cannot be taken as a decisive factor since there may have been many factors to account for the increase other than the reduction of economic insecurity. However, the figures do indicate that the reduction of economic insecurity was not, as a matter of fact, accompanied by a reduction of labor productivity.

If we are to deal directly with the question of the relationship between human incentives and economic security, we must move beyond statistical correlations to a reflective consideration of this relationship. John Dewey has made an excellent contribution to such a consideration in pointing out that in an age of scarcity, in an age when material abundance is simply beyond the scope of man's power, economic insecurity may well function as an impetus to human effort. However, in situations in which insecurity is generated not by forces of nature that are beyond human control but by man-made institutions and arrangements, which can be controlled by man, insecurity no longer functions as an incentive to work, but becomes the soil for despair.[61]

The reason for this difference may be grounded in the different effects on the relationships between an individual and his society that economic insecurity produces in the two contexts. In the context of material scarcity caused by natural factors beyond human control, economic insecurity does not function as a factor that alienates an individual from his fellow man, but may function as a unifying bond among the members of a given community. In such a situation economic insecurity is seen as part of the unavoidable condition of mankind and an individual sees himself united with the rest of the human community in the struggle to defeat the common foes—scarcity and poverty. However, in a context of material abundance in which economic insecurity is a function not of presently uncontrollable natural forces, but of human institutions, those who suffer from such insecurity may lose that sense of unity with their fellow man and of being involved in a common struggle that would appear to be a significant aid to human initiative.

---

[60] See footnote 114, Chap. IV, pp. 95–96.
[61] See footnote 55, *Liberalism and Social Action*, pp. 59–60.

It seems to me that the argument that man's incentive to work will be destroyed if he is granted economic security is based on a rather simplistic view of human motivation and of the character of human existence. The argument fails to see that the springs of human motivation run much deeper than a simple concern with economic security. The lives of economically successful people such as corporation executives and wealthy entertainers, who do not stop working despite the fact that they have achieved an economic security that certainly will last through their lifetime and almost as certainly the lifetime of their children, provide evidence indicating that the end of economic insecurity does not mean the end of human effort and striving. The same point is brought out if we consider the political activities of members of very wealthy families here in the United States. Moreover, business corporations in our own day try to attract young people to work for them not by offering only economic security, but by offering work that is challenging, that will provide them with the opportunity to use their talents to the maximum, and that will make a contribution to advancing the good of the community. Thus, it seems clear that human fulfillment is not simply reducible to economic security and that there are many other factors capable of fulfilling and, therefore, of motivating man.

Those who have argued that economic insecurity is necessary to motivate man have grossly underrated, if not totally ignored, the character of man as a being who finds fulfillment in expressing and manifesting his capacities in the world. To be engaged in what one considers a meaningful enterprise, to be working at a task that fits one's talents, to share the problems and successes of common undertakings with other men, to make one's own contribution to these ventures—these are sources of human fulfillment that are not simply reducible to economic security. Some might argue that this view of man applies only to a very small percentage of mankind and that society could not depend on these factors to motivate the vast majority of its members. It is undoubtedly true that the majority of mankind working under the conditions of scarcity and economic insecurity have been unable to view their work in terms of the type of human fulfillments mentioned above. However, this point should not mislead us into thinking that these sources of human motivation are the possession of only the wealthy.

To be a man is to be a being who can grow and perfect himself only through activity, only through the exercise of his various capacities. In so far as labor, whether it be primarily of the intellectual variety or primarily of the more physical variety, involves the exercise of human capacities, it itself can be a source of human fulfillment not only for the man of wealth, but for any man. In taking this position, I cannot deny that there will be men who will abuse economic security, to their own and society's detriment, just as Hayek could not deny that there are those among the wealthy who abuse their economic security. There is no institutional framework that is immune to human abuse. Granted this point, we must ask ourselves whether we are going to build a society that is so concerned with avoiding an abuse of economic security that it will deprive many men of the opportunity for human growth offered by such security.

Finally the fact that all citizens may be free from the suffering of economic insecurity as regards such basic factors in human well-being as health, food, clothing, and education does not mean that there will be absolutely no difference between the man who is successful in his work and the one who is not quite so successful. The successful man will be distinguished from his less successful coworker not only by his own sense of accomplishment and by the respect of his fellow workers, who will seek and take his advice in matters pertaining to their tasks, but also by his promotions to more challenging and responsible positions, and by the financial rewards, which he will receive, enabling him to buy more and better quality clothes, a bigger house in a better section of the city, and to pay for more extended travel than his less successful coworkers. In short, to try to build a society in which a man need not worry that he will be financially destroyed if one of his children must be hospitalized over an extended period of time, or that his old age will be marked by a constant struggle against poverty is not to destroy all the differences that separate the successful worker from the less successful. As we indicated in the section on justice, the meeting of the welfare demands of justice need not entail a denial of the claims of meritarian justice.

b. THE MARKET, HUMAN FREEDOM, AND THE RULE OF LAW IN AN AFFLUENT SOCIETY

In a 1953 speech, Albert Camus noted that modern man seems to be the victim of a vicious dialectic in which he is offered justice without freedom by the representatives of Marxist socialism or freedom without justice by those opposed to such socalism. He asks, "How then can this infernal circle be broken?" and answers,

> Obviously, it can be done only by reviving at once, in ourselves and in others, the value of freedom—and by never again agreeing to its being sacrificed, even temporarily, or separated from our demand for justice. The current motto for all of us can only be this: without giving up anything on the plane of justice, yield nothing on the plane of freedom.[62]

As Camus himself clearly recognized, this is an easier motto to proclaim than to put into practice. Undoubtedly, those sharing Hayek's views would argue that the justice that was discussed in the preceding subsection can be secured only by the surrendering of human freedom. The contention of this subsection will be that such a surrender need not be involved in the pursuit of justice.

If we are to make any philosophical advance in dealing with this issue, it is necessary that we be clear on the meaning of the words "justice" and "freedom," and on the values that these words are meant to convey. We have already given

[62] Albert Camus, *Resistance, Rebellion, and Death* (New York: The Modern Library, 1960), p. 68.

a good deal of attention to the meaning of justice in Chapter V and in the preceding subsection. The position to be taken in this subsection will also be grounded in the notion of freedom as self-determination that was developed in Chapter II. As we deal with the major issue of this subsection, it will be necessary to expand our discussion of freedom to include a consideration of political freedom.

It may be true, as Hayek suggests, that there have been those whose defense of the need for an equal distribution of wealth was based on a confusion of freedom with wealth. However, the position taken in the preceding subsection was not founded on such an error. The conception of freedom advanced in Chapter II certainly did not identify freedom with wealth. Human freedom, involving as it does the exercise of man's rational capacities, is not a commodity that can be bought. Man must make himself free. It must, however, also be noted that the analysis of human freedom in Chapter II indicated that man does not develop his freedom in a vacuum. He becomes free in an environment that can be either helpful to, or destructive of, the exercise of his capacities to be free.

This latter point is important to the issue concerning the relationship between economic power and human freedom. Poverty must be included among those factors that are detrimental to the development of man as a free being. Thus, a child's opportunity to become free is certainly not helped if his family lacks the financial resources to feed him a proper diet and to provide him with proper medical care, if his parents must be so concerned with finding ways and means to acquire the bare essentials of life that they have little or no time to give him the love and care he needs to attain emotional maturity, or if his psychological environment is permeated with the sense of despair and hopelessness that characterizes the existence of those whose lives are economic disasters.

It is possible that a man may become free despite the poverty-stricken conditions under which he lives. However, the acknowledgment of this possibility cannot logically ground the conclusion that an affluent society is contributing to the growth of human freedom by failing to use its abundance to try to alleviate these conditions. If it is an error to equate economic power with freedom understood as self-determination, as it surely is, it is also an error to imply, as I believe Hayek does, that poverty is not detrimental to the existence of man as a free being.

It is only because Hayek has an excessively narrow view of the threats to human freedom that he can move from the view that a market economy works according to impersonal forces to the conclusion that such an economy cannot possibly be a threat to human freedom. Working out of the analysis of freedom in Chapter II, one can say that coercion under the will of another is not the only factor in man's life which constitutes a threat to the emotional and intellectual growth that is essential to the development of human freedom. A man who has suffered brain damage and is unable to use his rational capacities cannot act freely, whether the damage was caused by the impersonal force of a falling tree or by a deliberate and intentional blow of another man. Similarly, a man who does not have the economic resources for the proper development of his rational capacities may not be free, whether his lack of economic resources is a result of the impersonal forces of the market or the deliberate act of another human being. Hence, the mere fact that the market functions impersonally does not justify the conclusion that it cannot be a threat to freedom.

Hayek has also tried to link the market to individual freedom by arguing that it is only through an analysis of the market that a man can know whether his actions are of sufficient social significance to warrant whatever effort and sacrifice the proposed action may require. The market is thus presented as the intelligible yardstick that free men can use to lead their lives by means of their own judgment. This position presupposes that the free market is the only criterion that a free man can use in judging the social worth of his acts. This presupposition cannot be sustained. The fact that a man can command a larger salary as a salesman or executive in the cigarette industry than he can as a fund raiser for the American Cancer Society does not mean that his work in the cigarette industry would be of greater social value than his work for the Cancer Society. Similarly, there is no reason to think that the work of a rock-and-roll singer, whose salary may be in the six-figure bracket, is of greater social value than the work of a minister, who is trying to help the poor in a slum area gain a sense of hope and of their own dignity and whose annual salary is many thousands of dollars less than that of the singer.

The fact of the matter is that the market is able to function as a criterion for judging the *economic* value of an enterprise, but not its *social* value, if this is taken to refer to the moral or humane good for society brought about by the enterprise. It is possible that a given enterprise may be both economically and socially valuable, but the two values are by no means identical. Hayek himself acknowledges that the market mechanism does not provide the sole criterion for judging the social value of human activities in defending the social value of the man of independent means on the grounds that such a man can concern himself with securing values that are not measured by the market.[63]

It is now necessary to evaluate Hayek's defense of the view that socialism inevitably leads to the destruction of democracy and to the establishment of totalitarianism, and that socialism and a certain type of welfare legislation are not compatible with a rule of law. The economist Henry C. Wallich, who was a member of the Council of Economic Advisers in the Eisenhower administration and whose basic outlook on the issues being discussed is more compatible with Hayek's position than with the position being offered in this section, disagrees with him concerning the inevitable union of socialism and totalitarianism.

History, which can prove no rules but often does prove the exceptions, has already handed down rebuttals to the indictment, [that socialism inevitably means the end of democracy and the beginning of dictatorships] as in the cases of Britain, the

[63] See footnote 4, p. 125.

Scandinavian countries, and Australia. In these and other countries much exposed to planning, democracy and freedom have survived without serious difficulty.[64]

Of course, Hayek can brush aside these instances that seem to contradict his position by holding that these countries have not as yet become totalitarian, but that they will at some future date, if they continue in their socialistic ways.

If such a prediction is to be anything more than a blind act of faith, Hayek must advance reasons to justify it in the face of existing evidence that does not support it. Hayek thinks that he does have such reasons, and perhaps these reasons have led him to conclude that the "unforeseen but inevitable consequences" of the pursuit of socialism will be totalitarianism.[65] He accepts this conclusion despite the fact that, in opposing the view that capitalism inevitably leads to the establishment of monopolies, he sees the intellectual history of the West from the mid-nineteenth century as providing "a perfect illustration of the truth that in social evolution nothing is inevitable but thinking makes it so."[66] Unless one is going to hold that Hayek is involved in an open and blatant contradiction in taking these two positions, one must think that he has satisfied himself that he has valid reasons to sustain the inevitable link between socialism and totalitarianism. The time has come to evaluate these reasons.

We have seen that Hayek is certain that socialism is incompatible with democracy because a socialistic economy cannot be managed efficiently under the restraints of democratic institutions. Hence, the people will inevitably become dissatisfied with democratic procedures and will place the management of the economy under the total control of a man or a group of experts. Wallich also raises a valid objection against this aspect of Hayek's thought. Although it may be true that a socialistic economy will advance the cause of totalitarianism in a country that has no strong democratic traditions, it need not be true that the same thing will occur in countries in which such traditions are strong.[67] Let it be granted for the sake of discussion that a country may find that the economy could be managed more efficiently if democratic procedures were put aside, it does not follow that the procedures must inevitably be put aside. It is certainly conceivable that the nation would recognize the value of democratic institutions and would decide to accept a less efficient economy rather than to sacrifice these institutions.

The game of thinking up the possible combination of factors that will be destructive of democracy is an endless one in which many can participate. Hayek has indicated that a democatic statesman will inevitably be confronted with the choice of surrendering his plan or assuming dictatorial powers. Such a situation is certainly conceivable. However, it is also conceivable that a democratic states-

[64] Henry C. Wallich, *The Cost of Freedom: Conservatives and Modern Capitalism* (New York: Collier Books, 1962), p. 57.

[65] See footnote 2, p. xvii.

[66] *Ibid.*, p. 48.

[67] See footnote 64, p. 57.

man working in a capitalistic country might decide that he must either suffer a defeat in his foreign policy or assume dictatorial powers. It is also conceivable that the differences of the distribution of wealth within a capitalistic country will lead those who find themselves left out of the country's abundance to revolt under a demagogue who will then establish himself as a dictator. The fact that all this, and more, may be conceivable does not mean that it must inevitably happen.

These bare possibilities become probabilities in a country that is weak in democratic institutions and traditions, and that does not place the free exchange of ideas in highest esteem. Granted a strong traditional commitment to democracy on the part of the people and granted a framework of political institutions, which gives these people an effective voice and influence in the wielding of political power, it is far from inevitable that such a people will be willing to sacrifice democracy to economic efficiency.

Hayek does not restrict himself to arguing that socialism will lead to totalitarianism at some future time. As we have seen, he also holds that a socialistic state is by *its very nature* incompatible with the demands of a rule of law which functions as an institutional safeguard for the freedom of individual citizens. He maintains that a socialistic government is committed to making decisions that *in principle* cannot be made in accordance with a rule of law because it can meet neither the demand that legal rules be of an abstract, general nature nor the demand that all be treated equally before the law. Because these two points are perhaps at the very heart of Hayek's view that socialism is necessarily totalitarian, it will be necessary to consider each in its turn. In defense of his first point, Hayek argues that a government which runs the economy of a nation must make particular decisions concerning concrete issues and thus cannot restrict itself to making the type of abstract general rules that is in keeping with a rule of law.

There can be no denying that a government which controls the means of production must make particular decisions concerning the standards that men must meet to be accepted for a particular job, how many men are to be hired, where plants are to be located, what shifts are to be established in a particular factory. Before drawing back in horror at such a state of affairs, it should be noted that in moving from the type of capitalism that is found in the United States today to government ownership of the means of production, we are not moving from a situation in which these decisions are made by no one to a situation in which they are made by certain men.

The market does not decide where General Motors plants are to be located, how many men are to be employed in a particular plant, or how many automobiles are to be produced. These decisions are made by those who have authority and power in the corporation. The corporation lawyer Adolf A. Berle, Jr. calls attention to a certain aspect of contemporary corporations that is relevant to the point now being considered. Berle's study of present-day corporations has led him to conclude that within certain limits there is "an enormous field in which managements act in their 'discretion'—which is merely a lawyer's way of saying that their power is uncontrolled."[68] Moreover, he points out that there is a need to give management wide discretionary powers in running a business.[69] If no decision could be taken by management unless it were previously reviewed from all sides by some court, or reviewing agency, management simply could not run the business.

Hayek also recognizes the need for discretion in the management of a business. He acknowledges that in so far as government is involved in administering its own resources, it cannot be bound by fixed general rules, but must be allowed as much discretion as any corporation would need in similar circumstances.[70] The fact that corporations in a capitalistic economy require and possess a good deal of autonomous power in the conduct of their affairs indicates that a socialistic economy need be no more totalitarian than is a capitalistic economy. It is true that a government, which uses its legal and coercive powers to enforce its discretionary economic decisions, will differ from a private corporation that does not have these legal powers to enforce its decisions. An acknowledgment of this point need not mean that a socialistic nation cannot meet the demand that laws be of an abstract and general nature. It simply means that a socialistic government must avoid trying to establish laws concerning those economic activities that are of such a nature that they cannot fit the demands of a rule of law.

It seems to me that one must admit that it is possible for a socialistic government to separate its legal coercive powers from its unavoidably discretionary economic activities. A government would thus be in the same position as private corporations in trying to work out a *modus vivendi* with the workers through their unions concerning such matters as general working conditions in a plant, hiring, firing, seniority, and vacation policies. It would be necessary to be explicit in stating that the government could not threaten imprisonment or any other legal penalties against union leaders or members for disagreeing with certain policies, just as it must be clear in a capitalistic economy that management cannot dismiss union leaders or threaten members with the loss of their jobs if they express their disagreement with management through proper and established channels. This is not to deny that it may be necessary for a socialistic government to assert its authority in dealing with labor disputes that may involve grave danger to the public interest. One could hardly maintain that governments functioning within a capitalistic economy have not found it necessary to do the same thing at times.

It is now necessary to evaluate the charge that neither a socialist state nor a welfare state, which does not use a means test, can fulfill the requirement of the equality of all before the law. Because Hayek rightly does not interpret this requirement to mean that the law can make absolutely no discriminations among

[68] Adolf A. Berle, Jr., *The 20th Century Capitalist Revolution* (New York: Harcourt, Brace and World, Inc., 1954), p. 65.

[69] *Ibid.*, p. 64.

[70] See footnote 4, p. 213.

people, it is necessary for him to provide a criterion on the basis of which one can distinguish between those discriminations that conform to the demand of equality and those that do not. There is a lack of clarity to the criteria he offers, which weakens his case and which also makes it difficult to respond to his position. It will be recalled that one of the tests that he offered was whether one could or could not foresee how the law might affect particular people. This criterion is understandable and reasonable if it is interpreted as meaning that a law ought not be passed to help any given individual. For example, a president ought not seek changes in the draft law simply to keep members of his family out of military service. However, if the criterion is interpreted in this way, I see no reason why one should hold that socialistic states or certain forms of welfare legislation cannot avoid this type of abuse.

Whether the legislators are acting in a socialistic or a capitalistic state, they will be making laws in a context and not in a vacuum. Working within the given context, they will certainly be aware of the types of people that they may be helping by a proposed law and the types of people who may find the law contrary to their interests. For example, laws granting certain special tax benefits to the legally blind were passed with the knowledge that these laws would be beneficial to blind persons. There was no knowledge concerning the names of all the individuals so helped or who, because of human accidents or natural misfortunes, might be helped by such a law in the future.

There would appear to be the same combination of ignorance and knowledge behind Medicare legislation. Although the legislators did not know the names of all those who would benefit now and in the future from this legislation, they did know that it would benefit people in a certain age group. Because Hayek explicitly includes legislation concerning the blind among those laws that he finds in keeping with the demand for the equality of all before the law, it is difficult to see why he thinks that laws within a socialistic state, or welfare legislation, could not meet this same demand.

The second criterion is no more helpful than the first in providing a reasonable ground for Hayek's criticism of socialism and of welfare legislation. It will be recalled that this criterion was that the proposed law be acceptable both to the majority of those who stand inside and outside that class. This criterion is clearly a very helpful tool in the hands of a legislator who is trying to decide whether or not a proposed law has broad popular acceptance, but it is not a criterion for judging the moral acceptability of a law. The fact that a piece of welfare legislation may fail to pass this test is no more reason for saying that such legislation is immoral in principle than is the fact that it may pass the test, a reason for holding that it is in principle moral. Because Hayek himself does not accept the notion that acceptance by a majority makes a law morally right, he cannot advance this criterion as a way to test the morality of welfare legislation or of socialism.

A twofold criterion based on the notions of equalitarian and welfare justice advanced in Chapter V can be established to help decide whether a proposed law in the area presently under discussion is in keeping with the demand for the equality of all before the law. If it can be shown that certain unregulated practices or institutional arrangements in a society deprive a segment of that society of the financial means necessary to meet pressing human needs, and if it can also be shown that a proposed piece of welfare legislation can provide these means without at the same time seriously undermining the chances of others in the society to meet these same needs, then that legislation is compatible with the equalitarian rule and with the demand for equal justice before the law. For it tries to do justice to the conditions for human well-being of both those who are in need and those whose taxes will provide the money to finance the program.

At this point, there would appear to be a major conflict between the demands of justice and of freedom in that the attempt to do justice to those in need involves the denial of the freedom of those who are taxed to pay for the program, because the latter are forced to contribute to the program. The dialectic between justice and freedom can never be resolved in a morally acceptable manner so long as freedom is defined simply as an individual's right to do whatever he pleases, because this right will inevitably come into direct conflict with the rules of justice, which regulate the relationships among men, and which limit what a man can do in the social dimensions of his existence.

Granted this definition of freedom, such laws as those which deny me the legal right to play my stereophonic record player so loudly that it disturbs my neighbor's sleep or which deny me the right to drive through a school zone at whatever speed I desire, are seen as being denials of my freedom. It is difficult to see how any law could be acceptable to one taking this conception of freedom because all law places some restriction on what man can do in the world in so far as his actions adversely affect the possibilities for physical and moral well-being of other human subjects existing in the world.

There may well be times when it will be very difficult to resolve a conflict between an individual's freedom and the demands of justice. However, the conflict presented in the preceding paragraph is exacerbated by an exaggerated notion of human freedom. If we see that the character of human freedom consists in the knowledge that one has of one's self and of one's situation, together with the psychological stability to be able to deal with a situation in a deliberative and reflective way and to pursue the good revealed by this deliberation, we may not be so quick to characterize every restriction on our physical ability to act in the world as a denial of human freedom.

No government or law can make a man a knower or can make him emotionally stable, but it can provide the conditions that either help or hinder his development in these areas. Once an individual realizes this point and also realizes that he is not the only center of freedom in the world and that what he does can affect for good or ill the possibilities for freedom of other persons, he will have a more adequate basis to judge the legal restrictions imposed on his physical ability to act in the world than the basis that simply equates human freedom with an individual's right to do whatever he pleases. For example, working out of the context of the notion of freedom accepted in this book, it is clear that it is not essential to the development of man as a free subject that he be allowed to travel at whatever rate of speed he desires, but that it is essential to the children's growth as free subjects that they be protected from being injured by an automobile.

It is now necessary to consider the relevance of these considerations to the question of whether or not there are valid moral grounds for opposing legislation that taxes one segment of a society to care for the needs of another segment. If we are agreed that an individual's right to do whatever he pleases must be limited by considerations of the effect of his actions on the subjectivity of others, it would seem that there could be no objection on moral grounds to a law which tries to regulate an institutional framework that may be functioning in such a way as to deprive a significant number of individuals living under that institution of the conditions that are essential to their growth as human subjects. Thus, if a market economy is seen to provide a context that is perfectly suited to the talents of many in the population—allowing them to accumulate more than what is essential to their development as human subjects—but in which there are a significant number of other persons who are deprived of such things as adequate medical care, economic security, and adequate housing facilities, we would have prima-facie evidence for the conclusion that some regulation of this context—such as a system of taxation on those reaping the benefits of living under this context—is morally demanded.

It should be emphasized that this conclusion does not depend on showing that those who are thriving under the institutional dynamics of a market economy are immoral, dishonest, or guilty of willfully and maliciously depriving others in the society of that which is essential to their human well-being. It is not the morality or immorality of those who benefit from the market economy that grounds the moral demand for legal regulation of the market or for a different type of economic arrangement, but the character of such an economy, which seems to deprive a significant segment of the population of the financial resources necessary to their physical and/or moral well-being in that society.

It is undeniably true that any regulation of the market economy will restrict the ability of those who have profited from the market economy to use their economic resources as they please. A moral evaluation of such a restriction must consider the context in which the activities are restricted and the influence of the restriction on the subjectivity of both the person who is restricted and the person who directly benefits from the restriction. Working out of the context of Aquinas' and Marx's insights summarized in the introduction to this section, I have argued that a limitation of man's right to manage all of his financial resources as he pleases does not necessarily deprive him of what is essential to his growth as a human subject, and I have tried to depict the type of situation in which such a limitation would be morally justified.

This emphasis on the notion of freedom as self-determination must be connected with the discussion earlier in this section concerning the possibility within a socialistic framework for what may be termed "political" freedom, which consists in an institutional order that allows citizens of a nation to participate effectively in the political processes of that nation. Both types of freedom must be preserved within a nation. To demand that a nation's institutions be established with a view to their possible contribution to the development of freedom as self-determination is simply to demand that these institutions be in keeping with the character of man as an end in himself. The demand for political freedom is grounded in the realization that a government that is not open to the influences of its citizens is likely to use its power to secure its own aims at the expense of the well-being of its citizens. It appears to be essential to the preservation of political freedom that the institutional arrangements of a nation allow for the public exchange of ideas and for peaceful and public changes of government. There must be an institutional framework that allows those who disagree with the government in power to bring their case before the people and that allows the people to affect peaceful changes in governmental policies and personnel.

Whereas Hayek has argued that a socialistic government will inevitably mean the end of such freedom because it will be able to use its economic power to so control its citizens that they will be faced with the alternative of doing exactly what the government demands or of suffering the loss of indispensable goods and/or services, I have maintained that this position is true only if there is no way in which citizens can exercise an influence on government by deciding who is to hold office and by having an effective voice in the making of laws limiting the powers of government officials. I do not think that Hayek has proved that this condition is necessarily implicated in a socialistic type of government. Moreover, as we have seen Wallich point out, there are historical situations that indicate political freedom is compatible with such governments.

Because this is an important point, it will be well to examine the type of considerations that the economist Milton Friedman thinks indicate that an institutional framework allowing for the public exchange of ideas is not compatible with a socialistic economy. We shall consider three examples that he uses to sustain this view. First, he points out that in a capitalistic society it is possible to find wealthy capitalists who will provide the financial backing necessary to give public exposure to minority views, but that the wealthy citizens of a socialistic economy are so much a part of the socialistic establishment that they will not be willing to support views that criticize this establishment. His second example concerns screen writers who had been blacklisted by the movie industry in Hollywood in the late 1940's because of alleged communist affiliations. Friedman holds that the vitality of capitalism is shown in this case by the fact that there were those in the industry who allowed the blacklisted men to continue to work under pseudonyms. One of the people who cooperated with these writers is quoted as saying that he had an obligation to his stockholders to buy the best scripts possible and that one of the blacklisted writers brought him an excellent script. Friedman interprets this situation as showing how the market works to preserve freedom by making it costly for people to comply with the blacklist. Finally, he questions whether a procapitalistic paper would be able to purchase whatever it needs in a socialistic economy as easily as communistic papers such as the *Daily Worker* have been able to purchase their supplies in a capitalistic country.[71]

I do not think that any of these arguments sustains the view that political freedom is impossible in a socialistic economy. Friedman offers no conclusive evidence to ground the premise which underlies his first example, namely, the view that men who have reaped enormous profits in a state that is congenial to capitalism will be willing to support anticapitalistic views, whereas men who have enjoyed financial success under a socialistic government will not be willing to support antisocialistic views. Precisely why successful capitalists should be more open-minded than successful socialists is a point which Friedman does not adequately explain. Just as we need not accept the communist view that in a capitalistic society all government officials are lackeys of industrial and banking interests so also we need not accept the view that in a socialistic economy all wealthy men are lackeys of the government in power. It seems to me that Friedman's distinction between the open-minded capitalist and the reactionary socialist presupposes that the socialist, unlike the capitalist, is living in a totalitarian system in which an individual's place of economic prominence is determined not by the character of his work, but by whether or not he agrees with the government in power. In short, his example presupposes the very point it purports to prove.

Moreover, it should be noted that the problem of the relationship between economic resources and the public dissemination of ideas is not one that is peculiar to a socialistic country. It seems to me that it is a problem that should be a matter of concern to those presently living in the United States. For example, the cost of financing political campaigns is becoming so expensive that we seem to be moving toward a situation in which only men of independent means can run for high public office, if we have not already reached such a situation. Friedman has clearly pointed to a significant problem in modern society, but in presenting it as if it were a problem only for a socialistic country, he has failed to get to the heart of the matter.

Much of his case is built on the premise that the amount of money necessary to publicize ideas is so great that one cannot realistically expect to raise this money from a number of people who are not independently wealthy. Accepting the fact that the public exposure of ideas is dependent on wealthy patrons, he has tried to show that one is not likely to find that ideas differing from those of the government in power will be given public exposure in a socialistic country. It seems to me that the public exchange of ideas is too important an ingredient in the political freedom of a nation to be left to the benevolence of a wealthy class whether that class be of the capitalistic or socialistic variety.

[71] Milton Friedman, *Capitalism and Freedom* (Chicago: The University of Chicago Press, 1962), pp. 16–20.

Seen from this perspective, the root problem is one that confronts both a capitalistic and a socialistic nation. I see no difference in principle between a society that is dependent on the benevolence of its wealthy capitalists for the communication of ideas and one that is dependent on the benevolence of its wealthy socialists. If Friedman is right in holding that such a large number of men of moderate financial means would be required to finance the publicizing of a political point of view that it would be unrealistic to expect political ideas to be publicized without help from men of great wealth, then citizens committed to a democratic form of government must search for ways to change this situation so that the public communication of ideas is not so totally dependent on the very wealthy class in a society.

Friedman was too quick in giving credit to the market as a stimulus to freedom in the case of the blacklisted writers. The case indicated that men who take the responsibilities of their work seriously will not reject a good piece of work for extraneous reasons. It is true that an individual was quoted in the example as saying that he accepted the script because of his responsibilities to his stockholders, but there is no reason to think that it would be impossible for a man in a socialistic economy to accept the script of a blacklisted writer because of his sense of responsibility to the public or to his art, unless one is going to take the position that a man can act out of a sense of responsibility only to his stockholders. The example showed that so long as there are men in a country who are willing to acknowledge the talents of men whose beliefs may not conform to those of the majority, there will always be an opportunity for such men to exercise their talents.

If one grants that a given socialistic state is totalitarian and is limited by no legal restrictions in the way it uses its economic resources, it is clear that a newspaper opposing the government in power would not be permitted to use government facilities. However, if the government is not totalitarian, if it is legally prohibited from making conformity to a certain ideology a condition for the use of government facilities, a newspaper with the proper financial backing could make use of these facilities despite its antigovernment stance. In short, the socialistic character of a state is not the decisive factor in this issue. What is decisive is the commitment of the people to the value of the public exchange of ideas and their willingness and ability to embody this commitment in an institutional framework.

c. HUMAN REASON AND MAN'S FUTURE

This subsection will deal with that aspect of Hayek's position that emphasizes the limited character of human reason in relation to the richness of man's historical existence. There are certain features of this position with which I can fully agree. Hayek is clearly right in holding that human reason is limited and in pointing out that the present status of human civilization is not the development of a single human plan, but has developed from the complex interaction of many forces that were beyond the power of individual human reason. Anyone reflecting on human history must acknowledge that the future has not always conformed to the ideal projections formed by the reason of individual human reformers. Hayek is also right in opposing a position that holds that an institution cannot work for the good of man unless it is a result of a conscious plan.

The question that will be considered in this subsection is whether Hayek's views on the limitations of human reason would invalidate the arguments that have been presented thus far in defense of a moral perspective on man's socio-economic life, which differs from one presented by Hayek. More specifically, it is necessary to ask whether the views on justice and freedom advanced in this section must be rejected on the grounds that the attempt to implement them will mean the end of human progress. In short, once the questions of justice and freedom are placed in an historical context, once we note that we have moral responsibilities to mankind in the future as well as to mankind in the present, we may see that we must surrender the conceptions of justice and freedom developed above because, as Hayek has pointed out, we can make our contribution to mankind in the future by submitting to the impersonal forces of the market.

A preliminary point that ought to be made in evaluating this aspect of Hayek's position is that man is in danger of becoming so enamored with his past and present achievements that he refuses to change his economic system even when he sees that it is stifling the lives of many men. One can picture a defender of feudalism arguing that feudalism has been successful in providing all the achievements of which man was aware during the feudal period and that therefore the system ought not be changed, although it may be presently harmful to the human good of many citizens, because by submitting to the forces of feudalism, man is contributing to the construction of a better tomorrow.

It is true that many, although certainly not all, of the advantages that we presently enjoy were developed by men in the context of a market economy, but we must not allow the acceptance of this truth to blind us to the possibility that what worked successfully for human advancement in the past may no longer contribute to such advancement under the new conditions of the present. It may well be that the market economy which gave birth to the economy of abundance may stifle the possibilities for further human advance inherent in such an economy. This book can only call attention to such a possibility. It would be necessary to move into the area of practical wisdom and to reflect on concrete economic issues and prospects to decide whether this possibility is actually realized in any given society.

The major point which I shall try to establish in this subsection is that an appeal to the unknown possibilities for a better future is not an adequate moral basis for rejecting a program that we know will contribute to the physical and/or moral well-being of human beings presently in our midst. Hayek's position that no one plan can encompass all the possibilities for human improvement inherent in man's existential situation is true, but it has no validity as a premise for the conclusion that man ought not interfere with the impersonal forces of the market. Man's moral responsibility reaches as far as does his knowledge of the possibilities inherent in the situation in which he finds himself and as far as his power to act on the basis of such knowledge. Thus, if it becomes clear that a significant segment of society is being deprived of certain goods or services essential to their well-being as persons and if a plan is developed to help them justly acquire these goods, an appeal to unspecified and unknown possibilities for a better future that may be stunted by putting the plan into effect does not constitute a sufficient reason for rejecting the plan.

This opposition to what appears to be a willingness to sacrifice man in the present for the unspecified glories of an unknown future does not commit one to the position that the future ought to be entirely ignored in considering whether or not we are morally justified in interfering with the forces of the market. Because we are beings who can look ahead to the future, our moral decisions must involve a consideration of the future *in so far as that future comes within the scope of our knowledge.* The italicized words are important in that if one can show that the implementation of a certain welfare plan will destroy a country's economy in a year or so, or will seriously endanger the well-being of a number of citizens in two or three years, one would have presented strong moral evidence against such a program. In short, if we are to oppose a program on the basis of an appeal to the future, we should deal with the program on the level of practical wisdom. If one can point to some specific feature or some omission in the legislation that would have results at some future date whose evil would outweigh the good to be achieved in the present, one would have an excellent case against such legislation.

Hayek's emphasis on unspecified possibilities for human advancement that may be stunted by any attempt to interfere with the forces of the market appears to make it unnecessary for anyone opposing such interference to point to specific bad results that would follow if a given plan were put into action. He seems to be trying to defend the market on the basis of man's ignorance of the future. It seems to me that Hayek would be more consistent in his emphasis on the limitation of human reason, if he acknowledged that neither he himself nor the man advocating a plan to change a given economic structure knows what the long-range results of this plan will be. It is true that the planner may not know what will become of society in the distant future if his plan is put into effect, but it is equally true that the man who opposes the plan on the grounds that submission to the market contributes to a society greater than any one of us can grasp through reason does not know what will become of society in the distant future if the plan is not put into effect. Such an acknowledgment of our common ignorance in the face of the long-range future would hopefully contribute to a lessening of the use of this future as a justification for not meeting our moral responsibilities to our fellow men in the present.

We must not allow the awareness of the fact that our actions provide a legacy for future generations to lead us to undertake the impossible task of trying to live the lives of these generations. If we can meet the demands of justice in our time without sacrificing political freedom, we ought not to be deterred by the observation that those coming after us will be willing to sacrifice their freedom. Having tried to make ourselves as clear as possible to those who will follow us concerning the value that we find in political freedom, and having tried to incorporate this value in the institutions that we will pass on to them, we must humbly accept the fact that what future generations will decide to do with this legacy is out of our hands. We must try to meet our own responsibilities in our own time and hope that such behavior may provide a firm foundation for unknown future generations as they face the problems and prospects of their existence.

Turning to the specific issue of this chapter, if we know that a significant segment of society is presently lacking certain resources essential to their physical and/or moral well-being, if we know that we can justly provide them with these resources, and if there is nothing in the proposed legislation in itself or in its relationship to other legislation already passed which will involve consequences in the foreseeable future whose evil outweighs the good to be achieved by the legislation, we have strong prima-facie evidence that we have a moral responsibility to support the legislation.

This position need not mean that man is being condemned to stagnation in the name of his moral responsibilities to his contemporaries. Because human beings are the prime source of novelty in the created world, an institutional arrangement, which provides men with the resources and conditions essential to the growth of human freedom understood both as political freedom and as self-determination, may claim to be working to release the most potent force of novelty in nature, namely man, from the bonds of economic insecurity, hopelessness, and despair. Because knowledge of the long-range future is no more available to me than it is to Hayek, I cannot guarantee that such institutional arrangements will lead to a more creative society in the future, but I certainly see no reason to hold that attempts to meet the moral responsibilities engendered by an affluent economy necessarily mean stagnation.

Hayek has tried to identify planning with stagnation by holding that man has only two choices in dealing with the economic order. Either he allows the forces of the market to work without any interference or he tries to control the economy in such a way that he will prohibit the asking of any questions and the performing of any experiments that do not appear to be significant to ruling opinion. Hayek has built into this second alternative the most extreme shortcomings and restrictions of an inflexible bureaucratic system in which those who administer the system exercise such complete control that points of view, which differ from theirs, have no possibility of being tested and of being able to show their worth. I have already acknowledged that socialism appears to be prone to the problems of bureaucracy. To acknowledge this point is not to say that planning is by its very nature antithetical to creative activity.

Planning that allows those who have the talent and inclination in a certain area of human endeavor to pursue their tasks in an atmosphere of open inquiry appears to be conducive to human creativity. Thus, it seems to me that we should add this type of planning as a third alternative to Hayek's two. Adding this third alternative does not guarantee that any given planned economy will be free from the excesses of bureaucracy, but it should help us to avoid identifying planning with the possible abuses of planning. It challenges the defender of a planned economy to show that his particular plan provides a context for the exercise of human creativity.

It should be noted that a market economy has also been criticized for stifling human creativity. For example, the philosopher Richard Lichtman who favors a planned economy points to two practices of the drug industry in the United States to substantiate his charge that a market economy frustrates the forces of human progress. He points out that researchers for drug companies devote a good part of their time to trying to produce medications that are not better than those of their competitors from the point of view of their effectiveness in fighting illness and disease, but that are sufficiently different from them to avoid patent problems.[72] Research time that could be spent in producing medications for illnesses or diseases for which we presently have no effective medication is thus devoted to altering, but not improving, existing medication so that a company can place this medication on the market under its own brand name.

Lichtman's second point also uses the drug company as an example of how a market economy can hinder human progress:

> Its corporatized researchers are prevented from carrying out significant discussion with each other, so that we are continually faced with the fact that the information possessed by a given scientist, which might, if generally shared, unlock the thwarted efforts of others, must remain his exclusive and infertile possession. There is no way of knowing how much progress in the development of drugs has been curtailed by this procedure.[73]

It might be argued in defense of a market economy that there is enough selfishness among men that they will hoard their knowledge for their own benefit and in disregard of the public good in any type of society. This point may be true, but it cannot be used validly in defense of a system which provides an institutional justification for such selfishness.

Lichtman's second point leads one to ask whether the contributions to the advancement of human good made by corporations working in a market economy resulted from the fact that there is a good deal of organization, planning, and cooperation within the individual corporations themselves. If the answer to this question is affirmative, as I believe it must be, it would not be the unplanned

---

[72] Richard Lichtman, *Toward Community: A Criticism of Contemporary Capitalism* (The Fund for the Republic, 1966), pp. 34–35.

[73] *Ibid.*, p. 43.

character of a market economy that contributes to human creativity, but the fact that there are many corporations working within this economy that are organized and planned in a way that allows men of differing talents to pool their resources in the pursuit of a common goal. The advocate of a planned economy must show that the efficiency found in many corporations will not be hampered by bureaucratic red tape if these corporations are united in a single nationwide organization. Because this raises a question that can be resolved only by reflecting on a particular organizational structure, it is a matter for pracitical wisdom and falls outside the scope of this book.

Because I have been primarily concerned with the validity of Hayek's moral perspective on the question of the merits of capitalism and socialism, I have not questioned the accuracy of Hayek's description of a market economy as one that is determined by the impersonal forces of the market, when this description is compared to the current economic situation in a country such as the United States. Although a complete treatment of this issue is clearly beyond the scope of this book, I think it is necessary to note that there is some question as to whether capitalism in an advanced industrial nation such as the United States is controlled by the impersonal forces of the market.

For example, in his book *The New Industrial State*, John Kenneth Galbraith sets out to show the accuracy of the following description of the contemporary American economic situation:

> We have an economic system which, whatever its formal ideological billing, is in substantial part a planned economy. The initiative in deciding what is to be produced comes not from the sovereign consumer who, through the market, issues the instructions that bend the productive mechanism to his ultimate will. Rather it comes from the great producing organization which reaches forward to control the markets that it is presumed to serve and, beyond, to bend the customer to its needs.[74]

Moreover, it is Galbraith's contention that this situation is not the result of any ideological victory on the part of socialism, but is rather demanded by the complex character of modern technology.[75] If private corporations are to make use of this technology, they cannot put themselves at the mercy of the impersonal forces of the market. They have been able to use this technology precisely because they have been able to exercise control over these impersonal forces.

It is beyond the scope of this book to consider the validity and accuracy of Galbraith's position. I can only call attention to the following point. *If* Galbraith is right, our alternatives are somewhat different from those that underlie Hayek's defense of capitalism. If we choose the type of capitalism described by Hayek, namely, one which is truly determined by the impersonal forces of the market,

[74] John Kenneth Galbraith, *The New Industrial State* (Boston: Houghton Mifflin Co., 1967), p. 6, also pp. 211–212. See also footnote 55, *Free Men and Free Markets*, pp. 19, 27.

[75] *The New Industrial State*, pp. 11–21.

we must surrender all that modern technology has to offer us because this technology cannot be employed with any degree of efficiency in market economy of this type. If we choose the type of capitalism that is currently being practiced in the United States, then we ought to recognize that what we are defending is not a system in which individuals are free from the control of other men, but one which upholds the corporation's right to manage the individual.[76] Finally, it should also be noted that if Galbraith's assessment of the modern industrial state is correct, the defenders of socialism will also be confronted with difficulties. For Galbraith contends that the complexity of modern technology is such that it cannot be controlled by government officials if it is to function efficiently.[77]

In concluding this chapter, it might be well for me to try to state what I consider to be the major point of difference between Hayek's position and the position taken in this section. Perhaps the ultimate point of difference between the two positions is that Hayek's position is based on a faith in the impersonal forces of the market for which I see no philosophical justification. Describing himself as a liberal and those who disagree with him as conservatives, Hayek states that the conservatives face the future lacking the "faith in the spontaneous forces of adjustment which makes the liberal accept changes without apprehension, even though he does not know how the necessary adaptations will be brought about."[78] He describes the liberal attitude as one that assumes that the self-regulating market forces will somehow succeed in producing whatever adjustments to new conditions may be required, although there is no way of foretelling how these forces will achieve such adjustments in any given case.[79] The issue here is not as Hayek implies whether one accepts changes with or without apprehension. The issue is rather whether one ought to ignore what his knowledge, which is admittedly limited, tells him about these changes and about the forces, personal or impersonal, influencing these changes.

One need not hold that human reason is all-powerful to take the position that a plan, which interferes with the functioning of the market, ought to be put into effect, when a reasoned assessment of a situation tells us that men are being deprived of essential goods and/or services and when this assessment reveals how the deprivation can be alleviated by the implementation of a plan, but fails to discover how this is to be accomplished through the forces of the market. In making such an assessment, one must guard against an overly hasty decision by allowing a proper amount of time for the development and maturation of the thinking process which should underlie it and must also guard against a one-sided decision by allowing for the expression of many different viewpoints in this process.

Admittedly after all precautions have been taken, we may come to see that reason's analysis of a particular situation was mistaken, but it should be recalled

[76] *Ibid.*, p. 217.
[77] *Ibid.*, pp. 98–108.
[78] See footnote 4, p. 400.
[79] *Ibid.*

that the defense in Chapter IV of the central role of reason in man's moral life was not grounded in the claim that it is infallible. Although Hayek has explicitly stated that he does not advocate "irrationalism" or "an abdication of reason,"[80] his act of faith in the workings of the impersonal forces of the market clearly seems to call for an abdication of reason in dealing with the problems engendered by a market economy. The thrust of my argument has been that there is nothing intrinsically moral about a market economy and that, especially in a time of affluence, we may be morally obliged to interfere with the market forces because they may be hindering the development of human freedom understood as self-determination or because they may be functioning in such a way that there is an unjust distribution of essential goods and/or services in a society.

Although I have tried to show in opposition to Hayek that socialism may be a morally viable alternative for man, I have not tried to prove that we are morally obliged to work for the establishment of a socialistic economy. I have tried to establish the validity of a certain general moral perspective on man's economic situation. The response to the question of the precise institutional arrangements that will conform to this moral perspective must be left to the man of practical wisdom.

[80] *Ibid.*, p. 69.

CHAPTER VIII

Morality and the Political Order

The purpose of this chapter is to investigate the moral dimensions of certain significant features of man's political life. It will proceed from a consideration of the relationship between the political and moral dimensions of human existence, to an investigation of the moral issues surrounding the practice of capital punishment, and conclude with an examination of certain significant moral issues relating to the conduct of war.

1. MORALITY AS AN ESSENTIAL FACTOR IN THE CONDUCT OF POLITICAL LIFE

A great deal of difficulty can be avoided in discussing the issue of the relationship between politics and morality by specifying what one means by the terms "politics" and "morality." Because we have already dealt with the meaning of the term "morality" in Chapters II and VI of this book, we shall begin this discussion with a consideration of what is meant by the term "politics." This term will be used in the following discussion to refer to the art of politics and not to the study of politics, or what is referred to in our day as "political science." Hence, we shall not deal with the methodological question of whether the political scientist does or ought to make moral judgments in his study of political phenomena. Although I am willing to acknowledge that the political scientist may restrict himself in his formal studies to such activities as explaining the dynamics of Soviet political life or to accumulating statistical data on the voting patterns of certain racial or ethnic groups without undertaking any moral evaluation of these phenomena, I shall try to make a case for the position that moral issues are inextricably bound up with the actual conduct of political life and that a man is not released from his moral responsibilities when he is actively engaged in resolving issues in the political order.

In the last chapter we spoke of man's dependence on the nonhuman things in nature for his continued existence and development. As a social being, man is also dependent on his fellow man. He finds himself in a world with other men who have interests, aims, and abilities that differ from his own. If he is to fulfill his aims, which may include the good of others as well as his own good, he will often find that he must discover some way to organize and control these interests, aims, and abilities so that they contribute to the realization of his aims. For example, the task of insuring that the wealth of this nation be put to more effective use in providing adequate medical care for the poor cannot be completed by any individual working in isolation from society. The art of politics involves the use of those techniques that are effective in helping a man so influence others that they will be useful to the achievement of his purpose.

This description represents a broad use of one of the forms of the word "politics." A more restricted use of the term refers to the influence over others that an individual is able to exercise in more formally structured social arrangements, such as religious, acedemic, and business organizations. Finally, the word "politics" and its derivatives are used to designate that area of human life that centers on the problem of the influence that individuals or groups are able to exercise on the governing of a nation, state, city, town, or village.

The man who is able to influence others so that they will be helpful to the realization of his aims is said to exercise power over these others. Intelligence, wit, beauty, friends, money are only some of the factors that may give an individual or group political power over others.

It is clear that power and politics are inescapable facts of life in so far as they are part and parcel of man's social existence. If one were to say that the mere fact that one man exercises power over another is contrary to the character of a person as an end in himself, it would seem that he would be logically forced to conclude that the only way in which men could live in conformity with their beings as ends in themselves is by completely closing themselves off from one another. However, there are many examples that can be taken from our daily lives to show that we use our economic power to purchase the services of other men and that such use need not be immoral. When I go to the barber shop with the price of a haircut in my pocket, I am counting on the barber's interest in money and his willingness to cut my hair for that money. I acknowledge him as a being capable of setting goals for himself and I try to find some way of meeting these goals so that he will choose to work in a way that will be helpful to me. One could work with a more complicated example, but it seems to me that this one serves the purpose of pointing to a type of power relation that need not be immoral. There need be no immorality involved in my using my money, my intelligence, or my social position in a way that will fulfill another's goals and at the same time prove useful to my purposes.

Even in those cases in which parties hold conflicting goals, the use of power to influence one or both of the parties to redirect their goals need not necessarily be immoral. The mere fact that one person is able to influence another in such a way that the latter is required to change his goals or is unable to achieve a particular aim does not mean that he is reduced to a mere means, unless one wants to hold that the person's character as an end in himself means that he must always achieve what he set out to achieve, which would be a confusion of being a person with being unlimited.

At this point, it becomes necessary to try to sketch a distinction between power and violence or force. Power is most obviously distinct from physical violence, which consists in one man asserting direct control over the body of another, with such control being exemplified by such acts as choking, stabbing, or twisting another's arm. Power leaves the control of one's own body to one's own consciousness. It works with another person as a being capable of setting his own goals and is not directed to denying or destroying this capacity.

Power should also be distinguished from a more covert type of violence that exerts a type of pressure on others, which renders them unable to use the rational capacities that make them free beings. This means that power, as understood in this discussion, does not try to destroy the emotional stability necessary to human freedom, nor does it try to place others in a situation in which reflection or thought, which is essential to freedom, is extremely difficult, if not impossible. In short, in conflict situations, I am using what may be morally accepted power, not violence, if I frustrate the goal of my opponent or render his opposition ineffective with regard to the point of contention, but without reducing him to such dire straits that his continued existence as a person is endangered. I am using power when I frustrate the achievement of another's goal, without, however, destroying or hindering those capacities that constitute him as a being capable of setting his own goals. The question of whether resort to military force is ever morally justified as a way to resolve differences among nations will be discussed later in this chapter, and should not be confused with the present question concerning the relationship between political power and morality.

Having tried to clarify what is meant by "politics," it is now necessary to consider whether there is an opposition between the ethical and the political dimensions of human existence. It is clear that there is a difference between a political question and a moral question in so far as political questions are concerned with discovering ways and means of influencing others so as to realize one's aims in society. Just as a man does not become a technically competent physician by being morally good, so also he may not become a technically competent politician by being morally good. The man who wants to become a proficient physician must study the functioning of the human body, the diseases which may befall man, and the factors which can be employed to combat these diseases. Talk about the nature of justice and of human freedom does not tell him how to perform open heart surgery. Similar points can be made with respect to the moral and political dimensions of human existence. A politician must be acquainted with the various sources of power available in a society and must know which sources can be used most effectively in a concrete situation to bring into existence or to avoid certain consequences. He does not learn such political facts of life by considering the nature of justice.

It would be a mistake to conclude from this difference that either medical or political issues as they actually confront an individual in a concrete situation are devoid of moral significance. Granted that a physician is an expert in heart transplant operations, he does not have the moral right to kill a man so that he can use his heart to save the life of a loved one. Thus, the fact that we can separate moral and medical issues in our conversations and studies ought not lead us to the mistaken conclusion that the exercise of one's medical proficiency in a concrete existential situation has no moral dimensions to it. In so far as one's actions significantly influence the possibilities for physical and/or moral well-being of others, or in so far as actions are seen to be in accord with, or contrary to, the character of one's self or others as human subjects, there is a moral dimension to such actions. This point holds true whether the human actions occur in a medical or political context.

A consideration of what the sociologist Daniel Bell terms "a basic dilemma of ethics and politics," in trying to account for the failure of the socialistic movement in the United States will shed further light on the question of the relationship between politics and ethics.[1] The movement apparently exemplified this dilemma in that the way in which it stated its goals and its rejection of capitalism made it impossible for the movement to relate itself to the concrete situation in which it found itself or to participate in the give-and-take of political action. It found itself in the world, but not of the world, and consequently could not effectively deal with this world.[2]

Bell takes another tack in dealing with the question of the relationship between ethics and politics by describing politics as the concrete way of distributing rewards and punishments in a society, which involves a struggle for power between organized groups for control over the system of distribution. Ethics is described as being concerned with what ought to be the system of distribution in terms of some theory of justice. Working out of this conception of ethics and politics, he asks whether politics is concerned with giving reality to ethical ideals, or with securing certain advantages, with ethics in this case being accepted as providing the limits within which the struggle for advantages is to be pursued.[3]

Bell seems to think that a position that sees ethics as providing the aims of political action is congenial to a closed, absolutistic society. The conception of ethics as the limit within which politics is played is more in keeping with a pluralistic society because it does not transform the political arena into a battleground on which issues become a matter of life and death. To base politics

[1] Daniel Bell, *The End of Ideology: On the Exhaustion of Political Ideas in the Fifties,* New Revised Edition (New York: Collier Books, 1962), p. 278.

[2] *Ibid.,* pp. 278–279.

[3] *Ibid.,* p. 279.

on a dedication to absolute ends is to surrender the notion of politics as an attempt to reconcile various positions in favor of the notion of politics as an attempt to create "true believers" who find themselves unable to accept any compromise.[4] Those who accept this latter view have surrendered the tension between politics and ethics and expect to change the world in a flash. They are exemplified by the Bolsheviks who, identifying themselves with what they conceive to be the laws of history, reject all notions of compromise.[5]

Bell's observations on the relationship between ethics and politics provide us with an opportunity to be more specific in describing what ought to be the relationship between these two dimensions of human existence. The conceptions of an ethics of ends and of the moral man as being in, but not of, the world seems to be grounded in a position that excludes practical wisdom from the realm of ethics. If "ethics" is understood simply as moral philosophy, it is clear that ethics alone cannot resolve the complex, concrete issues that daily confront man in a political situation. Such an outcome is in keeping with the position developed in this book.

The treatment of practical wisdom in Chapter V was undertaken with the acknowledgment that the abstract, general principles developed in moral philosophy are not sufficient in and of themselves for meeting the concrete challenges of human existence. It was pointed out that if man is to meet these challenges in a moral way, it is necessary that he develop the virtue of practical wisdom, which enables him to reach the proper moral decision concerning what he ought to do in a particular situation. The basic dilemma of ethics and politics discussed by Bell is one aspect of the problem of the relationship between abstract, general moral principles, and the demands of practical wisdom. If one accepts the solution offered to this problem in Chapter V, it is clear that the dilemma need not be interpreted to mean that one ought to leave his morals at the gates when he enters the political arena.

Moreover, the description of an ethics of ends as being congenial to an absolutistic society is true only if this ethics is separated from the ethics of limits. Such a separation is to be rejected for the same reasons that were advanced against a utilitarian position in Chapter IV. We must not allow the goodness of our ends to blind us to the fact that our means may not be in keeping with the subjectivity of others who may be affected by our actions. Because the ethics of ends and of limits need not be mutually exclusive, it is possible to unite them in such a way that the ethics of ends will lose its absolutistic character. For a morally acceptable ethics of limits is grounded in the awareness that no matter how good one's aims may be, the fact remains that when one enters the political sphere, he is dealing not with puppets whom he has the right to manipulate as he wills, but with other human beings who have moral rights that may place a moral limit on what one can do to achieve one's aims.

[4] Ibid.
[5] Ibid., p. 297.

If one were to try to deal with political issues exclusively in terms of an ethics of limits, it is difficult to know what standard one would use to evaluate possible conflicting ends. It is true that political considerations must play a role in deciding issues concerning possible ends, if the notion of "political considerations" is understood to mean that a man must decide whether or not he has the power to achieve one or other of the ends in question. However, if we exclude an ethics of ends from the political enterprise, we seem to be saying that moral considerations are to play no role in deciding between two ends that are within the realm of political possibility. It is clear that in so far as these aims influence the physical and/or moral well-being of human beings, they are matters that must be submitted to a moral evaluation. The politician who is making decisions relating to the physical and/or moral well-being of men cannot avoid making value judgments. As a matter of fact, he may make judgments that are opposed to what he himself considers to be moral values, but this only means that he is asserting that certain other values are to be given priority in a political situation over what he himself considers to be moral values.

It must be acknowledged that Bell has put his finger on possible sources of difficulty in the relationship between the political and moral dimensions of human existence. The difficulty with his position is that it is not sufficiently clear in distinguishing between the moral demands of human existence and possible misunderstandings of these demands. If we are to avoid contributing to the mistaken notion that there is a total separation between the political and moral dimensions of human life, we ought to accept Bell's criticism as applying to a "moralistic" approach to politics, with this term being used to describe a situation in which failures to recognize the full complexities of man's moral existence have made the effective integration of the moral and political dimensions of human life extremely difficult, if not impossible. Bell's descriptions of an ethics of ends and of moral man as being in, but not of, the world provide excellent examples of a moralistic approach to politics.

2. UTILITARIAN AND RETRIBUTIVIST APPROACHES TO CAPITAL PUNISHMENT

a. THE CASE FOR CAPITAL PUNISHMENT

Capital punishment has been defended on both utilitarian and retributivist grounds. The utilitarian defense holds that capital punishment is justified because it serves to deter those other than the executed person from committing capital offenses. The retributivist defense argues that capital punishment is a demand of justice. The American philosopher Sidney Hook's views on capital punishment exemplify the importance that has been attached to the question of deterrence in the debate on capital punishment. He believes that if one could provide conclusive evidence to show that capital punishment does deter crime, the practice would be morally justified.[6] The Director of the Federal Bureau of Investigation, J. Edgar Hoover, who favors retention of the death penalty, acknowledges that statistical evidence concerning the effect of abolishing the death penalty is inconclusive, but he also points out that it is impossible for anyone to say with any degree of authority that capital punishment is not a deterrent.[7] We simply do not know how many crimes have not been committed out of fear of the death penalty.[8]

An attempt has been made to bypass the problem of statistical evidence in defending the death penalty. Common sense alone provides convincing evidence that man's behavior is most fully influenced by that which he loves most and which he fears most to lose. It is clear that a man's life must be included among these influential factors and that the possibility of the loss of his own life would certainly exercise a strong restraining influence on a person contemplating murder. Those who argue that capital punishment does not deter crime might ask themselves why every criminal sentenced to death seeks to have the sentence changed to life imprisonment.[9]

Immanuel Kant has given what is perhaps the classic defense of capital punishment on retributivist grounds. He holds that the determination of the kind and degree of punishment to be inflicted on a condemned criminal must be grounded in the "principle of equality," which demands that one side not be treated more favorably than the other. According to Kant, there is no substitute for the death penalty in murder cases that would satisfy this principle because there is no similarity in kind between death and life, even if one is living under the most wretched conditions. Hence, there is no equality between the crime and the punishment if the criminal is not condemned by a court of law and put to death.[10]

The depth and extent of Kant's commitment to the demands of retributive justice is seen in the following example that he uses to illustrate his point. If the members of a state were to agree that they ought to dissolve their union and disperse to different areas of the earth, they would be obliged to execute the last murderer remaining in prison before carrying out the agreement. In meeting this obligation, the citizens will be fulfilling the obligation to give to each what his actions are worth and will also avoid incurring the guilt of the murderer on themselves. For their failure to carry out the punishment would make them

[6] Sidney Hook, "The Death Sentence," *The Death Penalty in America: An Anthology*, edited by Hugo Adam Bedau (Garden City, New York: Doubleday and Co., Inc., 1964), p. 147.

[7] J. Edgar Hoover, "Statements in Favor of the Death Penalty," *The Death Penalty in America*, pp. 132, 134.

[8] *Ibid.*, p. 131.

[9] Edward J. Allen, "Capital Punishment: Your Protection and Mine," *The Death Penalty in America*, pp. 135–136.

[10] Immanuel Kant, *The Metaphysical Elements of Justice*, trans. by John Ladd (New York: The Library of Liberal Arts, 1965), p. 101.

accomplices to the criminal's violation of legal justice.[11] Contemporary defenders of capital punishment try to strengthen their case on retributivist grounds by accusing abolitionists of not having a sufficiently vivid grasp of the pain and horrors to which criminals have subjected their victims.[12]

b. A RETRIBUTIVIST REJECTION OF CAPITAL PUNISHMENT

Before dealing directly with the issue of capital punishment, it might be well to distinguish two questions, the confusion of which might lead us astray in dealing with the issue of capital punishment. What is the moral justification for the establishment of a legal order? What is the moral justification for making punishment a factor in this order? The discussion of the place of law in human life in Chapter II has given a utilitarian response to the first question. The moral justification for the establishment of law is to be found in the fact that a legal order provides the framework within which human beings can work to achieve their moral and/or physical well-being. There is no intrinsic moral goodness to a legal order. Its moral value lies in the contribution that it is able to make to the realization of such values as freedom and justice.

Legal punishment may be morally justified on the grounds that it is a practice that has proved useful to making the legal order more effective in the life of man. Part of the task of law is to make known to those who are living under it the limits within which they may act without harming the well-being of others. Because man is at times motivated to act in his own self-interest and to the detriment of others, a system of punishment is included in the legal order to appeal to this self-interest.[13]

Granted that punishment is an effective instrument for law and order, does this effectiveness alone give the state the moral right to punish any man or is there some consideration other than the usefulness of punishment that limits this moral right? A strictly utilitarian defense of legal punishment would hold that so long as punishment makes a contribution to the good of the community or to the greatest good of the greatest number in this community, it is morally justified. The difficulty with this defense is that it appears to justify the punishment of an innocent man if such punishment could be shown to be productive of socially beneficial consequences. For example, if the emotions of a community have been aroused by a brutal crime known to have been committed by a member of one race against a member of another race, and if it becomes apparent that a race riot will occur unless the police capture the criminal, it would appear that the police would have strong utilitarian reasons for fabricating a case against an innocent person who happens to belong to the same race as that of the criminal.

[11] *Ibid.*, p. 102.

[12] See footnote 7, pp. 130, 133.

[13] Edmund L. Pincoffs, *The Rationale of Legal Punishment* (New York: Humanities Press, 1966), pp. 119–120.

MORALITY AND THE POLITICAL ORDER

J. J. C. Smart has acknowledged that there may be situations in which his act utilitarianism would sanction the punishment of an innocent man as the lesser of two evils.[14] The example that we are presently considering would appear to be such a situation in that one working out of Smart's quantitative approach to moral issues would tend to see the moral injustice done to a single innocent man as being a lesser evil than the injuries and possible loss of lives that might result from a race riot. The position taken in this book has emphasized that in so far as man is a being capable of freedom, capable of controlling his own life, there are moral limits to what can be done to him by others in the name of some more inclusive good. The fact that the police are interested in avoiding a race riot does not give them a moral right to treat any individual as if he were nothing but an object that is useful to fulfilling their interest.

It has been pointed out that utilitarians could offer two reasons based on utilitarian considerations against punishing the innocent. First, the practice of punishing the innocent ought not be allowed because it would allow for no limitations of those in power, thus setting the stage for their use of this power for their personal ends rather than for the good of the community. Secondly, punishment of the innocent would undermine the deterrent effect of punishment, because a man could be punished whether he committed a crime or not. Hence, he might think that because he is liable to punishment whether he breaks or obeys the law, he might as well take his chances by at least enjoying whatever goods or pleasures he might receive by breaking certain laws.[15]

This type of utilitarian approach to punishment fits into what was described as rule utilitarianism in Chapter IV. The criticism of this brand of utilitarianism made in that chapter also applies to the particular problem now under discussion. Rule utilitarianism may be able to oppose the general practice of punishing the innocent, but it seems to have no reasonable basis to oppose an individual act of such punishment, which one has reason to believe will never become a matter of general practice.

It is now necessary to move from the negative task of trying to show that the morality of legal punishment cannot be validly grounded in the purely utilitarian considerations of the social benefits to be derived from the practice to the positive and more difficult task of trying to establish a moral basis for the state's right to punish a man who has been proved guilty of a crime. It seems to me that the resolution of this issue lies in the retributivist view that legal punishment is morally justified because, far from denying the criminal's character as a free being, it asserts that he is a being capable of taking responsibility for what he has done. The criminal, who is punished, is treated as a being capable of bearing the burden for the evil he has performed. Legal punishment is thus seen not as a wholly arbitrary imposition of evil on the guilty man, but as the public

[14] J. J. C. Smart, "The Methods of Ethics and the Methods of Science," *The Journal of Philosophy*, Vol. LXII (1965), pp. 347–348.
[15] See footnote 13, pp. 38–39. See also D. F. Thompson, "Retribution and the Distribution of Punishment," *Philosophical Quarterly*, Vol. 16 (1966), pp. 59–63.

manifestation and expression of the burden that he bears as the source of evil in the life of another person or persons.

Seen from another perspective, legal punishment does not deny that the criminal is a free being existing in a community of free beings. It is the criminal who has acted as though he were outside of the human community in so far as his actions involved a denial that the rights of others placed limits on what he could do. Legal punishment is a way of asserting that the criminal does not enjoy sovereignty over his fellow man and that he cannot pass beyond the moral limits placed on his actions by the rights of others without himself suffering evil repercussions for his actions. Thus, the guilty man who is legally punished is treated as a member of the human community, sharing with other men the rights and limitations of this membership.

This view of the moral ground for legal punishment puts me in the retributivist camp. It is possible to accept this view and, without becoming involved in any contradiction, to disagree with Kantian retributivism on two important points. First, if it could be shown that legal punishment in no way contributed to the law's function of establishing a framework within which individuals could work to achieve their moral and physical well-being, the state would not be under obligation to exercise the moral right to punish. This position is grounded in the notion that the state has a more humble task than that of being the embodiment or expression of the moral law among men. It is based on a view which sees the state as being limited and guided by moral considerations in fulfilling its task of providing an institutional order that will allow its citizens to pursue their moral and/or physical well-being in peace and security.

Without going into a full-scale defense of this conception of the state, it seems to me that to charge the state with the task of being the embodiment of the moral law among men is to engender a situation in which the powers of the state will be used to try to enforce morality in both the public and private spheres of human life. When a state takes on such a role, the citizens of that state are in danger of losing their character as moral agents and of becoming puppets carrying out the moral beliefs of those who control government power.

Granted this view of the state's limited task, there are at least two questions that ought to be considered in trying to decide whether a certain legal practice ought to be instituted. First, does the practice contribute significantly to the maintenance of an order in which citizens can live in peace and security? If it does not, it ought not be put into law. If it does, there is the second question to be considered. Will this practice be contrary to the character of man as an end in himself, will it be destructive of man's capacity for freedom? If it is, the practice ought not be introduced into law, even if it passed the test of the first question.

A second point of disagreement between myself and Kant concerns his contention that the "principle of equality" demands that a man, who has been legally convicted of murder, must be executed. If this principle is interpreted as demanding similarity for similarity's sake, it would appear that the state should try to determine precisely how a murderer killed his victim and should proceed to execute the murderer in exactly the same manner. If the criminal killed his victim after subjecting him to torture over a period of hours, representatives of the state would be required to repeat the same process in executing the criminal.

Kant himself has provided a view that indicates that the principle of equality ought not be interpreted in this manner. We saw in the discussion of egoism and altruism in Chapter IV that he holds that man's duty of respect to his fellow man rules out such punishments as having a man quartered or torn by dogs.[16] He has also stated that the execution of a convicted criminal must not involve any maltreatment that would constitute a degradation of his character as a human subject.[17] Finally, Kant directly confronts the problem of principle, which I have raised, by noting that there are certain crimes such as rape and pederasty to which the principle of equality cannot be applied "because they would themselves be punishable crimes against humanity in general."[18] My disagreement with Kant's defense of capital punishment is that he has used the principle of equality without paying sufficient attention to man's duty of respect to his fellow man.

Kant's notion of man's duty of respect to his fellow man was meant to emphasize that one cannot deny the respect that belongs to a man in his character as a man, even if this man is immoral. Capital punishment, which is the direct and deliberate killing of a presently defenseless man who is neither harming nor endangering the life of another human being, seems to be totally incompatible with man's duty of respect to his fellow man. Hence, it should be included among those acts that by their very nature constitute a degradation at least of the humanity of the person who is made the object of this act, and perhaps also of those who must administer the punishment. The description in the previous sentence of the criminal marked for execution was not an attempt to work on the reader's emotions. It was a factual description of the murderer's situation as he is prepared for execution.

To assert that the state has a moral right to put a man to death in such a situation is to deny that the criminal is an end in himself. If the state's moral control over a man is such that it can decide the time, place, and way he is to be put to death, that man can no longer be said to exist as an end in himself. His existence is totally in the hands of the state. If a man's very right to life places no limit or exercises no claim on the state, then that man is said to exist simply as an object, which the state can dispose of at its convenience. The argument, which states that a man who has murdered another man has lost the right to life, is saying, in effect, that the murderer has ceased to be a man. For the moral right to life is certainly an essential and indispensable dimension of being a man. However, the fact is that a murderer has not lost the rational capacities

---

[16] See footnote 34, Chap. III, p. 133.
[17] See footnote 10, p. 102.
[18] *Ibid.*, p. 133. Kant holds that the punishment for these crimes should be castration.

that make him a being capable of self-possession and that constitute his character as an end in himself.

This argument against capital punishment has tried to show that the practice of capital punishment is incompatible with the duty of respect man owes to all men, even to those who have been found guilty of committing serious crimes. This position might lead one to inquire whether imprisonment is compatible with this duty. This is certainly a legitimate subject for discussion. Unfortunately, we cannot do full justice to it within the limitations of this book. We can, at best, provide a general framework for a more thorough discussion of this issue. Without denying that the restriction of one's freedom over a period of years is an evil, it is clear that it need not be as great an evil as the deliberate killing of a man. It may well be that conditions in many prisons in the United States today tend to degrade and brutalize the inmates. If such is the case, those in charge of our penal institutions must accept the responsibility of changing these conditions so that inmates do not suffer the brutalization of their persons, in addition to the evil of the loss of their freedom of movement.

The philsopher J. D. Mabbott has made some helpful observations concerning this issue:

> When a man is sentenced to imprisonment he is not sentenced also to partial starvation, to physical brutality, to pneumonia from damp cells and so on. And any movement which makes his food sufficient to sustain health, which counters the permanent tendency to brutality on the part of his warders, which gives him a dry or even a light and well-aired cell, is pure gain and does not touch the theory of punishment. . . . If it is said that every such reform lessens a man's punishment, I think that is simply muddled thinking which, if it were clear, would be mere brutality. For instance, a prisoners' aid society is said to lighten his punishment, because otherwise he would suffer not merely imprisonment but also unemployment on release. But he was sentenced to imprisonment, not imprisonment *plus* unemployment.[19]

This statement calls attention to the need to distinguish legal punishment from state-sanctioned brutality. In addition to the suggestions made by Mabbott to give reality to this distinction, one might also suggest that married inmates be allowed to share some time in privacy with their spouses at certain intervals. These observations have been made not to justify imprisonment as it currently functions in the United States, but to indicate that there are possibilities inherent in the prison system of punishment which, if actualized, may make such a system a just and humane form of punishment.

This discussion is also pertinent to the question of whether the state should replace punishment with reform in its handling of convicted criminals. Although punishment is not reform, there is no need to see these two aims as mutually exclusive. The state could and should use the moral right that it has in dealing

[19] J. D. Mabbott, "Punishment," *Mind*, Vol. 48 (1939), p. 165.

with convicted criminals as a means of helping such people become responsible citizens. However, it should be noted that there are moral limits to what the state can do in pursuing its reformatory aims.

Although I disagreed with Kant's interpretation of his principle of equality, I do think that he was right in indicating that this principle has a role to play in determining the character and amount of punishment to which the criminal is to be subjected. More specifically the principle may function as establishing the upper limit beyond which the state ought not go in punishing a criminal for a given crime, thus protecting the criminal from the possible excesses of the state. This means that the view which advocates that the state should be given the right to control criminals for whatever length of time it may take to reform them is to be rejected. If one were to accept this view, a man who was convicted of stealing a television set from a large department store might be jailed and subjected to compulsory psychiatric treatment for a period of thirty years because it was only after this period that the state psychiatrists thought that he was cured.

This interpretation of the place of the principle of equality in legal punishment was not advanced with the idea that it will provide legislators and judges with a magic formula that they can apply mechanically in deciding the type of punishment that ought to be established as a maximum for a certain type of crime. It is admittedly not always an easy matter to gauge the gravity of a certain crime and to establish a punishment that is proportionate to this gravity, without itself being guilty of committing the same atrocity as the crime. Because the principle of equality is interpreted as establishing a maximum punishment that can be handed down for a certain crime, it leaves a certain area of discretion open to the judge, who may take factors other than the principle of equality into consideration, in the sentencing of a certain criminal. For example, if the judge thinks that in a given case to hand down a maximum sentence is to do more harm than good to the criminal's future possibilities for a more responsible life, he might decide in favor of a lighter sentence. Thus, the retributivist position presented in this section does not exclude the possibility that deterrent and reform considerations may play a role in punishment practices.

c. Problems with the Statistical Evidence and with the Moral Justification of the Deterrent Argument

J. Edgar Hoover was right in holding that the statistical evidence concerning the deterrent effect of capital punishment is inconclusive. The available statistics indicate that there is no great difference in the homicide rate between states that have abolished the death penalty and neighboring states with similar sociocultural environments in which the death penalty is retained. In certain years the homicide rate of the abolition states will be somewhat lower than the rate in those states retaining the death penalty, whereas in other years the reverse will be true. For example, the homicide rate per 100,000 of the population in the state of Michigan, which abolished the death penalty, was 4.6, 4.5, 4.1, and 4.4 for the years from 1948 to 1951, whereas the rate in Ohio which retains the death penalty for the same period of years was 5.3, 5.3, 4.1, and 4.3.[20] The statistical data provide no evidence to sustain the view that capital punishment is a more effective deterrent than is imprisonment.

Although the inconclusiveness of the statistical data cannot validly be used to prove that the death penalty is not a more effective deterrent to crime than imprisonment, it does seriously weaken the case of those who defend the use of this penalty on the grounds of its deterrent value, because the burden of proof rests on them. Granted the inconclusiveness of present statistical evidence and the severity of the death penalty, it seems more reasonable to abolish it rather than retain it.[21]

It is now necessary to consider the view that statistical evidence is not necessary to prove the deterrent effect of capital punishment because we know that men prize life so highly that they will go to any lengths to preserve it. The example of the criminal trying to have his sentence commuted from death to life imprisonment certainly shows that when a man finds himself under the sentence of death, he will be willing to accept almost any other penalty in its place, but it tells us nothing about the man who is not in the iron grip of the law and who is contemplating murder. As equally well known as the fact that all men fear death is the fact that they are very adept at putting all thoughts of their own deaths out of their minds. I see no reason for holding that the criminal in thinking about his crime should be excluded from this latter well-known fact. The situations in which a man finds himself in the direct and immediate danger of death with almost no possibility of escape and those in which death, if considered at all, is seen as a possibility at some future date are so different that it is fallacious to conclude that men will react in exactly the same way in both situations.

Moreover, Cesare Beccaria made an excellent point in his treatise On Crimes and Punishments, first published in 1764, when he stated that the certainty of punishment, even if the punishment be only of a moderate nature, is a more effective deterrent to crime than is a very severe penalty which the criminal thinks he may be able to avoid.[22] One can easily make this position look ridiculous by suggesting that those who use this position to argue against the death penalty are willing to reduce the penalty for rape to a $25.00 fine.[23] As was

[20] George B. Vold, "Extent and Trend of Capital Crimes in the United States," The Annals of the American Academy of Political and Social Sciences, Vol. 284 (November, 1952), p. 4. This issue is devoted to the study of murder and the death penalty. See also Thorsten Sellin, "Death and Imprisonment as Deterrents to Murder," The Death Penalty in America, pp. 280–283.

[21] Hugo Adam Bedau, "Death as a Punishment," The Death Penalty in America, p. 214.

[22] Cesare Beccaria, On Crimes and Punishments, trans. by Henry Paolucci (New York: The Library of Liberal Arts, 1963), p. 58.

[23] See footnote 9, p. 141.

indicated earlier, one who opposes the death penalty can hold that there should be some proportion between the severity of the punishment and the gravity of the crime. There is no reason to accept the implication that we are restricted to a rather nominal monetary fine and the death penalty in establishing the legal punishment for crimes such as rape. One wonders how a reasonable man contemplating rape (if such a man can be said to be reasonable) could decide that the momentary pleasure he might derive from criminally assaulting a woman is worth a ten- to twenty-year prison sentence. It seems clear that if the man were to consider his options in a reasonable manner and if he were certain of being apprehended, the thought of losing his freedom for the next ten or twenty years would be as effective a deterrent against rape as capital punishment.

Beccaria also made another point that ought to be considered in discussions of the possible deterrent effect of capital punishment.

> The death penalty cannot be useful, because of the example of barbarity it gives men. If the passions or the necessities of war have taught the shedding of human blood, the laws, moderators of the conduct of men, should not extend the beastly example, which becomes more pernicious since the inflicting of legal death is attended with much study and formality.[24]

Although I would not rest the bulk of my case against capital punishment on this point, I think that it deserves serious consideration. Not only is there no statistical or reflective evidence to prove that capital punishment is a more effective deterrent to crime than is imprisonment, but there is reason to think that the death penalty may weaken a society's respect for human life. It is difficult to see how the state can be said to contribute to an abhorrence against the direct and deliberate taking of human life when it itself has established a procedure for the calm, deliberate, and unemotional killing of a presently defenseless person who is not a threat to the life of any other person.

I have tried to show in this subsection that if we restrict our evaluation of the morality of capital punishment solely to the question of its deterrent value, there is no evidence to sustain the view that it is a more effective deterrent than imprisonment. However, it should be noted that if my argument against capital punishment in the previous subsection is accepted, it would be necessary to condemn capital punishment as being immoral even if evidence were available to support the view that it is a more effective deterrent against crime than is imprisonment. We must not become so concerned with the question of what is the most effective deterrent to crime that we will become blind to every other consideration in weighing the morality of a particular type of punishment. For example, giving enough tranquilizers to every member of the human race so that everybody would be too drowsy to commit a crime would probably be a more effective deterrent to crime than either capital punishment or imprisonment.[25]

[24] See footnote 22, p. 50.
[25] See footnote 13, p. 121.

However, there is more involved in a moral evaluation of types of punishment than questions of their possible deterrent values. I have tried to show that what Kant refers to as our duty of respect to our fellow man must also be taken into consideration in making such evaluations and that capital punishment is contrary to the claims of this duty.

3. JUST-WAR THEORY: EMPTY RATIONALIZATION OR RATIONAL MORAL PRINCIPLE?

Writing in 1877, Frederick Engels criticized a fellow socialist for having failed to realize the positive role that force has played in human history and for admitting "only with sighs and groans," that man may be required to resort to force as a necessary evil in order to overthrow an exploitative economic system.[26] With the possible exception of the Chinese communists, it is doubtful that anyone today would criticize an opponent for viewing war as an evil or for having grave misgivings in acknowledging that there may be times when war is necessary to overcome some evil.[27] It is true that once a nation is engaged in a particular war, one hears about the good that will be achieved as a result of victory, but such defenses do not try to prove that war in general is a good and noble thing for mankind.

The sobering knowledge of two world wars and of the destructive power of thermonuclear weapons has deepened man's sense of war as one of the greatest of human evils. This deepened awareness seems to have made it easier for militarists and pacifists to agree on one point, namely that any attempt to distinguish between moral and immoral behavior in the conduct of war is a meaningless exercise in hairsplitting. Since war is so obviously evil, there are no rational grounds for distinguishing between moral and immoral acts of war.

The just-war theory, which was given its first systematic intellectual expression in the writings of St. Augustine, has tried to formulate principles to help distinguish between morally justifiable and unjustifiable resorts to wars and acts of war.[28] This section will not concern itself with a historical account of the development of this theory, but will attempt to see whether the principles of this theory relating to such problems as the initiation and the conduct of war are viable intellectual tools for dealing with the moral questions relating to modern warfare.

[26] Frederick Engels, *Herr Dühring's Revolution in Science,* trans. by Emile Burns (New York: International Publishers, 1939), p. 203.

[27] For a brief discussion of whether the Chinese communists actually are exceptions see Robert E. Osgood and Robert W. Tucker, *Force, Order, and Justice* (Baltimore: The Johns Hopkins Press, 1967), p. 196, footnote 2.

[28] On the development of the just-war theory and St. Augustine's contribution to it see Paul Ramsey, *War and the Christian Conscience: How Shall Modern War Be Conducted Justly?* (Durham, North Carolina: Duke University Press, 1961), pp. xv–xxii, 15–33.

As we begin to deal with the problem of the morality of violence among men, we should note that man cannot always depend on using appeals to reason or to human emotions as a means of securing what he needs and desires from his world. The reason for this is that man is dependent not only on his fellow man for his well-being, but also on animals, plants, and chemicals that are not responsive to such appeals. Therefore, he must depend on force if he is to make use of these things to his advantage. Force, as understood in this context, refers to man's bodily strength and to the augmentation of this strength by such things as stones, clubs, fire, bows and arrows, rifles, explosives, and machinery run by water, steam, electric, or atomic power.

It is true that much of this force would not have been available to man had he not exercised his rational capacities, and it is also true that he must often depend on both his force and his reason to achieve his goals. Thus, man cannot build a house by relying solely on the force necessary to fell trees and to shape them, but it is equally true that he cannot complete this task by relying only on the power of rational persuasion or emotional appeal.

When force is seen in this general context, it is clear that man's ability to use force is an indispensable means to the achievement of his well-being in the world. The moral issue that must now be considered is whether man has the moral right to use force against his fellow man who, unlike animals and plants, is able to respond to rational persuasions and emotional appeals. The term "violence" is often used to describe man's use of force against other men. Prima-facie evidence indicates that the use of violence is immoral because it involves the denial of the victim's character as a being capable of freedom. However, there are circumstances in which this prima-facie moral prohibition is open to question. There are men who are willing and able to use force or the threat of force against other men without any regard for the limits which the moral rights of the latter place on them. The aggressor-victim relationship as understood in this discussion is one in which the aggressor is trying to use the victim as a mere means to that over which he (the aggressor) has no moral claim. Thus, the relationship is different from one in which there is a conflict of interest between two human beings, each having an equal moral claim to the good at issue.

'If a man finds himself in a situation in which another man is using force against him, the individual under attack or another individual, who is in a position to help the intended victim, have the moral right to use whatever force may be necessary to protect the life and well-being of the victim. It must be acknowledged that this right is difficult to establish on the basis of the view that is taken in this book. However, this difficulty need not constitute a shortcoming of an ethical theory, because the moral right to use violence must certainly bring us to the very border separating moral from immoral behavior. The man trying to treat his fellow man as an end in himself finds himself confronted with difficult alternatives when dealing with aggression. Is he to allow violent men to achieve their immoral ends at the expense of innocent human beings or is he himself to employ whatever violence may be necessary against these men?

If one could frustrate the immoral work of an aggressor and prevent innocent human beings from being victimized by aggressors through the use of nonviolent means, he would certainly be obliged to employ these means, but we are now considering situations in which the employment of such means would not be effective.

The moral right to use violence against an aggressor is grounded in the view that the general prohibition against the use of violence does not mean that an intended victim is morally required to permit the aggressor to use him in the achievement of his immoral task. Granted that a victim has been unjustly placed in a situation in which violence is the only way of combating one who has ignored the moral limits of human existence and who hopes to use the situation to his own immoral advantage, it would appear to be unreasonable to deny the moral man the right to turn the aggressor's violence against him and to the advantage of man's moral existence.

The difficulty with trying to justify the use of violence in some cases is that it appears to be an intrinsically immoral means because it appears to fail to treat man as a being capable of freedom. However, in the case of aggression, the victim is confronted with a man, who not only refuses to treat the potential victim as an end in himself, but who also hopes to take advantage of the fact that he can place himself beyond rational persuasion and emotional appeal in order to complete his immoral task. The situation in which both he and his aggressor have been reduced to something less than human subjects is not of his own making. He must ask himself whether there is any way to salvage something of human value out of this situation. Granted that the aggressor has decided to place himself beyond moral influences, it is unreasonable to hold that the victim, who uses whatever violence is necessary against his aggressor in order to preserve his own character as a human subject, is guilty of treating the aggressor as a mere means. There are times when it is simply beyond one man's power to help another human being live up to his character as a moral being. It is the aggressor who has reduced himself to a mere object by his refusal to accept the moral limits that ought to regulate the relationships among men. Granted that the aggressor confronts the intended victim as a force that will not be controlled by the moral rights of the victim and granted that such behavior constitutes a present and serious threat to the life or well-being of the latter, it seems unreasonable to hold that the intended victim is morally blameworthy for taking whatever steps may be necessary to prevent the aggressor from transgressing his rights as a moral being.

Although we have not spoken of a nation's right to resort to war, it is clear that if man's moral right to use violence in certain circumstances has been established, this right may also be applied to relations among nations. However, it should be noted that the situation in which a nation may be said to possess this right is much more complicated than the relationship existing between individuals. In the case of individuals, one can usually restrict the use of force to the aggressor himself, whereas in the case of relations between nations, a defensive response will endanger the lives of many innocent people in both the defending and attacking nation. There is also a problem concerning the criterion for what constitutes a defensive war that will be discussed later in this chapter.

There are those who see an inconsistency in a position that denies the morality of capital punishment, but that defends the possible morality of war.[29] What saves the position from inconsistency is the differences in the circumstances surrounding capital punishment and the use of violence against an aggressor. Capital punishment does not involve the use of force against a man whose present use of force or threat to use force constitute a direct threat to the life of another human being. This situation is clearly different from the aggressor-victim relationship.

a. Three Problems Concerning the Principle of Noncombatant Moral Inviolability

This subsection will summarize three criticisms directed against attempts to restrict the conduct of warfare by an appeal to the principle of the moral inviolability of noncombatants against direct attack.

(1) The first criticism points out that the way of conducting war in modern times seems to have rendered the principle of noncombatant immunity meaningless. There are three factors involved in the modern conduct of war that have contributed to the erosion of this principle. First, modern weapons systems, which include aerial bombers and nuclear missiles, are indiscriminate in their killing effect in comparison with the sword, bow and arrow, and rifle of earlier days. The use of these modern weapons often involves an "unavoidable, intrinsic violation of the principle of the inviolability of noncombatants."[30]

Secondly, the dependence of modern armies on the industrial output of a nation means that an entire society must be mobilized for the conduct of war, thus rendering the distinction between combatants and noncombatants meaningless.[31] Finally, the fact that wars in modern times have been fought not for such rather uninspiring purposes as keeping a balance of power, but for great ideological purposes—such as keeping the world safe for democracy—has also contributed to a scrapping of the principle.[32] When defeat is seen as involving the crushing of all of man's highest ideals, when victory is seen as involving the prospect of "lasting or even perpetual peace and happiness,"[33] is it reasonable to worry about destroying an entire city, or three, or six? It is pointed out that we should not be too quick to scoff at these great ideological purposes.

[29] Jacques Barzun, "In Favor of Capital Punishment," *The Death Penalty in America*, p. 156.

[30] William V. O'Brien, "Nuclear Warfare and the Law of Nations," *Morality and Modern Warfare*, ed. by William J. Nagle (Baltimore: Helicon Press, 1960), p. 136.

[31] *Ibid.*

[32] *Ibid.*, p. 137.

[33] From a statement by Marshal Lin Piao, the Chinese communist defense minister. Quoted in *Force, Order and Justice*, p. 233, footnote 18.

For example, most people would agree that the power of Naziism had to be destroyed. The destruction of Naziism meant war, and the fighting of war in those years meant the use of aerial bombers. We are thus confronted with the question of whether we are willing to hold that because the conduct of war in our time means the use of weapons that unavoidably and intrinsically violate the principle of the inviolability of noncombatants, every modern war is immoral no matter what its objective may be, even if that objective includes the destruction of Nazi power. Although it may be clear that it would have been immoral for a medieval knight to kill a defenseless old woman, it does not appear to be quite so clear that the saving of civilian lives in Germany was more important than the defeat of Naziism.[34]

(2) The principle of double effect, which was used in dealing with the issues raised by induced abortions, has also played a role in the just-war theory. We shall present one difficulty, which the political scientist Robert W. Tucker finds in attempts to use this principle to evaluate the moral character of the conduct of modern war, and his attempted resolution of this difficulty. He is concerned with discovering some sort of criterion that would help decide whether the death and injury sustained by noncombatants was or was not the means used to achieve an otherwise legitimate military objective.

Tucker holds that an effect is ordinarily viewed as a means to a certain end, if the end cannot be achieved without that effect and if this dependence of the end on the effect is known. Understood in this light, the noncombatant deaths that occur in the course of an attack on a military objective are as much a means to military victory as is the destruction of the objective itself. The only difference between them is that the noncombatant deaths are an indirect means to victory, whereas the destruction of the objective is a more direct means to the same end.[35] Thus, Tucker concludes that so long as the just-war theory allows for the death and injury of noncombatants in the course of an attack on a military objective, it cannot claim to be in accord with the demand of the principle of double effect, in so far as that principle requires that the evil of the noncombatant deaths not be a means to the attainment of an otherwise legitimate military objective.

The surrender of this demand of the principle of double effect need not mean that there are no moral limits to be placed on the conduct of war. The conduct of war may be restricted by the principle of proportionality, which demands that there be a reasonable proportion between the evil of noncombatant deaths and the good to be achieved by means of this evil. Thus, the issue is no longer one of not using an evil means to achieve a good result; the issue is how much evil may be morally permitted in order to achieve the good that is military victory. There comes some point at which we say that the number of noncombatant deaths and injuries resulting from a military operation is an evil that is not outweighed by

---

[34] See footnote 30, pp. 137–138.

[35] Robert W. Tucker, *Just War and Vatican Council II: A Critique* (New York: The Council on Religion and International Affairs, 1966), p. 30.

the number of lives that one can expect to save or preserve from misery and suffering through the very operation that caused the evil of the death and injury of noncombatants.[36] In short, the problem of the morality of means is primarily a matter of quantitatively weighing the good and bad consequences that flow or may be expected to flow from the employment of the means in question.[37]

Tucker acknowledges that moralists who speak about man as an end in himself may find it difficult to accept his quantitative interpretation of noncombatant inviolability because it justifies practices that achieve the well-being of some by causing the death and injury of others. However, he points out that if we were to accept the moralist's view, we would be forced to surrender statecraft itself, because war is simply the clearest expression of what is involved in all political action, namely, bringing about the happiness of some by means of sacrificing the happiness and well-being of others.[38]

Tucker also notes that his quantitative approach was accepted by both critics and defenders of the general practice of strategic bombing in World War II, and also of the atomic bombing of Hiroshima and Nagasaki. The defenders of the latter actions presented as their principal justification the view that the Japanese government would be so overwhelmed by the awesome display of the United States' destructive power that it would surrender, thus saving many more American and Japanese lives than the number that would be killed by bombs. Critics did not dispute the principle of numbers upon which this decision was based, but questioned whether the bombings were actually necessary to force the Japanese to surrender. Similarly, critics of strategic bombing denied that it was necessary to achieve victory, but the great majority of them were willing to concede that had victory been impossible without terror bombing, such bombing would have been justified.[39]

(3) The pacifist Gordon Zahn presents a sociopsychological criticism of attempts to use the principle of double effect as a criterion for distinguishing between moral and immoral means of warfare. Describing this principle as "a principle that is fast becoming a moral slide rule by which almost any act of war can be justified," he states that those who depend on it to restrain men in the conduct of war are wholly unrealistic in thinking that military men are concerned with weighing the good and bad effects of an operation.[40] Whatever attention they might pay to the problem of evil effects will be restricted to the possible casualties that their own men might suffer, the possible damage to their equipment, or the possibility that a certain operation might strengthen the enemy's will to fight.

To think that men caught in the passions of war, overcome by a nationalistic

---

[36] See footnote 27, p. 247.

[37] See footnote 35, p. 31.

[38] See footnote 27, p. 241.

[39] *Ibid.*, pp. 200, 240.

[40] Gordon C. Zahn, *War, Conscience and Dissent* (New York: Hawthorne Books, Inc., 1967), p. 36.

pride and filled with a hatred of the enemy, are likely to be objective in distinguishing between the good and evil effects of bombing an enemy city is to show "a hopeless ignorance of human psychology."[41] Zahn points to the bombing of Hiroshima, the decisions of the Nazi high commands, and the allied bombing of Würzburg as examples of the inadequacies of philosophical distinctions, which do not take into account the way in which war hysteria tends to turn men into beings that are "somewhat less than human."[42]

b. THE VALUE AND LIMITS OF A RATIONAL PRINCIPLE IN EMOTIONAL SITUATIONS

We shall consider Zahn's criticism first, since the acceptance of his views would appear to lead to the conclusion that one is wasting his time worrying about the validity of a principle that everyone will ignore. Before dealing directly with this criticism, it should be noted that it may involve, or lead to, a certain confusion. Zahn's use of such examples as the bombing of Hiroshima may be accepted as a reason to reject the principle of double effect by those who are under the misapprehension that the defense of a principle as providing a valid tool for distinguishing between moral and immoral behavior constitutes a prediction that men will actually act in accord with that principle. If the test for the validity of a moral principle were whether or not examples could be found of behavior that did not accord with the principle, it would probably be safe to say that no moral principle would be able to pass this test, since I doubt that there is any immorality that man has not done at some time or other.

It should be noted that to require that a moral principle be submitted to such a test is to be guilty of the naturalistic fallacy, because the test implies that in order to defend the value of x as that which ought to be done, one must be able to prove that as a matter of fact x is always done, or negatively, is never violated.

One who has accepted the views expressed in Chapters I and V of this book concerning the relationship between human reason and human emotions would have no difficulty accepting Zahn's views in so far as he holds that philosophical distinctions are not adequate in themselves to regulate human behavior. As was pointed out at the beginning of Chapter V, human emotions are certainly sources of man's behavior, and in stress situations, they are probably the principle source of human action. However, as we also tried to point out in Chapter I, to acknowledge the inadequacy of reason alone to function as a principle of human action need not lead one to conclude that man ought to ignore what he is able to discover about the moral dimensions of his existence through the use of his reason. The response given in Chapter I, Section 10 to Stevenson's criticism of an ethics that claims to appeal only to reason is pertinent to the point now at issue.

---

[41] *Ibid.*, pp. 36–37.
[42] *Ibid.*, pp. 36–37, 56.

Working out of the context of that response, it is possible to distinguish between two tasks that man may be asked to perform as he confronts the problem of the role of the principle of double effect in placing moral limits on the conduct of war. First, it is necessary to ask whether there is any rational basis upon which one can justify placing certain moral limits on the means that can be used in the pursuit of military victory. If a rational basis for specifying certain limits is discovered, man may then be confronted with a second task, namely, finding ways to make these limits effective in the conduct of a war. Providing evidence to show that man has failed to meet the demands of the second task, as Zahn has done, says nothing about his success or failure in handling the first task.

If one can rationally justify the placing of moral limits on the conduct of war and if Zahn is right, as I think he is, in holding that an overbearing nationalistic pride and a hatred for the enemy stunts man's use of reason, man must look for some way to make the work of reason effective in war situations. The American experience of the Viet Nam war indicates that close television coverage of a war and the ability of a people to become acquainted with the ideals for which the enemy may be fighting through the writings of enemy leaders, through interviews with these leaders, or through the reports of objective newsmen who have had an opportunity to visit the enemy's country may help to moderate the chauvinism and hatred for the enemy that distort a people's judgment. I make this point not to defend the justice of the Viet Nam war—such an issue is beyond the scope of this book—but only to indicate the resources that may be available to help a nation moderate the emotions described by Zahn.

It is conceivable that one sharing Zahn's view might hold that it is nonsensical to be concerned about finding some rational basis for placing a moral limit on the means of warfare because it is simply impossible to moderate the passions generated by war in a way that would permit man to follow the dictates of reason. The acceptance by a pacifist of a position that takes such a dim view of human reason's ability to play a significant role in human life would appear to be paradoxical, if not downright inconsistent, in view of the fact that the same pacifist shows an almost unbounded faith in man's power to control his passions when he is in the process of making his case for the effectiveness of the nonviolent resolution of conflicts.

For example, in describing how an ordinary man who is being trained in nonviolence must be prepared to endure seeing others about him violently killed without himself resorting to violence, Zahn states that an effort must be made to bring "the softer sensibilities and spiritual inclinations of human nature" in this man "to the threshold of self-sacrificial fulfillment," and to control "to the point of elimination, if possible, that part of man's nature which is ever too ready to repay evil with evil."[43] It seems to me that anyone who thinks that man is capable of exercising such control over himself in situations of severe stress when

[43] Gordon C. Zahn, *An Alternative to War* (New York: The Council on Religion and International Affairs, 1963), p. 16.

he is responding to a conflict situation nonviolently cannot reasonably deny the possibility that he may be able to make the findings of reason effective in the stress of a war situation.

Although the type of issue raised by Zahn is explicitly directed toward an aspect of the just-war theory, it should be clear from our discussion that it touches the deeper and more general issue of the possible role of reason in man's social or national existence. This point is worthy of note because it indicates that one way to contribute to making the life of reason more effective in a nation's response to a war situation is to give it an opportunity to grow and develop in other situations. A nation whose domestic affairs are controlled by racial prejudices or by narrow sectional interests is not likely to become a citadel of reason in time of war. It is true that it is much more difficult to make reason effective in the life of a nation than it is in the life of an individual, but we must constantly be working at the unending task of making it more effective in times of peace as well as in times of war, in domestic as well as in foreign affairs, if we want to establish a political environment that will contribute to the moral and physical well-being of mankind.[44]

If Zahn is right in holding that the principle of double effect is becoming a moral slide rule that can be used to justify any act of war, the loss of the moral perspective incorporated in this principle means that man may no longer be able to distinguish between moral and immoral attempts to combat social injustices, whether these attempts be of a violent or nonviolent nature. An observation made by the Protestant theologian Reinhold Niebuhr is pertinent to this point.

> Gandhi's boycott of British cotton results in the undernourishment of children in Manchester. . . . It is impossible to coerce a group without damaging both life and property and without imperilling the interests of the innocent with those of the guilty.[45]

Because the innocent and the unjust live in one world, because the institutions that the unjust use for their own aims are also institutions upon which many of the innocent depend for whatever well-being they may enjoy, an attack on the unjust, an attempt to render the institutional structures upon which the unjust depend ineffective will inevitably have some evil consequences for the innocent—and this is true whether the means employed be of a violent or a nonviolent nature.

For example, although I think that many of the nonviolent demonstrations and acts of civil disobedience that this country has witnessed in recent years were morally justified, it seems to me that they have been a contributing factor—

---

[44] For an excellent examination of the problem of the place of reason in man's social life see Reinhold Niebuhr, *Man's Nature and His Communities* (New York: Charles Scribner's Sons, 1965).

[45] Reinhold Niebuhr, *Moral Man and Immoral Society* (New York: Charles Scribner's Sons, 1960), p. 172.

though certainly not the sole contributing factor—to a lack of respect for law and to the civil disorders that have resulted in the death and injury of innocent people, not to mention the nights of terror to which many such people were subjected during these disorders, and the loss of homes and the destruction of property upon which many people depended for their livelihood. The principle of double effect, described in Chapter VI, Section 10, can be a useful intellectual tool in helping man find a moral way to deal with a complex social world—a world in which he will often find that his most noble undertakings cannot avoid leading to consequences that are a mixture of good and evil. This principle tries to find a middle way between the reactionary response to this complex situation, which opposes every movement toward reform by pointing to the evil consequences—thus paralyzing the forces of justice while allowing injustice to flourish,—and a radical response which holds that because innocent people will be hurt in any case, any and every means is morally justified in the pursuit of a morally good goal.

c. In Defense of the Principle of Noncombatant Moral Inviolability

Tucker's interpretation of the principle of double effect provides an excellent example of the reasoning that would lead one to such a radical response. Because the just-war theory acknowledges that the death of noncombatants may be morally permissable if they occur as a result of an attack on a legitimate military target, he concludes that the theory cannot consistently hold that evil not be used as a means to achieve the good result. His is a modified radicalism in that he acknowledges that the principle of proportionality imposes a moral limit on the means that may be employed in the conduct of war. If one were to accept Tucker's interpretation of the principle of double effect, he would conclude that there is a redundancy in the usual formulations of the principle, because the rule that the good effect must not flow from the evil result is reduced to the principle of proportionality.

Tucker assures us that this interpretation does place a meaningful limit on the amount of death and injury that may be morally permitted. However, it seems to me that the limit is so broad as to be meaningless. It would appear that in any purely quantitative analysis of how much evil can be permitted to a nation at war in order to bring about a future good, everything short of the total destruction of the world would be morally justifiable. The present and those living in the present are reduced to insignificance when compared with the almost infinite expanse of the future. Because one's vision of the future can always include more people than are presently living, if one simply extends this vision over a sufficient number of years, one can justify the total destruction of any number of nations in the present in the name of the future happiness of human beings who will certainly outnumber those being killed if we include a sufficient number of years in our notion of the future.

The discussion of the morality of therapeutic abortion in Chapter VI, Section 10 was based on an interpretation of the principle of double effect, which saw a difference between the demand expressed in the rule that the good effect should not flow from the evil result, and the demand expressed in the principle of proportionality. The criterion that was presented there as an aid to distinguishing between morally justifiable and unjustifiable abortions can also be helpful in distinguishing between situations in which the death of noncombatants is an unavoidable consequence of an attack on a military target and those in which the death of noncombatants is an instrumentality for the achievement of military victory. Let us see how it would work in evaluating the morality of the bombing of Hiroshima.

Tucker quotes former President Truman as saying that he wanted the atomic bomb that was eventually dropped on Hiroshima to be dropped on a military target, on an important production center. He also quotes the former President as saying that he wanted to avoid as far as possible, the killing of civilians.[46] Our task is not to judge the person of President Truman, but to consider how a moral decision on the bombing of Hiroshima would be made by one who accepted the view that the death and injuries of noncombatants ought never be used as an instrumentality for the achievement of victory and who tried to use the criterion presented in Chapter VI to distinguish between those bombings in which the death and injury of noncombatants is an unfortunate, but unavoidable byproduct of an otherwise legitimate military operation and those attacks in which such deaths and injuries are the instrumentalities to an otherwise good military objective.

Such a person would want to take a careful look at how the dropping of the atomic bomb on Hiroshima could be expected to contribute to the noble purpose of shortening the war. What military installations or munitions plants was this bomb expected to destroy? How much explosive power would be needed to destroy the military objectives and to keep the noncombatant deaths and injuries at a minimum? Could these objectives be destroyed by bombs of less destructive power than the atomic bomb? What if, by some stroke of fortune, the atomic bomb destroyed only the military objective without causing any noncombatant deaths or injuries would it have served our noble purpose of shortening the war? It seems to me that when questions such as these are asked it becomes clear that if the atomic bomb were to serve its purpose of bringing the Japanese to the peace table, it was absolutely essential that it cause an awesome and terrifying amount of noncombatant deaths and injuries. On the basis of these considerations, the type of person whom we have described would reject the dropping of the bomb on Hiroshima as being immoral.

It might be well to list the kinds of issues that would be raised by one accepting the position being proposed. First, he will want to be sure that the object of attack is either the enemy's forces, his military installations, or such things as

---

[46] See footnote 27, p. 247, footnote 35.

shipbuilding facilities and war-plane plants that are directly involved in the enemy's use of force. Having satisfied himself that the object of attack is morally acceptable, he will then sanction only the use of such force as can be realistically expected to destroy the military target. He will reject as immoral any suggestion that he take advantage of the opportunity to increase his use of force so that he will not only destroy the military objective, but also cause as much civilian damage as possible. It seems to me that these issues are intelligible enough in their own right and are not reducible to the principle of proportionality. They are clear enough to distinguish between morally acceptable counterforce warfare in which a nation directs its armed might against an enemy's military force or against those production facilities engaged in making the enemy's weapons of war and morally unacceptable counter-city or counter-people warfare in which an enemy's entire cities and noncombatant population are made the direct object of attack.

It is now necessary to evaluate the view that because entire societies must now be mobilized for war, the distinction between combatants and noncombatants is no longer meaningful. The Jesuit theologian John C. Ford, writing in 1944 in opposition to the practice of obliteration bombing, used an excellent technique in responding to this view by enumerating a list of hundreds of occupations and stations in life that could not be reasonably described as mobilizations for the war effort.[47] The following list is not taken from Ford's, although his more extensive list includes most of those mentioned here. Are we to say that the following can no longer be considered noncombatants, that they have been mobilized for, or are directly engaged in, the war effort?

> Infants, school children, the aged, the mentally and chronically ill, housewives, grammar school principals and teachers, barbers, hair dressers, window washers, garbage collectors, house painters, plumbers, janitors, mail carriers, accountants, lawyers, bank clerks, bill collectors, grocers, druggists, undertakers, waiters and waitresses, bartenders, insurance agents, photographers, ministers, priests, rabbis, nuns,—those engaged in manufacturing, advertising, and selling such items as beds, desks, air-conditioners, television sets, and countless other items,—cab drivers, bus drivers,—those engaged in doing medical research on such health problems as cancer and mental retardation.

The list could be expanded, but I believe it is long enough to indicate the spuriousness of the view that the combatant-noncombatant distinction must be abandoned because modern industrial conditions make everybody a combatant.[48]

It is clear that these conditions do not involve all the citizens of a nation directly in such violent tasks as the bearing of arms, the manufacturing of arms, or the planning and supervision of military operations. Such innocent tasks as

---

[47] John C. Ford, "The Morality of Obliteration Bombing," *Theological Studies,* Vol. V (1944), pp. 283–284.

[48] See footnote 27, pp. 208–209.

the collecting of garbage, the caring for children, the burying of the dead, the selling of groceries, and the delivery of the mail are part of the daily life of modern industrial states, whether these states are at war or at peace. The direct and deliberate use of force against people engaged in such tasks is immoral because it goes beyond the moral limits that prohibit the use of force against men who are not themselves using violent means to threaten the peace and well-being of others.

If it is not modern conditions that render the combatant-noncombatant distinction meaningless, it may be that the indiscriminate character of modern weapons produces the same result. If the word "indiscriminate" is taken in an extended sense, it does not serve to distinguish between ancient and modern weapons, because the cave man's stone can be said to be indiscriminate in that it would crack the skull of an innocent man as well as that of an aggressor, depending on the one against whom it was aimed and the accuracy of the thrower. The problem with modern weapons is that man does not have as much control over their destructive power as he may have had over the bow and arrow or even the rifle. However, this lack of control need no more constitute an "intrinsic violation of the principle of the inviolability of noncombatants," than does a surgeon's inability to remove a cancerous uterus without at the same time killing the fetus constitute an intrinsic violation of the child's right to life.

Just as the surgeon cannot be morally obliged to save the lives of both mother and child as he engages in the morally good act of attacking a uterine cancer because it is simply beyond his power to save both lives, so also the military planner cannot be morally obliged to save the lives of noncombatants who are in the neighborhood of a legitimate military objective if he simply lacks the capacity to save these lives as he is engaged in the morally permissible task of destroying a legitimate military objective. In short, just as not every activity that results in the death of a child can be validly described as an intrinsic violation of that child's right to life, so also not every activity that results in the death of noncombatants can be validly described as an "intrinsic violation of the principle of nonviolability of noncombatants." Those situations in which the performance of a morally good or permissive act results in the death of some human being cannot be said to be an intrinsic violation of that being's right to life so long as this morally good or permissive act is directed to the achievement of a good that is reasonably proportionate to the evil that results from that act.

It is only after one has settled the point that it is a military objective being attacked that one confronts the issue raised by the principle of proportionality. Granted that one is attacking a morally permissible target, he must now ask himself whether the death and injury done to noncombatants as a result of such an attack will be at least equalled by the good to be expected from a successful destruction of the target. I know of no clear-cut mathematical rule or formula that can help a person decide what constitutes a reasonable proportion in such cases. It would be necessary to weigh the importance of the military objective to the enemy's war effort against the amount of noncombatant death and injury that might be expected to result from an attack on that objective. It would also be necessary to be sure that one is being realistic in using destructive force that is sufficient to cause maximum destruction of the military objective and minimum noncombatant death and injury. In short, one must be sure that he is not in the position of a man who tries to kill a fly (a legitimate target) that happens to be on another man's head with a sledge hammer.[49]

According to this position, a direct attack on a noncombatant population is immoral, no matter how good the consequences of causing noncombatant deaths may be expected to be. Such attacks are immoral no matter what purposes they are expected to serve—whether to show the people that its government does not control the cities, or to weaken the people's will to resist, or to carry the war to the enemy, or to shorten the war, or for reasons of reprisal. Thus, if Tucker is right in stating that both critics and defenders of the bombing of Hiroshima and of the bombing of such German cities as Hamburg agreed in applying only the principle of proportionality in their evaluations of the morality of such acts, the position being taken here is in opposition to the majority view.

Man is indeed a being capable of noble ends, whether these ends be to make the world safe for democracy, to establish the earthly paradise of a classless society, or to shorten the agonies of war, but the nobility of his ends does not give him an unlimited moral right over the lives of his fellow human beings. If there has been one theme that has run throughout this book from the criticism of utilitarianism, to the opposition to abortion on demand and to capital punishment, and now the opposition to counter-city warfare, it is that there are moral limits to what man may do to achieve his aims, however noble they may be.

Much of this book has been concerned with investigating the rational ground for principles that might help in the establishment of such limits. Because in our day man has been able to achieve so much power not only in the form of bombs, but also in such areas as medical technology, it is necessary perhaps now more than ever that he not be so blinded by the splendor of his aims that he use this power in a morally indiscriminate manner—a manner that sees no sense in a moral evaluation of how these noble aims will be achieved, whether the aims concern the social and economic well-being of a pregnant woman's family or the defeat of "atheistic communism" or of "imperialistic capitalism" (depending on the aim from which one views the world).

Such an approach is so convinced of the morality of its aims that it sees no reason to waste time with any other moral consideration and is interested in what becomes only a question of technique: How can this noble aim be achieved? The view taken in this book is concerned with insuring that innocence never becomes an insignificant matter in this world. As the discussion of the principle of double effect indicated, I realize that because of the limitation of man's power and because of the complex relations that constitute his world, he

[49] John C. Ford, "The Hydrogen Bombing of Cities," *Morality and Modern Warfare*, p. 101.

may find himself in situations in which even when he does a morally good thing such as operating on a cancer that threatens the life of a woman, he may not be able to avoid causing the death of an innocent child, but his limitations and the complexities of his world do not give him the right to do anything and everything to the innocent so long as his vision of a future state of affairs is noble enough and so long as he feels certain that his actions will be effective in bringing this state of affairs into existence.

A position such as Tucker's provides an excellent example of how one can proceed from the limitations and complexities of human existence to the conclusion that man ought to surrender the concern with avoiding evil and should ask himself only how much evil he is permitted to do. I can only refer to the discussion of the relationship between politics and ethics in Section 1 of this chapter and the discussion of the principle of double effect both in this section and in Chapter VI, Section 10 as presenting an alternative to Tucker's stand that politics, or statecraft, is impossible for one who does not accept his interpretation of the principle of double effect.

That the nobility of his ideals does not give a man unlimited moral rights over the lives of his fellow man must also be emphasized against those who maintain that the great ideological purposes for which modern wars have been fought have rendered the distinction between combatants and noncombatants meaningless. This latter position may be true as a statement of fact, but I hope that I have made a beginning in showing that it does not express a valid moral rule. The noble purpose of defeating Naziism did not morally justify the deaths of noncombatants in Hamburg, if these deaths were the result of a direct attack on them.[50]

It should be emphasized that the moral perspective that has been defended in this section applies to the use of nuclear weapons as well as to the use of conventional weapons. Counter-city warfare is immoral, whether conducted with hundreds of the types of bombs used in World War II or with one nuclear bomb. Counter-force warfare has been acknowledged as being morally permissible, and this remains the case whether nuclear weapons are used or not.

Those who condemn the use of all nuclear weapons without any qualification as being immoral have failed to take into account the fact that there are nuclear weapons that are not of the high megaton yield. There may be low-yield nuclear weapons, which may require fewer sorties to be effective in destroying a military target, and which, therefore, may hold out the promise of causing fewer noncombatant casualties than conventional weapons, because an increase of the number of sorties may mean an increase in the possible death and destruction that may be brought to noncombatants. To go into this matter more thoroughly would be to take us beyond the limits of this book. I have simply raised the issue to point out that the moral condemnation of nuclear weapons cannot be of an unqualified

[50] See footnote 30, p. 138. O'Brien implies that it was more important to defeat Hitler than to save noncombatant lives in Hamburg.

nature. It is possible to envisage situations in which the use of a certain type of nuclear weapon would be more in keeping with the moral limits set on the conduct of war than conventional weapons would be. However, it must be admitted that there is a danger that man will not stop with low-yield nuclear weapons once he begins to use them. This danger is one of the factors that the man of practical wisdom must weigh carefully as he tries to reach a decision concerning what he ought to do in a concrete existential situation.

There are certain types of atomic and hydrogen bombs which are so destructive that it is difficult to conceive how their use would not be contrary to the moral prohibition against counter-city warfare. To use such bombs in any situation would appear to be similar to using a sledge hammer to kill a fly on a man's head.

The position taken in this section logically leads to the conclusion that an all-out nuclear exchange, or a total nuclear war, is immoral no matter what excuse or reason might be offered in attempted justification of such an exchange. This view is taken not only as a logical development of the prohibition of counter-city warfare, but I think it can also be justified by pointing out that there could be no goal that would morally justify such an exchange. It should be emphasized that the position that I am about to defend leaves open the possibility for all types of counter-force warfare that does not make the noncombatants of a nation the direct object of attack.

Any attempt to give a rational justification for the morality of an all-out nuclear war will inevitably argue that the destruction wrought by such a war is morally justified because it is undertaken in defense of human freedom and justice. I am willing to admit that limited wars may be justified by some such goal. For despite the destructive feature of all wars, it is possible that men will have the conditions available for the realization of freedom and justice at the conclusion of a limited war. However, the result of a total nuclear war would be such as to render the goals of freedom and justice meaningless abstractions.

A nation that engages in such a war is pursuing a line of action that defeats the very goals that it offers as a moral justification for its behavior. As we have already seen, the realization of moral values in this world depends on the agency of man, but it is doubtful that the human race would survive the result of a total nuclear war, and if there were survivors, it is doubtful that they would be in a better position to achieve the moral and physical well-being of mankind than would have been possible had the world not been subjected to such a war.

Some might argue that the view of the results of an all-out nuclear exchange that grounds my conclusion is overly pessimistic, because it is possible that there may be millions of survivors alive after the last bomb has been exploded and the last fire has died. Hence, a total nuclear war is justified on the grounds that its aim is to preserve and develop a free society for these millions of survivors. However, the validity of this point of view is questionable, if we stop to consider the condition of these survivors and of their earthly environment. They will find themselves in a world poisoned by radioactivity. Where, then, will they find their food? From rotting animals and destroyed crops? From the surviving animals and plants, which are themselves poisoned by nuclear fallout and which, if eaten, could transmit this poison to the human body? The water, as well as the very air, which man breathes, would be contaminated. In short, man would find himself living in a world in which the animals, plants, water, and air upon which he depends would provide little, if any, support for his bare subsistence.

We have said nothing about the physical conditions of the survivors themselves. Their bodies would also be poisoned by radiation so that if they managed to survive and to generate offspring, these would also be in danger of suffering serious handicaps. These survivors could not expect much in the way of medical care, since many medical facilities would have been destroyed, not to mention the death and injury that trained physicians and nurses would have suffered. It is difficult to see how a war known to lead to results such as these can be justified on the grounds that it will contribute to man's physical and/or moral well-being.

To acknowledge the possibility that a situation may arise in which the use of military violence may defeat the very moral goals for which it was to lay the groundwork is not to hold that a nation must passively surrender to those who would impose a form of government on them that they think would be detrimental to the character of man as a free being. A nation confronted by such a prospect must be ready to use every morally acceptable violent and nonviolent means to frustrate those who have been placed in positions of power by the conquerors. Guerrilla type attacks on enemy troops stationed in the country and enemy installations would be among the more obvious morally acceptable violent means available.

The nonviolent means would consist in attempts to disrupt the day-to-day administrative activities of government by disrupting telephone comunications between officials, by making sure that written communications between them either never get to the intended person or are received only after it is too late to fulfill the purpose of the letter, by sabotaging the heating and lighting facilities in government offices. Other nonviolent means of combat would be work slow-downs, high absentee rates, not to mention strikes in vital industries. These suggestions are not made with the idea that they can be realized without great difficulties, without much suffering and losses of life, but it must be recalled that they are offered as an alternative to an all-out nuclear war, which would threaten the very survival of the human race, and to the passive acceptance of a dictatorial power that has been forcibly imposed on a people.

I have not raised this problem because I think that there is a good chance that we shall someday find ourselves in a situation in which we must make one of the choices outlined. Others may play the role of prophet if they wish. I have raised it simply to draw out the logical implications of the position taken in this section and to show that far from it being true that all would be lost if this position were pushed to its logical conclusion, it provides a viable alternative to the concept of unlimited war, which, if pushed to its logical conclusion, could involve nations in a war whose only end would be destruction for destruction's sake.

d. Defensive Wars and the Role of the Nation-state in Human Life

The discussion up to this point has been concerned with the question of the moral limits within which war may be conducted. There is another moral question that must be considered by those legitimately holding power in a state and the citizens of that state as they try to evaluate and to contribute their own thinking to the positions of their leaders. It is necessary to ask under what conditions is a nation morally justified in going to war against another nation. The conditions that seem to constitute the most acceptable answer to this question in our own day are first that the good that can reasonably be expected to result from a given war must outweigh, or at least be equal to, the evil that war can be expected to involve (the principle of proportionality), and secondly that the war must be defensive rather than aggressive.

Robert Tucker has done a fine job in bringing out the problems that are involved in these conditions which may appear to be so obviously reasonable to some that they are hardly worth discussing. We shall restrict ourselves to those problems raised by Tucker which appear to be most pertinent to a course in moral philosophy. He points out that even if man were to accept the principle of proportionality, even if he knew with certainty the consequences for good or evil that would result from initiating a particular war, the principle would be too empty and abstract to be of any significant help to him. No one would deny that in evaluating a possible line of action, a nation ought to consider whether the good that can be expected to result from the venture will at least be equivalent to, if not outweigh, the evil that may also be expected to accompany or result from it. However, the principle is of no help in providing a tool for discovering what would be good and what would be evil in the situation.[51]

There are two points that can be made with respect to this criticism. First, a principle that is hardly worth mentioning in the reflective, unemotional atmosphere of one's study or of a classroom may become a principle that not only ought to be mentioned, but ought to be given as much emphasis as possible when a nation is in a highly emotional state over some real or imagined wrong that it has suffered, and is trying to find some way to respond to this wrong. If just-war theorists thought that they need only state this principle to make it effective in such situations, they were indeed guilty of manifesting, in Zahn's words, "a hopeless ignorance of human psychology." However, if they realized that nations are in danger of allowing their emotions to run away with them in such

---

[51] See footnote 35, pp. 18–19, footnote 13.

situations, and if they stated this principle in their reflections on the morality of war to call attention to the need to make the outlook expressed by this principle effective in these situations, they are to be congratulated for knowing enough human psychology to recognize that one way to contribute to the possibility that man may act reasonably in situations of emotional stress is by calling to his attention in his reflective moments the reasonableness and validity of principles he is in danger of ignoring in moments of stress.

Secondly, Tucker's criticism provides a concrete example of the truth of a position taken in Chapter V, Section 7. It will be recalled that the defense of the practical significance of moral philosophy offered there quoted John Dewey's statement that any moral principle will cease being an effective intellectual tool if it is not subjected to the free play of reflective inquiry. If any putative moral principle is treated as a thing in itself, wholly isolated from a more fully elaborated moral theory, it will become a meaningless abstraction. The meaning of the principle of proportionality will differ, depending on whether one sees it within a utilitarian context, a deontological context, or a context that makes the good of the state the ultimate criterion of value. It is because of this fact that moral philosophy, which subjects these various contexts to reflective critique, is a matter of practical significance to the conduct of human life.

This brings us to the central issue of this subsection. Whereas the previous section dealt with the rather restricted, but certainly important, issue of noncombatant inviolability, this section will try to summarize the role to be given war within the context of a reflective naturalism. Granted that this ethical theory acknowledges that a nation may have the moral right to use force against another nation, does this theory place any limits on this right other than that imposed by the principle of noncombatant inviolability? That latter principle limits the manner in which a war may be conducted. Does reflective naturalism hold that so long as a nation does not violate the principle of noncombatant inviolability, it may go to war anytime it feels strong enough? It seems to me that the ideals of man as an end in himself and of the human community, which have been developed through the various themes discussed in this book, should serve to give the principle of proportionality the type of content that one can reasonably expect from a principle, which is presented not as a substitute, but as a tool, for further reflection.

For example, one accepting these ideals cannot ignore the injuries and deaths, which a potential enemy may be expected to suffer, in weighing the evil that may be expected to result from the outbreak of a war. They must be given the same weight as is given to one's own citizens in considering the evil that a possible war may entail. More importantly, one accepting the position developed in this book would not base his moral evaluation of whether to go to war solely on this principle. Unlike the utilitarian, he would recognize that a nation does not have the moral right to exercise force against another nation merely because it sees that the goodness, which one could reasonably expect to result from this war, would outweigh the evils to be expected from the waging of the war. This sort of consideration leads to the conclusion that there must be some factor in addition to the principle of proportionality that must be taken into account in trying to decide whether it is morally permissible to use force against another nation. Most people in the United States would probably agree that a nation is morally justified in declaring war against another nation only if this war is necessary as a defensive measure against aggression.

We shall restrict ourselves to examining two difficulties that Tucker points out in this position. First, he has clearly seen that the contemporary concern with whether or not a war is defensive has tended to reduce moral evaluations of war to this one issue. Against this reduction, he points out that a war may be defensive, but immoral because the good that one may reasonably expect to result from a given defensive war may be outweighed by the evil that may also be reasonably expected.[52] He also rightly points out that this reduction blinds some to the need to consider the morality of the means used in the conduct of war and of the ends for which the war is fought. There are those who seem to think that once it has been established that a nation did not fire the first shot, and is thus fighting a defensive war, anything that nation does must be considered defensive and thus moral—whether these actions are restricted to simply repelling the enemy, or involve attempts to annihilate him as a nation by a policy of counter-city warfare.[53]

This exclusive concern with defining a nation's role in a war by asking whether it fired the first shot may also have served to make men unaware of the incompatibility between a nation's claim to be fighting a defensive war and its goal, which is to secure the unconditional surrender of the enemy. It is possible that such a nation's declaration of war was a defensive measure, but it is difficult to see how the objective of securing unconditional control over the enemy nation can be said to be a defensive measure.[54]

The tendency to evaluate the morality of a war solely on the basis of whether a nation made the first aggressive move has undoubtedly contributed to a lack of proper concern with such issues as the morality of the way in which the war is conducted and the goals for which it is conducted. Thus, the fact that the Japanese fired the first shot against the United States in World War II seemed to justify everything that this country did in the conduct of this war. The general outlook behind this position is similar to the general outlook behind the position that defends the morality of capital punishment. Once a man is proved to have done something wrong, there are practically no moral limits to what can be done to him.

If this outlook is morally unacceptable when one is dealing only with the criminal who has been proved guilty, it is certainly unacceptable when one is dealing with a nation and when one's conduct of a war will cause the death and

[52] *Ibid.*, p. 10, footnote 6.
[53] Robert W. Tucker, *The Just War: A Study in Contemporary American Doctrine* (Baltimore: The Johns Hopkins Press, 1960), pp. 157, 162.
[54] *Ibid.*, p. 64.

injury of many who were unable to mount an effective opposition to the evil policies of their leaders, or who were unaware of these policies, or who were victimized by the propaganda of these leaders, or who, finally and most importantly, were not guilty of directly engaging in the evils perpetrated by their leaders. Thus, the dropping of the atomic bomb on Hiroshima cannot be morally justified by a position that claims the bomb was being dropped on those who were guilty of the sneak attack on Pearl Harbor, of beating American prisoners of war, and of refusing to obey the international laws of war.[55]

It should also be noted that there is some question as to whether a position such as the just-war theory, which places moral restraints on the conduct of war, can with any consistency accept unconditional surrender as a morally justified objective of war. If it did accept such an objective, it would be in the position of demanding that limited means be used to pursue an unlimited end. It may be logically possible to take a position that finds nothing wrong with the objective of unconditional surrender, but insists that this objective can only be sought by means that are kept within certain limits. However logically possible such a state of affairs may be, it certainly places man in a difficult situation. It would appear to be more in keeping with the just-war theory to hold that a nation contemplating war establish certain rather definite and limited objectives that it hopes to achieve through this war. Such a practice will not absolutely insure that the war will be conducted within moral limits, but it will make such a conduct more likely.

The second problem raised by Tucker concerns the question of what criteria one is to establish to judge whether a war is or is not defensive. The fact that a nation did not fire the first shot need not mean that its entrance into the war was defensive. It may have deliberately provoked the other nation to violence by threatening a nation's peace and security with means short of armed aggression. This indicates that we cannot resolve the problem of defining a defensive war by defining it as a response to aggression, unless we are prepared to define what is meant by aggression.[56]

The fact that a nation has the right to resort to force not only in defense of its territorial integrity, but also in defense of its independence and security raises the question concerning what constitutes a threat to a nation's security and independence.[57] For example, was the United States right in threatening the use of force in the Cuban missile crisis in view of the fact that one nation, the Soviet Union, and another nation, Cuba, came to a mutual agreement that the latter would provide the former with missiles?[58] Finally, it should be noted that if a nation were to wait until a hostile nation fired the first shot, it might find that

---

[55] Tucker quotes former President Truman as mentioning these three points in an apparent attempt to justify the destruction of Hiroshima. See footnote 27, p. 210.

[56] See footnote 35, p. 13, footnote 8; p. 14.

[57] See footnote 27, p. 274, footnote 40.

[58] See footnote 35, p. 15.

it was no longer able to defend those values such as independence and security which are said to justify a resort to arms.[59]

Tucker has put his finger on one of the most difficult problems confronting man as he tries to develop moral principles that will be helpful in ordering the relations among nations. It seems to me that some progress might be made toward resolving this issue by viewing it without specific reference to such terms as "defensive" and "aggressive," because these terms do not appear to be able to capture an intellectual center of focus that is useful in distinguishing between a moral and an immoral resort to force. A more helpful approach to this issue may lie in distinguishing between two types of good toward which a war effort may be directed, namely a *good of rectification* and a *good of aggrandizement*.

A war effort is said to be directed toward a good of rectification, and therefore, to be moral (at least, with respect to the aim of this effort), if a nation has undertaken this effort against another nation in response to activities on the part of the latter, which are directed to seriously endangering the former's security and independence, and if all attempts to use peaceful means to convince this nation to cease and desist from these activities have failed. This means that the good toward which a war is directed ought not be simply a matter of adding to a nation's territory or to such things as its political and economic interest, i.e. a war ought not to be directed to achieving only a good of aggrandizement.

It should be emphasized that the distinction between these goods is to be used in conjunction with the principle of proportionality as a nation tries to decide whether it is morally right in initiating a certain war. The establishment of these principles is no more presented as a substitute for personal reflection on concrete issues than were any of the other principles offered in this book. However, it is hoped that they will be helpful in deciding whether a nation has a moral right to initiate the use of force in concrete situations. Thus, one could not hope to properly evaluate the actions of the United States in the Cuban missile crisis by using these principles apart from a knowledge of the concrete historical circumstances surrounding these actions. However, the use of these principles together with such knowledge would hopefully help one make a proper moral evaluation of this action.

Tucker has indicated that if the protection of a nation's independence and security is made a major factor in justifying the resort to war, it will be necessary to define what is meant by a nation's "self."[60] For example, if we are to defend the independence and security of the United States, and if we hold that these values are not reducible to this nation's territorial integrity alone, it will be necessary for us to define what we understand to be the "self" of the United States. Such a task would be beyond the scope of this book. However, Tucker's emphasis on this task does indicate that a morality of war is not complete without

---

[59] *Ibid.*, p. 13.
[60] See footnote 27, pp. 274–276.

a discussion of the role of the nation-state in human life. It may well be the case that the role which a person gives to the nation-state in his system of values may play a more decisive part in his concrete decisions concerning matters of war and peace than the principles that have been discussed thus far because his view of the nation-state may determine the meaning he gives to these principles.

There would appear to be no need, especially in a democratic society, to consider whether the good of the nation-state should function as man's ultimate criterion of value. However, Tucker has made an excellent point in noting that the insistence with which citizens in such a society maintain that the nation is only an instrumental value does not appear to be consistent with their willingness to take whatever measures may be necessary to preserve the state's independence and survival. Such a willingness indicates that the state provides these people with a feeling of self-respect and of their own worth.[61]

Tucker also is able to show how a person need not subscribe to the position that the state is the ultimate source of all value in order to arrive at a position that, for all practical purposes, equates the state with all human value. So long as the state is taken to be the indispensable means for the protection of all human values, it takes on a role in the practical order that is no different from that of the ultimate basis of all value. Once the state is seen as the indispensable means to all human values, there are no limits to what may be done in the name of the independence and security of the state, since one has committed oneself to the view that no values are possible apart from the conditions established by the state.[62]

It is true that man needs some sort of authoritative institutional framework such as the nation in order to preserve and promote his moral and physical well-being. However, to acknowledge that some sort of institutional order similar to the nation is an indispensable means to the protection of human values is not to say that any given national order, whether it be that of the United States or of the Soviet Union, is an indispensable means for the protection of all human values. This means that we must acknowledge that any given state, any given political order, may be replaced by another political order without there being a total loss of all human values. Any given state is no more the sole and complete embodiment of all the possibilities for human goodness than is any individual man the full realization of such goodness.

Although no responsible person today would try to defend the doctrine of the divine rights of kings, this doctrine is by no means dead in the practical life of the modern nation-state. There is a tendency for the most powerful of these to view themselves not as human institutions shaped by men who, for all their greatness, were not infallible and were not without the peculiar limitations that are part of the lives of all human individuals, but as divinely inspired institutions with a messianic calling. This characterization is no less true of an explicitly

[61] *Ibid.*, p. 284, footnote 48.
[62] *Ibid.*, p. 284.

atheistic nation-state such as the Soviet Union than of the United States.[63] This tendency to deify one's own nation is matched by the tendency to demonize any strong nation that is opposed to one's own policies.

A marvelous technique has been developed that permits these tendencies to play a significant role in the relations among nation-states without making the processes of deification and demonization too obvious. It is the technique of comparing the highest ideals of the nation-state one favors with the most blatantly immoral part of the history of the nation-state one opposes. One using this technique seems to suffer from a severe moral myopia when viewing the history of the nation he favors, but enjoys super sensitive moral vision when viewing the history of a hostile nation. For example, communists see the history of the United States simply as a long history of the oppression of Negroes and of the poor, ignoring this nation's attempts to implement the high ideals expressed in its Declaration of Independence and in its Constitution. Similarly, many citizens of the United States tend to think of the Soviet Union solely in terms of the atrocities of Stalinism, ignoring the humanistic ideals in the Marxist world-view and the real advances that this country has been able to make toward improving the living conditions of its citizens in the relatively short time since 1917 and despite having been subjected to the devastation of the invading German armies during World War II.

The comparison of these two countries is beyond the scope of this book. I have used the examples simply to emphasize the need to compare ideals with ideals and history with history in any attempt to appraise the relative moral merits of a nation-state one favors and of a nation-state to which one is opposed. Such an appraisal will not necessarily lead one to want to canonize the country to which he is opposed; nor will it do away with all conflicts that may exist between the countries. It is hoped that such an appraisal will help to keep the conflicts that do arise within more managable limits than is likely to be the case if one nation views itself as the embodiment of all that is good and holy and its opponent as Satan Incarnate. Such a more realistic appraisal of the histories and ideals of nation-states in conflict may also have the added advantage of uncovering additional alternatives for the resolution of conflicts short of war.

This discussion of the just-war theory has tried to show the rationality of certain principles that may be useful to men as they try to make decisions concerning the morality or immorality of certain wars or of certain acts of war. The proper use of these principles requires not only a knowledge of the concrete circumstances pertinent to a given problem, but also an appreciation of the sufferings and tragedies that are inevitably involved in all wars.

---

[63] On the messianic character of Russian communism see the following works by Nicholas Berdyaev, *The Origin of Russian Communism*, trans. by R. M. French (The University of Michigan Press, 1960) and *The Russian Revolution* (The University of Michigan Press, 1961). See also the characterization of Marxism as a religious system in Robert C. Tucker, *Philosophy and Myth in Karl Marx* (Cambridge: Cambridge University Press, 1961), pp. 22–26.

CHAPTER IX

Toward an Open
Ethical
Naturalism

The purpose of this chapter is to explore the question of the relationship between man's moral experience and the existence of the Personal and Eternal God of theism. There are three basic stances that one can take with respect to this issue. It might be argued that the existence of God has nothing to do with the moral dimensions of man's existence. A second possible stance is that the existence of a Personal God destroys, or at best, impoverishes the moral enterprise. This position carries the implication that the character of man's moral life disproves, or at least casts serious doubt on, the existence of a Personal God. A third alternative is that the existence of such a God is in keeping with the moral character of human life and that His existence is a positive and enriching factor in this life.

The major concern of this chapter will be with the second and third alternatives. The discussion of these two will bring out considerations that appear to be destructive of the first alternative as a philosophically viable one. The first part of the chapter will be devoted to an exposition of John Dewey's position concerning the place of God and the supernatural in man's moral life. This position represents a defense of the second alternative. The remainder of the chapter will involve a criticism and evaluation of Dewey's position and an attempt to make a case for the third alternative. The phrases *closed naturalism,* and *open naturalism* will be used to describe the two alternatives, with closed naturalism being applied to Dewey's position in that this position is intent on keeping the whole moral enterprise within the limits of man in nature, and on opposing any position that would expand this enterprise to include a reference to a Personal and Eternal God. The position taken in this chapter will be denominated an open naturalism, with the word *naturalism* being used to emphasize that there are basic areas of agreement in moral philosophy between the position taken in this book and Dewey's moral philosophy, and the description *open* being used to emphasize the view that man's moral life can be expanded to include reference to a Personal and Eternal God and that such an expansion constitutes an enrichment of this life rather than a threat to it.

The position that will be taken in this chapter can be specified further by distinguishing it from other positions that could also fit into the third alternative mentioned above. Those who see the existence of God as an essential ingredient in man's moral life might argue that a knowledge of the existence of God is indispensable to morality in that it provides the ultimate norm for distinguishing between moral good and moral evil. Closely related to this interpretation of our third alternative is the view that man cannot be said to obligate himself and that, therefore, God must be used to ground moral obligation. The differences between these views and the position taken in this chapter will be considered later in the chapter.

It is also possible that the ethician will find that the existence of God is a conclusion that he must draw from his reflections on the moral dimensions of human existence. This view is more in keeping with the position to be taken in this chapter. However, I must emphasize that I have not seen any proof for the existence of God drawn from man's moral experience that seems to me to be philosophically conclusive. Hence, the position taken in this chapter will hold that although the existence of God may not be philosophically demonstrated from a reflection on man's moral experience, a case can be made to show that the existence of a personal God contributes to and enriches man's moral life. Having made this point, I shall also try to show that the existence of such a God is not wholly alien to man's moral experience and that there are factors within this experience that raise the question of the existence of such a being.

The work of this chapter will be conducted under the following headings: (1) John Dewey's Transition from a Theocentric Ethics to a Closed Naturalism, (2) Dewey's Case Against Supernaturalism, (3) The Religious As Naturalistically Based, (4) Dewey on the Place of "God" in Human Endeavors, (5) Open and Closed Naturalism: The Common Ground, (6) Critique of Dewey's Case Against Supernaturalism, and (7) The Case for an Open Ethical Naturalism.

1. JOHN DEWEY'S TRANSITION FROM A THEOCENTRIC ETHICS TO NATURALISM

The purpose of this section is to sketch the moral considerations which led John Dewey from the view that God is essential to man's moral endeavors to the view that the acceptance of the existence of God detracts from these endeavors. It is hoped that this sketch will contribute to a more appreciative and firm grasp of Dewey's mature naturalism, which will be dealt with in the next section. In an article published in 1887, Dewey argues that the exclusion of God from reality necessarily involves the exclusion of moral and ideal factors from reality.[1]

---

[1] John Dewey, "Ethics and Physical Science," *The Andover Review*, Vol. VII (June, 1887), pp. 576–577.

He states that his conviction of the inextricable union between the cause of God and of ethics is based not merely on the need for supernatural sanctions and restraints in man's pursuit of his moral task, but on the view that a purely physical conception of the universe, one which excludes God from reality, cannot account for the principles and ideas that are fundamental to the moral enterprise.

He acknowledges that a complete defense of this position would require the establishment of two points. First, it would be necessary to show that moral philosophy and moral conduct are not compatible with purely physical reality as depicted by science. Secondly, it would be necessary to prove that both moral philosophy and conduct are compatible only with a spiritual conception of reality, which is essentially identical with the theological tenets of Christianity.[2] He limits himself to the first of these tasks in the article here being considered.

Basically, the type of scientific ethics which Dewey is considering is one that holds that science has shown man to be a being in nature, that there is no need to look for a supernatural origin of man, and finally that evolutionary theory provides man with a social ideal in showing that the universe of which man is a part is moving toward the development of a social organism. Hence, the man whose behavior is such as to contribute to the growth of a harmonious community is moral whereas he whose acts are detrimental to or destructive of such a growth is immoral.[3]

The following quotation presents the aspect of Dewey's case that is relevant to this section.

> It [the defense of scientific ethics] is painted with colors which are borrowed from the school of spiritualism, and to which it has no claim; it is filled in with the shadows of figures who live only in the realm of Will and Reason; it reflects a light which has its source in God himself. . . . If we grant the postulates of the ideal conception of the world, if we assume the primacy of reason, if we acknowledge the supremacy of will,—then we may see a certain truth in this scientific ethics, we may see how it aids here and there our account of the moral life, how it supplies, here and there, needed fulcra for the moralization of man. But, denying these conceptions, as in consistency with a mechanical theory we must do, the whole scheme empties itself of value.[4]

Dewey's point is that the view of reality as moving toward a social ideal can be justified only if one accepts the premise that it proceeds from the Reason and Will of God. However, because the defenders of scientific ethics deny this premise, they have no right to posit the reality of ethical ideals for which man ought to work.

Dewey makes the same point from a slightly different perspective in carrying out his critique of scientific ethics. He holds that those defending this position

[2] *Ibid.*, p. 577.
[3] *Ibid.*, pp. 578–579.
[4] *Ibid.*, p. 579.

can be seen to have presupposed what they set out to prove, i.e. the existence of an identity of interests among men. It is this identity that constitutes the character and meaning of the moral order. A moral order is given once the unity and solidarity of interests among men is granted. However, Dewey maintains that the attempt to ground this moral order or community in the physical community of origin among men fails. That animals have a common physical origin does not prove that they share a common interest in life. They may all be interested in survival, but it is survival at all costs, meaning at the expense of the lives of other animals.

Physical processes alone are not sufficient to establish that sort of community of interests that grounds a moral community, a community in which benevolence and altruism have a role. Dewey does not deny that there is a solidarity existing among men, which allows for the postulation of a good in which all men may share harmoniously. However, this identity and harmony "is a spiritual principle, an ideal, which cannot be got out of the physical processes by any amount of manipulation."[5] The significant feature of this position for the present discussion is Dewey's insistence that a moral community must be given in reality if we are to account for the moral character of human life. At this point in his career, Dewey appears to be identifying the "natural" with the "physical" and arguing that it is necessary to move beyond the physical to the spiritual in order to account for the moral order in which "sane men live, move, and have their being in varying degrees of completeness."[6]

Dewey also holds that a purely physical order of reality cannot account for an order of reality that is fulfilling some sort of purpose. A purely scientific ethics is based on the view that the whole universe is heading toward an end. However, there can be no such purpose in a purely physical universe. If the universe is to be said to fulfill a purpose there must be a unity binding together the whole temporal order of reality.

> The end, in any intelligible sense, must have the same reference to an event which occurred a million years ago, as to one which will occur ten million years from now. In other words, it is that which interprets, which gives meaning to, which unifies all processes. And such a unity cannot be an object which exists in some place, or an event which occurs at some time. It cannot be one conditioned existence in a series of conditioned existences. It can be only an idea, a spiritual, an ideal unity of purpose and meaning.[7]

In short, the notion of an underlying world-purpose, which the scientific ethicians acknowledge to be essential to accounting for man's moral life, can be grounded only in a world that is seen as embodying reason and manifesting intelligent purpose. Thus, we have seen two points which Dewey made in this

[5] *Ibid.*, p. 587.
[6] *Ibid.*, p. 588.
[7] *Ibid.*, p. 589.

early article. First, the existence of a moral community among men cannot be accounted for apart from a spiritual principle of unity that cannot be engendered by physical processes. Secondly, the existence of an ethical ideal or end toward which man's moral endeavors are directed demands that the universe be seen as possessing an ideal unity of purpose and meaning and as "the embodiment of reason, and the manifestation of intelligent purpose."[8]

In an ethics textbook published in 1891, Dewey still sees a place for God in man's moral life, although the conception of God does not play a very significant role in the actual development of his position. The notion of a moral community continues to play a central role in Dewey's ethical thought. The moral perfection of oneself is the perfection of oneself as a member of a certain society.[9] "The basis of moral conduct is a faith that moral self-satisfaction means social satisfaction—or the faith that self and others make a true community."[10] This faith maintains that whenever one performs the service of which he is capable, it is not he alone that is satisfied, but the whole moral order is satisfied and the community in which one lives is advanced.[11] This faith thus maintains that there is a thoroughgoing and permanent unity of man's moral world. Dewey states that to probe the basis of this faith or moral postulate is to move beyond the scope of the book, which deals with issues *in* moral philosophy, to a "metaphysics of ethics," which would underlie this philosophy.[12]

He is most emphatic in pointing to the positive contribution that Christianity made to man's moral life when it made him aware of the importance of the social order to the achievement of his moral perfection and to the overcoming of his past evils. Christianity thus emphasized the *active* character of man's moral task. It placed morality not in some thing or in conformity to some external law, but in the individual's active engagement in a social order. The individual was taught that he is to overcome evil not by an isolated struggle, but by engaging in the world of social relations.[13] Thus, Dewey still saw a place for Christianity in man's moral endeavors. Although the major emphasis of the book is placed on the intrinsic values of man's social existence, Dewey did acknowledge the need to provide a metaphysical foundation for this existence.

The book does contain a criticism of a certain way of trying to ground moral obligation in the existence of God. Dewey points out that there is a danger connected with making a Divine Being the author of moral obligation in that this position can reduce such obligation to a matter of purely external constraint, and hence, destroy its moral character, which demands that it arise out of man himself. Moreover, if duty is grounded in God as separated from human activity, it

---

[8] *Ibid.*
[9] John Dewey, *Outlines of a Critical Theory of Ethics* (New York: Hillary House, 1957; an exact reprint of the 1891 ed.), p. 118.
[10] *Ibid.*, p. 128.
[11] *Ibid.*, pp. 129–130.
[12] *Ibid.*, p. 130.
[13] *Ibid.*, pp. 224–225.

becomes a purely empty and abstract affair, possessing no content. There is a further more serious difficulty involved in this position. In placing the source of moral duty wholly external to man's environment, the position seems to deny that there is any intrinsic moral significance to the human condition, with this denial implying a denial of the dignity and worth of human life in the exercise of its free activity.[14]

This criticism is significant in light of Dewey's later opposition to a supernatural order. However, he is still willing to admit at this time that there may be a place for God in an account of moral obligation, provided that the "Divine Being is shown to be organically connected with self."[15] Having mentioned this point, he drops it and spends his time in showing how moral obligation arises out of the social character of human existence.

In the same year that the book was published (1891), Dewey published an article dealing with the relation of moral theory to moral conduct in which he criticized the notion that moral obligation must be injected into man's situation from some external source.

> There seems to be an opinion that obligation, the 'oughtness,' is something super-added to the analysis of the act itself; that we may have examined never so thoroughly the content of a proposed act, of some suggested end, without the idea of obligation ever presenting itself, the result being some intellectual judgment regarding bare fact. Some machinery, the exact nature of which I have never found stated, is then called in to clap on the 'ought,' and thus give a moral aspect to a hitherto coldly intellectual matter. The creaking, lumbering *Deus ex machina* which in nick of time projects its proper entity upon the stage of human knowledge has, however, so often been replaced by the smooth, swift workings of a single intelligence, that we may gather courage for the hope that the 'ought' too is from intelligence rather than a somewhat let down from supernal flies or sprung from an unearthly trap.[16]

The context of the article from which this statement was taken is important to understanding Dewey's movement to a naturalism that has no place for a supernatural God in morality.

This attack against the use of a *Deux ex machina* to ground moral obligation is part of a more extensive criticism of the view that it is the task of moral theory to uncover some principle beyond the social relations among men that would ground the moral values exhibited in these relations.[17] Dewey thinks that such a conception of moral theory implies that there is no moral significance *intrinsic* to the human condition, or to man's ordinary activities in meeting the problems of his time and place. In short, whatever the search for the foundations of moral activity may mean, it does not mean that there must be something outside of

[14] *Ibid.*, p. 154.
[15] *Ibid.*, p. 150.
[16] See footnote 74, Chap. V, pp. 201–202.
[17] *Ibid.*, p. 187.

man's intellectual dealings with the facts of his experience. These dealings are not morally neutral, awaiting the injection of some external factor to render them moral.

There is no evidence that I have found to indicate that in 1891 Dewey saw any incompatibility between this position and the acceptance of Christianity. Up to 1894, when he left his position at the University of Michigan to join the faculty at the recently established University of Chicago, he seems to have taken the stand that Christianity does not reveal to man some sort of esoteric truths standing outside of the ordinary stream of human life, but that the truths of Christianity are to be worked out of the establishment of a democratic process, which will enable man to discover these truths through his involvement in this type of social process.[18]

Whereas in his 1891 book, Dewey left open the possibility of grounding his own conception of an ethical community in a metaphysical investigation into the basis for such a community, in an article published in 1896, he opposes the need to ground morality in a metaphysics. He investigates the possibility that a metaphysics, which establishes the existence of an "Ideal End, or Ultimate Good," provides a firm metaphysical foundation for man's moral life.[19] He points out that the one taking this position is forced to admit that man does not possess sufficient knowledge of this Ultimate End to permit him to know what he ought to do under particular circumstances. Hence, he must discover what is the right end to achieve here and now by an examination of the particular circumstances. Dewey finds this conclusion acceptable. However, he points out that the conclusion destroys any need for a metaphysical foundation for moral behavior in some Ultimate End.

A possible response to Dewey's stand is that the knowledge of the Ultimate End is helpful to the individual moral agent in that no matter how abstract and formal this knowledge may be, it does give him further knowledge of what he is about in his concrete undertakings. Dewey meets this response with the following position. What increases man's moral awareness of what he is about in dealing with particular ends is a broader and larger view of what is involved in the present act, as this act is related to the present society, which is sustained and/or developed by the act.[20]

Dewey contends that it is not the perfectly realized community distant an infinite length of time that gives content and meaning to my present acts. Rather, it is the larger and broader view of the implications of my present act for the society in which I live that gives content and meaning to the former community. Another difficulty entailed in attempting to ground ethics in a metaphysically established Ultimate End is that such a grounding depreciates the value of the present act, making it a mere means possessing no intrinsic value.

---

[18] George Dykhuizen, "John Dewey and the University of Michigan," *Journal of the History of Ideas,* Vol. 23 (1962), pp. 513–544; espec. pp. 541–542.

[19] John Dewey, "The Metaphysical Method in Ethics," *Psychological Review,* Vol. III (1896), p. 187.

[20] *Ibid.,* pp. 187–188.

If the present exists simply as one stage in bringing about an infinitely remote goal, it presents no imperative claims and affords no ends. Such a doctrine simply denies the doctrine that every collocation of circumstances has its *own* best. It makes rainbow chasing the essence of the doctrine of moral ideas. For my own part, I believe that an ethical doctrine with less 'foundations' under it is likely to go further and last longer.[21]

This quotation expresses a theme that will remain central to Dewey's philosophical outlook. He sees the establishment of any end outside of the social context in which man finds himself as necessarily involving a denial of the intrinsic value of this context or of the need to explore this context to uncover the possible ends inherent in it.

Finally, whereas in the 1887 article considered in this section Dewey intimated that there could be no moral community without the existence of God, in the 1896 article now being considered he rejects this position. He opposes the argumentation that a moral system not grounded in religious ideas cannot stand because it can give no explanation as to why man should love his neighbor as himself and is unable to justify the idea of a common good.

According to this position, it is only God who can act as a transcendent principle uniting men into that union of spirit, which is the ultimate basis of man's practical life. Dewey restricts himself to pointing out the dialectical difficulty embodied in this position. One cannot say, on the one hand, that all individuals are united in the divine self, and, on the other, that there are isolated individuals. Although Dewey is not explicit on this matter, I think he is pointing to the following difficulty. If the community of man is actually established by God, then it is given, and there is no need to talk about overcoming the isolation and exclusiveness of individuals because, granted God, there is no such isolation. If there is an isolation to be overcome, then there is no given community of men established by God.[22] He acknowledges that one way out of this difficulty is to hold that man considered naturally is wholly evil, being unable to move outside of himself to form any sort of meaningful community and that such a community can come into existence only through the workings of supernatural grace, which has its source wholly outside of man. However, the position that he is considering does not take this tack. Hence, Dewey does not consider it.[23]

Dewey's conclusion to this article indicates the line of development he himself will take in the future in developing his moral philosophy. He states that ethical theory needs an adequate "psychological and social method, not a metaphysical one."[24] Thus, whereas Dewey once saw the existence of God as necessary to establish a spiritual groundwork for the moral community among men, he finds difficulties in this position in 1896.

[21] *Ibid.*, p. 188.
[22] *Ibid.*, p. 186.
[23] *Ibid.*
[24] *Ibid.*, p. 188.

The major ingredient in Dewey's moral thought, which led to his disenchantment with God as essential to morality, was a growing idea that the role of the Christian God in morals removed any intrinsic moral significance from man's dealings with nature and his fellow man. He began to move toward the conclusion that the unity and integrity of man's moral experience was threatened by the acceptance of the existence of a supernatural God. Thus, in an article published in 1898, he disagrees with certain theologians and moralists who see a separation or dualism between the forces of nature and man's moral life as likely to strengthen this life.

> But I question whether the spiritual life does not get its surest and most ample guarantees when it is learned that the laws and conditions of righteousness are implicated in the working processes of the universe; when it is found that man in his conscious struggles, in his doubts, temptations, and defeats, in his aspirations and successes, is moved on and buoyed up by the forces which have developed nature; and that in this moral struggle he acts not as a mere individual but as an organ in maintaining and carrying forward the universal process.[25]

The further development of this theme will require an exposition of Dewey's case against supernaturalism.

2. DEWEY'S CASE AGAINST SUPERNATURALISM

The purpose of this section is to present Dewey's major moral arguments against the acceptance of supernaturalism as a factor in man's moral life. These arguments, which are spread throughout the very extensive *corpus* of Dewey's writings, are gathered together in the book *A Common Faith*, published in 1934. This book will be used as the unifying text of this and the following section, with material being taken from other Dewey writings in order to round out the positions taken in *A Common Faith*. The charges, which are leveled against the introduction of supernaturalism into morality, center in two closely related points: (1) the appeal to supernatural forces shows a lack of moral faith, and (2) supernaturalism is guilty of escapism and of weakening man's concern with the natural order.

The supernaturalist's lack of moral faith is seen in his belief that such values as justice, beauty, and truth are valuable because they are already existent in some supernatural realm. This position implies that man ought to pursue these values only because they are securely and permanently existent in a realm that transcends the dangers and changes of the natural order. A true faith in moral ideals is shown by one willing to pursue them because he sees them to be intrinsically valuable and not because they are existentially given in a supernatural order. Those committed to proving the prior existence of these values show themselves to be more interested in power than in the values themselves, because

---

[25] John Dewey, "Evolution and Ethics," *The Monist*, Vol. VIII (April, 1898), p. 341.

such prior existence adds to these values only a power to reward or to punish.[26]

Against the supernaturalist's lack of moral faith, Dewey points out, "The demand of righteousness for reverence does not depend upon the ability to prove the existence of an antecedent Being who is righteous."[27] He holds that even if one were to admit for purposes of argument that the natural world is indifferent to values in the sense that values are "mere incidents, transitory accidents," in the process of nature, he would not be forced to surrender the moral enterprise.[28] The acknowledgment that there is not an all-Good principle underlying nature and that thus the whole of nature does not work for the good does not imply the end of morality. It implies rather that man must use his intelligence to discover how he can use the natural factors available to him to render the admittedly unstable and transitory values of his world more stable and more readily available to more men.[29]

Dewey recognizes that those whom he has charged with lack of moral faith may object to his position on the grounds that it asks man to pursue values that may be illusory. He meets this objection by pointing out that the question of whether the values that are a part of human experience are real or illusory arises only if one presupposes the existence of some reality that transcends human experience. Once this presupposition is dropped, man accepts what is an immediate factor in his experience, viz., the existence of goods and evils.[30]

The natural world as found in human experience is a *complexus* of goods and evils. Hence, one cannot argue that nature as given to man is morally good. The moral dimension of human existence is accounted for by man's ability to select among the goods and evils that are involved in his transactions with nature and to work for the more stable and wide-spread establishment in nature of these values that enrich human life. Thus, there is no need for a being transcending the natural order to account for the moral character of human existence.[31]

Moreover, Dewey contends that the view that nature is included in an all-embracing spiritual and ideal whole adds nothing to man's moral task.

Is any value more concretely and securely in life than it was before? Does this perfect intelligence enable us to correct one single mis-step, one paltry error, here and now? Does this perfect all-inclusive goodness serve to heal one disease? Does it rectify one transgression? Does it even give the slightest inkling of how to go to work at any of these things? No; it just tells you: Never mind, for they are already eternally healed in the eternal consciousness which alone is really Real.

[26] John Dewey, *A Common Faith* (New Haven: Yale University Press, 1960), p. 44, also pp. 21–22, 23, 49. See also *Experience and Nature,* pp. 415–416.

[27] See footnote 73, Chap. V, p. 304.

[28] John Dewey, "Nature and its Good: A Conversation," *The Influence of Darwin on Philosophy: and other Essays in Contemporary Thought* (Bloomington: Indiana University Press, 1965), p. 23.

[29] *Ibid.,* pp. 23–24.

[30] *Ibid.,* pp. 26–28.

[31] *Ibid.,* pp. 42–44.

> Stop: there is one evil, one pain, which the doctrine mitigates—the hysteric sen-
> timentalism which is troubled because the universe as a whole does not sustain
> good as a whole. But that is the only thing it alters.[32]

Not only does the conception of an all-inclusive Good underlying nature fail to help man in his moral project, but it hinders him in that it leads to a moral quietism in which all evils are eternally resolved in the Real. It also leads to such a quietism in assuring one that the universe as a whole sustains the good as a whole.

Perhaps this lack of moral faith on the part of the supernaturalist would not be of much consequence, if it did not entail an escapist and defeatist practical response to man's situation in nature, and a weakening of man's concern with exploring the natural resources available to him to better himself in this world. Having evacuated the natural order of any intrinsic moral significance, the supernaturalist turns to some power external to his natural condition to resolve the difficulties of his life.[33] The belief that moral truths are grounded in some supernatural order and that this order is not accessible to ordinary human intelligence has diverted human intelligence from the task of reflecting on man's natural situation in order to discover how to preserve, develop, expand, and deepen the standing of the values that man finds in nature and conversely to destroy, stunt, narrow, and lessen the hold that evils have in nature.

Furthermore, the supernaturalist's emphasis on the supernatural origin and locus of values has led to the depreciation of natural social values. The practical consequence of this emphasis is that men have neglected and passed over the values inherent in the natural relations existing between married partners, between parents and children, between friends and neighbors, and between men sharing in common enterprises such as manufacturing, sciences, and the arts. These values have not simply been played down. They have also been viewed as threats to higher supernatural values and as man's revolt against the divine.[34]

This position has contributed to the brutalization of man's natural relationships. Granted that one comes to these relationships with the attitude that they are not *really* or *ultimately* of any value, or, what is even worse, that they are intrinsically depraved and corrupt, he is not very likely to participate in them with any concern to render them more humane. They have already been condemned out of hand. Hence, the supernaturalist will play his role in these relations because he cannot avoid them, but he will accept whatever inhumanity and corruption he may find in them as simply confirming his supernatural orientation.[35]

The attempt to ground morality in some factor that transcends the natural

---

[32] *Ibid.*, pp. 24–25.
[33] See footnote 26, p. 46.
[34] *Ibid.*, pp. 71–72.
[35] John Dewey, "Antinaturalism in Extremis," in *Naturalism and the Human Spirit*, ed. by Yervant H. Krikorian (New York: Columbia University Press, 1944), p. 15.

order is pushed toward defending the *status quo*. Because a transcendent principle is so remote from the practical moral issues of man in nature, the defenders of this principle, who maintain that it is absolutely essential to man's moral endeavors, try to compensate for the isolation and remoteness of their principle by readily accepting whatever values happened to be held by a society as those which are in keeping with the transcendental principle of morality. Having thus sanctified existing moral codes, they contribute to frustrating the work of intelligence in reflecting on the customary moral codes in order to find out what is worth preserving and expanding in these codes and what ought to be put aside as constituting an impediment to human progress.[36]

Finally, dependence on a supernatural power presents man with the practical alternatives of being either wholly pessimistic or naively optimistic in meeting the challenges of life. The pessimism arises out of the feeling of the corruption and impotency of natural resources that underlies the belief that all value and power exists in an order that is beyond man's reach. The only alternative to this pessimism is an exaggerated optimism that leads a man to the belief that a power beyond nature will in an instant transform his situation for the better. This belief in the possibility of a sudden transformation and in the efficacy of prayer provides man with an easy way out of his difficulties, because he feels no responsibility to do the type of reflection necessary to discover those resources that may advance the human condition. Once again, the supernaturalist's belief is seen as leaving matters in about the same unhappy state of affairs as they were before the conversion.[37]

In concluding this section, it will be well to see the two contrasts that Dewey sees as separating the naturalist and the supernaturalist approach to values. Whereas the supernaturalist states that the human condition separated from a relationship to the supernatural is morally no different from that of the brutes, the naturalist sees natural social relations as the matrix from which all significant values and all the resources for stability and peace have proceeded, and maintains that the values given a supernatural locus are in fact natural goods that have been idealized by man's imaginative grasp of his natural world. Moreover, whereas the supernaturalist holds that the supernatural is the only dependable source of motivation and that it has been directly and indirectly the motivating force behind every serious attempt to rectify man's life on earth, the naturalist maintains that the goods experienced by man in his natural environment such as those of family, citizenship, and the pursuit of scientific and artistic endeavors, have been the forces upon which man has depended for guidance and support and that the reference of these goods to a supernatural order has weakened their motivating power and has served to obscure their real nature.[38]

[36] "Intelligence and Morals," *The Influence of Darwin on Philosophy*. See footnote 28, pp. 75–76.
[37] See footnote 26, pp. 46–47.
[38] *Ibid.*, p. 70.

3. THE RELIGIOUS AS NATURALISTICALLY BASED

Dewey does not limit himself to the purely negative task of criticizing the effects of a belief in the supernatural on man's life. His naturalism has something of positive value to offer man.

> The fact of the case is that naturalism finds the values in question, the worth and dignity of men and women, residing in human nature itself, in the connections, actual and potential, that human beings sustain to one another in the natural environment. Not only that, but naturalism is ready at any time to maintain the thesis that foundation within man and nature is a much sounder basis than is or can be any foundation alleged to exist outside the constitution of man in nature.[39]

The purpose of this section is to present the central premises that Dewey offers in defense of this position.

He maintains that the liberation of man from concerns with a supernatural realm will broaden and extend the scope of the "religious" character of human existence. Instead of restricting the religious area of his life to the times when he is dealing with the supernatural in church, in prayer, or in his participation in certain rites and cults, man will come to see, "that experiences having the force of bringing about a better, deeper, and enduring adjustment in life are not so rare and infrequent as they are commonly supposed to be."[40] The experiences mentioned in this statement provide a good beginning for exploring the meaning that Dewey gives to the term religious. Experiences having the features mentioned in the quotation are religious, according to Dewey. Because religious refers to "a quality of experience,"[41] that may belong to all types of human undertakings such as aesthetic, political, and scientific, it is clear that the denial of the supernatural frees this quality from its restricted and exclusive reference to a supernatural power.

In order to grasp the full significance of this position, it will be necessary to probe more deeply into Dewey's conception of the religious. He distinguishes three ways in which man may relate to his world, viz., through accommodation, adaptation, and adjustment. Man is said to accommodate himself to his environment when he changes his attitudes in the face of conditions that are beyond his control. Accommodation is marked by two characteristics. First, it is mainly a passive response. Secondly, it is a restricted mode of behavior, one that does not involve the whole self. Adaptation involves a more active response to the environment, one in which the self changes certain conditions so as to bring them into line with one's own needs or attitudes. This sort of response is also

---

[39] See footnote 35, p. 9.
[40] See footnote 26, p. 14.
[41] *Ibid.*, p. 10.

of a particular and restricted nature, and does not involve a deep seated and enduring change of the whole self.[42]

Adjustment refers to those types of change in the self's relations to its world that are more deeply rooted and more inclusive than are the changes described by the terms *accommodation* and *adaptation*. The changes that are referred to by the term *adjustment* are described as follows.

> They relate not to this and that want in relation to this and that condition of our surroundings, but pertain to our being in its entirety. Because of their scope, this modification of ourselves is enduring. It lasts through any amount of vicissitude of circumstances, internal and external. There is a composing and harmonizing of the various elements of our being such that, in spite of changes in the special conditions that surround us, these conditions are also arranged, settled, in relation to us.[43]

Dewey acknowledges that there is an element of passivity or of submission in adjustment, but he points out that it also involves an outgoing dimension, a joyful readiness to meet the challenges of the world. Finally, it involves a voluntary element, but this element must be understood as "a change *of* will, conceived as the organic plenitude of our being."[44]

Once the habitual identification of the religious with belief in a supernatural power is surrendered, we may come to see that what is truly religious in man's life involves a fostering of "natural piety, the sense of the permanent and inevitable implication of nature and man in a common career and destiny."[45] Dewey finds that both supernaturalists and militant atheists lack such natural piety. The supernaturalist's lack of natural piety is seen in his conception of the whole drama of sin and redemption as being carried on within the soul of the isolated individual. There is no appreciation of the continuity between man and nature. Nature considered apart from man is held to be negligible, at best, or accursed, at worst. It is given no positive role to play in human redemption. The militant atheist shows the same lack of natural piety in viewing man as existing in a world that is completely hostile and alien to his needs and desires.[46]

The practical outcome of these apparently wholly contradictory positions is very similar in that both lead men to ignore the natural resources available to him for bettering man's situation in the world. The militant atheist is reduced to "issuing blasts of defiance," against the world, which leaves the world pretty much in the same shape as he found it.[47] The supernaturalist does the same

---

[42] *Ibid.*, pp. 15–16.

[43] *Ibid.*, p. 16.

[44] *Ibid.*, p. 17.

[45] John Dewey, "Religion in Our Schools," *Character and Events: Popular Essays in Social and Political Philosophy*, Vol. I, ed. by Joseph Ratner (New York: Henry Holt and Co., 1929; article originally published in *Hibbert Journal*, July, 1908), pp. 515–516. As we shall see, Dewey develops this notion of "natural piety" in *A Common Faith*.

[46] See footnote 26, p. 53.

[47] *Ibid.*

thing with respect to the world by placing his hopes in a supernatural power, and thus relieving himself of the responsibility of working with those factors in his world that could enrich the human condition.

Dewey gives a good description of what he means by natural piety in explaining the religious feeling aroused in man by intense aesthetic perception:

> We are, as it were, introduced into a world beyond this world which is nevertheless the deeper reality of the world in which we live in our ordinary experiences. We are carried beyond ourselves to find ourselves. I can see no psychological ground for such properties of an experience save that, somehow, the work of art operates to deepen and to raise to great clarity that sense of an enveloping undefined whole that accompanies every normal experience. This whole is then felt as an expansion of ourselves. For only one frustrated in a particular object of desire upon which he has staked himself, like Macbeth, finds that life is a tale told by an idiot, full of sound and fury, signifying nothing. Where egotism is not made the measure of reality and value, we are citizens of this vast world beyond ourselves, and any intense realization of its presence with and in us brings a peculiarly satisfying sense of unity in itself and with ourselves.[48]

Once man rids himself of the conception of some power beyond nature, he will be in a position to develop this sense of natural piety, which will make him aware of his continuities with his fellow man, and with his natural environment, and of the possibilities inherent in these continuities for the enrichment of human life.

Natural piety need not be a fatalistic acceptance of whatever happens in nature, nor need it be a romanticized conception of nature.

> Nature may not be worshipped as divine even in the sense of the intellectual love of Spinoza. But nature, including humanity, with all its defects and imperfections, may evoke heartfelt piety as the source of ideals, of possibilities, of aspiration in their behalf, and as the eventual abode of all attained goods and excellencies.[49]

It rests upon man's realization that he is a part of the whole of nature and upon his recognition that his possession of intelligence and purpose gives him the power to try to work with natural conditions in order to make them more consonant with what is humanly good.[50]

Before proceeding further into the exploration of the sense of wholeness and continuity that marks the religious perspective, it might be well to consider the factors within nature that ground this perspective. Dewey acknowledges that when he speaks of the wholeness of the Universe and of the self, he is not speaking of any existent reality that is given to man in observation. This whole-

---

[48] John Dewey, *Art as Experience* (New York: Capricorn Books, 1958, originally published 1934), p. 195.

[49] See footnote 73, Chap. V, p. 306.

[50] See footnote 26, pp. 25-26.

ness is an ideal, not a reality already accomplished. The whole self and the "Universe (as a name for the totality of conditions with which the self is connected)," are imaginative ideals, projections of the human imagination.[51] This position does not necessarily reduce the wholeness of the self and of the Universe to a purely fanciful status, mere daydreams.

The ideal projections of the imagination have a naturalistic basis. The imagination is able to grasp the possibilities for action and thought given in the existential situation, possibilities that are not yet realized, and to have them function as motivating ideals in the life of man.

> There are values, goods, actually realized upon a natural basis—the goods of human association, of art and knowledge. The idealizing imagination seizes upon the most precious things found in the climacteric moments of experience and projects them. We need no external criterion and guarantee for their goodness. They are had, they exist as good, and out of them we frame our ideal ends.[52]

It is only those, described in the previous section as lacking moral faith, who want to find these ideals already existent in some omnipotent reality. Against such people, Dewey points out that the claim, which an ideal exercises over human conduct, is precisely the claim of an ideal and not of a fact.[53] It is the values expressed and captured in the ideals that place a demand on man to work for their realization.

Every attempt to bring a better situation into existence is motivated by faith in possibilities, not by an adherence to what is given as actual. The motivating power of such faith is not a cognitive assurance that the ideals being worked for will necessarily come into existence. A man may realize that the final outcome of his endeavors rests with factors beyond his control. However, the intrinsic value of the ideal leads him to try to mold those conditions that are in his control so that they will work for the realization of the ideal.[54] This faith in ideals becomes specifically religious when it involves the wholehearted, complete, and persistent commitment of the self to ends that are so inclusive that they serve to unify the self in his relations to the Universe grasped as an ideal whole.[55]

Dewey points out that the element of natural piety in his conception of religious faith also serves to call man's attention to the unity that binds men together, thus compensating for the disruptive influence introduced into the life of man by Christianity. Historic Christianity has emphasized the separation between the saved and the lost, the sheep and the goats. The talk about the brotherhood of man has often been nothing more than mere lip service. Moreover, even when the common brotherhood of mankind was mentioned, there

[51] *Ibid.*, p. 19.
[52] *Ibid.*, p. 48.
[53] *Ibid.*, p. 21.
[54] *Ibid.*, p. 23.
[55] *Ibid.*, pp. 22–23, also p. 33.

was always involved in this notion of community a separation between those who accepted a belief in the supernatural and those who did not, with the latter being regarded as "only potential brothers, still requiring adoption into the family."[56] The naturalist stressing the common matrix of man in nature heightens man's sense of community with his fellow man by making him aware that all are "in the same boat traversing the same turbulent ocean."[57] Dewey sees in this fact a matter whose potential religious significance is infinite.[58]

This stress on the community of man as found in nature gives concrete expression to the naturalistic ideal. For this ideal gives the individual man a sense of sharing in a humanity that reaches back to a remote past and whose roots are deeply embedded in nature. Man comes to see that the things that he now holds as most dear to him have come to him as a legacy from his fellow man's past dealings with nature. It is because man is a part of the human community that he is now able to share in the values and goods that were mined by the men of the past. Our task and responsibility is to conserve, pass on, rectify, and expand the heritage that we have received so that those who come after us will find these values more securely and solidly grounded in the actual state of affairs and so that they will be more widely and more fully shared by those who follow us than they were in our own time.[59]

Dewey's conception of the way in which this naturalistic frame of reference will influence man's life is seen very clearly in the following statement:

> From the standpoint of its *definite* aim any act is petty in comparison with the totality of natural events. What is accomplished directly as the outcome of a turn which our action gives the course of events is infinitesimal in comparison with their total sweep. Only an illusion of conceit persuades us that cosmic difference hangs upon even our wisest and most strenuous effort. Yet discontent with this limitation is as unreasonable as relying upon an illusion of external importance to keep ourselves going. In a genuine sense every act is already possessed of infinite import. This little part of the scheme of affairs which is modifiable by our efforts is continuous with the rest of the world. The boundaries of our garden plot join it to the world of our neighbor's and of our neighbors' neighbors. That small effort which we can put forth is in turn connected with an infinity of events that sustain and support it. The consciousness of this encompassing infinity of connections is ideal. When a sense of the infinite reach of an act physically occurring in a small point of space and occupying a petty instant of time comes home to us, the *meaning* of a present act is seen to be vast, immeasurable, unthinkable. This ideal is not a goal to be attained. It is a significance to be felt, appreciated. Though consciousness of it cannot become intellectualized (identified in objects of a distinct character) yet emotional appreciation of it is won only by those willing to think.[60]

[56] *Ibid.*, p. 84.
[57] *Ibid.*
[58] *Ibid.*
[59] *Ibid.*, p. 87.
[60] John Dewey, *Human Nature and Conduct: An Introduction to Social Psychology* (New York: Random House, 1930), pp. 262–263.

It is important to note that the ideal of a naturalistic human community gives meaning to an act as it is occurring *here and now*. Dewey explicitly opposes a position that sees an act as being significant *only in its* relationship to the future and thus evacuates the act as presently occurring of any intrinsic significance.

To place the religious significance outside the act itself is to place man in a situation in which the activities, which he is presently performing, are always seen as necessary evils that he must endure in order to achieve that harmony and unity of self and nature that characterizes religious experience. Dewey's naturalistic humanism is directed toward expanding man's consciousness and appreciation of the present activities in which he is involved so that these activities themselves are seen as possessing a meaning that is "seen to be vast, immeasurable." Our experience is truly religious "in so far as in the midst of effort to foresee and regulate future objects we are sustained and expanded in feebleness and failure by the sense of an enveloping whole."[61] Thus, man's religious experiences do reach out toward the future, but in such a way as to include a sense of wholeness and unity in man's present efforts. It is "peace in action not after," that the ideal contributes to man's undertakings.[62]

The naturalistic humanist can provide man with a basis for this peace in action by showing him the naturalistic roots of such peace. We are now in a position to appreciate the full force of Dewey's contention that the naturalistic grounding of values in man in nature provides a firmer foundation for these values than any foundation alleged to exist outside the natural order. The naturalist works at the task of securing and developing these values more whole-heartedly and with a greater sense of fulfillment than does the supernaturalist, because he is able to appreciate the intrinsic religious significance of this task, whereas the supernaturalist, lacking natural piety, finds the task to be something of a chore, at best, in so far as it requires any sort of involvement in natural social affairs.

4. DEWEY ON THE PLACE OF "GOD" IN HUMAN ENDEAVORS

Dewey's rejection of the supernatural as a foundation for moral values does not lead him to conclude that a conception of God has absolutely no role to play in man's life. Although he is not unaware of the possibility that his use of the term *God* may give his position a supernaturalistic tone, which he rejects, Dewey is hesitant to reject its use out of hand. The purpose of this section is to present his meaning for the term, and, perhaps more importantly, to see the reasons that he advances for the retention of the word *God* in a naturalistic philosophy. A question, which has been considered earlier in this chapter, is significant to the

[61] *Ibid.*, p. 264.
[62] *Ibid.*

issue of what one means by God. If one takes the view that ideals are of value because they point to an already existent realm of being in which these ideals are existentially given, then the conception of God refers to a particular being. However, if one takes Dewey's position that ideals are valuable because of the inherent values which they contain, although these values may not as yet be actually existent, the conception of God will denote the unity of all ideals that move men to action.[63] This latter conception does not make God a being existing in some realm transcending nature. God is the ideals as unified that move men to act.

Expanding on this conception, Dewey points out that the ideals that motivate men are not mere fantasies. They have some roots in nature. There are natural and social forces that generate and ground them. Furthermore, these ideals, which exist in a somewhat inchoate and disconnected form in nature, take on a unity, coherence, and solidity through actions undertaken in their behalf. Dewey would give the name *God* to this "active" relationship between the ideals and the natural order as actual, which contains both the soil for the realization of these ideals and the agents, men, who can cultivate this soil so that the ideals can become more firmly rooted in the actual course of nature.

Dewey justifies this use of the term *God* on the grounds that the relationship, which is meant by the term, is a reality and that there is need to focus all of man's resources on this relationship. For in addition to the factors in nature that can foster and contribute to the realization of ideals, there are other factors present in nature that threaten their realization.

> In a distracted age, the need for such an idea [an idea of the union of ideal ends and the actual conditions of nature] is urgent. It can unify interests and energies now dispersed; it can direct action and generate the heat of emotion and the light of intelligence. Whether one gives the name 'God' to this union, operative in thought and action, is a matter for individual decision. But the *function* of such a working union of the ideal and actual seems to be identical with the force that has in fact been attached to the conception of God in all the religions that have a spiritual content; and a clear idea of that function seems to be urgently needed at the present time.[64]

Dewey's reluctance to give up the use of the word *God* seems to be based on a recognition of the need to appeal to the whole man—to man as an emotional as well as a rational being—if man is to engage wholeheartedly in the process of so reconstructing his natural world that human ideals will be more easily, more completely, and more universally realized and developed. Such a reconstruction requires an emotional, as well as an intellectual, point of focus.

There is a further value that Dewey sees in using the word *God* to refer to the union of the ideal with the actual. Such use will serve to foster that natural

[63] See footnote 26, pp. 41–42.
[64] *Ibid.*, pp. 51–52.

piety that we saw earlier was lost sight of by both militant atheism and supernaturalism. Man will come to see his connection with and dependence on the
enveloping whole, which the imagination presents as a universe, in such a way
that he is protected from the sense of isolation from the world and the feeling
of despair or meaningless and unproductive defiance that follows such a sense.[65]

5. OPEN AND CLOSED NATURALISM:
THE COMMON MORAL GROUND

The purpose of this section is to emphasize the areas of agreement existing
between what I have termed "closed," and "open" ethical naturalisms. The question, which we saw Socrates raise in Chapter I, provides a good starting point for
this section: "The point which I should first wish to understand is whether the
pious or holy is beloved by the gods because it is holy, or holy because it is beloved of the gods."[66] Whatever may be the case with the gods, the ethical naturalist holds that the cognitive basis for distinguishing between morally good and
morally evil acts cannot be grounded in any prior philosophical knowledge of the
existence and nature of God.

My defense of this position is grounded in two points. First, there is an ethical
intelligibility involved in man's dealings with the finite beings of his direct experience. The proof for this point is to be seen in the preceding chapters of this
book, especially beginning with Chapter IV through Chapter VIII. Secondly, the
position is grounded in the view that the philosophical knowledge of the existence and nature of God, which man may be able to achieve, is much too limited
to serve as a standard of morality. Man's philosophical knowledge of the existence
of God must be indirect, i.e. achieved through his reflections on the finite beings
found in his direct experience.[67] To maintain that a philosophical knowledge of
God can function as a standard of morality is to imply that man possesses a more
complete, direct, and intimate knowledge of God than he possesses of the distinction between moral good and evil, because this position would make the
knowledge of God a premise from which one could draw moral distinctions.
Thus, if the knowledge of God were advanced as an alternative to the standard
presented in this book, it would be necessary to show that man has a more
intimate knowledge of God than he has of himself.

It would be possible to challenge this position by holding that man's knowledge of God is not achieved indirectly through his knowledge of finite beings,
but is direct and immediate. If this view could be validated, the criticism ad-

---

[65] *Ibid.*, pp. 52–53.

[66] See footnote 11, Chap. I, p. 391.

[67] I am willing to allow that the existence of God may be open to philosophical proof.
For an excellent historical survey of the various views taken with respect to this issue in
the Western philosophical tradition, Nicholas Cusanus to the present, see James Collins,
God in Modern Philosophy (Chicago: Henry Regnery Co., 1959).

vanced in this section against the possibility of using the knowledge of God as a moral norm would collapse. However, I see no way of validating it in view of the fact that man's knowledge is grounded in his experience of finite beings and of the values that are implicated in his relations to these beings.

Perhaps those who center their lives around doing what God wants see the criticism advanced in this section as contradicting their own moral experience. Two points can be made with respect to this issue. First, if such people would examine their reasoning processes, they would discover that in many cases they characterize a certain act as being in accord with God's will because they have seen the act to be moral. In short, it is often the case that the moral goodness of an act functions as the premise for the conclusion that God wants one to perform an act rather than a knowledge of God's will functioning as the premise for the conclusion that the act is morally good. Thus, in these cases, it is only because one possesses some way of judging the morality of an act that is distinct from God's will that he can know whether an act is moral and therefore in keeping with what God wills.

Secondly, I have denied only that a knowledge of God grounded in man's reflections on his experience could function as a standard of morality. Those who maintain that the Bible or a certain Church is the Word of God may build their lives around these. For example, they may maintain that adultery is wrong because it is condemned by God, presenting passages from the Bible as evidence that God has condemned this type of act. As far as the work of this book is concerned, the role of the Bible or of a Church as moral teachers is an open question. However, two observations may be in order with respect to this matter. Those who would condemn out of hand reliance on the Bible or a Church as sources of moral instruction should recall that no man has the ability or the time to become his own expert on every facet of human life. There are times when the most intelligent thing a man can do is to follow the advice of those whom he trusts. This does not mean that the man with the ability and time for reflection on moral issues should rely on a Church or the Bible out of an intellectual laziness.

This brings us to our second point. Those whose task it is to present the moral outlook of a Church or of what they find in the Bible must be careful to avoid an excessively "positivistic" approach to moral issues. Such an approach would consist in defending a moral stand by simply pointing to the bare fact that a Church has said that X is immoral, with no attempt being made to point to the factors in human experience that might serve to give this position some sort of experiential validation. I am rather certain that it was this sort of approach that Dewey had in mind when he said that a naturalistic approach to moral values would render these values more secure than a supernaturalistic approach. For if the supernaturalist makes no attempt to show the relevance of his moral judgments to man's life, but takes his stand on authority alone, these judgments will lose their power over men in the long run.

To say that a moral judgment is true simply because a Church says it is so places the judgment outside the realm of dialogue and reflection. Far from safe-guarding the judgment, this practice contributes to reducing it to a meaningless and empty exhortation. The position taken up to this point is clearly in agreement with Dewey's criticism of the possibility of using a conception of God as man's Ultimate End as a cognitive principle that would help man distinguish between moral good and moral evil.

The second area of agreement between open and closed naturalism is found in the account of moral obligation given in Chapter IV. It will be recalled that I maintained that moral obligation is not something imposed upon man by some force or power external to him, but arises out of the use of his own rational resources. This position places the naturalism developed in this book in opposition to the view that moral obligation can be accounted for only by the existence of a supreme lawgiver who is God. Such a view amounts to a denial that man is a being capable of morality. What difference is there between saying that obligation is grounded only in the State or in God. I see no difference between the man who says that the *only* reason I ought not do X is that the State prohibits it, and the man who says that the *only reason* I ought not do Y is that God prohibits it. So long as a man sees his obligations only as duties imposed upon him by another, whether this other be the State or God, he is acting in a purely legalistic order.

To say that a man is unable to obligate himself and that obligation is meaningful only if it is grounded in some source external to the man obligated is to say that man can act only within a legalistic sphere. For the essence of legalism is to perform an act simply because someone in authority has said that the act ought to be performed. A person is said to act legalistically when the only answer that he gives to the question, "Why do you think that you ought to perform this act?" is, "Because X said I ought to." Anyone taking the position that the only basis for moral obligation is the existence of God as a supreme lawgiver is saying that the only reason that a man can advance for saying that it is his duty not to commit adultery is that God forbids it. This position does not account for moral obligation, but reduces it to a purely legal obligation.

Moreover, those who would substitute God for the naturalistic grounding of moral obligation presented in Chapter IV are taking a position that implies that man can stand only in a purely legalistic relationship to God. Man's response to God will be limited to a response to Him as Power, and Power alone. Unless man possesses the resources whereby he acknowledges the claims and obligations imposed upon him by possibilities, persons, or ideals precisely in so far as any of these is good, he cannot be said to respond to what he may see as the goodness and love of God in a moral way, i.e. in a way in which God's claim on man is seen to lie not in his power, but in his goodness and love. Once it is granted that man is able to respond to ideal goods and possibilities as exercising a claim over him simply because they are goods, the realization of which bring out what is best in him, man can be acknowledged to respond to God as Good and not simply as Power. Hence, I do not see that this account of moral obligation impoverishes man's relationship to God; indeed, it lays the groundwork for a deeper relationship than could be established by making God alone the basis of moral obligation.

Thus, there is no disagreement between the position taken in this book and Dewey's naturalism in so far as both find the cognitive resources for a norm of morality and for moral obligation in man's interaction with the finite beings of his experience. However, the acceptance of these positions does not necessarily entail the conclusion that the existence of the theistic Personal God is incompatible with man's moral existence. The justification of this position requires an evaluation of Dewey's case against supernaturalism and a consideration of the positive ethical significance of theism. The treatment of these points will be taken up in the two sections that follow.

6. CRITIQUE OF DEWEY'S CASE AGAINST SUPERNATURALISM

The purpose of this section is to evaluate Dewey's criticism of the role of supernaturalism in man's moral life. An admonishment given by John Stuart Mill to the critics of utilitarianism provides a good starting point for this section. Mill, who shares with Dewey a distrust of supernaturalism, makes the following point against those who base their criticism of utilitarianism on what he considers to be the weakest expressions of the position.

> No one is entitled to found an argument against a principle upon the faults or blunders of a particular writer who professed to build his system upon it, without taking notice that the principle may be understood differently, and has in fact been understood differently by other writers. What would be thought of an assailant of Christianity, who should judge of its truth or beneficial tendency from the views taken of it by the Jesuits, or by the Shakers? A doctrine is not judged at all until it is judged in its best form. The principle of utility may be viewed in as many different lights as every other rule or principle may. If it be liable to mischievous misinterpretations, this is true of all very general, and therefore of all first, principles.[68]

Without becoming involved in Mill's evaluation of the Jesuits or Shakers as representatives of Christianity, it must be admitted that Mill has emphasized a point worth remembering in the evaluation of any position. Mill's statement is especially pertinent to the work of this section because the controversy among naturalists and those whom Dewey terms supernaturalists has often been marred by a tendency of the defender of one of these positions to take the worst possible statement of the opposing position as representative of that position.

It is indeed very easy to condemn naturalistic ideals out of hand by taking the

[68] See footnote 3, Chap. IV, p. 124.

activities of such men as Stalin and Mao Tse-Tung as representing these ideals. However, a naturalist in the Deweyan tradition can point out that what these men did represents a perversion of the naturalistic ideal. This possible response indicates that one must move beyond the cataloguing of atrocities committed by those who have claimed to represent a naturalistic ideal. It is necessary to consider this ideal itself, as it is presented by one who, we think, presents it in its strongest and best light. An evaluation of the ideal will ask such questions as whether it is in conformity with the character of human existence, whether it does full justice to the richness of this existence, whether it is helpful to man in his day-to-day living, and finally whether it does involve certain necessary implications that, if carried out in practice, would be destructive of some human good.

Of course, what is good for the goose is good for the gander. The same ground rules should apply to the naturalist's evaluation of the supernaturalist's ideal. He also must be aware of the possibility that the atrocities committed in the name of the supernatural are perversions and abuses of this ideal. He also must take the responsibility of trying to discover the strongest and best expression of the supernaturalist's ideal before condemning it as sapping man of his drive to make a better and more humane world. Although Dewey has said that the naturalist would not dare engage in the type of intellectual carelessness that he found in the supernaturalist's camp, I am not certain that his treatment of supernaturalism in *A Common Faith* bears him out on this point.[69]

For example, one of his major criticisms of supernaturalism is that it so emphasizes man's dependence on the supernatural that it tends to blind man to the natural powers that are within his grasp and that can be used to better man's situation in nature. However, toward the very end of the book, he merely mentions in passing that "the old-fashioned" belief that man must assume the responsibility of making God's will prevail on earth is logically and practically more acceptable than the supernaturalism that he has criticized.[70] No matter how old-fashioned this belief may be, it certainly seems to represent a type of supernaturalism that does not fit into the supernaturalistic mold that Dewey criticizes throughout the book. It would seem that a careful intellectual critique of the influence of belief in the supernatural on man's moral endeavors ought not to pass over such a conception of the supernatural, especially when this conception would appear to contradict the basis of one's criticism.

Admittedly, there is a great deal of difficulty in trying to decide on which expression of supernaturalism one is going to focus his attention. Dewey does a fine job in pointing out this difficulty when he emphasizes the vast differences to be found in the conceptions of the supernatural, in the rites and cults, and in the moral perspectives that have characterized various religions in different times and different places. These differences lead Dewey to conclude that the attempt

[69] For Dewey's statement see footnote 35, p. 5.
[70] See footnote 26, p. 79.

to define religion in general reduces religion to such a lowest common denominator that the definition becomes almost meaningless.[71] One of the weaknesses of Dewey's criticism of the moral significance of supernaturalism is that much of his case is built on this lowest common denominator conception of the supernatural as something that is powerful and unseen.

More specifically, I maintain that Dewey's charge of the moral poverty of supernaturalism is not valid with respect to the Judeo-Christian conception of God. The justification of this criticism will require that I refer to certain passages in the Bible. I do this with some hesitation because this procedure opens one to the charge of confusing theology with philosophy. However, I think that William James's approach to religion in his *Varieties of Religious Experience* was basically sound in so far as he recognized the need to study the writings of those representing religious points of view if one is to evaluate these points of view. I hope to show that there is a good deal of textual evidence in the Bible to show that the Judeo-Christian world-view does not conform to Dewey's characterization of religions. I shall also point to positions taken by writers in this tradition that do not fit this characterization. Because Dewey's criticism has touched on many points, it will be necessary to subdivide this section under the following headings: (a) The "World," (b) Social Man, (c) The Role of Human Intelligence, (d) Man in Nature, and (e) Institutionalized Christianity.

(a) *The "World."* Considered from the point of view of moral philosophy, one of Dewey's most serious charges against supernaturalism is that it detracts from man's commitment to the natural order, and that it depreciates natural values. There are certainly passages in the Bible that would seem to justify this criticism. For example, in Matthew 16:26, we are asked, "What does it profit a man, if he gains the whole world, but suffer the loss of his own soul?"[72] However, before drawing conclusions from texts of this kind, it will be necessary to note that some of the texts throughout the Bible complicate the issue. For example, in the book of Genesis, God is said to have looked upon his work and seen that it was good.[73]

In the book of Isaias, the people of God are told that the Lord is not satisfied with sacrifice alone, they must "relieve the oppressed, judge for the fatherless, defend the widow."[74] The same book issues a warning to those who make unjust laws, who oppress the poor, and who take advantage of widows.[75] Turning to the New Testament, the same emphasis on involvement in the world is found. Perhaps, the most striking call to such involvement is seen in Christ's picture of the last judgment in which those who have fed the hungry, clothed the naked, cared for the stranger, visited the sick are welcomed into the Kingdom of Heaven. There is no unbridgable gap drawn here between the natural and the

[71] *Ibid.,* pp. 1–5.
[72] See also Luke 9:25.
[73] Genesis 1:25, 31.
[74] Isaias 1:17.
[75] Isaias 10:1–2.

supernatural.[76] The parable of the talents also is a call to make use of the resources that a man possesses. That man is condemned who out of fear of his master wrapped his talent in a napkin in order to retain what he had. Those who tried to build on what was given to them are praised.[77] The Pharisees are taken to task for failing to do justice in their concern with performing the proper sacrifices.[78]

If we take the Bible as representative of a supernaturalist position, it would appear that it is involved in a contradiction with respect to the issue of involvement in the world. The notion that man must reject the world has certainly been a part of the Judeo-Christian tradition, but it is equally clear that there has been a strong emphasis on becoming involved in this world so as to make it a more just and moral order. Once again, John Stuart Mill, who is certainly no supernaturalist, may help clarify the issue. Mill meets the criticism that utilitarianism is to be rejected because it is grounded in a worldly standard by distinguishing two senses of worldly.

He points out that the description *worldly* is often used in a pejorative sense to refer to an excessive concern with wealth, power, or social position. However, the word need not necessarily carry this pejorative sense. It may refer simply to that which occurs in the world. Mill states that the utilitarian does judge the morality of acts in terms of their worldly consequences, with worldly taken in this second sense. Thus, to save a man from death, to heal the sick, to clothe the naked, to shelter the homeless—all these are acts that involve worldly consequences. Mill rightly states that both the utilitarian ethician, who may or may not be Christian, and the specifically Christian ethician agree in rejecting a worldly ethics understood in the first sense, and in accepting the type of worldly ethics understood in the second sense.[79]

Mill's description of the ambiguity connected with such words as the *world* and *worldly* indicates that one should be rather careful in interpreting texts that call man to give up things of the "world." It is possible that such advice does not mean a wholesale surrender of the natural order. The texts quoted above which clearly call for man's involvement in the world indicate that the Judeo-Christian message does not advise such a wholesale rejection. The warning that there is no profit in gaining the whole world at the expense of losing one's soul can be interpreted as calling man's attention to the possibility that he may become so engrossed in his quest for fame, honor, or fortune that he may reduce his humanity to the status of a mere means for the attainment of these things.

[76] Matthew 25:34–40.
[77] Luke 19:12–26.
[78] Luke 11:42. Add to these statements, the admonition to let one's light shine before the world so that his good works might be known and call others to give glory to God. Matthew 5:14–16.
[79] See footnote 3, Chap. IV, pp. 151–153. As Mill sees matters, the only difference between his utilitarianism and Christianity on this issue is that the latter holds that an act cannot be meritorious unless it is done from a motive that is concerned with the Supreme Being.

It might be argued that the Bible is much too complex a document from which to take selected texts that seem to invalidate the view that supernaturalism necessarily involves a denial of natural values. However, it is not the Bible alone that provides evidence that Dewey's characterization of supernaturalism does not apply to the Judeo-Christian message. For example, Thomas Merton quotes Saint John Chrysostom, a Church Father of the fourth century, to the effect that fasting, sleeping on the ground, weeping are meaningless, if one is of no use to another person, and that one must give alms if he is to enter the Kingdom of Heaven.[80]

Turning to a more accessible source, Thomas Aquinas sees no incompatibility between his belief in God and the study of nature, a position that does not fit Dewey's description of the supernaturalist, who is so concerned with the supernatural order that he does not engage in a wholehearted investigation of the natural order. Aquinas sees the study of nature as a way in which man may come to admire God's wisdom and power, and to appreciate His goodness. In opposition to the view that nature is wholly depraved, he points out that the beauty, delightfulness, and goodness of nature provide man with a way to God, the source of all goodness.[81] Perhaps, what is as important as Aquinas' words is the attitude which underlies them. Whereas Dewey has depicted the supernaturalist as viewing nature and supernature as opposites so that concern with one is seen as necessarily involving a denial of the other, Aquinas' words convey the idea of an integration of the two, of their compatibility. He does not think that the goodness of God is to be established only by denying the beauty and goodness found in nature.

(b) *Social Man.* Dewey has also charged that historic Christianity's emphasis on the separation between the saved and the lost, the sheep and the goats has blinded man to his unity with his fellow man. Whatever may be the case with historic Christianity, the Christian ideal is rather clearly directed to making man aware of his brotherhood with his fellow man. Certainly the parable of the good samaritan and the call to love one's enemies cannot be legitimately interpreted as blinding man to his unity with his fellow man.[82] Moreover, the major thrust of the parables of the lost sheep, of the prodigal son, and of the lost coin is to make man aware of establishing a single community among men. The prodigal son is to be accepted into the community wholeheartedly and joyously, not grudgingly and with an "I-told-you-so" attitude.[83] There is an element of separation of the sheep and the goats in Christianity, but it is clear that this separation is to be done by God and not by man. The task of man on earth is to work for the realization of an integrated human community under God.

[80] Thomas Merton, *Life and Holiness* (New York: Image Books, 1964), p. 15.

[81] *ScG* II, 2; see footnote 9, Chap. II, Bk. II, pp. 30–32.

[82] For the good Samaritan parable see Luke 10:30–37. For the command to love your enemies see Luke 6:27–38.

[83] For the parable of the lost sheep see Luke 15:3–7, the lost coin, Luke 15:8–10, and the prodigal son Luke 15:11–32.

Whereas Dewey sees all supernaturalism as setting up an opposition between man's social relations and the supernatural order, Aquinas maintains that man needs his fellow man if he is to achieve his union with God. He points out that men can be of mutual assistance in the attaining of knowledge and truth and that man needs his fellow man if he is to grow in knowledge and love.[84] He also finds biblical support for this position, quoting from the book of Proverbs, and from Ecclesiastes. "As iron sharpens iron, so man sharpens his fellow man."[85] "Two are better than one. . . . If one falls, the other will lift up his companion. Woe to the solitary man. For if he should fail he has no one to lift him up. So also, if two sleep together, they keep each other warm. How can one alone keep warm? Where a lone man may be overcome, two together can resist. A three-ply cord is not easily broken."[86] It is difficult to see how the charge that Christianity has denigrated the social relations among men can be substantiated in the face of these texts.

After stating that supernaturalism leads man to ignore and pass over the values inherent in such human relations as those existing among friends, husbands and wives, parents and children, and neighbors, Dewey notes that the use of such terms as *Father* and *Fellowship* have projected the values inherent in these natural relations into a supernatural realm for safekeeping. However, I find that this latter point is open to another interpretation. Christianity may have incorporated these values in its beliefs, because it recognized their importance to the religious life of man. Not accepting the dualism between the natural and the supernatural, which Dewey attributes to religions, Christianity, far from passing over the values of natural associations, may have recognized the values inherent in these associations—values that are not threats to man's relationship to God, but that are resources available to man in his journey to God.

(c) *The Role of Human Intelligence*. This defense of the social awareness of a certain type of supernaturalism is not adequate to meet a principle that may underlie Dewey's criticism. This aspect of Dewey's criticism may be grounded in his view that supernaturalism tends to lead man to ignore the value of intelligence as a tool to explore man's world. He seems to connect the dogmatism of supernaturalism with its socially divisive character. "The association of religion with the *supernatural* tends by its own nature to breed the dogmatic and the divisive spirit."[87] The problem before us is to consider the evidence which Dewey offers for this contention.

The appeal that he makes to "what seems to be almost a common place of history," cannot of itself validate the position.[88] It must be acknowledged that

---

[84] ScG III, 128; see footnote 9, Chap. II, Bk. III, Part II, pp. 159–160.

[85] Proverbs 27:17.

[86] Ecclesiastes 4:9–12. See also Ecclesiasticus 6:14–16.

[87] John Dewey, "Experience, Knowledge and Value: A Rejoinder," *The Philosophy of John Dewey*, ed. by Paul Arthur Schilpp (New York: Tudor Publishing Company, second ed., 1951), p. 595.

[88] *Ibid.*

there have been, and there are at present, dogmatic supernaturalists, just as there are dogmatic naturalists, e.g., the communists. However, such evidence does not justify the view that the "association of religion with the *supernatural* tends *by its own nature* [italics mine] to breed the dogmatic and the divisive spirit." The only way that this could be established on historical grounds is through a complete and exhaustive induction showing that all believers in the supernatural are dogmatic, a requirement that is impossible for man to fulfill. Even if the requirement were met, it would prove only that Dewey's position was true as regards past associations between religion and the supernatural, and not that it must necessarily be true in the future. Unless this latter point is established, the view that the association of religion with the supernatural tends by its own nature to breed the dogmatic and the divisive spirit is not sustained.

Dewey does present a stronger argument to justify his criticism. Belief in the supernatural is seen as limiting man's access to truth to certain specified roads or channels. Many religionists are thus depicted as seeing any faith in human intelligence's ability to push back the forest of human ignorance as a threat to their fixed supernaturalistic beliefs. Whereas the supernaturalist is committed to the view that there is only one access to truth, the naturalist places his faith in what can be achieved by continuous and rigorous inquiry.[89] Because the supernaturalist is committed to dogmas that do not permit him to engage wholeheartedly in cooperative, reflective inquiry, it is open to the charge of generating a divisive spirit.

There is evidence to show that Dewey's characterization of the supernaturalist as lacking faith in human intelligence does not apply to the supernaturalism of the Judeo-Christian tradition. For example, Alfred North Whitehead sees the medieval conception of God as stimulating rational inquiry. He maintains that the medieval period's greatest contribution to the formation of the scientific enterprise was "the inexpugnable belief that every detailed occurrence can be correlated with its antecedents in a perfectly definite manner, exemplifying general principles."[90] He sees this belief as that factor which provides man with the hope and motivation necessary to undertake the scientific quest. The scientist is motivated by the strong conviction that "there is a secret, a secret that can be unveiled."[91] Whitehead finds the basis for the existence of this conviction in the European mind in the medieval conception of God.

> When we compare this tone of thought in Europe with the attitude of other civilisations when left to themselves, there seems but one source for its origin. It must come from the medieval insistence on the rationality of God, conceived as with the personal energy of Jehovah and with the rationality of a Greek philosopher. Every detail was supervised and ordered: the search into nature could only result in the vindication of the faith in rationality. Remember that I am not talking of

[89] See footnote 26, p. 26. See also pp. 29, 32.
[90] See footnote 10, Chap. V, p. 12.
[91] *Ibid.*

the explicit beliefs of a few individuals. What I mean is the impress on the European mind arising from the unquestioned faith of centuries. By this I mean the instinctive tone of thought and not a mere creed of words. In Asia, the conceptions of God were of a being who was either too arbitrary or too impersonal for such ideas to have much effect on instinctive habits of mind. Any definite occurrence might be due to the fiat of an irrational despot, or might issue from some impersonal, inscrutable origin of things. There was not the same confidence as in the intelligible rationality of a personal being. I am not arguing that the European trust in the scrutability of nature was logically justified even by its own theology. My only point is to understand how it arose. My explanation is that the faith in the possibility of sciences, generated antecedently to the development of modern scientific theory, is an unconscious derivative from medieval theology.[92]

One need not accept Whitehead's views on Asia to see the strength of his case with respect to the influence of the medieval conception of God on the development of science. Although Whitehead does not want to say that the trust in the scrutability of nature was logically justified by medieval theology, it seems to me that one can safely point out against Dewey's position, that a person is not acting consistently with his belief in an intelligent, personal God, if he refuses to use his own intellectual resources to explore the mysteries of God's world.

A. C. Crombie's massive study of the development of science in the West from the fifth to the seventeenth century presents a good deal of specific evidence, which sustains Whitehead's observation and which indicates that Christians found their belief in God to be compatible with a reflected inquiry into nature. For example, Adelard of Bath, a scholar and cleric of the twelfth century, when asked if it would not be better to account for all operations of the universe by attributing them to God is quoted as giving the following response: "I do not detract from God. Everything that is, is from him and because of him. But [nature] is not confused and without system and so far as human knowledge has progressed it should be given a hearing. Only when it fails utterly should there be recourse to God."[93] Adelard is also quoted as saying that he was unable to discuss issues with those who were "led in a halter [by past writers] . . . Those who are now called authorities reached that position first by the exercise of reason. . . . Wherefore, if you want to hear anything more from me, give and take reason."[94] These are not the words of a man whose beliefs in a supernatural God have led to a lack of faith in the use of intelligence.

Moreover, the work of Thomas Aquinas shows a very healthy faith in the work of intelligence. He points out that the study of nature is not restricted to the theologian and that it is the task of the philosopher to study nature in terms of natural causes. With respect to the question of the morality of fornication, Aquinas maintains that to say that such activity is immoral because it injures

---

[92] *Ibid.*, pp. 12–13.

[93] A. C. Crombie, *Medieval and Early Modern Science: Science in the Middle Ages, V–XII Centuries*, Vol. I (Garden City, New York: Doubleday Anchor Books, 1959), p. 26.

[94] *Ibid.*, pp. 26–27.

God does not appear to be an adequate explanation, because man offends God only by doing something contrary to his own good.[95] Perhaps, more to the point, it should be noted that Aquinas is well aware of the distinction between a theological explanation and an explanation in moral philosophy. He states that the moral philosopher considers sin as that which is contrary to reason, whereas the moral theologian considers it as an offense against God.[96] He also shows an awareness of the fact that an appeal to authority cannot do the work of reason. Thus, he states that if a teacher resolves an issue by an appeal to authority alone, the student will have gained information about the authority, but he has not acquired a scientific grasp of the issue, and is thus left empty-handed so far as science or wisdom is concerned.[97]

Aquinas is very explicit in stating that things prescribed by the divine law are good not simply because they are so prescribed, but also because they are suitable to advancing the human good. Acts that are naturally suitable to man are good in themselves, and not good simply because they have been prescribed by the divine law.[98] Aquinas also takes the position that virtue is a good in itself and that to depart from virtue is evil in itself.[99] One may agree or disagree with Aquinas' views on the morality of fornication, adultery, suicide, lying, birth control, and other matters.[100] However, if one takes the time to examine the arguments, he will find that Aquinas does try to show the disorientation that these acts introduce into man's relationships with his world and/or his fellow man. This procedure does not of itself automatically make the arguments rationally sound, but it does show a concern with the influence of certain activities on man's situation in the world, and a willingness to use intelligence to explore this situation—a concern and a willingness that Dewey maintains is not and cannot be present in a supernaturalist's position.

In more recent times such men as the Protestant theologian H. Richard Niebuhr and the Jesuit archeologist, theologian Pierre Teilhard de Chardin have also stressed the Christian's commitment to a wholehearted probing of man's world. Niebuhr remarks,

Any failure of Christians to develop a scientific knowledge of the world is not an indication of their loyalty to the revealed God but of their unbelief. . . . Re-

[95] ScG III, 122; see footnote 9, Chap. II, Bk. III, Part II, p. 143.

[96] S.T. I–II, Q. 71, a.6, ad.5; see footnote 36, Chap. I, Vol. II, p. 568.

[97] Quodlibet IV, a.18. The text cited here was found in M. D. Chenu, Toward Understanding Saint Thomas, trans. with authorized corrections and bibliographical additions by A. M. Dandry and D. Hughes (Chicago: Henry Regnery Co., 1964), p. 139, footnote 20. This book contains valuable chapters on Aquinas' commitment to the use of human intelligence. See especially Chapters IV and V, pp. 126–199.

[98] ScG III, 129; see footnote 9, Chap. II, Bk. III, Part II, p. 163.

[99] Ibid., 139; p. 202.

[100] On fornication and birth control, see ScG III, 122; see footnote 9, Chap. II, Bk. III, Part II, pp. 142–147. See also S.T. II–II, Q. 154, aa.2, 3 on fornication. On adultery see S.T. II–II, Q. 154, a.8. On suicide see S.T. II–II, Q. 64, a.5. On lying see S.T. II–II, Q. 110, aa.1–5.

sistance to new knowledge about our earthly home and the journey of life is never an indication of faith in the revealed God but almost always an indication that our sense of life's worth rests on the uncertain foundations of confidence in our humanity, our society, or some other evanescent idol.[101]

It is Niebuhr's contention that the Christian's faith in the value of what God has created allows him to engage fully and wholeheartedly in the scientific enterprise.

Against those who state that the Christian faith leads man to ignore the natural order, de Chardin makes the following point,

> Our faith imposes on us the right and the duty to throw ourselves into the things of the earth. As much as you, and even better than you (because, of the two of us, I alone am in a position to prolong the perspectives of my endeavour to infinity) I want to dedicate myself body and soul to the sacred duty of research.[102]

He points to the belief in the creation of the world by God and in the Incarnation (the belief that Christ, the second person of the Trinity, was born, lived, worked, and died on this earth) as factors which, for the Christian, make this earth and man's work on this earth sacred.[103]

There is another dimension of the Judeo-Christian conception of God that ought to be considered in evaluating Dewey's charge of anti-intellectualism. The emphasis on the fact that God can never be fully grasped by the human intellect in this life serves to balance off the emphasis on the rationality of God that Whitehead noted. The first emphasis need not involve a denial of the second. The acknowledgment of the mysteriousness of God should serve to soften man's confidence in reason so that this confidence never degenerates into a rationalistic smugness, which is as destructive of a truly cooperative intellectual enterprise as is a total lack of confidence in reason. This smugness leads one to maintain that he possesses the full truth. The Christian's belief in the inexhaustible richness of the divine existence should also lead him to acknowledge that man must work with many methods and from many paths if he is to gain even a partial glimpse of God and of his world.

These elements in the Christian conception of God show that there are resources within the Christian faith to meet a very legitimate requirement that Whitehead places on religion.

> Religion will not regain its old power until it can face change in the same spirit as does science. Its principles may be eternal, but the expression of those principles requires continual development. This evolution of religion is in the main

[101] H. Richard Niebuhr, *The Meaning of Revelation* (New York: The Macmillan Co., 1952), pp. 173–174.

[102] Pierre Teilhard de Chardin, *The Divine Milieu: An Essay on the Interior Life* (New York: Harper and Brothers, 1960), p. 39.

[103] *Ibid.*, p. 35.

disengagement of its own proper ideas from the adventitious notions which have crept into it by reason of the expression of its own ideas in terms of the imaginative picture of the world entertained in previous ages.[104]

The belief in the inexhaustible richness of God and his world indicate that there are factors in the supernaturalist's perspective that call for the type of evolution described by Whitehead. Granted these beliefs, the Christian supernaturalist is committed in principle to an acknowledgment that he can never merely "sit on" whatever truths he may have received from the past, as if these represented the final word on the matter. This is an important point in view of Dewey's contention that the supernaturalist's allegiance to "an irreducible minimum of belief so fixed in advance that it can never be modified," conflicts with an allegiance to the scientific method.[105]

In the thirteenth century, Thomas Aquinas pointed to a factor in man's quest for truth that makes it imperative for those living in the present to move beyond a mere restatement of the views taken by their predecessors. He sees no reason to be shocked by the fact that the sayings of the saints contain elements that appear to be doubtful to those of his own time. He sees this as being understandable because the intellectual environment out of which they were working was not as extensive as the one out of which he and his contemporaries worked. For example, one cannot expect those who wrote before the time of Arius (who taught that Christ was not divine) to have as full and as explicit a statement of the unity of the divine essence as is to be found in the Church doctors writing after the time of Arius. Aquinas concludes that since the early Church doctors worked out of a more limited intellectual context than the one out of which he and his contemporaries worked, it is not surprising that the positions of the early doctors do not show the caution, refinement, and precision that marks the work of those who came after them. Because the problematic context of the early doctors was a more limited one than that in which Aquinas worked—more limited in the sense that they were not as fully aware of the possible difficulties that their own positions might engender through certain interpretations—their positions lacked the precision that could come only after one has faced these difficulties.[106]

When this position is added to Aquinas' observation that the study of philosophy is directed not to knowing what men have taught, but rather to know how the truth itself stands, it is difficult to see how one can justify characterizing this type of supernaturalism as being committed to beliefs so fixed in advance that they can never be modified.[107] Aquinas himself does not think that it is his task to repeat what others have said, and his observations on the early Church doctors

[104] See footnote 10, Chap. V, p. 189.

[105] See footnote 26, p. 39.

[106] Contra err. Graec. Proem. in Opusc. theol. Marietti, ed., Vol. I, p. 315, n. 1029. This statement was also taken from Chenu, pp. 148–149.

[107] For Aquinas' statement see In 1 De Caelo lect. 22. Also taken from Chenu, p. 154.

certainly point to the need to modify the teachings of the past in light of the constantly developing problematic context.

The outcome of this discussion indicates that there are supernaturalists in the Judeo-Christian tradition who do not show the lack of faith in intelligence and in the significance of developing inquiry with which Dewey charges supernaturalism. What is more significant than this historical point is that there are factors in this tradition that enable one to say that *in principle* and by *their very nature* the central beliefs of this tradition call for the humble use of human intelligence and involve an acknowledgment that man's quest for truth is an endless affair so long as he inhabits this earth. This part of the discussion cannot be concluded without acknowledging the obvious historical and present fact that an intellectual arrogance is found among many Christians and Christian communities. Such arrogance would lead one to think that they had engaged the Lord Almighty Himself in a tête-à-tête concerning every last detail in the life of man in his world. I leave them to Dewey. My concern has been to sketch out those dimensions of the Judeo-Christian message that foster in man that humble confidence in human intelligence that is an essential ingredient to cooperative attempts to come to an understanding of man and his world.

(d) *Man in Nature.* Dewey has also accused supernaturalism of sharing with militant atheism a lack of natural piety in that it regards the whole drama of salvation as going on in man in isolation from nature. However, there is certainly a bond established between man and nature when man is told in the Book of Genesis to fill the earth and subdue it, and have dominion over every other earthly creature. Commenting on another part of Genesis in which God is said to make man out of the dust of the earth, the Lutheran theologian Dietrich Bonhoeffer points to the close union between man and the earth that is signified by this text.

> The man whom God has created in his image, that is in freedom, is the man who is formed out of earth. Darwin and Feuerbach themselves could not speak any more strongly. Man's origin is in a piece of earth. His bond with the earth belongs to his essential being. . . . The man who renounces his body renounces his existence before God the Creator. The essential point of human existence is its bond with mother earth, its being as body. Man has his existence as existence on earth; he does not come to the earthly world from above, driven and enslaved by a cruel faith. He comes out of the earth in which he slept and was dead; he is called out by the Word of God the Almighty in himself a piece of earth, but earth called into human being by God.[108]

This interpretation of man's involvement in and dependence on nature is not one that suddenly appeared in Christian circles in the twentieth century. Thomas Aquinas' treatment of private property discussed in Chapter VII cer-

[108] Dietrich Bonhoeffer, *Creation & Fall: A Theological Interpretation of Genesis 1–2* in *Creation and Fall: Temptation: Two Biblical Studies* (New York: The Macmillan Co., 1959), pp. 46–47.

tainly indicated that he was fully aware of the bond between man and nature and that man's continued earthly existence depended on his use of the things of this earth. This bond between man and nature is also seen as being necessary to man if he is to acquire such goods as knowledge and virtue. Thus, Aquinas points to the soul's need of its body for the attaining of its perfection, because it must make use of the body to acquire both knowledge and perfection.[109] Moreover, Aquinas' discussion of the place of man in nature often emphasizes the point that man is a being capable of freedom, of ruling over himself, of being master of his own actions.[110] This point is brought up to indicate that Dewey's charge that supernaturalism involves escapism and defeatism is open to question. A position that is so emphatic in depicting man as capable of ruling himself would hardly lead one to conclude that he ought to surrender the task of trying to improve himself and his world.

At this point it might be well to state the reason for my reliance on the writings of Thomas Aquinas to show that Dewey's charges against supernaturalism are not valid against all those who accept the existence of a God who is the Creator of the universe. The statement that was made above after the quotation from Bonhoeffer to the effect that Bonhoeffer's interpretation of man's union with nature is not one that first made its appearance in the Christian tradition in the twentieth century is the key to my reliance on Aquinas and on Biblical texts. References to these writings were meant to highlight the fact that a concern with the natural order is deeply rooted in the Judeo-Christian tradition. The writings of a man such as Pierre Teilhard de Chardin may also have served as an example of a thinker whose acceptance of a Personal God, who is Creator of the universe, did not lead him to denigrate the natural order. However, the use of these writings may have given the erroneous impression that the recognition of the value and importance of the natural order is something wholly new in Judeo-Christian circles, a recognition that had no roots in the Judeo-Christian heritage and that represents something of an *ad hoc* position fashioned wholly in this century to meet the challenges of nontheistic naturalisms.

There is a principle underlying Dewey's criticism of supernaturalism that has not been fully dealt with by the texts cited to show that there are those writing out of the Judeo-Christian heritage that simply do not fit the Deweyan mold of supernaturalism. This principle is that an opposition exists between the supernatural and natural orders, with the result that a man who believes in a supernatural order must necessarily ignore the natural. If this were true, it could be argued on Dewey's behalf that a man such as Aquinas, who does not surrender his concern with the natural order, is simply not being consistent with his supernatural orientation. However, Aquinas sees no opposition between the natural and supernatural orders. He holds that grace does not destroy or do

---

[109] *ScG* III, 144; see footnote 9, Chap. II, Bk. III, Part II, p. 214.
[110] See *Ibid.*, 1, 78; see *Ibid.*, Part I, pp. 32, 262. See also *ScG* III, 111, 112, and 113; see footnote 9, Chap. II, Bk. III, Part II, pp. 114–122.

away with nature, but perfects and completes it.[111] Thomas Merton points to the logical consequence that flows from this principle. "The axiom that grace builds on nature has often been misused. But the fact remains that, if nothing is left of nature, there is nothing for grace to build on, there is nothing left to be sanctified and consecrated to God."[112] Acceptance of the principle that grace builds on and completes nature commits a man to engaging wholeheartedly in every humane natural enterprise, for the principle envisions a continuity rather than an opposition between the natural and the supernatural dimensions of human existence. This means that a supernaturalist's concern with the natural order is not simply a matter of expediency, something that the exigencies of living force him to acknowledge in his practical life, but that cannot be justified by either his theological or philosophical world-view.

Finally, Martin Buber points out that it would be nonsensical for anyone accepting the existence of God as the Creator of the world to set up an opposition between God and the world. To see the "religious" man as a person for whom the world no longer counts is to suppose that "God has created his world as an illusion and man for frenzied being."[113] In another book, Buber criticizes the view that God can be reached only by renouncing man's essential relations to the world, to community, and to other individuals. "A God reached only by renunciation of the relation to the whole being cannot be the God of the whole being, cannot be the God who has made and preserves and holds together all that is."[114] Buber's statements also serve to emphasize the exigencies within the supernaturalist's position that lead one accepting this position to take on the burdens and responsibilities of dealing with the natural order. One does not accept God by a full-scale renunciation of the world that He has created. Furthermore, it should be noted that the theist, as distinct from the Judeo-Christian, can also use the point made by Buber to show that his position calls for his involvement in the world.

The importance to this section of the principle that grace builds on and completes nature and of Buber's observations cannot be overemphasized. For they present a view of the relationship between God and nature which *by its very nature and in principle* demands a concern with the natural order. It is not because of their loose thinking that Aquinas and Buber do not fit into Dewey's conception of supernaturalism. Their conception of God as the maker and preserver of the natural order militates against the acceptance of any radical opposition between God and nature, an opposition that would confront man with the dilemma of accepting God and rejecting nature, or of accepting nature and

[111] See *S.T.* I, Q. 1, a.8, ad.2; see footnote 36, Chap. I, Vol. I, p. 14.

[112] Thomas Merton, *Conjectures of a Guilty Bystander* (New York: Doubleday & Co., 1966), p. 16.

[113] Martin Buber, *I and Thou* (New York: Charles Scribner's Sons, 1958, second ed.), p. 108.

[114] Martin Buber, *Between Man and Man* (New York: The Macmillan Co., 1965), trans. by Ronald Gregor Smith, p. 179.

rejecting God. Aquinas' notion of grace as building on and completing nature, together with his conception of a cause-effect relationship existing between God and nature, lead him to see nature not as a threat to man's relationship to God, but as man's way to reach God.

Similarly, the discussion of the role of intelligence in a Judeo-Christian super-naturalism was meant to point out that the conception of God and of man's relationship to God demanded *in principle* that humble confidence in the use of human intelligence that was spoken of above. Thus, the use of the writings of such men as Aquinas, Buber, De Chardin, and Bonhoeffer was not meant simply to provide historical examples of thinkers who do not fit neatly into Dewey's supernaturalistic mold. The prime purpose in using them was to emphasize that there is a supernaturalistic conception of God and of man's relationship to this God which by its very nature demands that man be concerned with the natural order, with his fellow man, and with the use of human intelligence.

(e) *Institutionalized Christianity*. It might be pointed out that texts from the Bible, from Thomas Aquinas, and from Martin Buber do not meet Dewey's charge that *historic* Christianity—Christianity as it has been practiced and not as it has been preached—has weakened man's awareness of his community with his fellow man. It may also be pointed out that these texts do not meet the charge that supernaturalists have paid only lip service to the notion of the brotherhood of man.

It has not been the purpose of this section to whitewash the evils perpetrated in the name of Christianity down through history. However, in fairness, it should be noted that the history has certainly not been all black, as Dewey himself noted when he observed that a complete account of the rise of a humanitarian spirit as a motivating force behind nineteenth-century industrial reforms cannot ignore the contribution of religious leaders drawn both from the Established Church and from dissenting religious groups.[115] Church groups certainly have played a role in helping the poor, in establishing hospitals, and in trying to rehabilitate the criminal. They may not have been as effective as one might wish, and they may not have carried as much of the burden as one might expect, but it would not be historically accurate to deny that they have played any role. However, the issue in this section revolves around the ethical significance of the Christian ideal and not around historical issues. More specifically, I have argued against the view that Christianity involves *in principle* a depreciation of natural social values, and in favor of the view that *in principle* it calls for an involvement in the natural order that will improve the human condition.

Dewey's criticism of supernaturalism undoubtedly often hits the mark when it is seen as directed against the institutionalized forms of supernaturalism. Thus, although the textual evidence gathered from the Bible does not bear out his contention that Christianity sets up as an ideal the separation of men and a denial of the community among men, it is true that there has been a separation

---

[115] See footnote 114, Chap. IV, pp. 20–21.

among men brought about by institutionalized Christianity, which has made it difficult for them to cooperate in a common human venture. That this situation is changing today does not wash away this historical fact.

Before condemning supernaturalism out of hand because of this fact, it might be well to consider a distinction that William James suggests be drawn in any consideration of religion.

> The baseness so commonly charged to religion's account are thus, almost all of them, not chargeable at all to religion proper, but rather to religion's wicked practical partner, the spirit of corporate dominion. And the bigotries are most of them in their turn chargeable to religion's wicked intellectual partner, the spirit of dogmatic dominion, the passion for the laying down the law in the form of an absolutely closed-in theoretic system. The ecclesiastical spirit in general is the sum of these two spirits of dominion; and I beseech you never to confound the phenomena of mere tribal or corporate psychology which it presents with those manifestations of the purely interior life which are the exclusive object of our study.[116]

This section has been concerned with meeting Dewey's criticism of religion in so far as that criticism is based on the supernaturalistic character of religion. It was not concerned with evaluating Dewey's position in so far as it could be interpreted as being directed against religion as institutionalized. Using James's distinction, I would maintain that Dewey's charges have a good deal of validity in so far as they are seen as applying to what James has referred to as the ecclesiastical spirit, a spirit which is certainly not in keeping with the type of supernaturalism defended in this section.

Although it is beyond the scope of this book to deal with the question of institutionalized religion, it should be noted that the forces of corporate and dogmatic dominion are not restricted to ecclesiastical organizations. They are endemic to any institution. They are present, to a greater or lesser degree, in any area of human life that has taken on an institutionalized form—whether the area be political, economic, military, educational, or religious. Dewey himself certainly experienced the difficulties in overcoming the forces of corporate and dogmatic dominion in trying to have his educational theories put into practice by the educational establishment of his own day. Moreover, there are those who would maintain that the forces of corporate and dogmatic dominion are to be found among those in the educational establishment who profess to be putting Dewey's educational views into practice today. The work of science itself has not been free of these two forces in so far as it has become a part of the political and military institutions of certain countries.

The naive response to these observations is to get rid of institutions and all their laws, constitutions, officers or hierarchies, and established procedures. However, Dewey himself is certainly not ready to accept a wholesale dismissal of all forms of institutionalized living. "To give up the institutions is chaos and an-

---

[116] William James, *The Varieties of Religious Experience: A Study in Human Nature* (New York: Mentor Books, 1958), pp. 263–264.

archy; to maintain the institutions unchanged is death and fossilization. The problem is the reconciliation of unbridled radicalism and inert conservatism, in a movement of reasonable reform."[117] Thus, when considering the role of institutions apart from a specific study of religious institutions, Dewey saw both the need for institutions and the dangers that they held for human life. Institutions are necessary conditions for human growth in that they represent the funding of the experiences of the past that permits men to move beyond past achievements. They provide the stable framework that keeps man from running off in all directions with no sense of what he is trying to accomplish and with no leverage from the past that he might use to try to accomplish a definite aim if he had such an aim.[118]

In an article published in 1924, ten years before the publication of *A Common Faith*, Dewey placed the following question before the religious liberals of that day: "What is the relation of a specially organized community and institution like the Church, whatever be the church, to religious experience?"[119] Dewey's position in *A Common Faith* indicates that he was given no satisfactory answer to this question. For in this work, institutionalized religion is always seen as a hindrance and encumbrance to the development of the religious dimensions of human life. Dewey certainly is right in challenging institutionalized religion to show its credentials. The defenders of institutionalized religion must show how their institutions, with their rites, dogmas, and organizations, serve to focus man's attention on the religious character of his life and provide him with a leverage, which he can use to deepen and expand the religious quality of his life, allowing this quality to permeate every aspect of life. If their rites are not to become mere formalities, it is necessaray that the members of these institutions be made aware not only of the historical justification of these rites, but also of their contemporary significance.

Dewey's criticisms of institutionalized religion are not without their own difficulties. It is easy enough to criticize any institutionalized form of life. Having finished with the criticism, Dewey must indicate how he intends to preserve and to foster that sense of wholeness with nature that he refers to as the religious quality of experience. What mechanism is he going to use to keep that idea of "God" before the eyes of man, an idea which he said must be kept before man in a distracted age? If there is anything worth preserving in his own view of the religious character of experience, how is he going to preserve it and pass it on to the great majority of mankind who are not philosophers? In short, can the naturalist provide a substitute for institutionalized religion without himself setting up some sort of institution? Does he want the state to function as his answer to institutionalized religion? The point of these questions is to indicate that the preservation and development of any significant aspect of human life, which

---

[117] See footnote 25, p. 335.
[118] See footnote 60, pp. 166–167.
[119] John Dewey, "Fundamentals," *Characters and Events*, Vol. I, p. 458.

is to touch the lives of all men, would seem to require some sort of institutionalized framework.

After the festivities of listing the evils of institutionalized religion, comes the Monday morning when one must decide what to put in place of that which was so easily done away with on the previous evening. Dewey closed his *A Common Faith* with the remark that the view of man in nature, which he defended in that book, has always been the implicit common faith of mankind and that the task that remained was to make this faith "explicit and militant."[120] It would appear that some sort of institutionalized framework would be necessary to achieve this task.

This discussion of the problems of institutionalized religion should not lead one to lose sight of the major thrust of this section. It is not necessary that every form of supernaturalism be an antinaturalism. There is a supernaturalism that is by its very nature and in principle committed to nurturing and expanding the values to be found in man's existence in this world.

7. THE CASE FOR AN OPEN ETHICAL NATURALISM

Having tried to show that the existence of a supernatural God need not deprive the natural order of its moral significance, it is necessary to try to sketch the positive role that a Personal God plays in man's moral life, unless one is willing to agree with those French thinkers of the nineteenth century who, according to Jean-Paul Sartre, held that "nothing will change if God does not exist; we shall rediscover the same norms of honesty, progress, and humanity, and we shall have disposed of God as an out-of-date hypothesis which will die away quietly of itself."[121] This position indicates that it is not enough to show that the acceptance of the existence of God does no harm to man's moral life. A God who lends no positive significance to man's moral endeavors is, at least from the perspective of these endeavors, an "out-of-date hypothesis which will quietly die of itself." Moreover, unless one shows the positive significance, which the existence of God holds for man's moral existence, one is guilty of what Dewey once described as the "current unreality of philosophy," which is the view that "great generalizations may be, as it were, plastered over life to label its contents, and not imply profound practical changes within life itself."[122]

If Dewey can be said to have disproved the existence of a supernatural God on moral grounds, he did so by establishing two points. There was a negative and a positive dimension to his position. On the negative side, he tried to show

---

[120] See footnote 26, p. 87.

[121] Jean-Paul Sartre, "Existentialism is a Humanism," in *Existentialism from Dostoevsky to Sartre* ed. with an intro., prefaces, and new translations by Walter Kaufmann (New York: Meridian Books, 1956), p. 294.

[122] See footnote 45, pp. 505–506.

how the existence of a supernatural order impoverished human existence. On the positive side, he tried to sustain the view that a philosophical reflection on a reality, which includes only man and nature, shows that such a reality can do full justice to the value and richness of human existence. His description of the purpose of *A Common Faith* captures this positive side of his undertaking. He states that the book was an attempt to show those persons who have abandoned supernaturalism "that they have within their experience all the elements that give religious attitude its value."[123] In short, he set out to show that his naturalism is not to be included among those atheistic philosophies that reduce man to issuing empty blasts of defiance against the world.

In the immediately preceding section, I have presented a response to the negative side of Dewey's position. This section will deal with the positive task of attempting to show that the very values that Dewey tried to incorporate into his own naturalism can be philosophically grounded only in a world that includes the Personal God of theism. Even if this undertaking is successful, it will not have demonstrated the existence of God. Before rejecting the task of this section as being insignificant because it fails to provide such a proof, it should be noted that what we saw of Dewey's position was not concerned with the question of any theoretical proof for the existence of God. The basic message of Dewey's treatment of a supernatural order is that the existence of a Personal God, if not harmful to man's endeavors in the world, is, at best, irrelevant to them.

This section will try to deal with this message by attempting to give a philosophical answer to the question, "What positive difference does the existence of a Personal God make to human existence?" Such a philosophical answer will not concern itself with the factual question of whether those who do not believe in God can have the same feeling about their lives and their work as believers have. This is a matter of personal histories that does not fall within the scope of philosophical inquiry. What the section will try to show is that values such as natural piety, which Dewey saw as important to human existence, are philosophically groundless and are simply metaphors or purely romantic representations of man's true existential situation in the world, if this situation does not include a Personal God.

I shall try to make a second point in this section. I shall try to show that a reflection on the quality of man's moral existence raises the possibility that the world in which man lives may not be wholly reducible to the purely temporal and passing state of affairs that is perhaps the most obvious feature of our experience of the world. Although this point does not demonstrate the existence of God any more than did the first, it does indicate that there are factors in man's moral encounter with his world that are compatible with the existence of a Personal and Eternal God. It may well be that metaphysical or epistemological considerations that are beyond the scope of this book may lead one to reject open naturalism, but, if this section is successful in making its point, one must

[123] See footnote 87, p. 597.

admit that this rejection and his consequent acceptance of closed naturalism mean that he is forced to accept a lowest common denominator view of man's moral life—one that sees this life as lacking the significance and adventure that are to be found in an open naturalism.

Alfred North Whitehead was right in pointing to the disservice done to religion and God as significant aspects of human life by attempts to excite fear of divine wrath and by attempts to show that religion makes for a comfortably organized society through sanctions that it can hold over man. Against such characterizations of religion, he offers his own characterization, "The worship of God is not a rule of safety—it is an adventure of the spirit, a flight after the unattainable. The death of religion comes with the repression of the high hope of adventure."[124] Although the conception of God that underlies this section is not that of Whitehead's, I hope to show that the conception used does introduce this high hope of adventure into man's moral endeavors.

Dewey's closed naturalism is able to introduce this hope of adventure in man's life only because he has done what he accused the defender's of scientific ethics of doing, i.e., he has painted man's situation in nature in colors borrowed from the very view of reality that he has rejected. Specifically, when Dewey talks of man finding the expansion of himself in an enveloping undefined whole, of man as a citizen of this vast world beyond himself, and of man being sustained and expanded in feebleness and failure by the sense of an enveloping whole, he is to overcome man's sense of alienation and to unify and give meaning to man's endeavors only by personifying this whole, giving it the character of a Personal God. Dewey's description of natural piety as "the sense of the permanent and inevitable implication of man and nature in a common career and destiny," also makes sense only if nature is itself personified or is seen as coming from a Subject who is concerned with man in nature and toward whom man in nature is moving.

If nature is taken out of the context of being the work of a Personal God, all talk about man being sustained by the sense of an enveloping whole, and of being engaged with nature in a common career and destiny becomes pure metaphor, with no substance behind it. For then the whole becomes a whole of "things," "objects" that can be manipulated or used by man. It is difficult to see how mankind can be said to be engaged in a common career or destiny with chemicals, stones, or vegetables. The subjectivity that is implicated in being a man seems to alienate him from the rest of nature when the rest of nature is seen to be mindless process or dumb objects. There can be no sharing between man and nature so considered. Martin Buber's distinction between the I-Thou relationship, which is a relationship between persons, and the I-It relationship, which is a relationship between a person and the world of things, is important to the criticism of Dewey's position that is being offered at this point.

There is no communication in an I-It relationship between man and the

---

[124] See footnote 10, Chap. V, p. 192.

world of objects. Buber gives the following description of man's dealings with objects:

> He perceives what exists round about him—simply things, and beings as things; and what happens round about him—simply events, and actions as events; things consisting of qualities, events of moments; things entered in the graph of place, events in that of time; . . . he perceives an ordered and detached world. . . . Its organisation can be surveyed and brought out again and again; gone over with closed eyes, and verified with open eyes. It is always there, next to your skin, if you look on it that way, cowering in your soul, if you prefer it so. It is your object, remains it as long as you wish, and remains a total stranger, within you and without. You perceive it, take it to yourself as the 'truth,' and it lets itself be taken; but it does not give itself to you.[125]

The world of objects is simply "there" to be used, be manipulated, to be talked about, and to be described to other selves. It has the organization and stability that allow man as a seeker of truth to be able to deal with it as an object of truth. However, for all his dealings with the world of It, for all its closeness to man, he finds himself a stranger with respect to it. It is a world that permits itself to be taken and to be used, but it does not communicate with man.

Because the natural world of a closed naturalism is a world without a personal God, it is a world of "it." Man is certainly involved and immersed in the natural order of objects. However, because there can be no community and no sharing between man and the world of objects, there appears to be no philosophical justification within Dewey's naturalism for the view that man and nature are implicated in a "common career and destiny." Unless Dewey is willing to introduce a note of subjectivity in the natural order of objects and processes, apart from man, it would seem that he would be forced to acknowledge that man and the world of objects do not share in a common career and destiny, because there is no real possibility of their sharing in anything.

Moreover, it is difficult to see the philosophical justification for the view that we are "sustained and expanded in feebleness and failure by the sense of an enveloping whole," in view of Dewey's own observation that modern science has shown that "nature has no preference for good things over bad things; its mills turn out any kind of grist indifferently."[126] Man may use a certain chemical to save himself, or the chemical may so react on him as to kill him. It makes no difference to the object what the outcome of its use may be. It is difficult to see how man can be sustained and expanded in feebleness and failure by the sense of an enveloping whole, when this whole is seen to involve man as part of a world of objects and processes that are wholly indifferent to him. Man may well be sustained and expanded in feebleness and failure by the sense of an enveloping whole, but once the closed naturalist has described the natural world in

---

[125] See footnote 113, pp. 31–32.
[126] See footnote 44, Chap. III, p. 112.

which man exists, there appears to be no philosophical justification for this expansion.

It will be recalled that Dewey suggested that the word *God* be applied to the active relationship existing between man's ideals and the natural order as actually given to man—an order containing both the soil for the realization of these ideals and the agents, men, who can cultivate this soil so that the ideals become more firmly rooted in the course of nature. If the natural order in which man finds himself is the mindless process that it must be in Dewey's closed naturalism, the use of the term *God* to describe the relationship between this order and God is certainly misleading in that it gives the relationship a personal character that it simply does not have. Although Dewey has explicitly denied it, it seems to me that he has romanticized nature in order to invoke man's heartfelt piety to nature as the source of all ideals. When the enveloping undefined whole that accompanies all experience is seen to be a series of mindless processes in which man finds himself implicated, there is no philosophical ground for the natural piety that is so important to Dewey. The nature of a closed naturalism, a nature that is evacuated of a Personal God, simply cannot carry the unifying, sustaining, and expanding role that Dewey would give to it.

It may justly be pointed out that Dewey has grounded natural piety in an *idealized* conception of man in nature, and not in the actual situation in which man finds himself. It is the *ideal* sense of man as a part of the great whole of nature that is to overcome man's sense of isolation from nature. In taking this tack, Dewey has missed an essential factor involved in man's sense of isolation. The fact that man possesses ideals is an essential ingredient in constituting this sense of isolation. Man with his ideals finds himself in a nature that goes its merry way, without the slightest concern for these ideals. The values, which man finds in his ideals, and the mindless indifference of nature as found in a closed naturalism are two essential factors in man's sense of isolation from nature. A nature that is simply "there," that mindlessly permits itself to be used for moral or immoral purposes, and that mindlessly and indifferently brings about the death of all men whether moral or immoral seems to be totally alien to man as the being in nature who is the bearer of moral ideals. Such isolation or alienation is not done away with by a more inclusive ideal, because it is the fact that man has ideals in a universe of mindless processes that brings home to him the full force of his estrangement from these processes.

The existence of a Personal and Provident God as the Creator of man and nature provides a basis for overcoming this estrangement. This does not mean that chemicals, minerals, physiological, and biological processes of nature are automatically transformed into thinking subjects. However, there is a transformation of man's relationship to these mindless realities, when this relationship is seen to occur in a universe created by a Personal God. Dewey himself provides material that can be used to explain this transformation. "Shared experience is the greatest of human goods. In communication, such conjunction and contact as is characteristic of animals become endearments capable of infinite idealization."[127] In this statement, Dewey is beginning an account that indicates that man's ability to share meanings with another person, his ability to communicate his joys, sorrows, and purposes to another, transforms sexual acts that are mere conjunction and contact on the animal level to acts that are charged with meaning and that are capable of infinite idealization on the human level.

The insight that Dewey shows in this account can be used in explaining the transformation that occurs in man's relationship to his natural environment, when both are seen to be creatures of a personal God. The objects and processes that are involved in man's natural environment remain objects and processes when the existence of such a God is acknowledged, just as human sexual intercourse continues to involve physical contact. However, within the context of an open naturalism, man's involvement in these processes and his dealings with them are seen to be his way of sharing in and with the Divine Person. Man can now truly be said to *share* in the whole of nature in that his involvement in nature is seen to be a reaching out toward, and a meeting with, the Person whose Providence extends over the whole of nature. Man's moral endeavors are now seen to be factors in a shared experience, a communication with this Person. Man is no longer seen as cast adrift in a vast sea of mindless events and processes, for his dealings with them and their implications in the whole of human affairs are now grasped as man's way of responding to God.

The open naturalist can also speak of man being carried beyond himself to find himself, but he is not restricted to speaking of this expansion as being felt to reach to an enveloping undefined whole. For the open naturalist, man is carried beyond himself to find himself as sharing in the life of an Eternal Person. Man is now seen to be an I, who through his works and activity in nature, as well as through his dealings with other men, is responding to and sharing in the life of an Eternal Thou. Whereas talk about the implication of man and nature in a common career and destiny seems to be empty rhetoric devoid of philosophical justification when considered within the boundaries of a closed naturalism, such talk is seen to have some philosophical grounding when seen within the context of an open naturalism. Man and nature are implicated in a common career and destiny in that they are both created by God and man's activity in nature is seen as his way of giving himself and his world to God.

Moreover, Dewey's contention that in "a genuine sense every act is already possessed of an infinite import," takes on a more meaningful moral dimension in an open naturalism than it can have in Dewey's closed naturalism. It will be recalled that Dewey's account of this infinite import was grounded in the fact that the "little part of the scheme of affairs which is modifiable by our efforts is continuous with the rest of the world," with the result that the "small effort which we can put forth is in turn connected with an infinity of events that sustain and support it." Dewey holds that acts, which, from the standpoint of

[127] *Ibid.*, p. 202.

their definite aim, are petty in comparison with the totality of natural events, are seen to have an infinite import in that they are involved in a web of infinite connections. The infinite import of an act lies in the infinite number of relations into which it enters. This would seem to mean that such acts as the curing of one alcoholic, the solace offered to a dying man, and parents' care for their children, are all seen to be petty when their definite aim is compared to the totality of natural events, but that they are also seen to have an infinite import when it is recognized that they are parts of this totality and that they are thus caught up in a web of infinite relations.

It is difficult to see how the consciousness of this sort of infinity can contribute to that "peace in action," which Dewey is concerned with establishing or how it can sustain and expand man in feebleness and failure. If anything, the awareness of this sort of situation should serve to bring home to an individual person the insignificance of his moral endeavors precisely in their moral character, i.e., in so far as they can be placed within the sphere of his moral responsibility and control.

Of course, Dewey's conception of the infinite import of man's acts may be the only type of infinite significance available to man. If this be the case, let us be free of the possible illusion that it has anything to do with the moral import of man's acts. Let us be clear that, at best, this type of infinity adds nothing to this import and, at worst, it emphasizes that aspect from which the moral import of an act is seen to be petty and insignificant. As distinct from this state of affairs, the moral import of an act as it occurs here and now can never be slighted in the context of an open naturalism by comparing it with the total sweep of events over which a moral individual has no control. Within this context, an act can be said to be of "infinite" import not only in the rather quantitative sense described by Dewey, but also, and more importantly, in a qualitative sense in so far as it occurs in the knowing and loving presence of the Divine Person, who in his own Being is lacking no value and before whom the whole of being and value stand totally revealed.

The solace that an individual offers a dying man is not met by the moral dumbness and blindness of a mindless universe. It reaches in its moral character to the very source of the universe in so far as it occurs in the provident presence of that Person who is the unlimited source of all being and value. That an individual's activity occurs in a small point of space and occupies a petty instant of time does not affect the moral import of the act. The moral character of an act as it occurs here and now can be said to take on an infinite import in so far as it is man's free response to the Infinite Person who in his providence is concerned with every act.

There is a further enrichment found in the quality of man's moral task if the existence of an eternal God and of human immortality are accepted. There is a permanence and endurance present in this task that cannot be found in the universe of closed naturalism. Such a naturalism can point to the fact that a man's acts may influence the course of history long after he has died. These acts thus have a certain permanence about them. The open naturalist need not deny this position. However, one does not give an eternal significance to acts by stringing together a series of transient and evanescent acts, with each act dying and through its death passing into another. That which has died and no longer exists, though with its death it has laid the groundwork for what now exists, is not said to be eternal.

The eternal significance of man's moral task means that there is a coming to fruition of man's acts so that what he does *here and now* lives on not only by passing into some other men, but lives on in him in the sense that he is never free of the responsibilities of what he does freely here and now. A man's acts live on not only in others, but also in himself. From the perspective of open naturalism, every individual man is seen to be embarked on an eternal career in that his life does not end in the grave, but comes to an unending fruition. Thus, what is at issue in every moral decision is not simply a course of action that is here today and gone tomorrow or that may or may not influence the course of human history, but an eternity. Man is seen to be in the process of making a self that is eternal. This point is not made with the hope of frightening anyone into being moral, a hope that is self-contradictory. It is made rather to emphasize the depth and significance that is found in man's moral life within the context of an open naturalism.

The closed naturalist may argue that the emphasis on the immortal character of man's moral task tends to detract from his concern with the historical significance of his acts. It is said to logically lead to the sacrifice of all natural values in the name of eternity. That men have, as a matter of fact, committed moral atrocities in the name of eternity, I do not deny. However, I do deny that such sacrifices are logically implied by the emphasis on human immortality. Man's immortality does not begin after this life. His immortality is at issue here and now. It is what man does in time and in history that determines the character of his immortal existence. Granted this fact, it is nonsensical to think that a man enriches the character of his immortal existence by debasing himself or his fellow man, or by failing to meet the moral responsibilities of his own time and place. Thus, the emphasis on eternity does not lift the burden of moral responsibility from man's shoulders. Eternity is not offered as a way to escape the demands of temporal existence. Indeed, it is seen as denying the possibility that man can escape from the type of self that he has made of himself through time. What man has freely made of himself in time will come to fruition in eternity.

It is also sometimes argued that an emphasis on the immortality of man tends to make him egotistical and self-centered in the sense that his perspective is narrowed so that he is concerned only with himself to the exclusion of his fellow man. C. S. Lewis provides material for responding to this objection.

> It is a serious thing to live in a society of possible gods and goddesses, to remember that the dullest and most uninteresting person you talk to may one day be a creature which, if you saw it now, you would be strongly tempted to worship, or

else a horror and a corruption such as you now meet, if at all, only in a nightmare. All day long we are, in some degree, helping each other to one or other of these destinations. It is in the light of these overwhelming possibilities, it is with the awe and the circumspection proper to them, that we should conduct all our dealings with one another, all friendships, all loves, all play, all politics. There are no *ordinary* people. . . . It is immortals whom we joke with, work with, marry, snub, and exploit.[128]

Lewis has emphasized the social significance of the doctrine of immortality. The notion of man as an end in himself is certainly enriched when it is recognized that this man is immortal. The community of ends takes on an added significance when it is seen to be a community of immortals.

It was necessary to be rather positive in stressing the differences between open and closed naturalism. However, it should be noted that this positive tone was not grounded in any belief that there is no darkness or mystery in the universe of the open naturalist. To assert that there is an infinite meaning to man's life is not to say that this meaning is perfectly clear to man. To assert that man is embarked on an eternal career is not to assert that one has anything approaching a detailed description of the character of man's eternal existence. Man has a difficult enough time predicting tomorrow's weather, much less describing eternity. One can hope only that the statements made concerning these matters are sufficient to bring out their ethical significance. The rationalist, who seeks perfect clarity in all areas of life, will not be satisfied with this state of affairs, but I doubt that any position, which is true to the complexities and depth of human life, will satisfy him. Dewey himself certainly is not to be classified among these men. He describes the natural community of causes in which man finds himself enmeshed as the symbol of the *"mysterious* [italics mine] totality of being," which the imagination refers to as the universe.[129]

It might be well to draw together what has been said about open naturalism up to this point by trying to sketch out how it contributes to what Whitehead has referred to as the "high hope of adventure." The world of the open naturalist is filled with the hope of eternity and of man's sharing in the life of an Infinite Person in a more direct way than he now does. Man's moral achievements are seen not as passing, transient affairs, but as matters of an infinite and eternal significance. Man's task of building a moral character and of bringing nature under human control so that it contributes to the betterment of man is not a process that ends dumbly in the grave, but is rather a task that reaches beyond the grave toward an eternal union of the perfected human community with the Person who is the ultimate source of all being and value.

Whitehead has made the point that apart from religion, "human life is a flash of occasional enjoyments lighting up a mass of pain and misery, a bagatelle of

---

[128] C. S. Lewis, *The Weight of Glory and Other Addresses* (Grand Rapids, Michigan: William B. Eredmans Publishing Co., 1965), pp. 14–15.

[129] See footnote 26, p. 85.

transient experience."[130] Open naturalism need not deny the reality of pain and misery that is a part, and no doubt a very large part, of the human situation. However, at the same time, it asserts that human life is not a mere trifling of transient experience. For man's immortal destiny means that the moral good which he achieves is not a flash of occasional enjoyment, but a movement toward the building of an immortal human community, in which the good that man has effected in freedom will come into its own, will assert itself in the fullness of its being.

The difference between the open and closed naturalist can perhaps be seen when the eternal *vista* of the open naturalist is compared to the following description of humanity given by Dewey at a moment when he was not explicitly concerned with emphasizing values of his naturalism as compared to supernaturalism. "Humanity is but a slight and feeble thing, perhaps an episodic one, in the vast stretch of the universe. But for man, man is the center of interest and the measure of importance."[131] The naturalism advanced in this book has no argument with the last sentence of this statement. Indeed, the defense of the standard established in Chapter IV included an attempt to justify the central role which the human community should play in man's moral decisions. Moreover, I can also agree that man is a limited being and that seen in the perspective of the vastness of the universe and of his vulnerability to natural forces, he is a slight and feeble thing.

Having pointed to these areas of agreement, it must also be noted that the tone of Dewey's statement seems to confirm Whitehead's contention that human life apart from religion is a bagatelle of transient experience. Open naturalism differs from Dewey's naturalism in that it maintains that humanity is not an episodic thing, but is embarked on an adventure of immortal dimensions. Admitting the slightness and feebleness of humanity when compared to the vastness of the universe, open naturalism at the same time points to the greatness of man—to his freedom and subjectivity—which enables him alone of all the beings of nature to participate freely in God's creation, and through such participation to enter into an I-Thou relationship with God. This unique relationship existing between man and God thus serves to strengthen and enhance the central role given to man in the moral standard advanced in Chapter IV.

Dewey's case for a closed naturalism indicated that man's life would lose nothing of its wholeness and of its infinite import in a world evacuated of a Personal God. This section tried to point to what were considered to be philosophical shortcomings in Dewey's case and also tried to point to factors in a world that included a Personal God which serve to enrich the meaning of human life. There may be other considerations that may lead one to reject the existence of such a God. If such is the case, let us not fool ourselves in saying in our moral

[130] See footnote 10, Chap. V, p. 192.

[131] John Dewey, *The Public and Its Problems* (Denver, Colorado: Alan Swallow), p. 176.

philosophy that this rejection is of no great significance to man's moral endeavors.

Without a God, all talk of the infinite import of man's acts is, in the last analysis, empty rhetoric. Without God, man's life is a passing affair in a world of passing events, which are neither hostile nor friendly to him; it is a world that is mindlessly "there." Without God, man's life is a chain of events fluctuating between fulfillments and frustrations, leading nowhere but to the silence of the grave. Without God, the feeling of natural piety as "the sense of the permanent and inevitable implication of nature and man in a common career and destiny," is seen to be lacking philosophical grounding.

Moreover, it is also difficult to see any philosophical justification for the use of the word *permanent* in the description of natural piety. In a world in which eternity is denied can anything be said to be permanent? It would seem that, in the last analysis, everything must be said to be passing and transitory. Without God, the more man becomes aware of "that sense of an enveloping undefined whole that accompanies every normal experience," the less able will he be to justify the view that this whole is an expansion of himself. For it is difficult to see how this whole which, without God, can be only a mindless process, can be considered to be an expansion of the human subject.

If we must accept a closed naturalism, let us accept it without illusions, let us be clear in the knowledge that we have accepted a lowest common denominator conception of man's moral life. This description fits the closed naturalist position in that there is nothing that is positive and affirmative in this position that cannot be accepted by and included in an open naturalism. Whereas open naturalism is not predicated on a denial of the significance of human values, closed naturalism is characterized by its denial that these values have an eternal significance. Whereas closed naturalism, if it is true to its own world view, must insist on the passing and finite significance of human life, open naturalism sees this life as eternally and infinitely significant. In short, closed naturalism is open naturalism which has been evacuated of any philosophical ground for its high hope of adventure.

Dewey may be right in saying that the existence of a Personal God does not enable us to correct one single misstep, one paltry error here and now. He may also be right in holding that the existence of such a being does not give man the slightest inkling of how to work at rectifying one transgression or healing one disease. Perhaps, there are those who would say that Dewey has hit the mark against the open naturalism advanced in this chapter when he observed that the existence of God serves only to mitigate the hysteric sentimentalism that is troubled because the universe as a whole does not sustain the good as a whole.

If open naturalism is to be found guilty of trying to mitigate hysteric sentimentalism, then Dewey's own naturalism is also guilty. It will be recalled that Dewey was concerned with providing man with a basis for "peace in action not after," with showing that in "a genuine sense every act is already possessed of an infinite import," with so describing our situation in nature that we find ourselves "sustained and expanded in feebleness and failure by the sense of an enveloping whole," with pointing to the sense of unity that man can find in "that sense of an enveloping undefined whole that accompanies every normal experience," and finally with fostering in man's life a sense of "natural piety." The charge of hysteric sentimentalism must be applied both to Dewey's naturalism and to the open naturalism of this chapter because the case for this latter naturalism attempted to show that the existence of a Personal God can account for those very dimensions of human existence that Dewey wanted to incorporate into his closed naturalism.

However, there seems to be no justification for saying that every attempt to ground the eternal significance of human endeavors is reducible to an attempt to mitigate the hysteric sentimentalism that is troubled because the universe as a whole does not sustain the good as a whole. It ought to be noted that the defense of open naturalism did not include an attempt to show that the ideals for which man ought to work are valuable because they are already existent in an eternal realm. The existence of an eternal Thou was not presented as a guarantee for the moral success of any given human venture. The moral good and the moral evil that are realized in the world are the work of man. The preservation, development, and expansion of moral values in the world depend on the activities of man as a moral agent. God was not presented as a being who would do man's work for him, nor as a being whose existence guaranteed that everything man tried would be successful. To present God as providing such a guarantee is to deny the significance of human freedom and responsibility, because it would be saying in effect that no matter what man did or failed to do, he would be morally successful. What was at issue in this section was not whether the universe as a whole sustains the good as a whole, but whether what a man does in freedom is a transient event in a series of passing events or a matter of eternal significance.

Having tried to show how the existence of a Personal God enriches the significance of man's moral life, I now come to the issue of the philosophical evidence for the existence of such a being that can be gathered from a reflection on man's moral experience. As I indicated in the introduction to this chapter, I have not found any proof for the existence of God that can be grounded in this experience. However, the experience does involve factors that intimate, at least, that there is an absolute and permanent character to man's existential situation that militates against the reduction of the whole of reality to the more obvious transient character of his world. If the case for this view can be made, it will be seen that the discussion of the role of an Eternal God in mans' moral life was not something that was imposed on this life wholly from without. The remainder of this chapter will concentrate on the metaphysical implications of that quality of man's moral experience to which we referred in Chapter VI in calling attention to the distinction between the moral and aesthetic dimension of human existence.

There is an incongruity in the view that a being such as man can be both a wholly transient being existing in a wholly transient world and a being who is committed to ideals and values whose significance may call for a great deal of sacrifice and effort on his part. It would appear that a wholly transient being caught up in a wholly transient environment would be solely and exclusively concerned with taking the pleasure of the moment. The assertion of the absolute value of human subjectivity also appears to be incongruous with a view that sees man as a passing affair existing in a context that is nothing but a series of passing states of affairs. The human subject and the values such as freedom and justice that are to be preserved and expanded in the life of human subjects appear to have a significance that is not reducible to a passing existential state of affairs. As a man grows and develops into a moral agent he seems to be introduced into the deeper reality of the world in which we live our ordinary experiences. Thus the seriousness with which the moral agent confronts moral issues cannot be appreciated by a child whose life has not yet grown into this deeper dimension and who still lives in the more obvious and transitory realm of human existence.

The fact that man freely takes on responsibilities that may cause him a great deal of difficulty and personal suffering because he sees these responsibilities as meeting the moral demands of his existence, and the fact that man is capable of freely facing death in the name of moral values may not provide a fully conclusive philosophical demonstration that man is embarked on an eternal career, but they certainly give some intimation of his involvement in such a career. The absoluteness of moral demands and values, and the seriousness with which man meets these demands indicate that the moral man is reaching beyond the limitations of a transient and passing existence.

It should be noted that this position does not say that a man who does not believe in man's eternal career cannot possibly be moral. The evidence for the position was not drawn from what man believed or did not believe concerning eternity. Rather, it was argued that the quality of man's moral existence—involving as it does absolute demands and values and man's seriousness in making moral decisions—indicates that human existence is not a series of transitory events. Moreover, the position does not suggest that man ought to give up the moral enterprise if he is not convinced that he has an eternal destiny. It is not directed toward establishing or criticizing any moral standard, but is directed toward exploring the existential implications that can be drawn from the quality of man's moral existence. It argues that the character of man's moral existence does not seem to fit into a position that sees reality as a series of transient events and that allows only for that type of permanence that is the stringing together of a series of transient acts, a permanence that is, in the last analysis, no permanence at all.

Perhaps, the incongruity between the character of man's moral experience and such a view of reality can be gathered from the following considerations. A man who is vitally interested in advancing his career may find himself in a situation in which he can advance this career by committing an injustice against a colleague either by taking credit for the work done by this colleague or by remaining silent when he knows that the colleague is being erroneously accused of incompetence. A man in such a situation may try to side step the difficulty of his moral decision by shrugging his shoulders and asking, "What difference will it make a hundred years from now, or even fifty years from now?" Viewed from the perspective of man's lived moral experience, this appeal to the future is seen as an attempt to hide from oneself the moral significance and seriousness of the act to be performed here and now. For the moral man, there is a hollow ring about a man's attempt to shrug off his injustices to another man by saying that fifty years from now his injustice will make no difference either to himself, to his victim, or to anyone else for that matter. The hollowness of such an attempt and the feeling that it has missed the whole point of man's moral existence by introducing considerations that are simply not pertinent to the moral issue indicate that there is something about the character of this existence that does not fit neatly into a metaphysics that sees the whole existential order as a series of transient events. If the metaphysician is to take the character of moral existence seriously and if he is not committed to treating this existence as some second-class or pseudoreality, it would appear that his conception of reality must be broadened to include a permanence and endurance that would fit this existence.

There is in man's moral experience a value attached to the human subject that is not commensurate with a conception of his existence as a passing event. The significance given to the development and growth of the human subject as a free agent, the view that there is no good more precious than this good and that this good is not to be surrendered for any other good, no matter how much more readily and immediately available that other good may be, call into question any conception of the human subject as a passing event in a series of passing events. The very fact that man can take this stand concerning the value of a human subject indicates that he is not wholly caught up in a transient state of affairs and that his existence is not fully grasped when it is seen as a passing phenomena.

Admittedly, the above considerations do not prove conclusively that there is an eternal dimension to reality, but they do indicate that there are factors in man's moral existence that would seem to demand such a dimension. They certainly point out that references to man's eternal career are not completely alien to the character of man's moral experience. Having accomplished this, they also serve to open the human mind to the possibility that reality involves not only man in nature, but also an Eternal Thou from whom man and nature proceed. The pointing to the possibility of an eternal dimension to existence does not necessarily imply the existence of an Eternal God, but once the possibility of this dimension is acknowledged, it is certainly not unreasonable to admit the possibility of the existence of an Eternal God.

It will be recalled that Dewey opposed an attempt to provide a metaphysical foundation for man's moral life because such a foundation seemed to deprive man's situation in nature of any meaning intrinsic to it. Dewey was clearly right in taking this stand. The position taken in this section does not depend on denying the naturalistic basis for man's knowledge of moral values and for moral obligation. It is only if one sees a complete opposition between the natural and the supernatural that one concludes that the establishment of a naturalistic basis for man's moral life necessarily excludes any reference to a "supernatural," or, more properly, to a "deeper" dimension of reality. However, as I tried to show in the section preceding this, there need be no opposition between these two dimensions of existence.

Having already described the resources in man's interaction with his finite world that make him capable of morality, I have concerned myself in this last section with the quality or character of his moral existence. I have tried to indicate the way in which the existence of a Personal God enriches man's moral life, pointing out that the existence of this being gives philosophical substance to aspects of man's moral existence, which Dewey himself recognized, but which he could not adequately account for within the framework of his closed naturalism. Moreover, having discussed the resources that make man a moral agent, I have turned to a consideration of the character of the life that the exercise of these resources makes possible and have tried to point to evidence that can be gathered from this life that indicates that there is an eternal dimension to human life. Thus, the view that man's moral existence reaches toward an eternal order and a Divine Person was not grounded in a denial of the naturalistic foundation of this existence, but rather in a further reflection on the lived character of this existence.

The issues raised in this chapter push us beyond the study of moral philosophy to metaphysics and ultimately beyond the limits of philosophical speculation to life itself. Whether or not there is any substance to the position advanced in this chapter will be decided by each of us as he deals with the successes and failures, the triumphs and tragedies of his own life. Each of us must ask himself whether he finds in these aspects of his life any intimations of an Eternal, Personal God.

Bibliography

I. Selections, Surveys, and Histories of Ethics

ALBERT, ETHEL M.; DENISE, THEODORE C.; PETERFREUND, SHELDON P. (eds.):
Great Traditions in Ethics: An Introduction (New York: American Book Co.,
1953).

BOURKE, VERNON J.: *History of Ethics* (Garden City, New York: Doubleday and
Co., 1968).

BRINTON, CRANE: *A History of Western Morals* (New York: Harcourt, Brace and
Co., 1959).

BROAD, C. D.: *Five Types of Ethical Theory* (Paterson, New Jersey: Littlefield,
Adams and Co., 1959).

CLARK, GORDON H., AND SMITH, T. V. (eds.): *Readings in Ethics*, Second Edition
(New York: Appleton-Century-Crofts, Inc., 1963).

EKMAN, ROSALIND (ed.): *Readings in the Problems of Ethics* (New York: Charles
Scribner's Sons, 1965).

FOOT, PHILIPPA (ed.): *Theories of Ethics* (London: Oxford University Press,
1967).

GIRVETZ, HARRY K. (ed.): *Contemporary Moral Issues* (Belmont, California: Wads-
worth, 1963).

HILL, THOMAS E.: *Contemporary Ethical Theories* (New York: Macmillan, 1957).

JOHNSON, OLIVER A. (ed.): *Ethics: Selections from Classical and Contemporary
Writers* (New York: Holt, Rinehart and Winston, 1965).

JONES, W. T.; SONTAG, FREDERICK; et al. (eds.): *Approaches to Ethics: Representative Selections from Classical Times to the Present* (New York: McGraw-Hill
Book Co., 1963).

MANN, JESSE A.; KREYCHE, GERALD F.; et al. (eds.): *Approaches to Morality: Readings in Ethics from Classical Philosophy to Existentialism* (New York: Harcourt,
Brace, and World, Inc., 1966).

KERNER, GEORGE: *The Revolution in Ethical Theory* (New York: Oxford University Press, 1966).

MARGOLIS, JOSEPH (ed.): *Contemporary Ethical Theory: A Book of Readings* (New
York: Random House, 1966).

MARITAIN, JACQUES: *Moral Philosophy: An Historical and Critical Survey of the
Great Systems* (New York: Charles Scribner's Sons, 1964).

MELDEN, A. I. (ed.): *Essays in Moral Philosophy* (Seattle: University of Wash-
ington Press, 1958).

MOTHERSILL, MARY (ed.): *Ethics* (New York: The Macmillan Co., 1965).

SIDGWICK, HENRY: *Outlines of the History of Ethics* (Boston: Beacon Press, 1960).
WARNOCK, M.: *Ethics Since 1900* (London: Oxford University Press, 1960).

II. Ethical Theory

AIKEN, HENRY DAVID: *Reason and Conduct: New Bearings in Moral Philosophy* (New York: Alfred A. Knopf, 1962).
ARISTOTLE: *Nichomachean Ethics.* Translated, with an introduction and notes, by Martin Ostwald (New York: The Library of Liberal Arts, 1962).
BAIER, KURT: *The Moral Point of View: A Rational Basis of Ethics* (New York: Random House, 1965).
BARNES, HAZEL E.: *An Existentialist Ethics* (New York: Knopf, 1967).
BEAUVOIR, SIMONE DE: *The Ethics of Ambiguity* (New York: Philosophical Library, 1948).
BLANSHARD, B.: *Reason and Goodness* (London: G. Allen, 1961).
BOURKE, VERNON J.: *Ethics in Crisis* (Milwaukee, Wisconsin: The Bruce Publishing Co., 1966).
BRADLEY, F. H.: *Ethical Studies* (New York: Liberal Arts Press, 1951).
BRANDT, RICHARD B.: *Ethical Theory: The Problems of Normative and Critical Ethics* (Englewood, New Jersey: Prentice-Hall, 1959).
———— (ed.): *Social Justice* (Englewood Cliffs, New Jersey: Prentice-Hall, 1962).
BRONOWSKI, J.: *Science and Human Values* (New York: Harper and Row, 1956).
CARRITT, E. F.: *The Theory of Morals* (London: Oxford University Press, 1928).
DEWEY, JOHN: *Human Nature and Conduct: An Introduction to Social Psychology* (New York: The Modern Library, 1929).
————: *Theory of the Moral Life* (New York: Holt, Rinehart and Winston, 1960).
————: *Theory of Valuation. International Encyclopedia of Unified Science* (Chicago: University of Chicago Press, 1939).
EDEL, ABRAHAM: *Ethical Judgment: The Use of Science in Ethics* (New York: The Free Press, 1955).
EDWARDS, PAUL: *The Logic of Moral Discourse* (New York: The Free Press, 1955).
EMMET, DOROTHY: *Rules, Roles, and Relations* (New York: St. Martin's Press, 1966).
EWING, A. C.: *Ethics* (New York: The Free Press, 1953).
————: *The Definition of Good* (New York: Macmillan, 1947).
FIELD, G. C.: *Moral Theory: An Introduction to Ethics* (London: Methuen University Paperbacks, 1966).
FLETCHER, JOSEPH: *Situation Ethics: The New Morality* (Philadelphia: The Westminster Press, 1966).
FLEW, ANTHONY: *Evolutionary Ethics* (New York: St. Martin's Press, 1967).
FRANKENA, WILLIAM K.: *Ethics* (Englewood Cliffs, New Jersey: Prentice-Hall, 1963).
GILSON, ETIENNE: *Moral Values and the Moral Life: The System of Thomas Aquinas.* Translated by Leo Richard Ward (St. Louis, Missouri: B. Herder Book Co., 1931).

HARE, R. M.: *Freedom and Reason* (New York: Oxford University Press, 1965).

———: *The Language of Morals* (Oxford: The Clarendon Press, 1952).

HUDSON, W. D.: *Ethical Intuitionism* (New York: St. Martin's Press, 1967).

JOHNSON, O. A.: *Rightness and Goodness* (The Hague: Nijhoff, 1959).

KANT, IMMANUEL: *Critique of Practical Reason and other Writings in Moral Philosophy*. Translated and edited with an introduction by Lewis White Beck (Chicago: The University of Chicago Press, 1949).

———: *Foundations of the Metaphysics of Morals*. Translated with an introduction by Lewis White Beck. (New York: The Library of Liberal Arts, 1959).

———: *Lectures on Ethics*. Translated by Louis Infield (New York: Harper Torchbooks, 1963).

———: *The Doctrine of Virtue: Part II of the Metaphysics of Morals*. Translated by Mary J. Gregor (New York: Harper Torchbooks, 1964).

———: *The Metaphysical Elements of Justice*. Translated, with an introduction, by John Ladd (New York: The Library of Liberal Arts, 1965).

KLUBERTANZ, GEORGE: *Habits and Virtues* (New York: Appleton-Century-Crofts, 1965).

KOHLER, WOLFGANG: *The Place of Value in a World of Facts* (New York: The New American Library, 1966).

LEPLEY, R. (ed.): *Value: A Cooperative Inquiry* (New York: Columbia University Press, 1949).

LYONS, DAVID: *Forms and Limits of Utilitarianism* (London: Oxford University Press, 1965).

MARGENAU, HENRY: *Ethics and Science* (New York: D. Van Nostrand Company, 1964).

MAYO, BERNARD: *Ethics and the Moral Life* (New York: The Macmillan Co., 1958).

MOORE, G. E.: *Ethics* (London: Oxford University Press, 1912).

———: *Principia Ethica* (Cambridge: Cambridge University Press, 1959).

MILL, JOHN STUART: *Utilitarianism* (New York: The Library of Liberal Arts, 1957).

MUIRHEAD, J. H.: *Rule and End in Morals* (London: Oxford University Press, 1932).

NOWELL-SMITH, P. H.: *Ethics* (Baltimore, Maryland: Penguin Books, 1954).

OLSON, ROBERT G.: *The Morality of Self-Interest* (New York: Harcourt, Brace and World, Inc., 1965).

PERELMAN, CH.: *The Idea of Justice and the Problem of Argument*. Translated by John Petrie (New York: Humanities Press, 1963).

PERRY, RALPH BARTON: *General Theory of Value* (New York: Longmans, Green and Co., 1922).

———: *The Moral Economy* (New York: Charles Scribner's Sons, 1909).

PIAGET, JEAN: *The Moral Judgment of the Child*. Translated by Marjorie Gabain (New York: The Free Press, 1965).

PIEPER, JOSEF: *Fortitude and Temperance*. Translated by Daniel F. Coogan (New York: Pantheon Books, 1954).

———: *Prudence* (New York: Pantheon, 1959).

PRICHARD, H. A.: *Moral Obligation: Essays and Lectures* (Oxford: The Clarendon Press, 1949).

PRIOR, A. N.: *Logic and the Basis of Ethics* (Oxford: The Clarendon Press, 1949).

RAND, AYN: *The Virtue of Selfishness: A New Concept of Egoism* (New York: The New American Library, 1964).

RICE, P. B.: *On Knowledge of Good and Evil* (New York: Random House, 1955).

ROSS, W. D.: *Foundations of Ethics* (Oxford: The Clarendon Press, 1939).

————: *The Right and the Good* (Oxford: The Clarendon Press, 1930).

SESONSKE, ALEXANDER: *Value and Obligation: The Foundations of an Empiricist Ethical Theory* (New York: Oxford University Press, 1964).

SHIRK, EVELYN: *The Ethical Dimension: An Approach to the Philosophy of Values and Valuing* (New York: Appleton-Century-Crofts, 1965).

SIDGWICK, HENRY: *The Methods of Ethics* (New York: Dover Publications, Inc., 1966).

SINGER, GEORGE MARCUS: *Generalization in Ethics: An Essay in the Logic of Ethics, with the Rudiments of a System of Moral Philosophy* (New York: Alfred A. Knopf, 1961).

SMART, J. J. C.: *An Outline of a System of Utilitarian Ethics* (Victoria, Australia: Melbourne University, 1961).

STACE, W. T.: *The Concept of Morals* (New York: The Macmillan Co., 1937).

STEVENSON, CHARLES L.: *Ethics and Language* (New Haven: Yale University Press, 1960).

————: *Facts and Values: Studies in Ethical Analysis* (New Haven: Yale University Press, 1963).

STROLL, A.: *The Emotive Theory of Ethics* (Berkeley, California: University of California Press, 1954).

TOULMIN, S. E.: *An Examination of the Place of Reason in Ethics* (London: Cambridge University Press, 1950).

WADDINGTON, C. H.: *The Ethical Animal* (Chicago: University of Chicago Press, 1960).

WARNOCK, MARY: *Existentialist Ethics* (New York: St. Martin's Press, 1967).

WELLMAN, CARL: *The Language of Ethics* (Cambridge: Harvard University Press, 1961).

III. Religion and Ethics

AUER, J. A. C., AND HARTT, JULIAN: *Humanism versus Theism* (The Antioch Press, 1951).

BERGSON, HENRI: *The Two Sources of 'Morality and Religion*. Translated by Ashley Audra and Cloudesley Brereton with the assistance of W. Horsfall Carter (New York: Doubleday Anchor Books, 1954).

BONHOEFFER, DIETRICH: *Ethics*. Edited by Eberhard Bethge. Translated by Neville Horton Smith (New York: The Macmillan Co., 1965).

BUBER, MARTIN: *Between Man and Man*. Translated by Ronald Gregor Smith (New York: The Macmillan Co., 1965).

————: *Eclipse of God: Studies in the Relation between Religion and Philosophy* (New York: Harper Torchbooks, 1957).

————: *I and Thou*. Translated by Ronald Gregor Smith (New York: Charles Scribner's Sons, 1958).

COBB, JOHN B.: *The Structure of Christian Existence* (Philadelphia: Westminster, 1967).

CORKEY, ROBERT: *A Philosophy of Christian Morals for Today* (London: Unwin, 1961).

DEWEY, JOHN: *A Common Faith* (New Haven: Yale University Press, 1934).

FEUERBACH, LUDWIG: *The Essence of Christianity.* Translated by George Eliot (New York: Harper Torchbooks, 1957).

HAWKINS, D. B.: *Christian Ethics* (Englewood Cliffs, New Jersey, 1963).

KANT, IMMANUEL: *Religion within the Limits of Reason Alone.* Translated with an introduction and notes by Theodore M. Greene and Hoyt H. Hudson (New York: Harper Torchbooks, 1960).

KIERKEGAARD, SOREN: *Either/Or.* 2 volumes. Translated by Walter Lowrie (New York: Doubleday and Co., 1959).

————: *Fear and Trembling, and the Sickness unto Death.* Translated by Walter Lowrie (New York: Doubleday, 1955).

LEHMANN, PAUL: *Ethics in a Christian Context* (New York: Harper and Row, 1963).

LEPP, IGNACE: *Atheism in Our Time.* Translated by Bernard Murchland (New York: The Macmillan Co., 1963).

MARITAIN, JACQUES: *An Essay on Christian Philosophy.* Translated by Edward H. Flannery (New York: Philosophical Library, 1955).

NEWMAN, JOHN HENRY: *Grammar of Assent* (New York: Doubleday and Co., 1955).

NIEBUHR, REINHOLD: *An Interpretation of Christian Ethics* (New York: Macmillan, 1956).

NOVAK, MICHAEL: *Belief and Unbelief: A Philosophy of Self-Knowledge* (New York: The New American Library, 1965).

OWEN, H. P.: *The Moral Argument for Christian Theism.* (London: George Allen and Unwin, Ltd., 1965).

RAMSEY, IAN T. (ed.): *Christian Ethics and Contemporary Philosophy* (New York: Macmillan, 1966).

RAMSEY, PAUL: *Basic Christian Ethics* (New York: Charles Scribner's Sons, 1950).

————: *Deeds and Rules in Christian Ethics* (New York: Charles Scribner's Sons, 1967).

THOMAS, GEORGE F.: *Christian Ethics and Moral Philosophy* (New York: Charles Scribner's Sons, 1955).

TILLICH, PAUL: *Morality and Beyond* (New York: Harper and Row, 1963).

WHITEHEAD, ALFRED NORTH: *Religion in the Making* (New York: Meridian Books, 1960).

IV. Morality and Human Sexuality

ATKINSON, RONALD: *Sexual Morality* (New York: Harcourt, Brace and World, 1965).

BERTOCCI, PETER A.: *Sex, Love, and the Person* (New York: Sheed and Ward, 1967).

CALDERONE, MARY STEICHEN (ed.): *Abortion in the United States* (New York: Hoeber and Harper, 1958).

CARLSON, WADE: *Sex and Abortion* (Hollywood, California: The Gennell Corporation, 1964).

CHESSER, EUSTACE: *Unmarried Love* (New York: Pocket Books, 1966).

D'ARCY, M. O.: *The Mind and Heart of Love* (New York: Meridian Books, 1956).

FINNEY, PATRICK; O'BRIEN, PATRICK: *Moral Problems in Hospital Practice: A Practical Handbook* (St. Louis, Missouri: B. Herder Book Co., 1956).

FROMM, ERICH: *The Art of Loving* (New York: Bantam Books, 1963).

GEBHARD, PAUL H.; POMEROY, WARDELL B.; et al.: *Pregnancy, Birth and Abortion* (New York: Paul B. Hoeber, 1958).

GRUNWALD, HENRY ANATOLE (ed.): *Sex in America* (New York: Bantam Books, 1964).

HEALY, EDWIN: *Medical Ethics* (Chicago: Loyola University Press, 1956).

HOFMAN, HANS: *Sex Incorporated: A Positive View of the Sexual Revolution* (Boston: Beacon Press, 1967).

KIRKENDALL, LESTER A.: *Premarital Intercourse and Interpersonal Relations* (New York: Julian Press, 1961).

LADER, LAWRENCE: *Abortion* (New York: The Bobbs-Merrill Company, Inc., 1966).

LEPP, IGNACE: *The Psychology of Loving.* Translated by Bernard B. Gilligan (New York: The New American Library, 1965).

LEWIS, C. S.: *The Four Loves* (New York: Harcourt, Brace and World, Inc., 1960).

ORAISON, MARC: *The Human Mystery of Sexuality* (New York: Sheed and Ward, 1967).

PLANQUE, DANIEL: *The Theology of Sex and Marriage.* Translated by Albert J. La Mothe, Jr. (Notre Dame, Indiana: Fides Publishers, 1962).

ROSEN, HAROLD (ed.): *Abortion in America: Medical, Psychiatric, Legal, Anthropological, and Religious Considerations* (Boston: Beacon Press, 1966).

RUSSELL, BERTRAND: *Marriage and Morals* (New York: Bantam Books, 1959).

SCHUR, EDWIN M. (ed.): *The Family and the Sexual Revolution* (Bloomington, Indiana: Indiana University Press, 1964).

WILSON, JOHN: *Logic and Sexual Morality* (Baltimore, Maryland: Penguin Books, 1956).

V. Morality and the Politico-Economic Order

ANDERSON, PERRY; AND BLACKBURN, ROBIN (eds.): *Towards Socialism* (New York: Cornell University Press, 1966).

ARNOLD, THURMAN; BERLE, ADOLPH A. JR.; et al.: *The Future of Democratic Capitalism* (New York: A. S. Barnes and Co., 1961).

BARKER, ERNEST: *Principles of Social and Political Theory* (Oxford: Oxford University Press, 1951).

BECK, ROBERT N. (ed.): *Perspectives in Social Philosophy: Readings in Philosophic Sources of Social Thought* (New York: Holt, Rinehart and Winston, Inc., 1967).

BECKER, CARL: *Modern Democracy* (New Haven: Yale University Press, 1941).

BERLE, ADOLPH A. JR.: *The 20th Century Capitalist Revolution* (New York: Harcourt, Brace and World, Inc., 1954).

CAMUS, ALBERT: *The Rebel: An Essay on Man in Revolt.* A revised and complete translation by Anthony Bower (New York: Vintage Books, 1958).

CARR, EDWARD HALLETT: *The New Society* (Boston: Beacon Press, 1962).

CASSIRER, ERNST: *The Myth of the State* (New Haven: Yale University Press, 1946).

COHEN, CARL (ed.): *Communism, Fascism, and Democracy: The Theoretical Foundations* (New York: Random House, 1962).

CHILDS, MARQUIS W.; AND CATER, DOUGLAS: *Ethics in a Business Society* (New York: Mentor Books, 1954).

CROCE, BENEDETTO: *Politics and Morals* (New York: Philosophical Library, 1945).

DE GEORGE, RICHARD T. (ed.): *Ethics and Society: Original Essays on Contemporary Moral Problems* (New York: Anchor Books, 1966).

DEWEY, JOHN: *Freedom and Culture* (New York: Capricorn Books, 1963).

————: *Individualism Old and New* (New York: Capricorn Books, 1962).

————: *Liberalism and Social Action* (New York: Capricorn Books, 1963).

————: *The Public and its Problems* (Denver, Colorado: Alan Swallow, n.d.).

DRUCKER, PETER F.: *The Concept of Corporation* (New York: Mentor Books, 1964).

EWING, A. C.: *The Individual, the State and World Government* (New York: The Macmillan Co., 1947).

FINE, SIDNEY: *Laissez Faire and the General Welfare State* (Ann Arbor, Michigan: University of Michigan Press, 1964).

FINER, HERMAN: *Road to Reaction* (New York: Little, Brown and Co., 1945).

FRIEDMAN, MILTON: *Capitalism and Freedom* (Chicago: University of Chicago Press, 1965).

FROMM, ERICH (ed.): *Socialist Humanism* (New York: Anchor Books, 1965).

FULBRIGHT, J. WILLIAM: *The Arrogance of Power* (New York: Vintage Books, 1966).

GALBRAITH, JOHN KENNETH: *The Affluent Society* (New York: New American Library, 1958).

————: *The New Industrial State* (Boston: Houghton Mifflin, 1967).

GARRETT, THOMAS M.: *Business Ethics* (New York: Appleton-Century-Crofts, 1966).

GEWIRTH, ALAN (ed.): *Political Philosophy* (New York: Collier-Macmillan, 1965).

GREEN, T. H.: *Lectures on the Principles of Political Obligation* (Ann Arbor, Michigan: Ann Arbor Paperbacks, 1967).

HARRINGTON, MICHAEL: *The Other America* (Baltimore, Maryland: Penguin Books, 1965).

————: *Toward a Democratic Left: A Radical Program for a New Majority* (New York: The Macmillan Co., 1968).

HAYEK, F. A. (ed.): *Capitalism and the Historians* (Chicago: Phoenix Books, 1963).

————: *Individualism and Economic Order* (Chicago: University of Chicago Press, 1948).

————: *The Constitution of Liberty* (Chicago: University of Chicago Press, 1960).

————: *The Road to Serfdom* (Chicago: University of Chicago Press, 1944).

Hobhouse, L. T.: *Liberalism* (New York: Oxford University Press, 1964).

Hocking, William Ernest: *Man and the State* (New Haven: Yale University Press, 1926).

————: *The Lasting Elements of Individualism* (New Haven: Yale University Press, 1937).

Hook, Sidney (ed.): *Human Values and Economic Policy: A Symposium* (New York: New York University Press, 1967).

Kaplan, Abraham: *American Ethics and Public Policy* (New York: Oxford University Press, 1963).

Kirk, Russell: *The Conservative Mind.* Revised Edition (Chicago: Henry Regnery Co., 1960).

Lichtman, Richard: *Toward Community: A Criticism of Contemporary Capitalism* (The Fund for the Republic, 1966).

Lippman, Walter: *The Good Society* (New York: Grosset and Dunlap, 1936).

————: *The Public Philosophy* (New York: Mentor Books, 1955).

Locke, John: *Two Treatises of Government.* A critical edition with an introduction and apparatus criticus by Peter Laslett (New York: The New American Library, 1965).

MacIver, Robert M.: *The Web of Government* (New York: The Macmillan Co., 1947).

McCord, David: *Capitalism* (Chicago: Henry Regnery Co., 1962).

Maritain, Jacques: *Man and the State* (Chicago: University of Chicago Press, 1951).

Marx, Karl: *The Economic and Philosophic Manuscripts of 1844.* Translated by Martin Milligan. Edited by Dirk J. Struik (New York: International Publishers, 1964).

Mayo, Elton: *The Human Problems of an Industrial Civilization* (New York: The Viking Press, 1960).

Mill, John Stuart: *On Liberty.* Edited with an introduction by Currin V. Shields (New York: The Liberal Arts Press, 1956).

Morganthau, Hans J.: *Politics Among Nations: The Struggle for Power and Peace.* Third Edition (New York: Alfred A. Knopf, 1960).

Myrdal, Gunnar: *Beyond the Welfare State: Economic Planning and its International Implications* (New Haven: Yale University Press, 1960).

Neumann, Franz: *The Democratic and the Authoritarian State: Essays in Political and Legal Theory.* Edited with a Preface by Herbert Marcuse (Glencoe, Ill.: The Free Press, 1964).

Niebuhr, Reinhold: *Man's Nature and His Communities* (New York: Charles Scribner's Sons, 1965).

————: *Moral Man and Immoral Society: A Study in Ethics and Politics* (New York: Charles Scribner's Sons, 1960).

Nitze, Paul H.: *The Recovery of Ethics* (New York: The Council on Religion and International Affairs, 1960).

Pennock, J. Ronald: *Liberal Democracy: Its Merits and Prospects* (New York: Rinehart and Co., 1950).

Petit, Thomas A.: *Freedom in the American Economy* (Homewood, Illinois: Richard D. Irwin, Inc., 1964).

QUINTON, ANTHONY (ed.): *Political Philosophy* (New York: Oxford University Press, 1967).

RAND, AYN: *Capitalism: The Unknown Ideal* (New York: Signet Books, 1967).

RUSSELL, BERTRAND: *Human Society in Ethics and Politics* (New York: The New American Library, 1962).

————: *Roads to Freedom: Socialism, Anarchism and Syndicalism* (New York: Barnes and Noble, Inc., 1966).

SAMPSON, RONALD V.: *The Psychology of Power* (New York: Vintage Books, 1968).

SCHUMPETER, JOSEPH A.: *Capitalism, Socialism and Democracy*. Third Edition (New York: Harper Torchbooks, 1962).

SIMON, YVES R.: *Philosophy of Democratic Government* (Chicago: University of Chicago Press, 1951).

SOMMERVILLE, JOHN; AND SANTONI, RONALD E. (eds.): *Social and Political Philosophy: Readings from Plato to Ghandi* (New York: Anchor Books, 1963).

THEOBALD, ROBERT: *Free Men and Free Markets* (Garden City, New York: Doubleday and Co., Inc., 1965).

————: *The Challenge of Abundance* (New York: New American Library, 1962).

————. (ed.): *The Guaranteed Income* (Garden City, New York: Doubleday and Co., Inc., 1967).

THORSON, THOMAS LANDON: *The Logic of Democracy* (New York: Holt, Rinehart and Winston, 1962).

VEBLEN, THORSTEIN: *The Theory of the Leisure Class: An Economic Study of Institutions* (New York: Mentor Books, 1953).

WALLICH, HENRY C.: *The Cost of Freedom: Conservatives and Modern Capitalism* (New York: Collier Books, 1960).

WARD, BARBARA: *Spaceship Earth* (New York: Columbia University Press, 1966).

WEBER, MAX: *The Protestant Ethic and the Spirit of Capitalism*. Translated by Talcott Parsons (New York: Charles Scribner's Sons, 1958).

WEISSKOPF, WALTER A.; IYER, RAGHAVAN N.; *et al.*: *Looking Forward: The Abundant Society* (The Fund for the Republic, 1966).

WELDON, T. D.: *The Vocabulary of Politics* (Baltimore, Maryland: Penguin Books, 1953).

WINTER, GIBSON (ed.): *Social Ethics: Issues in Ethics and Society* (New York: Harper and Row, 1968).

VI. Law, Capital Punishment, and War

ARON, RAYMOND: *The Century of Total War* (Garden City, New York: Doubleday, 1954).

BECCARIA, CESARE: *On Crimes and Punishments*. Translated by Henry Paolucci (New York: The Library of Liberal Arts, 1963).

BEDAU, HUGO ADAM (ed.): *The Death Penalty in America: An Anthology* (New York: Anchor Books, 1964).

BENNETT, JOHN C. (ed.): *Nuclear Weapons and the Conflict of Conscience* (New York: Charles Scribner's Sons, 1962).

BOURNE, RANDOLPH S.: *War and the Intellectuals: Collected Essays, 1915–1919*. Edited by Carl Resek (New York: Harper Torchbooks, 1964).

COHEN, MORRIS RAPHAEL: *Reason and Law: Studies in Juristic Philosophy* (Glencoe, Illinois: The Free Press, 1950).

DAVIS, PHILIP E. (ed.): *Moral Duty and Legal Responsibility: A Philosophical-Legal Casebook* (New York: Appleton-Century-Crofts, 1966).

D'ENTREVES, A. P.: *Natural Law: An Historical Survey* (New York: Harper Torchbooks, 1965).

DEVLIN, PATRICK: *The Enforcement of Morals* (London: Oxford University Press, 1968).

FULLER, LON L.: *The Morality of Law* (New Haven: Yale University Press, 1964).

GOLDING, M. P. (ed.): *The Nature of Law: Readings in Legal Philosophy* (New York: Random House, 1966).

HART, H. L. A.: *Law, Liberty and Morality* (New York: Vintage Books, 1966).

———: *Punishment and Responsibility: Essays in the Philosophy of Law* (New York: Oxford University Press, 1968).

———: *The Concept of Law* (Oxford: Oxford University Press, 1961).

FINN, JAMES (ed.): *Peace, the Churches and the Bomb* (New York: The Council on Religion and International Affairs, 1965).

———. (ed.): *Protest: Pacifism and Politics* (New York: Vintage Books, 1968).

KAHN, HERMAN: *On Escalation* (New York: Frederick A. Praeger, 1965).

———: *On Thermonuclear War* (Princeton: Princeton University Press, 1960).

LAWRENCE, JOHN: *A History of Capital Punishment*. With a comment on capital punishment by Clarence Darrow (New York: The Citadel Press, 1960).

LORENZ, KONRAD: *On Aggression*. Translated by M. K. Wilson (New York: Harcourt, Brace and World, Inc., 1966).

MAYER, PETER (ed.): *The Pacifist Conscience* (New York: Rinehart and Winston, 1966).

MILLIS, WALTER; AND REAL, JAMES: *The Abolition of War* (New York: The Macmillan Co., 1963).

MURRAY, JOHN COURTNEY: *Morality and Modern War* (New York: The Council on Religion and International Affairs, 1959).

NAGLE, WILLIAM J. (ed.): *Morality and Modern Warfare* (Baltimore: Helicon Press, 1960).

OSGOOD, ROBERT E.; AND TUCKER, ROBERT W.: *Force, Order, and Justice* (Baltimore: The Johns Hopkins Press, 1967).

PINCOFFS, EDMUND L.: *The Rationale of Legal Punishment* (New York: Humanities Press, 1966).

QUESTER, GEORGE H.: *Deterrence before Hiroshima* (New York: John Wiley and Sons, 1966).

RAMSEY, PAUL: *The Limits of Nuclear War: Thinking about the Do-Able and the Un-Do-Able* (New York: The Council on Religion and International Affairs, 1963).

———: *War and the Christian Conscience: How Shall Modern War be Conducted Justly?* (Durham, North Carolina: Duke University Press, 1961).

RUSSELL, BERTRAND: *Has Man a Future?* (New York: Simon and Schuster, 1962).

SHKLAR, JUDITH N.: *Legalism* (Cambridge: Harvard University Press, 1964).

SIBLEY, MULFORD Q. (ed.): *The Quiet Battle: Writings on the Theory and Practice of Non-violent Resistance* (Garden City, New York: Doubleday and Co., 1963).

SPAAK, PAUL-HENRI; INOZEMSTEV, N. N.; *et al.*: *On Coexistence* (The Fund for the Republic, Inc., 1965).

TUCKER, ROBERT W.: *Just War and Vatican Council II: A Critique.* With commentary by George W. Higgins; Ralph Potter; *et al.* (New York: The Council on Religion and International Affairs, 1966).

————: *The Just War: A Study in Contemporary American Doctrine* (Baltimore: The Johns Hopkins Press, 1960).

WASKOW, ARTHUR I. (ed.): *The Debate over Thermonuclear Strategy* (Boston: D. C. Heath and Co., 1965).

WEINBERG, ARTHUR, AND LILA (eds.): *Instead of Violence* (Boston: Beacon Press, 1965).

ZAHN, GORDON: *An Alternative to War* (New York: The Council on Religion and International Affairs, 1963).

————: *War, Conscience and Dissent* (New York: Hawthorne Books, Inc., 1967).

Index